Jews on the Frontier

Jews on the Frontier

I. Harold Sharfman

Henry Regnery Company•Chicago

Library of Congress Cataloging in Publication Data

Sharfman, I. Harold.
  Jews on the frontier.

  Bibliography: p.
  Includes index.
  1. Jews in the United States—History—Addresses, essays, lectures.   2. United States—History—Addresses, essays, lectures.   I.   Title.
E184.J5S44   973'.04'924   76-55651
ISBN 0-8092-7849-9

Copyright © 1977 by I. Harold Sharfman
All rights reserved.
Published by Henry Regnery Company
180 North Michigan Avenue, Chicago, Illinois 60601
Manufactured in the United States of America
Library of Congress Catalog Card Number: 76-55651
International Standard Book Number: 0-8092-7849-9

Published simultaneously in Canada by
Beaverbooks
953 Dillingham Road
Pickering, Ontario L1W 1Z7
Canada

This history of Jews in the American West
is appreciatively dedicated
to Kosher Overseers Association of America, Inc.,
and to the concerns it serves
in this country and abroad
for their substantive contributory participation
in bringing this work to fruition

Contents

FOREWORD   ix

ACKNOWLEDGMENTS   xiii

INTRODUCTION   xv

PROLOGUE   xix

1: COLONIAL JEWISH-INDIAN TRADERS   1

A Jew Ventures into Indian Country
Fight for the "Land of the Forks"
"Wolfe's Jew" Helps Topple New France
Hebrew Captives of Pontiac Uprising
When Indiana was South of the Ohio
Trading "Sundries" for the Illinois Country

2: AMERICAN AND HEBREW REVOLUTIONS   55

The Seashore Aflame, the Frontier Ablaze
Revolt in the Jewish Community

3: JEWISH SETTLERS IN FRONTIER HINTERLANDS 79

Virgin West Open to Settlement (South of the Ohio)
Virgin West Opens to Settlement (North of the Ohio)
German Jews Migrate to the Ohio Valley
Ignorance, Indifference, Intermarriage

4: HEBREW PATRIOTS, PIONEERS, PIRATES 107

Hebrew War Hawks
Stalemate in the States
Hebrew Pirates—Heroes of New Orleans
Laffite Learns of his Ancestry
Vendetta with Spain

5: JUDAISM TAKES ROOT IN WESTERN WILDERNESS 155

Hebrews in Bondage
English Jews' Synagogue Adorns "Queen City"
Steamboating to the Crescent City
The Hebrew Godfather
"Acting Rabbis" at "Gates of Mercy"
Statue in a Synagogue Courtyard
Jewishness of the American Indian

6: THE ISRAELITES' ROLE IN THE CONQUEST OF THE SOUTHWEST 231

Spanish Land Grants North of the Rio Grande
By Gulf to Galveston
Spanish Jews of the Republic of Texas
Lone Star Orbits into Stars and Stripes
Mexico Surrenders Its Golden Treasure

EPILOGUE 279

SOURCES 283

INDEX 321

Foreword

THIS IS A BOOK that Frederick Jackson Turner, pioneer historian of the American frontier, would have loved. In his famed essay "The Significance of the Frontier in American History" Turner postulated that the successive Wests served as crucibles in which immigrants were "liberated and fused into a mixed race, English in neither nationality nor characteristics." There was the "region of most rapid and effective Americanization." Along the frontiers, he believed, a distinctly American civilization emerged, formed by the fusion of the cultural traits of the pioneers of differing ethnic and cultural backgrounds who met and mingled there. This was a distinctly American phenomenon, and it underlay the distinctiveness of American society.

Implied in this appraisal was an understanding that the unique ethnic and national characteristics of those who contributed to the emerging American civilization were abandoned in the process. The frontier, as Turner put it, was "a gate of escape from the bondage of the past." The peoples from differing backgrounds who met there created something new but in doing so abandoned something old. Ancestoral traits, habits, and practices were not completely submerged by the frontiering process, but they were robbed of primary importance as acculturation and the impact of the wilderness environment joined to create that "new man, the American." So Frederick Jackson Turner believed, and so his followers have believed down to the present.

Of the many ethnic groups who contributed to American expansion, the Jews would seem least likely to abandon their cultural heritage. For 40 troubled centuries they had clung to their faith and their identity in Europe. They defied prejudice, persecution, and the threat of expulsion for the right to live and worship as their fathers had lived and worshipped, whether in fifteenth-century Spain when monarchs sought to drive them from the land or in nineteenth-century Czarist Russia where bloody pogroms thinned their ranks and created folk martyrs. Surely such deep-rooted loyalties would defy all disintegrating pressures and guard the traditions of Judaism.

Yet not even the tenacity of the American Jewish immigrants could withstand the erosive pressures of the frontier. Rabbi Sharfman has made "The Vanishing Jew" the hero of this book—and rightly so. For the demands of pioneering decreed that no minority—ethnic or religious—could maintain its identity during the westering process. The primitive frontiers provided no clergy or teachers as a link with the past, no teachers to keep faith alive, no synagogues for worship, no leisure that would keep the Sabbath holy, no kosher foods necessary in upholding the dietary laws. Instead they hurried the disintegration of traditional practices in two ways. First, most Jews, in common with other minorities, tended to move westward as individuals, thus subjecting themselves to alien pressures and denying themselves the group strength needed to preserve inherited beliefs and practices. Second, men always outnumbered women along the western fringes. In fact, few Jewish women were among the early frontier pioneers. Marriage beyond the faith was common, and with that marriage a loss of Jewish identity. The lone Jew, denied the companionship of others of his faith and married to a Gentile with little sympathy for his religious beliefs, simply disappeared into the emerging social order.

This fate has denied Jewish frontiersmen the recognition they deserve for their role in the conquest of the West. Historians who read the records, unaware that many of the pioneers whose deeds they were chronicling boasted a Jewish ancestry, simply assumed that Jews were concentrated in eastern cities and played no part on the frontier. Few histories of the West mention their contributions, even though other minority groups—Negroes and Mexican-Americans, for example—have been given some of the credit they deserve. If a Jew does appear, he is usually an unnamed peddler who supplies the commercial needs of frontier towns or mining camps, but contributes nothing to the settlement process. Nothing could be farther from the truth. At the close of the era described in this book, only one half of one percent of the people in the Northeast were Jews, but in many western communities they numbered as high as one and one half percent of the population. It's clear then that Jews moved westward and played a sizable role in the occupation of frontier America.

Happily many who did so left behind clues to their Jewish origin, and happily they have at last found a historian with the energy and intelligence and persistence to rescue them from obscurity. Rabbi Sharfman has discovered an amazing—and important—gallery of pioneers, most of them unknown until now. The author explores the careers of many frontiersmen. A small sampling indicates the richness of his finds: Joseph Simon, David Franks and Levy Andrew Levy, whose trading activities helped shape Indian policy and opened much of the Trans-Appalachian West to commerce and settlement; Heyman Levy of New York, reported to be the leading Indian trader of his day; Samuel Sanders who accompanied Daniel Boone on his explorations and was at the siege of Boonesborough; David S. Franks who helped found one of the earliest communities in Ohio; the pirate Jean Laffite, whose exploits helped open much of the Southwest; Abraham Mordecai and his Indian wife who dominated the trade of the lower Mississippi Valley; David Kokernot, a Texas pioneer; Lewis Adler and Jacob Frankfort who were among the earliest California settlers; and Jacob Hirschorn, a hero in the Mexican War. These are typical of the hundreds of Jewish frontiersmen unearthed by Rabbi Sharfman from the forgotten records of the past—men who heralded the coming of civilization to the American West and in many instances sacrificed their Jewish identity in doing so.

The emphasis on individual achievement so properly stressed in this book guarantees exciting reading. Unlike their counterparts who remained in eastern ghettos, many of the Jewish pioneers ascended the social and economic ladder to become leading citizens. Their success stories have a Horatio Alger touch that adds to their fascination. Others were prominent explorers or military leaders, whose tales will captivate any armchair adventurer. But this is no mere collection of exciting narratives; this is a book of vast learning and Herculean research. The mere fact that most of his characters were relatively obscure forced Rabbi Sharfman into prodigious efforts to reveal their life stories. He has not only located tidbits of material in hundreds of local journals and other printed sources, but has explored every important archive, investigated dozens of obscure depositories, and searched the attics and basements of synagogues and county court houses for fragments of information. His has been a labor of love; only a thoroughly dedicated scholar would have invested the years of effort that make such a book possible.

The result is a volume that fills a long-neglected spot in the nation's history, and does so with such thoroughness that it should remain the standard source on Jews in the West for generations to come. With this book on their shelves, historians need no longer ignore the Jewish pioneer or write vaguely of his role in the commercial evolution of the frontier. Instead they can borrow from this wealth of information to assure proper recognition for the hundreds of Jewish pioneers who hurried the westward expansion of the United States—even at the risk of their own faith and tradition.

Ray G. Billington

Ray Allen Billington
The Huntington Library

Acknowledgments

I EXPRESS INDEBTEDNESS TO my many teachers: first and foremost, my father, Rabbi Hyman Sharfman, of blessed memory, who gave me the foundation in Talmudic and Rabbinic learning; to the many faculty members at Yeshiva University, eminent among them Rabbi Dr. Joseph Ber Soloveitchik whose instruction in Talmudic Tractates and Commentaries as well as Philosophy deepened and widened my insights into authentic Jewish law and tradition.

In the field of American Jewish History, Dr. Irving Agus of the Bernard Revel Graduate School, Yeshiva University, initiated, directed, and guided my doctoral thesis: "Responsa and Religio-Legal Documents from the Year 1636 to 1836 Relating to America," and Dr. Isidore S. Meyer, Editor Emeritus of the American Jewish Historical Society and Dr. Jacob R. Marcus, Director of the American Jewish Archives, both distinguished historians who constantly encouraged and assisted in various stages; the directors and librarians of archives and libraries in many states who closely cooperated. Special commendation is given to the staff of the history department of the Main Public Library of Los Angeles.

My deepest appreciation for their perceptive insights and invaluable direction towards perfecting this manuscript is expressed to the eminent historians Dr. Ray Allen Billington of the Huntington Library in San Marino; Dr. Andrew F. Rolle, Occidental College in Los Angeles; and Dr. Malcolm H. Stern, Hebrew Union College, New York City. Their scholarly contributions enabled a clear, accurate reconstruction of a pioneer element that disappeared along with the vanished frontier.

Most cherished has been the constant promotion by Mr. Joseph Jonah Cummins of historic articles authored by myself and illustrated by artist Kurt Friede. Mr. Cummins, publisher of *B'nai B'rith Messenger*, Los Angeles, California, is blazing a new path in Anglo-Jewish journalism.

Thanks is hereby expressed to Leo Guild of Los Angeles for his styling of the manuscript, and to Millisa Harmon for her technical assistance while serving as Secretary of Kosher Overseers Association of America, Inc., the organization I have the honor to serve as Rabbinic Administrator.

All the years I shall ever remember the great inspiration of that giant of American history, the late Dr. Allan Nevins, of blessed memory. His warm friendship sparked the initiation of this and other projects to be published, G-d willing.

Lastly, I salute the sponsors of this work, Kosher Overseers Association of America, Inc., H. Robert Weiner, president; and Xonics, Inc., Bernard B. Katz, chairman, Board of Governors. Their deep and abiding dedication and friendship was the indispensible catalyst in the final analysis.

Introduction

"GO WEST, YOUNG MAN!" exclaimed newspaper publisher Horace Greeley, popularizing the slogan that has fired the imagination of American adventurers since the mid-nineteenth century.

If anyone fulfilled that directive not once, but twice and thrice, it was my father, Hyman Sharfman. As a lad, he left Rublia, Russia (later Poland) and traversed the American continent from New York City to San Francisco. Then in Kansas City, Missouri, Hyman Sharfman graduated from the Southwestern Optical College as a Doctor of Optics.

But metropolitan New York was the fountainhead of rabbinic studies, so Dr. Hyman Sharfman returned to pursue his main interest, a rabbinical career, as had his father before him. Rabbi Hyman Sharfman served as spiritual leader of the Hebrew Educational Institute of South Brooklyn, but though he had been taken out of the West, the West could not be taken away from his adventurous spirit. He was soon westbound again, this time to the Old West, to West Virginia's Huntington where nearby the Ohio River receives the waters of the Guyan.

The beauty of the forested hills in and around Huntington, the cornfield next to our home where between the rows of stalks were scattered plump pumpkins, the myriad grasshoppers by day and lightning bugs by night—all presented to my young mind a country charm never-to-be-forgotten. And there flowed the clear waters of the river that awed me when it rampaged and Marshall College (which my father had attended) had to be reached by boat.

There was a time when with my father I visited Cincinnati and rode up its steep hills on those electric powered trolleys. The highlight of that visit was a meeting with one of my father's closest friends, Rabbi Eliezer Silver, the uncrowned Chief Rabbi of American Jewry.

My ambition too was to be a rabbi, and, according to our family tradition, I would be the thirty-sixth. Already I had learned of my descent from Rabbi Jacob Israel of Emden, Germany, and of his father, Rabbi Zebi Ashkenazi of Amsterdam, Holland. They were the leaders of world Jewry in the eighteenth century, and I was their ninth and tenth descendant respectively.

But I had other interests also. I wanted to sit in the cab of a steam-puffing locomotive and be its proud engineer and chug through the mountains into the unknown regions beyond. And I hoped to own one day a sporty Model A, or the like. Little did I then dream that someday I would explore the lands of the Ohio, rediscovering the long-forgotten Jews who first entered and pioneered the first American West.

After my ordination and studies in American Jewish history leading to a doctorate, I was amazed to learn that no book told the story of the Jews in the American West. When I began my search, I came across a few pages written in 1892 by Lewis N. Dembitz in an article entitled "Jewish Beginnings in Kentucky." Therein he noted: "I might have named a number of Jews and some Jewesses who, between 1820 and 1840, came here, became quite prominent in society or business circles, intermarried with the best Gentile families, and thus became lost to their race; but it is no part of my duty to tell their story."

Here was the key to the story of western Jewry that proved so elusive in writing their history. Only after years of gathering sources found in musty basements of old synagogues, historical societies, private and public libraries and archives, and as many years of organizing the mass of material, did it become apparent that in the West we were dealing with an era of Jewish history different from any other in its 4000-year past. Unlike his ancestors in the wilderness of Sinai, where the Jews moved as a nation, in the American wilderness the Jew moved alone. He came individually to make his way beyond the frontier. He lived apart from other Jews, married a Christian or Indian woman, and in time was lost to Judaism. Like the Jew, Simon, who in 1702 was baptized in Charleston, Massachusetts, assumed the name of Barns, and disappeared into the surrounding community, so would the names of pioneer western Jews be absorbed by their sons-in-law, so that identification by a Jewish surname was impossible and the name and heritage unknown to succeeding generations.

The greatest number of European Jews who went west came from Germany. Most of them were teenagers or young men who, from the time of American independence, braved the Ohio and Mississippian wilderness. Traveling alone, the German Jew stopped keeping the kosher diet aboard ship when during the long voyage he ate salt pork and the like to survive. When he took to the trail in the wilds of Kentucky and Ohio, he stopped observing the Sabbath, for there was nowhere to rest on the holy day. He chose not to identify with his people after taking a wife. Ninety-nine times out of a hundred she was a Christian, for there were no Jewish women in the West. The one hundredth married either an Indian, a Creole, or a free black woman.

Unlike the Portuguese Jew, who fled the Inquisition to live according to his ancient faith and married within the fold, the German Jew left his native land because of economic repression stemming from anti-Semitic attitudes. Young and uneducated in general studies, not fortified in his faith, he rebelled against poverty at the cost of his religion. Removed by an ocean and mountain range from parental and communal influence, he assimilated, baptized his children, and, although he did not convert, was laid to rest forever in city or church graveyards.

The free social mixing in the eastern cities had tended to facilitate a drift away from the Jewish community. In the free social atmosphere of American society, Jewish religious negligence became easy and observance difficult. The characteristically American absence of outward constraint inevitably eased marriage between Jews and Christians, for social circles that intersect intermarry, and love laughs at denominational strictures.

There would come the day when in a certain fashionable church on Fifth Avenue in New York City so many membership applications were received from Jews that for self-preservation the church established a quota of five percent for Jewish converts. The minister, when asked by a new Jewish convert to be introduced to the members of the congregation, presented her to other Jewish ladies who had recently entered.

As many as an estimated ten percent were intermarried at the time of the American Revolution in the nation's capital, Philadelphia, and later that percentage grew in eastern cities. The figure was much higher in the West where virtually all Jewish youths were assimilated in the early decades of the opening of the lands to settlement beyond the Appalachians.

Only in the "Queen City of the West"—Cincinnati—did English Jews settle and found in the 1820s a congregation that stood as a bulwark against assimilation, emulated by their brethren in the "Crescent City"—New Orleans.

Few Jews today can trace their ancestry to pioneers of the Old West, but many Christians will, upon reconstructing their family trees, learn (perhaps to their astonishment) that their pioneer patriarch in the first American West was an Israelite, most likely an Indian trader or peddler, or perhaps a farmer or plantationer, a professional or even a pirate.

According to Judaic religio-legal principle, the assimilated, apostate, or atheist Hebrew was nonetheless a Jew. Together with those who planted the ancient faith of Israel in the wilderness of western America, they shared in the opening and development of the Old West, transforming the wilds into farms and flourishing communities. This is their story—unique in the annals of Jewish history.

Harold Sharfman

Los Angeles, California
July 4, 1976

Prologue

TODAY IN THIS GREAT COUNTRY some six million Jews constitute less than three percent of the total population. When I mention this small figure to well-educated men they are usually surprised to find that there is so low a percentage of Jews in the United States.

I am certain they are surprised because the Jewish influence is dominant in almost all fields, in business, the arts, politics, sports, the professions and, in fact, in nearly every other realm of endeavor.

So, too, in the very beginning of American history. In the Old West, Jews constituted a small fraction of the pioneers. Of an estimated 100,000 settlers in the Ohio Valley by 1800, less than 100 were Jews. Almost a quarter of a century later in Cincinnati, a community of 45,000 inhabitants, less than 45 Jews founded the first synagogue in the West. When they first arrived, they were the objects of intense curiosity. People came from near and far to look at these descendants of the Hebrew patriarchs.

Even today there are localities in America where no one has ever seen a Jew. Yet they have all heard of Einstein, Kissinger, Brandeis, Salk, and many other leading Jewish Americans.

What is the history of the Jews in America and its early frontiers? How did they increase and multiply to achieve such prominence?

This book traces the beginnings, truly and objectively. It reveals the brawn, the business acumen, the loves and the lives of the first Jewish pioneers who were Indian traders, peddlers, adventurers, and settlers.

This has been a labor of love that I inherited from a family dedicated to learning. To better understand the famous Jews of this generation, as well as the average Jew, you will find clues in these surprising beginnings.

This story, told for the first time, is not only for Jews but for all religions and peoples who want to know—in the language of today—what is a Jew?

Jews on the Frontier

1

Colonial Jewish-Indian Traders

A Jew Ventures into Indian Country

In the days when 12 colonies and as many cities lay nestled along the Atlantic seaboard, the western frontier was but 100 miles inland at the foothills of the forested Appalachian Mountains. There on the distant border of Penn's Colony, from a newly built log cabin on an Indian trail leading from Conestoga Creek to Swatara Creek, blasts of a ram's horn pierced the air. Momentarily, clatter and chatter of the wild creatures were stilled.

The occasion was the ushering in of the Hebrew New Year, 5484, by a group of New Dunkers who in that year (A.D. 1724) built the first Jewish house of worship on the North American continent. In their synagogue, which they called "shul," those German Baptists who turned to Judaism celebrated Sabbaths, welcomed the advent of the new moon, and invoked blessings upon his majesty, George II. In their homes, they scrupulously kept the kosher diet. They named their settlement New Judea.

The inquisitive New Dunkers' interest in Judaism may have been piqued by the asceticism of a lad named Jacob, the first Jew born in Philadelphia. Seeking to learn the laws of nature, the universe, and its

Creator, Jacob left for the romantic setting of the Wissahickon to live with the "Woman in the Wilderness"—a German Pietist community of mystics formed there in 1694. There, the young wizard in mathematics and physics spent his days probing the depths of *Cabbala*—Hebrew metaphysics. There, too, he adopted for his new surname that of his native City of Brotherly Love. In time, Jacob Philadelphia would leave the community of mystics to settle among the Indians of the Upper Country, north of the Great Lakes.

But even more than asceticism, it was the Jew's continual sacrifices for his faith that inspired the New Dunkers. The very year they built their shul, 1724, the French expelled all Jews in their North American colonies from *La Nouvelle Orleans* in Louisiana to Louisbourg in New France. The few who sought to avoid that edict, contained in *Le Code Noir* (the Black Code), and who remained after the deadline for banishment, allegedly suffered martyrdom at improvised stakes. A few were reportedly burned at Fort de Vincennes, their ashes shoveled into the Wabash River.

Seventeen years passed and the New Judeans were delighted to learn that at Hickory Town, 20 miles south, a newly arrived Jewish Indian-trader opened in his cabin a 'Schul,' having brought with him a Scroll of the Law. That trader's cabin was easy to locate, for it was by the giant hickory tree not far from Conestoga Creek—the tree serving as the center pole of a large wigwam in which tribal chiefs gathered in council. That German-born trader, Joseph Simon, was 28 when he arrived from London in 1740.

Dressed in a checkered shirt, buckskin breeches, boots, and donning a coon-cap, the young Jew set forth with a heavy pack strapped to his back. He trudged the 10-mile trail to the Susquehanna River, then followed the up-river bank and inland creeks to barter with the tribes, exchanging colorful trinkets and a variety of eye-catching beads and the like for valuable furs.

Simon, like other successful tradesmen, had a simple formula—honesty and integrity. But not all traders of that time acted as Simon. An apostate Jewish predecessor, Isaac Miranda, opened his trading post not far from the giant hickory tree sometime before 1720. At the back door of the Miranda post was his 500-acre farm which drew its waters from Conoy Creek that coursed through it on its way to the Susquehanna.

Indian-trader Isaac, posing as a "fashionable Christian," gained the political appointment of judge, swearing his oath upon a New Testament, but His Honor was soon dismissed for defrauding the Indians. William Penn's Colony was founded on the ideal of its leader—to deal fairly with all men.

On the trails trudged by Isaac Miranda and his son George, through the wildernesses of the Conestoga Valley, now tramped Joseph Simon, returning home by way of the frontier village of Heidelberg (renamed Schafferstown), where stood the New Judean log cabin 'Schul'. Those Sabbatarians were dismayed to learn from Simon that though they circumcised themselves and their sons, though their wives separated meat and dairy dishes in conformity with the kosher diet, they were not Jews. Simon explained to them that conversion to Judaism required the sanction of an ecclesiastical court called a *Beth Din* (House of Law). At the same time, Simon affirmed that Judaism reckoned them among the "Pious of the Peoples of the World" who would merit the divine reward of a "share in the world to come."

For three years, Simon was the one and only Jew to live in Hickory Town. Happily in 1743 he welcomed Abraham de Lyon and Isaac Nunes Henriques who came to settle with their wives and families. These Spanish-Portuguese Jews having made good their escape from Lisbon to London made their way across the ocean to the New World to pioneer in Georgia in 1732 when it was founded as the thirteenth-colony. They developed plantations and operated ranches on the Savannah until 1742 when Spanish troops attacked from their bases in Florida. Portuguese and German Jews alike, with the specter of the Spanish Inquisition and its tortures and horrors looming before them, abandoned their property and fled to the northern colonies. De Lyon and Henriques opened shop in New York, but after one difficult year of eking out a bare existence they set out for the greater opportunities that beckoned in the western frontier. Upon the door of their emptied shop hung a sign, "gone to Conestoga."

Simon had a personal reason for most warmly welcoming Henriques. He was a *shochet* (licensed to kosher slaughter fowl and cattle). No longer would Joseph Simon have to await pickled kosher meats sent from New York but could regularly enjoy fresh hen as well as such treats as venison and goose.

In the following year, 1744, another *Shochet* arrived. He was London-born Joseph Solomon who was accompanied by his bonneted wife Bilah Myers-Cohen and their children. Solomon fared well and attracted his brother-in-law Hiam Solomon Bunn (Heim Bonn), like himself a *Shochet*, to settle in frontier Hickory Town. Bunn arrived in

1746, along with his wife Rachel Myers-Cohen and eighteen year-old daughter, Rose. The reunion of Rachel with her sister Bilah was a tearful but happy one.

Other Jewish families came too, as did those of various Protestant denominations. Hickory Town assumed the more prestigious name, Lancaster, and under the British flag became the leading inland city in colonial America.

During 1747, when the number of Jewish families had risen to ten, an infant child of one of these pioneer families died. Simon and Henriques purchased on that day half an acre of land for six pounds sterling (about fifteen dollars) to forever serve the Jewish community as a consecrated burial ground.

Simon, learned in Hebrew, spent much of the Sabbath studying the scriptures and the Hebrew commentaries. He talked with friends about his daring dream to cross the mountains into Indian country, taking the trail through the 4,000-foot high ridges of the Allegheny Mountains. He would become the first Jew to trod the paths that led into the virgin West.

Though he did not speak of financial gain on the Sabbath day, Simon knew that there was great potential in expanding his trade if he could but barter with the tribes in their own land.

The adventurous, ambitious Simon was, however, apprehensive about entering territory virtually uninhabited by white men. Though a few daring explorers and traders had penetrated the country beyond the mountains, it largely remained an unspoiled wilderness.

The unknown is more terrifying than any other terrors the mind can imagine: raging elements, savage beasts, hostile natives, even starvation. But Simon's apprehensions were mitigated as he began and ended his daily worship with the prayer:

> I rest my spirit in His hand;
> Asleep, awake, by Him I'm stayed.
> My body and my soul with God,
> I face my future unafraid.

Each and every sunrise Joseph Simon prayed in the parlor of his home. He swayed to and fro with prayerbook in hand as he worshipped in front of a Holy Ark set upon the east wall, facing in his prayer (according to tradition) the direction of the ancient Holy Temple of Jerusalem. Over the wooden ark extended a cornice across which was inscribed the Talmudic dictum: "Know before whom you stand" and above which was carved the Hebrew letters of the Ten Commandments.

One morning in the spring of 1747, 10 men gathered in Simon's shul, the minimum number allowed for public congregational worship. Although Simon's birthplace was Germany, he deferred to the Portuguese order of prayers instituted in all synagogues in the Western Hemisphere since earliest times.

Elated over the fact that a *minyan* was assembled and that the Scroll of the Law could be read in public worship, Joseph Simon proudly drew the plush curtain that draped the Holy Ark and opened its doors to reveal the velvet-covered scroll. He embraced the scroll adorned with a silver breastplate. As he carried it to the reading table the silver-bells jingled atop the two wooden handles.

After the worship was concluded, Reb Yosef (Mr. Joseph as they called him) served refreshments. Simon at last officially revealed to his fellow worshipers his decision to lead a pack train into the land beyond the mountains.

Everyone was stunned by his announcement. Beyond the mountains was the French dominated Ohio Valley. A New Judean reminded Simon of the Black Code. Abraham de Lyon recalled the sensational deportation of a confused French teenager who had unsuccessfully attempted to enter New France, disguised by sex as well as religion.

"Jacques la Farge," ostensibly a lad of 15 about to set foot on land ruled by Louis XV, was questioned by authorities at the port of entry, Quebec, and finally admitted being a girl. She was Esther Brandeau, the illegitimate daughter of a Jewish merchant of St. Esprit near Bayonne, France. She had run away from home and, disguised in masculine clothes, roamed the world for five years. Placed in custody and on trial, she was ordered to a convent. The nuns, unable to persuade the flighty girl to convert, declared her deranged and returned her to the court which decided that she be deported. The cost of passage back to France became a knotty issue, unravelled only when the King of France himself assumed the expense.

To Simon, and to all Jews attached to their faith, the French presence in the Ohio Valley posed a decided threat. But reports from Indians with whom Simon bartered convinced him that no French troops were stationed on the far slopes of the Alleghenies and that the nearest French forts would take a moon to reach. Fort Pontchartrain du Detroit was over 300 miles northwest, and Fort de Vincennes was more than 400 miles away.

Simon was then approached by Solomon Bunn, a fatherly man who one day, in fact, would become his father-in-law. So there are no French soldiers. Good! But what of the scalping savages who tortured and tomahawked even other tribesmen? Were they not feared even in the East, in the palisaded town of New York?

Though at least 20 years had elapsed since the Jew Louis (Lewis) Gomez and his son Daniel built their trading post in the wilds of Upper New York (11 miles north of the village of Newburgh), Dutch fur traders canoeing up the Hudson avoided that rocky headland jutting into the river—and for good reason. Many Indian trails converged there, the tribes gathering to perform their exotic chants and rites. Bunn quoted from memory a stanza of the "Devil's Dance Chamber"—a ditty about the mystic ceremonials performed there by the Algonquin Indians around great bonfires:

> For none that visit the Indian's den
> Return again to the haunts of men.
> The knife is their doom, oh sad is their lot.
> Beware! Beware of the blood-stained spot!

But Simon, who was well acquainted with Indian customs, calmed Bunn's fright and the alarm of all present. He explained that in the autumn, when the leaves turned color, the tribes assembled in ceremonial headdress to dance and pray for the success of their hunt. The rites concluded, they packed tepees and possessions into their canoes and paddled their families to winter campsites.

The Jewish Indian trader from Hickory Town, better than any other of his competitors, understood the Indian's contempt for the tamed life of the white man, a life as pale and bloodless as his skin. The whites were fearful of the elements and of nature, covering themselves with clothing from head to toe, sheltering themselves with wooden houses and log huts, sleeping behind barred doors, living in palisaded forts in the solitude of the wilds. Ever worried about the future, they had to store corn in barns, grow their own produce, and raise cattle in fenced pastures. They were only strong and appeared superior because they had rifles, axes, and horses. Despite all this, they were never at ease, never silent.

The Indian hated white settlers with a passion, for they hacked down trees, leveled roads where the deer trails ran, killed off their buffalo and deer, and drove away wild game.

Erect in his bearing, the Indian was free and proud. He knew the natural life, the wild country, the forest trails, the frosty salt licks where buffalo roads led beyond the mountains. He loved his ancestral hunting grounds and fishing waters and achieved mastery over all its challenges.

Bidding his friends farewell, Joseph Simon loaded his pack train with necessary commodities, rifles, and trinkets and set forth on the westward trail. Following the rising path through hillsides covered with forests of hickory, conifers, walnut, oak, and maple, he led his file of horses through the mountain passes and along narrow trails that frequently followed a cliff's edge. Called Traders' Path, it would in time be widened to accommodate wagons as large as the freight-hauling Conestoga.

From vantage points on the Allegheny ridges, Simon scanned a vast endless land that was actually but a small portion of the continent extending toward the setting sun. He could see even less of the dangers that might be posed by the terrain, by man or beast, or by the elements. With a sense of gratitude and achievement, Simon began his descent into the western foothills.

Following the landmarks described by the friendly Indians, Simon reached the arrowhead-shaped triangular strip of land that was narrowed to a point by the merging waters of the clear Allegheny River from the north and the muddy Monongahela River from the south. These combined to flow westward in what the Algonquin tribes called in their tongue Ohio, "Beautiful River."

On this first exploratory junket, Simon pitched his tent by the Shawnee village at the tip of that jutting headland overlooking the Ohio and its two mighty branches. Here, on the site of the future Fort Pitt and outlying Pittsburgh, Simon's presence soon became known to the Wyandotte and the other tribes, as well as to the Delaware and Shawnee as they returned from their winter hunt with bales of peltries. They displayed fox, coyote, lynx, marten, muskrat, otter, skunk, squirrel, weasel, wolf, and, in lesser numbers, black bear. The greatest number of pelts by far were those of the beaver, for the white barterers sought these in ever growing numbers as gentlemen in the colonies, as in the mother country and on the Continent, had begun to wear beaver hats as a sign of distinction.

The Jewish trader put aside some of the best beaver pelts for himself. These he planned to have fashioned into hats as gifts for the Hebrew New Year in the fall.

As Indians canoed into the "Land of the Forks" (as the trading spot between the Allegheny and Monongahela Rivers became called), Joseph Simon offered them fair exchanges in wampum and the sundries they sought for their furs. They would have a choice of beads, earrings, armbands, cheap laces, blankets, red cloth, tobacco, knives, hatchets, tomahawks, rifles, bullets, whiskey, or rum.

Simon never accepted bear, buffalo, wild turkey, or other meats the hunters offered him, only wild fruit and berries, complementing his kosher diet with the biscuits, hard-boiled eggs, and other edibles he carried with him. It was comparatively easy to obtain the fish he particularly sought for his Sabbath meals. It is an old Jewish tradition to add this delicacy on the special day of rest. The Ohio teemed with 10-pound trout and 40-pound perch, which also became his everyday diet.

Simon, living alone among the Indians, kept his religion as he had among his friends in Hickory Town. Feather-bonneted hunters entering his tent during the Sabbath morning found him wrapped in a prayer shawl intoning the Hebrew prayers. Afterwards he would chat with them but neither bargain nor barter.

On weekdays in the sunrise the Indians gazed in wonder upon the black boxes Joseph bound with leather bands round his arm and head as he swayed to and fro reciting prayers. Not until his obeisance was concluded would any waiting barterer be invited to join him and at the campfire conduct trade over a cup of steaming hot coffee.

As he squatted with the curious braves by the fire, Simon explained that he, like them, worshipped the Great Spirit. The black cubes contained strips of hides upon which were written that one should love the Great Spirit. The fringed shawl, he explained, was a reminder to keep His ways in thought as in deed, from the rising of the sun to its setting, from birth to death.

In friendship, Simon presented the braves with "segars" and told them that he believed the Indians to be of the same ancestry as his, the Hebrew patriarchs. They, like himself, observed the new moon with special incantations; in mourning they tore their buckskin and so would he. Simon also knew that they set up 12 stone altars, no doubt an ancient allusion to recall the 12 tribes of Israel, a past undoubtedly long forgotten to the Indians.

The chiefs may have wondered why their long lost brother had a pale face. They nonetheless felt a kinship in their trust of Joseph Simon. He was their friend.

Little did they realize, nor did Simon, that they were bartering away their civilization. The iron kettles, shooting irons, and sundries they acquired for furs meant that they had to kill for many pelts that exceeded their needs for clothing, food, and shelter. Dependency on the white man's whiskey led to quarrelsomeness and murder of fellow braves. They fell prey to the diseases of the pale faces for which they had no immunity—smallpox, measles and sexual diseases. Over the previous century they had bartered Manhattan Island and the eastern seaboard for colorful beads and trinkets, and in the century to come they would barter their Shawnee village and all the Ohio Valley.

But the Indians were naive, trusting, and generally friendly. In happiness over their colorful beads, trinkets, goods, and strong drink received for peltries, the tribesmen told Simon to revisit them the coming year, in the Moon of Greening Grass. Simon assured them he would and after puffing the calumet, bid them farewell.

Joseph Simon returned to Hickory Town in the late summer something of a hero. From far and near acquaintances and strangers came to see him, meet him, buy from him. He was happy to tell them tales of his adventures. He had accomplished everything he had set out to do, to cross the mountains, locate the "Land of the Forks," barter all his goods and return with loads of rich pelts. Invariably he would conclude by mentioning his resolve to return in the spring and again set up his tent on that tribal meeting ground at the arrowhead projection which pointed the "Beautiful River" westward from the Shawnee village at the "Land of the Forks."

Fight for the "Land of the Forks"

Many an evening the prospering young man visited the Bunns. In 1747, as he was approaching another birthday, Solomon and Rachel Bunn recalled to the bachelor the teachings of the ancient rabbis that man should marry at age 18. They noted that he was twice that.

Needing no further prompting, one particularly romantic spring night Simon proposed to their daughter Rose, called by the Sephardic townspeople Rosa. She was a healthy, adventurous, bright-eyed girl of 20, a fit wife for a man of Joseph's personality. They had a perfect understanding, and were able to speak the complete truth to each other.

The newlyweds moved into a stately three-story house at the southwest corner of Penn Square, a dowry from the Bunns. The roving Indian traders opened a store in the best location in Lancaster. Now Simon could spend more time in town and at home.

In their marriage, Rose proved to be a fine cook and seamstress as well as a superb hostess. As a couple, they were much in demand for all social occasions—better than a wood fire, it was said, to brighten up a party. She was a pretty girl and full of activity.

In their frame house, Rose busily engaged herself. Among the chores she undertook was setting up separate cabinet compartments for dairy and meat, two sets of dishes and silverware, cookware, and bakeware for year-round use and two sets for Passover, each of the four services readily identified by individual design and shape.

No sooner was their home in order when Joseph received a plea from his widowed sister, Mary Simon Levy, to take into their charge her 13 year-old son, Levy Andrew Levy. Seeing no future for him at home, she was ready to sacrifice her interests to those of her son. Furthermore, she was dependent on Joseph's aid. Rather than have two dependents, her son could work his way and learn a trade at Simon's shop. Why she did not go with her son to America remains unanswered.

Joseph and Rose Simon agreed to care for the lad and the Oxford-born boy arrived from England to apprentice as a clerk and serve as Joseph's English scribe. Uncle Joe could only write two words in that language—his name. But that was all he needed to sign and countersign notes and conduct business.

Simon, like his fellow Jewish traders, closed his shop every Friday before sundown for observance of the Sabbath. This was known throughout the country to farmers, townfolk, and Indians, as an Anglican missionary would learn.

One Saturday, Reverend David McClure and a companion rode into Lancaster, on their way to the Muskingum River country to convert the Indians. Short of wampum, they sought out the "Jew Merchant." Simon replied to them: "Gentlemen, today is my Sabbath, and I do not do business in it; if you will please to call tomorrow, I will wait on you."

The missionary objected that as a Christian he could do no business on Sunday, but apologized for the intrusion and promised to wait. Simon, realizing the clergyman's predicament, called in his neighbor, asked him to handle the financial transaction. The missionary was spared a two-day layover.

Simon did not lose trade by keeping his shop closed on the Jewish Sabbaths and Holy Days, but actually gained the respect of everyone and prospered as a result. He not only became the leading shopkeeper of Lancaster but also a prominent wholesaler, selling to other shopkeepers in town. He obtained his goods from Levy & Franks Company in Philadelphia. Those partners, Nathan Levy and David Franks (and their brothers) had arrived 20 years earlier to become distinguished merchants in the Quaker City. The Levys were David Frank's uncles and they were distantly related to Simon. Nathan Levy's uncle, Samuel Levy, had married Rachel Asher, who upon her husband's death was remarried to Samuel Myers-Cohen, uncle of Rose, wife of Joseph Simon.

Franks and Levy were merchant-shippers, importing from England on their own ships manufactured goods and exporting raw materials including furs sent by Simon in wagons operated by his neighbor, Mathais Slough. Simon sent his own pack trains which he outfitted with Indian goods over the mountains into the "Land of the Forks." Competition was rather keen between himself and fellow traders. Indians canoeing downstream on the Allegheny or Monongahela rivers would yululate across upon nearing the "Land of the Forks", and the trader who was the quickest would raft his goods across the river. There, the Indians moved from trader to trader looking for the best deal. Many traders used rum as their trump card. And so, Simon boated down the "Beautiful River", the Ohio as the Indians called it, to the "Father of All Rivers", the Mississippi—to be celebrated as one of the first English traders to reach the Illini tribes.

But all Indian trade in the future seemed in great danger. The French fur traders claimed the entire Mississippi Valley from the "Great River" eastward, even to the ridges of the Appalachians. They were incensed by such English fur traders as Joseph Simon who penetrated deep into the Ohio Valley, even to the Mississippi. One trader even established posts in Ohio Country, notably at the Indian village of Pickawillany on the Great Miami tributary of the Ohio in the very heart of French-claimed country.

Earlier that year, 1747, a group of wealthy Virginians, which included the brothers of the teenaged surveyor George Washington, formed the Ohio Company. Their objective was to obtain a land grant from the Crown along the Ohio River in western Virginia, build roads into that western colony, and there found settlements and establish farms and cities.

They initiated this move into the West in the face of the French who were fortifying the land bridge linking the east-west Maumee and Wabash rivers and between Lake Erie to the north and the Ohio River to the south. It was a warlike act but that year actual warfare was being waged overseas between the British and French—the third war they fought for the ownership of the Mississippi, Ohio, and St. Lawrence valleys. King William's War had been fought at the end of the seventeenth century; Queen Anne's War at the beginning of the eighteenth; and King George's War began in 1744 was almost at an end. Like the previous wars, it too ended in a draw.

The growing boldness of the English traders towards the mid-eighteenth century infuriated the French and would hasten a fourth and decisive war, this one to be fought on American soil. The French became daily more aware that they would lose all their North American possessions unless they closed the Ohio to the Pennsylvanians, who gained the favor of the Indians with their superior English manufactured goods.

With the gains of the Pennsylvanian traders, the French were indignant. They claimed all territory that stretched inland from the "Father of All Rivers" to the Appalachian Mountains, including the fur trade of the Ohio Valley. In response to the British counterclaims, the government of New France dispatched 200 soldiers and 30 Indians to transport in long, fast canoes a cargo of heavy lead plates and light tin strips.

Down the Allegheny River and into the Ohio the French and Indian contingent paddled. At intervals, the soldiers imbedded the plates along the riverbanks, an inscription upon each plate proclaiming the Ohio Valley as the soil of France. The tin strips, emblazoned with the French coat of arms and a warning to the English to depart, were nailed upon adjacent tree trunks.

Upon seeing the warnings, Joseph Simon and other Indian traders shrugged and continued to barter. The French were outraged that the furs sought by their *voyageur* Canadians who canoed and tramped in the Ohio Valley were in the hands of the Pennsylvanians on their way to Philadelphia and London instead of Montreal and Paris. Moreover, Ohio Company explorers were surveying a grant of 200,000 acres awarded them by the British Crown.

And as if to light the fuse, Sir Alexander Cuming of Culter, a Scottish nobleman, publicly urged the Duke of Bedford, secretary for the Southern Department (who had charge of colonial affairs) in the British Parliament, to approve a Hebrew colony in the British-contested American West. Sir Cuming told of his visit to the Tennessee Mountains 20 years earlier when Jews were among the pioneers of the then newly established thirteenth seaboard colony, Georgia. Sir Cuming urged that European Jewry, or 300,000 Jewish families of those lands oppressing them, be moved across the Cherokee Mountains into their western colony. As British subjects they would pay sufficient taxes to cover the national debt of England, which amounted in 1750 to 80,000,000 pounds.

At Lancaster, Simon was more interested in what the Indians had to say of conditions in the Ohio. They told him that in the French forts there was talk of war. The French were on one side, the British on the other, and the tribes were asked to take sides. To his amazement, Simon learned that most of the Indians were siding with the French. Though many had once been friendly with the British, they now felt it was these Britishers who would do to the Ohio as they did to the seaboard—cut down the trees, build cabins, fence the open land for farms, found cities, and force them and the wildlife out of their hunting grounds.

Actually the Indian looked upon the fight between the white nations as contesting the right to hunt, even as the Upper Ohio tribes fought those in the Lower Valley, the "Beautiful River," the Ohio, being the dividing line. The Indians did not grasp the white man's concept of land ownership. To the native American, the earth upon which he trod was as free as the air he breathed or the water he drank. He could not grasp the white man's concept of buying or selling land, his killing of animals not needed for food or clothing, or his despoliation of the natural landscape.

Though the French too had built cities in the East where the St. Lawrence flowed into the ocean and forts on the Wabash and Mississippi and Great Lakes in Indian country, they also lived in Indian villages, mated with Indian women, hunted and trapped with the braves. The Englishmen came to trade not only for furs but for land.

Simon's transactions with Levy & Franks developed by 1751 into a full partnership. The firm of Levy, Franks & Simon became the most daring and powerful merchant western-conglomeration of its time. Expanding his trade, Simon opened a second location, acquiring from Levy & Franks the two-story building on the southeast corner of Penn Square (2-4 King Street) across the street from his first shop. His status as a shopkeeper was enhanced by his association with the prestigious Levy & Franks, David Franks being respected as the merchant prince of Philadelphia.

In the first year of the partnership of Simon, Levy & Franks, 1752, a Levy and Franks trans-Atlantic vessel—the 10 gun, 250-ton *Myrtilla*

—transported from England to America the 2,000-pound bell which was installed in the Tower Room of the State House in Philadelphia.

The occasion was the celebration of the 50th anniversary of Penn's charter of liberties for his colony. Around that bell's upper perimeter protruded the letters that comprised the Biblical verse: "PROCLAIM LIBERTY THROUGHOUT THE LAND UNTO ALL THE INHABITANTS THEREOF."

That proclamation had yet to be heard in the American West where the French *Code Noir* was in force. Liberty for Jews within the great land arc that swerved from the St. Lawrence through the Ohio and Mississippi Valleys would be attained—but not without sacrifice.

In 1753, Virginia's governor, Robert Dinwiddie, sent a local militia major, George Washington, to the French military commander at Fort Le Boeuf (south of present-day Erie, Pennsylvania) who was then building its ramparts, with a message to depart the Ohio Valley. As expected, the French commander firmly refused.

Upon his return to Williamsburg, capital of Virginia, Washington urged Dinwiddie to build a fort in the Land of the Forks because of its commanding position and strategic location. This site was the key to the Ohio Valley.

There, where Simon set his trading post, the English began building a fort. French troops forced them to depart, and completed its walls and stockades, and named it Fort Duquesne. Determined to regain the strategic fort, Britain dispatched General Edward Braddock to command the British forces, over 1,200 strong.

Among the American Volunteers was Isaac Myers, a Jewish citizen of New York, who called a town meeting at the Rising Sun Inn and organized a company of bateau men, of which he became captain. Jacob Myer(s) and a Michael Franks were among the volunteers. The former, Jacob Myers, if a brother of Isaac, was the son of Mordecai and Esther Myers of Georgetown, South Carolina—Esther's brothers, Jacob and Abraham, would serve in the war for independence. As for the latter, Michael Franks, he may have been related to the prominent David Franks.

These young men labored on widening the trails westward to facilitate the movement of troops and supplies. Simon & Franks packtrains (Nathan Levy died in 1753 at the age of 50) moved over the completed portions. The success or failure of Braddock's expedition depended to a great extent on supplies reaching them on schedule. It took money and manpower to fulfill those needs.

The British highly respected David Franks for his loyalty to the Crown, as he raised 4,000 pounds to support the British war effort to drive the French out of the Ohio Valley and capture their fort in the "Land of the Forks."

David Franks and his brother, Moses Franks in London, as part of the English syndicate comprised of James and George Colebrook and Arnold Nesbitt, were a formidable force in Colonial troop supply. But this was more than a supply agency. It was a quartermaster corps and even more than that. It had a courier service to forward latest news dispatches and government baggage, and acted in an advisory capacity. Its prime task on the western frontier was to provide the troops with flour and cattle for food.

Franks's daring in the face of Indian depradations was attributed to his adventurous great-uncle Benjamin Franks, the first of his family to settle in America. A jeweler in England and determined to get to New York on the first sailing vessel, Benjamin Franks had sailed in 1696 as a privateer under the command of Captain William Kidd, on the galley *Adventure*. The famed pirate captain at this time was commissioned by the King of England to capture certain notorious pirates and seize their stolen goods. But disillusioned with Captain Kidd, the bad food, and rough treatment, Benjamin gifted swashbuckling Kidd with a beaver hat to lull any suspicions and then, when anchored at Bombay, India, he jumped ship. Eventually he reached New York.

Without delay, David Franks approved sending a pack train, probably the largest ever to head west and into hostile Indian country, and Joseph Simon joined in the venture. That Simon & Franks packtrain, reportedly valued at hundreds of thousands of pounds sterling, was proceeding along Braddock's Road in June, 1755, when General Braddock's forces were but 10 miles from Fort Duquesne. It reached Big Crossing at the Casselman River, tributary of the Youghiegheny, when Delaware and Shawnee attacked out of ambush. They had been friendly to the British but now sided with the enemy French. They fired arrows and musket balls and swung tomahawks, possibly the very hatchets Simon previously traded to them for their furs.

The braves did not neglect the redcoats for whom the supplies were intended. It was a bloody and brief battle. By the sheer weight of numbers and the element of surprise the Indians overwhelmed the British. More than 400 redcoats were wounded and over 500 massacred. General Edward Braddock was shot through the heart, but a few escaped including Colonel George Washington and David Hays, a Jewish farmboy from Westchester County in New York. David carried his own sword, a family heirloom brought to America by his grandfather Michael. Engraved upon it was the Spanish legend that translated to:

> Draw me not without reason—
> Sheath me not without honor.

The British "broke and ran as sheep pursued by dogs," said Washington. Upon returning to his farmhouse near Pleasantville in Westchester County, David Hays sobbingly told his parents and friends about the Indian victors holding aloft the raw scalps of his fellow soldiers on the bloody swords they had captured. It was a terrible defeat. Simon, Levy & Franks, as the firm continued to be called despite the loss of Nathan Levy, calculated its losses in multi-thousands of pounds. The British, however, refused to compensate, claiming that the French were responsible for the depredation.

Losses were suffered by the Heyman Levy Company of New York, the major Jewish competitor of Simon, Levy & Franks, and reputedly the leading Indian trader of his day. Though the Indians did not know what Levy offered when he advertised for sale: "A large Assortment of goods including Fustians and thicksets, Harrateens, Sagothees, Duroys, Shalloons, Messinets, Camblets, Callimancoes, Prussianets, Ducapes, Peelongs, Sad irons . . ." they appreciated his fair dealings in presenting them with quality "Striped Indian blankets, red, blue and black strouds, vermillion, beads, garterings, rings" and the like for their best northern beaver, old coast beaver, raccoons, dressed martin skins and deer leather, both Indian dressed and in the hide. Always there were heaps of black and white wampum on hand.

The tribes adored and revered Heyman Levy, actually worshipped him as a God. They felt differently about his agents in the forts. Two years after Braddock was defeated by the French and Indians, Heyman Levy set up at Albany a supply post, by permission from Lieutenant General Oliver de Lancey, married to David Franks' sister, Phila.

The Indians silently struck at the British forts on the eastern side of the mountains in Upper New York. There, at Fort Edward, Manuel Josephson, a Heyman Levy agent, operated a trading post. Josephson, who supplied the army with everything from canteens to weapons, was acknowledged by all as a gentlemanly trader, a man of high cultural attainments. All his Jewish friends recognized him to be the most erudite layman versed in rabbinic law.

Josephson, like David Franks, was suave, polite, respected, yet that genteel individual readily adapted to the rugged frontier.

At nearby Fort William Henry, a fellow Jewish trader, Benjamin Lyon, also a Heyman Levy agent, dealt in military goods including camp equipment and scarlet broadcloth for uniforms. Actually, he carried much of everything that Josephson supplied. For the Indians they obtained from Heyman Levy the best black and white wampum, hair pipes of conk shell, gordiots, broaches, ear-bobs, and moons. But the Indians were in a fighting mood. Levy, Lyon & Co. would suffer severe losses.

Josephson was not expecting a visit from Lyon during the summer of 1757 when on a hot day in August, Lyon staggered into Fort Edward on the verge of collapse, but not from the heat. Between gasps he told Josephson that Fort Henry had been attacked by the Mohawks and French. He had been most fortunate to remain untouched by arrows, bullets, and tomahawks. In Lyon's words:

> When our troops came away this morning safe from the French, the cruel Indians (of which 'tis said they have near 3000) fell in the first place among them, took out the women from among them, stript, and afterward scalpt them with their children and sucklings. Almost every young lad and boy amongst them shared the same most cruel fate. . . . They then began upon the officers and soldiers, stript them of their cloaths, shoes, shirts, money, and swords, several officers scalped. . . .

The Canadian Mohawks plundered and massacred as they ranged southward into Pennsylvania. There at a village called Wagontown, about three miles from Coatesville on the Old King's Highway, a group of young couples from the elite families of Lancaster were riding one Sunday in 1757 en route to a high society affair—a dance of the Assembly—at the State House in Philadelphia. The hostile Mohawks intercepted them at the ford of the Brandywine River. Surrounded by the war-painted braves, an Indian read off the names of the captured to his chief. Among the names was that of Franks. The hardened war chief, Le Loup Blanc, relaxed, a gleam of kindness sparkled from his eyes as he declared: "You, people of the blood of the Franks, Go! You free to go back to Hickory Town. Not come back!"

The youngsters scurried home. Everyone, even the warring chiefs, respected honest and friendly David Franks, who was an equally brave man to trade when tribes took to the warpath.

The Simon, Levy & Franks firm, despite the risks, continued to supply the troops in the West, looking forward to the time when they could reenter the Ohio Valley to trade with the Indians. In 1758, as he prepared to march on Fort Duquesne and avenge his and Braddock's disaster of three years earlier, Colonel Washington himself sent a communication to David Franks. In this letter he sought many articles that were in short supply, now that the French and Indian War was on.

May 1, 1758

Sir:

I shall be much obliged, if you would provide for me, and send immediately to this place by the Bearers waggon, the following articles: vizt.

As much green half-thick's, as will make indian-leggings for 1,000 men: if *green* can not be had, get white; if there is not enough of that, then get any other *colour.*

Two proper English pack-saddles, for carrying field-baggage on; and four wanteys (sic) suited to ditto. Three leading-halters. A travelling letter-case, with stands for ink, wafers, &c. A pair of light shoe-boots, round toes, without linings, and jockey-tops made of thin, english calf-skin, by the enclosed measure. A hair-cloth, (trunk) to go under a field-bed. Half a dozen *china* cups and saucers.

Unless those articles come to hand speedily, they will be useless to me. Mr. White, I believe, can furnish the *Leggings,* if you have them not by you; and may be usefully employed in providing the other Things (*Boots* and *china* excepted.) I sent a few weeks ago for 4 Pack-saddles; and the *dutchman* who undertook to procure them, brought common *saddles,* such as indian traders generally use, that were of little service to me.

Please to send your accompt with these things, and the money shall be paid to your order, or lodged with any person in this place, whom you shall think proper to direct.

I must beg to know how our paper money passes with you; for I suppose I shall be under the necessity of paying in that currency, having little of another kind with us. I hope you will excuse the liberty I have taken, without *first* knowing whether it would be agreeable to you

I am Sir,

Geo. Washington

While Washington led his force of 800 to Ford Duquesne, Franks maintained close contact. "I wish you a Successful Campaign," Franks wrote to Washington and in his letter enclosed the receipt:

> Recd philada. June 26th 1758 From Collo. George Washington Two pounds 19/ on accot. pr. Jn. Spore

This was counter endorsed in Washington's handwriting:

> David Franks Esqr. 27th June 1758. Inclosing two Rects.

David Franks and his partner Joseph Simon were overjoyed to receive word late in 1758 that on November 24, the redcoat troops, David Hays among them, and Colonel Washington, serving with General John Forbes, occupied Ford Duquesne, which they renamed Fort Pitt after the British statesman who had inspired them to victory.

Sutlers and traders rode the trail west to Fort Pitt; settlers followed. In the shadow of the fort's walls they built cabins, naming their settlement Pittsburgh. At Lancaster, Simon supplied the emigrants with wagon parts, hardware, guns, and other necessities. As the tempo of westbound pioneers rose in 1759, Simon purchased a second store at 20 King Street from Levy & Franks for 331 pounds. This seems to have been a warehouse. In the brick building to the rear Simon stabled his horses. That year Simon also entered into a number of partnerships to fill the growing demand for goods in the far West as well as supply the renewed Indian trade.

With Dr. Samuel Boude, Simon expanded the business to include the manufacture of silver brooches, earrings, arm bands, and all sorts of ornaments. For two years Simon & Boude engaged in the production of pot or pearl ash used to manufacture soap and glass in the building at the southwest corner of West Chestnut and Arch streets. Lazarus Isaac, a Jewish craftsman described as "a glass cutter and engraver upon glass," fashioned from Simon & Boude potash at William Henry Steigel's Elizabeth furnace, a glassware that became world famed as Steigel's.

For the Indian trappers, Simon in partnership with John Miller made beaver traps; and for white settlers they made horsebells and wagon parts.

Firewater in high demand by everyone including the troops, Simon decided to process hard liquor. In partnership with John Miller and brewer Mordecai Moses Mordecai, a Jewish newcomer to Lancaster, their "Distill'd Liquors" were brewed by blending "Annesses, Caraway seeds, Callamus, Cinnamon, Orange, Snake root and Spirits."

The army took notice of Joseph Simon the manufacturer, that very year, 1759, and Colonel Henry Bouquet, called upon him to make "Baggs" for the troops. With cloth from his warehouse, Simon engaged women to work in their homes. But transport was slow. Bouquet irked by the slow delivery complained: "Mr. Simon had no business to make all the Baggs at Lancaster. If he had sent according to my directions the stuff (cloth) to York, Carlisle or Reading, they would have been sooner ready and I would not have complaints every day for Baggs at these places."

Sensing that it was only a matter of time before there would be open warfare between the English and French for control of the Ohio Valley and Great Lakes fur trade Simon engaged in the making of guns. He entered into partnership with Lancasterian William Henry, who served as armorer for the British General Braddock.

Simon was impressed by the rifle Henry developed. It was lighter to handle and easier to fire than the smooth bore muskets, commanding a greater range and accuracy. Henry explained that its improvement was in the precision of the rifling (or bore), the fit of the rifleball, and the type of greased buckskin he used to seal the rifling grooves against the escaping powder gasses. Henry further detailed to Simon how he made the ball slightly smaller than the bore and encases it with a greased patch which fit easily into the grooves of the rifle. This, said Henry, imparted the spin to the bullet which was how his rifle attained greater range and accuracy. This "Pennsylvania Rifle" would be famed by successive generations as the "Kentucky Rifle."

In their homes, under Henry's direction, workmen would make the parts which would be assembled at the Simon & Henry Forge at Simon's trading post on Penn Square. But first he sent Henry to England to obtain not only whatever was needed for the forge but also a complete line of hardware. Upon Henry's return, Simon & Henry advertised a full line, including snuffers, augers, sconces, escutcheons, nail nippers, rotten stone, Negroe knives, horse fleams, steelyards, stone buckles, smelling bottles, "and numerous articles too tedious to mention."

Henry was surprised to find books shelved in their store, for Simon could neither read nor write. The books, as he would learn, were not for sale. They were being temporarily housed for the Juliana Library, which Simon had helped found the previous year—the third public library formed in America.

After the war when demand for rifles would drop, Henry fashioned at the Simon & Henry Forge the first sternwheel steamboat in America. It sank in Conestoga Creek, but one later built by his pupil, Robert Fulton, proved navigable. Fulton learned the art of gunmaking and draughting at the Simon & Henry Forge.

One of the largest shipments in tonnage by Simon & Henry was pig iron. A train lugging 100 tons went to Baltimore Town, a village of twenty-five scattered houses, two taverns, and a church. The ore was presumably destined for London.

Levy Andrew Levy seems to have accompanied that shipment to Baltimore for he returned to Lancaster with a sweet, affable girl of sixteen, who was very mature looking. He introduced her to uncle Joseph Simon as Susannah, but said little more. There was speculation that she was possibly Susanna Talome, a servant of one McNamara. Seven years earlier, in 1752, the Baltimorean "Jew Tailor" Henry Hart had been accused of an illicit relationship with her and was sentenced to serve McNamara for half a year "for the Damage Sustained . . . on Acct. of the said Henry Hart begetting a Bastard child on the body of Susanna Talome . . ."

Confronted with this rumor, Levy disclosed that his beloved was Susannah Magruder. The records remain silent though in all probability Joseph Simon arranged for her conversion to Judaism.

Levy Andrew Levy, now a man of responsibility, was given a partnership by Simon, to open a trading post at Fort Pitt. With his bride Susannah and their Negro female slave, Levy Andrew proceeded westward on horseback trailed by a file of horses laded with Simon goods. Once over the mountains the women breathed a sigh of relief as they neared Pittsburgh, a new settlement of about three hundred persons nestled in the "Land of the Forks."

Susannah liked the frontier town for it was little larger than her home town of Baltimore and far more exciting. She even felt more secure living within the shadow of strongly garrisoned Fort Pitt. Its blockhouse was a tower of strength to her and the hundred women and children of Pittsburgh. The army was erecting palisades to surround their dwellings, and the parapet of logs raised above the ramparts assured further protection. At Fort Pitt a log hospital was being built under the drawbridge, where patients would be safe from the arrows or musket balls of Indians whenever they might attack. Soldiers were constantly riding in and out of the fort.

In their newly built log cabin in Pittsburgh, Susannah worked hard. Her slave, one of the first blacks in Pittsburgh, was treated like a member of the family. Susannah sewed, baked, and rubbed the Sabbath candlesticks to give them a high polish. Her slave drew water, milked the cow, and cared for the horses. One night, however, she fled with an Indian lover into the forest, never to return. Filling the void was Susannah's deranged brother, Blizzard, who spelled his last name McGruder rather than Magruder. He came to live with them and performed all sorts of odd jobs until one day he, too, ran off.

Susannah never complained, a quality so typical of the pioneering women. Ofttimes her husband Levy Andrew was away from home many days, even weeks. His fur trading trips were limited to a southern trek into western Virginia for the French were entrenched in the Ohio Valley and Great Lakes. At home Susannah had a supply of kosher meats, salted and pickled in Lancaster or Philadelphia. Levy carried some with him but on one trip his supply ran out. Accompanying horsemen offered him bacon which he courteously refused.

At such times Levy wished that he had been a qualified *Shochet,* so that he could perform ritual slaughtering as did his uncle's partner, Benjamin Nathan, at Heidelberg. He would also regret his inability to perform ritual circumcisions as did Barnard Itzhak Jacobs, who operated a shop at Heidelberg.

In 1762 a son was born to Levy Andrew and Susannah. The Biblical law required that the boy be entered into the "Covenant of Abraham" on the eighth day. But Levy who fearlessly led pack trains into hostile Indian country with skillful rifle and hunting knife felt powerless to hone a circumcision knife and perform the rite. Two years after his son's birth, when the lad was strong enough and the weather ideal father and mother brought their child across the mountains to have the rite performed at Lancaster by the "Jew Rabbi" Barnard Jacobs.

The Heidelberg trader gained that honorific title from his townspeople because whenever he learned that a baby boy was born he immediately prepared to leave his residence and shop located on the Millcreek Road, two miles from Tulpehocken, jumped on his horse, and rode off to either Lancaster, York, Reading, Easton, or Philadelphia, always arriving by the eighth day to punctiliously perform the circumcision rite.

Simon's Heidelberg partner, Benjamin Nathan, would however be forced to depart the town in disgrace, the Simon & Nathan dissolving violently. After nonpayment of rent for a year, Simon investigated, learning that his partner had been gambling with their profits. His addiction was such that even when he lost an immediate member of his family he resorted to the gambling saloon instead of observing the first week of mourning in the traditional manner. Jewish custom required a mourner to remain in his place of residence, his garment rent, shoes removed, and seated upon a low stool. He was to recall the merits of the deceased and contemplate the purpose of life.

Simon rode off to Heidelberg, seized a surprised Benjamin Nathan by the collar, and shouting "Get out you dem sona vebitch!," ordered him out. Simon kept all the hardware stock as security, allowing Nathan to take only his "religious tools" which included his honing stones and ritual knives used for kosher slaughtering.

Levy Andrew Levy writing from Lancaster, justified his uncle's actions: "Benjamin Nathan could not wait until the eight days (of mourning) expired, but went to taverns drinking . . . his behavior here is most ridiculous. I need not say more, only that he is a worthless rascal; his character will go with him."

Levy Andrew Levy bemoaned his frontier isolation, concluding: "For a family to be removed from our (Jewish) society is shocking."

"Wolfe's Jew" Helps Topple New France

With British entrenchment in the Land of the Forks, springboard to a West yet under French rule, the impetus of the French and Indian War turned toward the French forts and inland cities along the banks of the Great Lakes and Saint Lawrence River.

British forces captured Isle Royale, largest island in Lake Superior, a key position from which to control the West.

Simon, Levy & Franks, like all colonial merchants and companies, were elated. Contrasting sharply with their buoyant mood were the depressed members of David Gradis & Sons, headquartered in Bordeaux, France, with branches in New France, New Orleans, the French islands in the West Indies—the firm that almost single-handedly provisioned the French and Indian allies for almost a decade.

David Gradis & Sons traded on a large scale, shipping cargoes from Bordeaux to Cayenne, Martinique, St. Domingo, and other West Indian islands. The Gradis company was said to be controlling that great trade. The cargoes consisted of wine, alcohol, and pickled meats, with return cargoes of sugar and indigo.

Founder of the firm, David Gradis, had escaped after the turn of the century with his family from the menacing agents of the Spanish Inquisition. Arrived from Portugal in France, these former Marranos were not expelled as were Jews who gained entry into the French colonies, for the Black Code was instituted primarily to regulate slavery in the American colonies. Portuguese Jews, traders and plantationers alike, also were expelled from the colonies even as they traditionally had been banished from France since the Middle Ages.

David Gradis was an exception. Not only was he allowed to remain in Bordeaux, but his rapid rise to fortune and popularity made him a favorite of men in high position. In 1731, he was singularly honored with citizenship in the city of Bordeaux.

In 1744 the firm of David Gradis & Sons became a power in the New World, too, when David's eldest son, Abraham, assumed leadership of the company. Without ever setting foot in New France, Abraham Gradis operated huge warehouses in Quebec, to which he shipped textiles, foodstuffs, and armaments under the name Society of Canada.

Abraham's devotion to the king, his charm and his personality earned him respectability at court, both as a Frenchman and as a Jew. As he walked on a Paris street one Saturday afternoon, the year long forgotten, the Duc de Richelieu waved to him and invited the Jew to ride in his carriage. Abraham declined, reminding de Richelieu that it was his Sabbath. "In that case," stated the duke, leaving his carriage and grasping Gradis's arm, "we shall both walk."

Recognizing the gravity of France's position in the New World after the English victories in 1758, Abraham Gradis took up his quill to write to an associate in charge of the office of David Gradis & Sons at Guadaloupe, French West Indies:

> For twenty months nothing has been done except to allow our marine to be destroyed. We have just lost Isle Royale, and now Canada is threatened. We have not a single warship left; they have all been captured. The price of foodstuffs is enormously high and it is impossible to send a single ship to the colonies.

Abraham Gradis had cause for concern. At that very moment the British were preparing for a full-scale invasion of New France. Abraham Gradis, troubled over the need for reinforcements, personally recruited 400 troops and shipped them to Canada in his fleet of 26 vessels laden with food, muskets, and munitions, to resupply the stronghold of Quebec. Without such replenishing of the diminishing supplies of gunpowder and foodstuffs, Gradis felt, even the formidable, impregnable fortress of Quebec could be starved into submission and surrender.

France would not forget Abraham Gradis's sacrifices and devotion. A royal letter would be issued on August 21, 1779, signed by King Louis XVI, commending "David Gradis et Fils . . . with the provisioning of Canada and of Isle Royale, from the year 1748 until the time when these last regions had the misfortune to fall into the hands of the English."

For the Gradis's industry in Canada's St. Lawrence and attempted development of the Mississippi Valley and for "the large sums of money and provisions" furnished to the generals and officers, France granted that family full freedom, the rights and privileges of French citizens throughout all its lands, and the right to own property. All this when *Liberté, Egalité, et Fraternité* for Frenchmen, save nobility and clergy, would not become a reality until the French Revolution. French Jews would have to wait for emancipation until 1791.

Even during the French and Indian War, the Gradis family enjoyed the right to trade in Canada and the French West Indies, a privilege in lands where the Jew was banned by *Le Code Noir*.

In 1759, 250 ships, carrying 8,000 British troops under the leadership of General James Wolfe, sailed across the Atlantic to Nova Scotia.

Aboard the fleet ships were the Jewish sutlers Abraham Chapman, Gerson Levy (Levi), Jacob de Maurera, and the cousins Ezekiel Solomons and Levi Solomon. Upon their landing in Halifax, Nova Scotia, they were to report to Commissary-General Aaron Hart, a cousin to Levi Solomon and Ezekiel Solomons. Hart would become further tied to them through the marriage of his brother, Moses Hart, to Esther Solomons, the sister of Ezekiel Solomons.

Aaron Hart had come to America as a lieutenant in the German Legion back in 1745. Under command of Sir Frederick Haldimand he supplied the English army. Seven years later he was appointed to the high post of Commissary-General by Sir Haldimand, commander of the British forces in Canada, and transferred from New York to Halifax. At that Nova Scotian port the British had established three years earlier a sea base to protect the New England colonies from the threat posed by the French from their fortress at Louisbourg, Nova Scotia.

Soon after his arrival in 1752, Hart was shocked to learn of the forced conversion of a Dutch Jew at Louisbourg earlier that year. A hapless Hollander had the misfortune of being discovered aboard the French vessel *La Frippone* en route to Acadia. The ship's officers compelled him to swear on the New Testament to be a true Christian "after he had been enlightened with the truth of the Roman Catholic and horror of the Judaic Religion in which he had hitherto confessed faith."

Upon landing at Louisbourg, he was formally baptized. In a solemn ceremony held at the Royal Chapel the terrified Jew was immersed in the presence of high dignitaries, including the Governor of Acadia, who acted as his Christian godfather and the wife of a naval lieutenant, acting as his godmother.

Hart silently vowed that he would avenge the French for their violation of his fellow Jew's religious conscience and looked forward to the day that other Jews would come to Canada. The 28-year-old Commissary-General, always optimistic and punctilious, responsibly carried his duties in troop supply, and engaged in Indian trade.

Believing himself to be the only Jew in Canada, he was surprised to learn that 20 years before his arrival in Halifax, Ferdinande Jacobs had come to the Canadian Northwest in the employ of the Hudson's Bay Company. Jacobs first served as Chief Factor at Fort Churchill, where the Churchill River emptied into the Hudson Bay in northern Manitoba, then at York Fort, where the Hayes River emptied into the Hudson Bay in northern Manitoba.

Jacobs carried on an extensive Indian trade. There, in the northland on the rim of the Arctic, in the late spring the ice broke up allowing tribesmen from all directions to converge at the fort. By summer, Chippewayan and Woods Cree from the south below the tree line, came in their canoes, and Eskimos from the icy northern cap rowed in their kayaks to make their welcome appearance with their peltries. At the same time, boats arrived from the mother country loaded with goods and supplies to depart before temperatures dropped to below freezing, in their holds packs of pelts destined for London.

A powerful British fleet stormed into the French port-fortress of Louisbourg to command the entranceway to New France.

At last, in 1758, Aaron Hart eagerly welcomed the British troops and sutlers, newly arrived to begin the conquest of New France. Louisbourg fell before their onslaught, and Commissary-General Hart complimented the sutlers for their role. In the following year, he welcomed New York sutlers Benjamin Lyon, who in the previous year escaped the Fort Henry massacre, Manuel Gomez, said to be a grandson of Indian trader Louis Gomez, and Isaac Miranda—grandson of the "Apostate Jew" of that name who traded in Penn's Colony a quarter of a century earlier. These men would assist in troop supply in the pending invasion of the redcoats and their Iroquois allies.

Early in June, 1759, Hart and the increased number of sutlers under his command sailed with the fleet up the Saint Lawrence, their major objective the fortress of Quebec.

Dominating Wolfe's ingress with 15,000 troops and scores of cannon poised in readiness in the heights, was French General Marquis de Louis Joseph Montcalm, who assumed leadership of the troops of the fleur-de-lis after they had defeated the British General Edward Braddock. Having captured Fort William Henry, the victorious Montcalm felt confident and secure as he peered from the plateau on which Quebec was perched. Commanding the all-important St. Lawrence waterway, the fortress-bastion appeared invincible as it overlooked the steep-sided cliffs and Montmorency River Falls that dropped 275 feet into the St. Lawrence River below.

The cunning General Wolfe pondered whether to storm the enemy's stronghold directly from the east near Montmorency Falls or attempt to run through the cannon fire and proceed upriver to assail the heights from the west. He decided to do both in one attack.

Each of the generals preparing for battle would turn to his Jewish aide in matters of strategy and leadership.

The French General de Montcalm had as his first aide Brigadier General Gastogne François de Lévis, a descendant of Henri de Lévis, the Duc de Ventadour, Viceroy of New France (1625-27). The de Lévis family were Marranos who openly hinted of their Jewish ancestry as represented by their centuries-old coat of arms. Proudly it displayed a lion—biblical symbol of the tribe of Judah from which King David descended—and three Stars of David. A more subtle hint was the portrait of the Virgin Mary that hung in the de Lévis family chapel. She was supposed to have spoken to a member of the de Lévis family standing before her, urging *"Couvrez-vous, ma cousin"* (Cover your head, my cousin). "I am more comfortable this way, my cousin," the Marrano Duc de Ventadour replied coolly.

Opposing Montcalm and de Lévis was the English General James Wolfe, who placed great faith in the leadership of the trusted commander of the frigate *Diana,* Captain Alexander Schomberg. A convert to Christianity, he was the son of the deist Meyer Loew Schomberg who had once served as physician to the Great Synagogue of London.

In July, Wolfe attacked from the east and, as expected, was repelled by Generals Montcalm and François de Lévis. The English army withdrew by order of General Wolfe to encamp at Point de Lévis, named in honor of the early viceroy of New France whose descendant was defending Quebec from the heights above.

As Montcalm concentrated his defenses toward warding off that attack in the moonless night, the tide quietly bore British flatboats down the St. Lawrence, past the French cannon, to the west of Quebec, to a cove called Anse du Foulon. In command was Captain Schomberg. He was the first to jump ashore, then gave the silent signal that brought the British troops to shore.

Muscular and steeled for the rugged life demanded of a navy man, Schomberg led the vanguard of soldiers in scaling the 275-foot bluff. They killed the unsuspecting guards, overcame an enemy post, and took the heights commanding strategic Montmorency Falls.

The capture of this key post was followed by the climb up the same cliff by General Wolfe and 5,000 armed troops. Silently, they took their positions. Led by Wolfe, they turned eastward to engage a surprised General Montcalm and his forces camped on the Plains of Abraham. In a battle that lasted but fifteen minutes, and in which both generals, Wolfe and Montcalm, lost their lives, the British scored a decisive victory.

The remnants of the French forces, nearly 7,000 men, rallied behind General de Lévis, who made a daring attempt to recapture Quebec before the ice was out of the St. Lawrence, in the spring of 1760; but lacking reinforcements to sustain his drive, he raised the siege and retreated to Montreal.

There, too, de Lévis prepared to give battle, but Pierre de Rigaud, Marquis de Vaudreuil, Governor and Lieutenant-General throughout New France and Louisiana, by order of King Louis XV, ordered de Lévis to submit instead of fighting a hopeless battle.

Sailing with Amherst towards Montreal, Commissary-General Aaron Hart kept a sharp lookout on the St. Lawrence northern riverbank, not only for the enemy but for a likely location to establish a supply house after the war. This site he spotted midway between Quebec and Montreal. It was the village of Trois Rivières (Three Rivers).

The powerful fleet approached. De Lévis, ordered to surrender, gave himself one bitter and last satisfaction. He ordered his troops to burn their colors, to spare themselves "the hard condition of handing them over to the enemy."

For his gallant conduct and loyalty, the French government would award General Gastogne François de Lévis the coveted title—Chevalier.

With the redcoats entering Montreal on September 8, 1760, the Jewish Commissary-General Aaron Hart enjoyed his chief moment of glory. It came as he rode proud and erect at the side of Major-General Jeffrey Amherst into the cowed city. As the French colors went up in flame and smoke, Hart saw the infamous "Black Code" consigned to oblivion. It was a supreme day for the Jews, a day of judgment for the French.

The war over, Hart lost no time in personifying his inherited family coat of arms—a fleeing hart, surmounted by a crown over the motto: "Schnell Fuss und Frei" (Run fast and free). He hastened to Three Rivers to open a general store in a town of less than 200 families numbering in all about 800 persons.

Eight years after he settled in Three Rivers, Aaron Hart sailed to London to marry his cousin, Dorothea Catherine Judah. After the American Revolution, Dorothea's niece Hannah married the patriot-rabbi of New York, Reverend Gershom Mendes Seixas. The rebel-rabbi had fled his ministry at the Portuguese *Shearith Israel* (Remnants of Israel) synagogue (its edifice erected in 1730, was the first on the continent) to help build in American-held Philadelphia the *Mikveh Israel* (Hope of Israel) synagogue.

Only one other synagogue stood in America before the revolt of the thirteen colonies. That was *Yeshuat Israel* (Salvation of Israel), New Port, Rhode Island, its edifice completed at the end of the French and Indian War, in 1763. Its tradition claimed that it was founded in 1650, four years before New York's *Shearith Israel*.

Just as New York's synagogue was named after that parent congregation in London, England, so too was Canada's first Hebrew congregation. Upon his return to Three Rivers with his bride, Hart assisted Montreal Jews in founding there the congregation *Shearith Israel*. Though he and his cousins and other Canadian Jews were of German origin, they accepted the Portuguese, rather than the German prayer book, in keeping with the Portuguese order of worship prevalent at New York, New Port, Philadelphia, and Lancaster.

Shearith Israel's fledgling congregation at Montreal worshipped in a hall on St. James Street until 1777, when they built their edifice, the third North American synagogue.

Aaron Hart, Dorothea, and children, the only Jewish family in

Three Rivers, strictly observed Sabbaths and Festivals and all the dietary laws. But not for his adherence to Judaism nor his support of the Montreal synagogue did Aaron gain the unsolicited title, "Pope of Canada," but rather because he numbered among his chief benefices Ursuline Convent in Three Rivers. His daughters attended the Convent for their secular studies.

Pious and honest, Aaron gained the confidence of his many customers, troops and settlers alike, even the Indian barterers. Alert for new opportunities, Hart invested his profits in vast acreages. He acquired several sections of Three Rivers, a seigniory of Grondines, Vieux-Pont and Sainte Marguerite, part of Trinity Island and the mouth of Sainte Maurice, and a fief in Bécancour. As Seigneur of Bécancour, Hart was entitled to recruit a battalion of volunteers from among the men who lived in his seigneury. These men wore on their caps a metal badge that bore the Hart coat-of-arms.

Grains harvested on his lands were stored in granaries Hart acquired and shipped on Hart boats. Respected for his integrity, Hart kept in his safe the earnings of farmers and lent money often without interest, eventually to build the Hart Bank.

In time Aaron Hart was spoken of in the "Gentlemen's Magazine" and other English publications of the time as one of the wealthiest British subjects living outside the British Isles and reportedly the wealthiest Jew in the British Empire. But his wealth was greatly exaggerated. His total worth at the end of the century amounted to a hundred thousand dollars.

Respected for his economic, social, and religious standing, Hart hosted Edward, Duke of Kent (father of Queen Victoria), when he came over to Canada as commander of the 60th Regiment. Aaron Hart received the royal visitor in his house at Three Rivers with all appropriate dignity.

The British government never forgot his role in supplying the British troops in the French and Indian War, thus gaining Canada for the Crown. Neither did the British forget the role of another Jewish hero of that war.

After the war, the reigning monarch, King George III, knighted the hero of Quebec, Alexander Schomberg, popularly called by the troops, "Wolfe's Jew."

Yet, Sir Alexander Schomberg preferred the sound of the backwoodsman's axe to that of the palace sword, the beauty of the St. Lawrence to the Thames. He petitioned his superiors to appoint him commissioner of an outpost in the Indian country of the Canadian wilds, the American West, or to assign him to any post His Majesty might prefer along the St. Lawrence or Great Lakes forts.

Appointing Sir Schomberg commander of a frigate in the Royal Navy, the Crown ignored his request presented by his admirer, the renowned English actor, David Garrick, who wittingly urged:

> Make him the tyrant of a fort
> He laughs no more of you or faith
> Surrounded by his scalping court
> What monarch would, be half so great.
>
> Send him where oft he fought and bled
> Again to cross the Atlantic sea
> To tomahawk and wampum-bred
> He's more than half a Cherokee.

Hebrew Captives of Pontiac Uprising

In the fall of 1760, the Union Jack waved over all the Canadian St. Lawrence Valley and Great Lakes forts. In the western foothills of the Alleghenies, Pittsburgh would within the decade supplant Lancaster as the last frontier outpost. Simon instinctively concentrated his trade in this westernmost supply center as the pivotal point of the fur trade. Together with Levy Andrew Levy, he would seek out the Indian tribes deep in the Ohio Valley as far away as the Mississippi.

Simon prepared well for his thrust into the far west. Half a year before the British triumphantly entered Montreal, and a few months before their conquest of Quebec, Joseph Simon was so confident of the outcome that he drew into formal partnership with his nephew, Levy Andrew Levy, to take charge of far western operations and with David Franks to transfer the furs to England. There was also a fourth partner, the famed Indian Agent Captain William Trent Jr., after whose father Trent Town, (the future Trenton), capital of New Jersey, was named.

On May 16, 1760, the firm of Simon, Levy, Trent & Company was founded officially; the "Company" being David Franks who remained a "silent partner" because of his high visibility as supplier of the British troops, a post which could only hurt the company's Indian trade for the tribes were subdued and sullen.

To further develop his Indian trade, Simon took in as an apprentice a former Franks clerk, Barnard Gratz, who would become a leading Indian trader of his day.

Barnard Gratz soon became related to his boss for in December, 1760, Barnard married Richea Myers-Cohen. Her aunt Rachel Myers-Cohen was Simon's mother-in-law. Hence Joseph Simon and Barnard Gratz had married girls who were first cousins.

Joseph Simon was a dynamic businessman. Though he possessed charm and warmth in his family and social relationships, these were not evident when he returned to his daily commercial dealings. Exactly one month after Barnard's wedding, Simon dictated to him the following letter:

Lancaster, 11th January, 1761

Mr. Barnard Gratz,
Merchant in Chesnutt Street,
Philadelphia.

Sir:

I beg you will let me know what you sold the beavor and racoons for, as I must give the people creditt. And as my waggons will be down this week, I beg you will get my things ready.that is for the stilling [distilling] bussiness.

You'll be kind enought to buy me half a galloon of lubbage water (Isaac Levy's wife knows where it is to be had), and ½ gall. of cinnamon water, one barrel of good muscavado (unrefined) sugar, 24 lbs. of chocolate, 25 lbs. good coffe, 1 lb. cinnamon, 1 lb. mace, 1 lb. cloves, and one barrel of Mr. Franks's white powder sugar, if he has any.

Please to send me up my deed of a house and lott in Carlisle (Pennsylvania) which I left in your house, and I have a watch at young Biddle's, which get for me. Any thing that you lay out for me in them triffles, don't book it, but let me know the amount and I will send you down the money by next post.

Lawrence has left me and I have kept Nicholson. My wife joins me in her love to you and Mrs. Gratz (my wife's cousin), and Mr. Bush and his wife and family. I am, sir,

Your humble servant,

Joseph Simon

Shall be obliged to you if you'll send me up two rock fish.

Simon's Indian trade boomed. He purchased a stopover house at strategic Carlisle, midway between Lancaster and Pittsburgh. There his trains could rest on their six-day journey over the mountains. A typical Simon pack train as that recorded on August 17, 1762, was laden with "975 fall deerskins, 501 raccoon pelts, 279 summer deerskins and 173 beaver pelts."

They now encountered a new rival force, the Canadian Jewish sutlers who opened Indian trading posts in former French forts round the Great Lakes. Chapman Abraham settled in Fort Detroit, the former Fort Pontchartrain du Detroit. Gerson Levy (not related to Levy Andrew Levy) opened his Indian post in Fort Sandusky, the former Fort Juandot. Ezekiel Solomons proceeded to the northern tip of the Michigan Peninsula, opening his trading post at Fort Mackinac, the former Fort Michilimackinac. And Benjamin Lyon arrived from New York to compete with him. All of these set out themselves to lead canoe paddling *voyageurs* and Indians in canoes loaded with kegs of rum and whiskey, powder and ball, trinkets and goods, into the Ohio, Illinois, and Wisconsin lands to barter for the Indian furs.

The British officers, however, took a different attitude. Unlike the French, who befriended the Indians and fraternized with them, the English despised them, called them "dogs and hogs," and warily regarded them to be as savage wild animals as wolves or boars. Stringent army regulations were posted in all the western forts. Traders were allowed to sell then only small quantities of powder and lead, insufficient for their hunt, and no rum or liquor. Upon firing the sunset cannon, all trade ceased, the Indians left the fort, and the gates closed.

For two hunting seasons Indian anger smoldered; their wrath kindled against the redcoats and their long rifles, the English settlers who cut down trees, built log cabins, fenced farms, and indiscriminately killed off buffalo, deer, and wildlife. With increasing alarm they wondered how they could preserve the forests from the white intruders.

Pontiac, Chief of the Ottawa, gave the answer in a most striking manner. He besieged Fort Detroit. His plan had been to launch a surprise attack from within the fort, massacre the troops and traders, burn the stockade. His secret plan had, however, been disclosed to Major Henry Gladwin, commander of that Great Lakes fort, by a Chippewa who was in love with him. She paid a high price for her treason. Though no one ever would say how it happened, Indians told that she "fell" into a vat of boiling maple syrup.

In the spring of 1763, as the Pontiac siege of Fort Detroit began, Chapman Abraham, having resupplied at Fort Niagara, was blissfully canoeing up the Detroit River to his trading post in Fort Detroit. His was the lead canoe. Four others followed, loaded with Indian trade goods, a goodly quantity of forbidden rum, foodstuffs, and seventeen barrels of gunpowder.

The sun was setting in a blaze of glory that Thursday, May 12. Though they could have made Fort Detroit in a few hours, chief *voyageur* Chapman Abraham decided to bank the canoes and rest until daybreak at the outpost of his friend, the Frenchman Saint Louis.

An alarmed Monsieur St. Louis greeted his friend with the news that Fort Detroit was under siege. Abraham ordered his men immediately to row back to Fort Niagara, unaware that Indians were attacking that and other Great Lakes forts as well. He had no idea how widespread was the Pontiac revolt. His fellow *voyageurs,* however, felt that it was no longer safe to be paddling in the middle of the river as perfect targets and refused to return to the canoes. Chapman had no alternative but to accept the welcome offer of his French benefactor and store his cargo inside St. Louis's cabin.

All goods and kegs of rum and sacks of ammunition safely stashed, the *voyageurs* sought out places to hide. Chapman Abraham found a cave that led beneath the cabin of a French woman, Madame Esperame. She, however, chanced upon him. Fearful that her own life would be endangered if he were discovered by the Indians, she demanded that he leave. Abraham, aware that he would emerge into certain death, offered his most valuable possession, a solid gold watch chain. She was not tempted and ordered his immediate departure.

The desperate Jewish trader scurried off towards the woods but was caught by Chippewa who ground out of him the information they sought. Brought back to the St. Louis cabin, he helplessly watched the Chippewa and Huron carry out his trade goods, gunpowder, and rum, which they gleefully distributed and divided amongst themselves.

The Chippewa, whose name meant "to roast until puckered up" and who ate the flesh of their captives when they took to the warpath, took a trembling Abraham to their tepee camp nearby. They tortured him with painful ordeals then tied him to a stake preliminary to his burning.

A remarkable drama then unfolded. As Abraham begged for a last drink, his wish was granted. It was Indian custom, previous to a captive being put to death, to give him what they called his last meal; a bowl of pottage or broth. Such kindness, they believed, would forestall any ill report by the victim of his slayers in the spirit world.

Abraham's hands were untied and a bowl brought to him by a brave. He raised the bowl to his mouth and the hot liquid scalded his lips. Instinctively he spit it out and flung the bowl and its broth into the face of the brave who had handed it to him. The superstitious Indians encircling the stake awaiting the burning were convinced that the paleface was mad, and therefore under the protection of the Great Spirit, as were all insane men.

At Fort Detroit, rascally Frenchmen told Commander Gladwin of Chapman Abraham's capture and said that its large cargo of ammunition was in the hands of the Hurons, all drunk from the rum they seized. Gladwin ordered 25 volunteers to board the sloop, go down and burn the Huron village, and rescue the powder. They rowed a short distance; then the wind shifted and blew against them. Gladwin signaled for their return. The commander later learned that more than a hundred Hurons, very sober, were waiting in ambush.

The besieged Gladwin was unable to dispatch men to rescue Abraham and others. After two months of captivity he was in the hands of the Potawatomi who brought him with trader Hugh Crawford (perhaps related to Colonel William Crawford, burned by Sandusky Indians in 1782), and seven soldiers, for exchange with a Potawatomi Chief.

During the fateful month of May, when the inflamed Pontiac revolt began with the seige of Fort Detroit, other western tribes—Ojibwa, Huron, Potawatomi—were likewise fired with the spirit of attack upon their return from the winter hunt and so, too, the Shawnee and Miami.

The Ojibwa arrived with their pelts at Michilimackinac, "Island of the Turtle." They brought in their furs at the fort, bartering with Ezekiel Solomons, Benjamin Lyon, and competing Christian trader Alexander Henry. They powwowed with some visiting Sauk and (as had been their custom) engaged in a game of baggataway (lacrosse) on the sand just outside the fort.

During an exciting moment of the contest, the ball was purposely tossed into the fort. Indian players rushed after the ball, snatching as they ran weapons from under the blankets draped about the squaws. Alexander Henry described the massacre: "The dead were scalped and mangled; the dying were writhing and shrieking under unsatiated knife and tomahawk; and from the bodies of some, ripped open, their butchers were drinking the blood, scooped up in the hollow of joined hands and quaffed amid shouts of rage and victory."

A search uncovered Ezekiel Solomons hiding in the loft of a cabin. Fortunately for him, an Ojibwa recognized him as a friend and took him captive. Ezekiel was released a few months later after receiving a ransom. Somehow Benjamin Lyon, who barely escaped the Mohawk scalpers at Fort Henry in 1757, managed once again to elude the Ojibwa and Sauk warriors thirsting for more of the white man's blood at the remains of Fort Mackinac.

The spontaneous revolt of the western Indians round the Great Lakes and river forts as they heard of Pontiac's attack had erupted with such suddenness that white settlers and traders traveling the rivers and trails had no knowledge of any uprising.

Two hundred and fifty miles south of Mackinac Island, and about 70 northwestward of Fort Detroit, trader Jacobs was on his way inland of Saginaw Bay, up the Saginaw River to trade at Saginaw. Arrived there, the Indians suddenly attacked. It is not known if Jacobs was a Jew but to the Indians all that mattered was that he was an Englishman. After being mortally wounded, Jacobs shot dead one of the Ojibwa.

On the trail near Fort Sandusky, Gerson Levy was captured by Wyandotte, but by some clever strategy escaped his captors. He may have been on his way to join Fort Pitt's Levy Andrew Levy, then en route to Fort Detroit.

Approaching Fort Sandusky, Levy Andrew Levy, leading his pack train from the Simon & Levy trading post at Fort Pitt to rendezvous with the Wyandotte at the shore of Lake Erie, was unaware of the Indian uprising. As he proceeded north coming close to his destination, the Wyandotte kept him and his pack train under surveillance. When it entered a forested terrain, they made their sudden appearance, dropping from the branches with shrill shrieks and tomahawks swinging. There was no time to defend themselves or the property. The Indians appeared from all over onto Levy's train and party of ten. A few were scalped and killed, others injured.

Appropriating what they could wear and carry, they set torch to the wagons, dragging into the woods their surviving captives.

Word reached Joseph Simon in Lancaster that "the Indians have begun a war near the Forts. They've killed and taken several people and traders and Levy is a prisoner." Levy's wife, Susannah, hoped and prayed for Andrew's safe return. Then his uncle Joseph received a second unfortunate report: "Levy A. Levy was killed this side of Cap d'Troit."

Her worst fears confirmed, Susannah mourned the loss of her husband. She was comforted by his bereaved uncle and aunt, Joseph and Rose Simon. Charitable offerings were pledged in his parlor-synagogue to the memory of *Yehudah Halevy,* the Hebrew name of Andrew Levy. Susannah spoke affectionately of *Leib Anshel,* as she endearingly called her husband by his Yiddish (Judeo-German) name.

At the end of the first week of mourning, the period of *shiva* (meaning seven), grief reverted to joy as news was received that Levy Andrew Levy was alive. On July 9, "Levey," along with Ensign Christy (who commanded at Presqu'Isle—an island near Lake Erie in northwestern Pennsylvania) and three soldiers, were beseiged at that stockade for three days by the Wyandotte. Upon their surrender the Indians allowed them to go to Fort Pitt but en route they were again attacked. An entry made by a Major Roberts in his diary on July 10 noted: "We heard today that the Miami Indians were gone off with Mr. Levy." Apparently the Miami acquired Levy from the Wyandotte. Levy made his escape (in his diary Levy Andrew Levy recorded the details of his captivity and escape).

As he made his way southward, Levy heard that Fort Pitt had withstood the Indian attacks. Simeon Ecuyer, commander of Fort Pitt, having learned of the Indian killing of a man, two women, and a child 25 miles south of Fort Pitt, and sensing the Indian mood, had ordered the outlying village of Pittsburgh, its 200 cabins and huts, burned to the ground to prevent attackers from operating under their cover. All the inhabitants were safe in the fort.

As Ecuyer surmised, the Delaware and Mingo attacked. Fort Pitt's fortifications were stronger than those at Fort Detroit, and defended by twice as many troops. It withstood the combined forces of the tribes, which included the Shawnee and Wyandotte, who in their usual battle plan returned again and again with intermittent attacks but lacked an all-out concentrated effort. After five weeks they withdrew and did not return.

During those five weeks the Indian siege made it impossible for sanitary conditions to be maintained within the walls. Refuse mounted, resulting in an outbreak of smallpox that almost reached epidemic proportions. When the siege ended, Captain Ecuyer informed Field Commander Colonel Henry Bouquet of the raging smallpox plague; he in turn notified his superior, General Jeffrey Amherst, Commander-in-Chief of the British forces in North America.

General Amherst, who loathed all Indians, recommended that Commander Bouquet engage in what would become termed germ warfare. The General wrote Bouquet: "Could it not be contrived to send the smallpox among the dissatisfied tribes?" Bouquets's response —to distribute infected blankets from smallpox sufferers at Fort Pitt to Indians around the fort—was relayed to Captain Ecuyer.

An opportune moment to implement Commander Bouquet's order presented itself on June 24 when a Delaware chief accompanied by his principal warrior arrived at Fort Pitt to inform the white chief, Simeon Ecuyer, that the Indians had captured the three forts between Fort Pitt and the Great Lakes Fort Niagara and urged his surrender of the garrison. Ecuyer politely thanked the Delaware Chief but insisted that he could ably defend his post against any combined onslaught. He urged them to make peace and gave them presents—each a blanket and handkerchief.

Captain Ecuyer then called upon Levy Andrew at his trading post. He told how he tricked the chief into accepting the deadly gifts and placed an order to replace the blankets and handkerchiefs. This grim invoice accompanied the new goods, receipt of which was duly acknowledged by Ecuyer:

> Debtor: The Crown to Levy, Trent & Co., for sundries had by order of Captain Simeon Ecuyer, Commandant . . . to sundries, got to replace in kind those which were taken from the people in the hospital to convey the smallpox to the Indians, viz.,
>
> | | |
> |---|---:|
> | 2 blankets @ | 2.00. |
> | 1 silk handkerchief @ | .10. |
> | 1 linen do. | 3.6 |
> | Total: | 2.13.6 |
>
> Fort Pitt, August 15, 1763
>
> I do hereby certify that the above articles . . . were had for the uses above-mentioned.
>
> S. ECUYER, CAPTAIN, COMMANDANT

Seventy Shawnee, Mingo, and Delaware, fell before the unseen enemy, smallpox. Many more undoubtedly died, for the Indians had no resistance to the white man's diseases.

As the siege of Fort Detroit wore on, Joseph Simon received urgent requests to dispatch supplies to sustain the 250 beleaguered troops. In short order, a Simon, Levy, Trent & Franks pack train, the largest they ever assembled, was readied. Levy Andrew set out to lead the train over the protests of his wife, in-laws, and partners, but he was adamant. As he set forth at the head of the well-armed train, he was joined by an equally formidable one outfitted by the Quaker firm, Baynton, Wharton & Morgan, operating out of Philadelphia. The Jewish and Quaker rivals in the western Indian trade for the moment joined forces for their security and to save the entrapped troops.

So from Philadelphia a giant soldier-guarded pack train combining the supplies of the two companies set forth together. Clothing, blankets, gunpowder, and—strangely enough—a large hand-made British flag were among the many commodities loaded aboard the train that wended northwestward. Without these necessities the men within the fort and their families and soldiers could not subsist.

It was a hot, stifling night, that July 21, as the Jewish-Quaker pack trains crossed the narrow timber bridge that crossed Paris Creek, just two miles from Fort Detroit. Not a leaf moved, not a blade of grass stirred, only the hoofs of the horses and mules broke the stillness when suddenly all the troop-guards were overwhelmed by the onslaught of Ojibwa, Huron, and Ottawa warriors. Fifty-eight soldiers were tomahawked to death, wounded, or taken prisoner. Among the captives was Levy Andrew. Among those killed was the army captain, James Dalyell.

The triumphant Pontiac invited to a grand celebration feast the Frenchmen living in the vicinity who helped provide the warring tribes with foodstuffs and supplies for the siege. The feast finished, the chief asked his guests, "How did you like the meat?" He did not wait for an answer, but added, "It was very good young beef, was it not? Come here. I will show you." Pontiac then opened a sack lying on the ground and took out the bloody head of the English captain who had been felled at Parent's Creek, appropriately renamed Bloody Run. The French had been tricked into partaking of the flesh of their enemies— an old Indian custom.

At Fort Detroit as at Fort Pitt, Pontiac's stranglehold weakened because his braves were human after all. They lost their patience waiting for victory. After six months, the impatient braves of undisciplined tribes left for their villages in order to prepare for their annual winter's hunt. The captured Fort Mackinac and others were abandoned to the astonishment of the English, the tribes all setting out to trap and hunt. Pontiac retreated into the far western Illinois Country.

Pontiac's uprising quelled in the Ohio Valley and Great Lakes, Great Britain created a vast reservation for the tribes. In October of 1763 King George III made it official. He advised "all loving subjects . . . on pain of our displeasure" not to cross the crest of the Appalachian mountains into the West. Troops were dispatched to the Great Lakes and Ohio forts and along the mountain passes. Only licensed Indian traders would be permitted entry to barter for furs, not land.

To obtain license to trade with the Indians, traders were required to invoice under oath the supplies they carried into Indian country. An Ezekiel Solomons invoice included "28 bales of dry goods (blankets, cotton goods, linens); 2 sacks of flour; 4 bales and 1 'role' of tobacco; 4 boxes of iron ware containing brass and copper kettles (an assortment of knives, needles, axes); 24 Indian guns, 600 pounds of gunpowder, 1,000 pounds of shot and ball." In addition to the solids, there were "256 gallons of rum and brandy, 64 gallons wine." This cargo, 18 months' supply of "sundry goods," was valued at 750 pounds.

All 16 of his French-Canadian canoemen, *voyageurs* all, none of whom could sign their names (unlike their leader Ezekiel), had to declare solemnly together that they would not stir up trouble with the Indians and to swear allegiance to the King.

Solomons also had to post bond of almost double the value of his wares as assurance that he would scrupulously observe all prohibitions governing relations with the Indians. Ezekiel Solomons was thereupon issued his license, permitting him to trade at "Michilimackinac and beyond. . . ."

All western barterers avoided entry into the Illinois Country. There, the unappeased Pontiac convinced the Illini, Cahokia, Kaskaskia, Kickapoo, and Piankishaw tribes to band under his leadership and keep the redcoats and English traders and settlers out of the Mississippi Valley.

Minor skirmishes flared between British troops and the Illini Confederacy. The far western tribes prevailed. French flags continued to fly over Fort du Chartres, as they had since the day it was founded in 1720. Fort du Chartres was the key post in the Mississippi Valley, situated halfway between the mouths of the Missouri and the Kaskaskia rivers, about midway up the "Great River"—the Mississippi. Rebuilt by the French in 1753, its wooden walls and barracks had been replaced with heavy stones. It guarded on its flanks the French settlements of Cahokia to the north and Kaskaskia to the south, all on the Mississippi's eastern riverbank in the Illinois Country.

The British considered Fort du Chartres as the finest fort in western America and were determined to occupy that bastion and raise over its grounds the Union Jack. In 1764 British authorities at Fort Mobile (the former French Fort Louis de la Mobile founded in 1702) prepared to send an expedition up the Mississippi to take Fort du Chartres. Major Robert Farmar, the British Commandant at Fort Mobile, turned to the leading western firm, the Jewish Monsanto Company headquartered in Spanish New Orleans to outfit troops and furnish bateaux to convoy them to Fort du Chartres on the Mississippi and Fort de Vincennes on the Wabash.

The Monsanto Company was well stocked to equip soldiers, plantationers, *voyageurs,* storekeepers, and everyone with everything. The firm engaged in the sale of a variety of goods, wholesale and retail, ranging from guns to calico, from canvas and lumber to sugar and lime, as well as cattle and slaves.

From New Orleans, the six-year-old Monsanto Company reached out that year (1764) to French Martinique as the official agent of David Gradis & Sons of Bordeaux; to Spanish Cuba; and to English Jamaica and other Caribbean islands. On the continent, its shipping reached into British West Florida on the Gulf and Spanish Louisiana. Its founder, Isaac Rodrigues Monsanto, himself a merchant-prince, lived even as a *voyageur,* canoeing up the Mississippi to Kaskaskia to barter with the Illini tribes.

The great Monsanto Company would not last another six years. Isaac Monsanto and his family and Jewish associates were the first Jews to reenter, in 1758, the French Louisiana from which country their predecessors were banished in 1724. Distracted by the French and Indian War and aware of the importance of Monsanto as representative of David Gradis & Sons in advancing supplies to the French troops, the Monsantos were allowed to remain.

Upon the defeat of the French in New France, to prevent New Orleans from being forfeited to the British, King Louis XV presented the city as a gift to his Spanish cousin, Charles III, in a secret treaty dated November 3, 1762. The Monsantos of New Orleans now came under the rule of the Inquisition, which forbade Jews from staying upon Spanish soil.

The Monsantos and their kinsmen were shocked when, in 1764, the secret was made public with the raising of the Spanish flag over New Orleans. Isaac Monsanto realized there was but little time before the Holy Office would single out him and his family, and other Jews, for persecution and worse. So it was important for these merchants to expend every effort to gain their fortunes quickly and quietly and depart.

In 1764, when the Monsanto Company outfitted the British convoy to the Illinois Country, the firm was at the height of its power and expanding its phenomenal development. During the four-year period that followed until Spain dispatched a governor to assume control, the Monsantos and New Orleanean Jews were lulled into complacency. They were therefore caught unawares upon the arrival in 1769 of General Don Alejandro O'Reilly, the governor of Louisiana Territory under Spain. He instituted a local Inquisition, stripped the Monsantos and other prospering New Orleans Jews of their wealth, and expelled them. The Monsanto Company emporium and its warehouse, one of the largest in the Crescent City, was expropriated.

In Monsanto outfitted and supplied canoes, Major Farmar dispatched Lieutenant John Ross to Fort du Chartres to attempt peaceably to persuade the tribes to accept the coming of a British garrison. But at the powwow held April 4, the Cahokia, Kaskaskia, Peoria, Michigamea, and other western tribal chiefs declared for war. The British decided to try yet another strategy.

General Thomas Gage, Commander-in-Chief of the British forces, called upon George Croghan, Deputy Superintendent for Indian Affairs, to smoke the peace pipe with the western chiefs and offer them gifts in exchange for peace.

Croghan arranged with Baynton, Wharton & Morgan to outfit an 81-pack-horse train to be shipped from Philadelphia to Pittsburgh, there to be reloaded aboard flatboats to be poled down the Ohio to Fort de Vincennes, where rendezvous would be set for his meeting with Pontiac and the chiefs of the Illini, presenting gifts and smoking the calumet.

The Quaker outfitted pack train was, however, ambushed on the Pennsylvania-Virginia border south of Pittsburgh by the "Black Boys" and burned. The "Black Boys" were white frontiersmen who cheated Indians and white traders alike. They were called "Black Boys" because they smeared a black pigment over their faces streaked with vermillion, donned breech clouts and leggings of animal hides, and bound red handkerchiefs around their heads to simulate the naked painted skulls and bodies of the Indians in order to cast suspicion upon them.

With only seventeen horseloads of goods salvaged out of the original 81, Croghan turned to Simon, Levy, Trent & Franks to replace the 64 horseloads destroyed. The Jewish firm filled the order calling for "Sundries for the Use of the Indians." It totaled 2,000 pounds. The items included beads, silver armbands, ear bobbs and bells, hair plates and hair trinkets, looking glasses (mirrors), blankets, tomahawks, axes,

36,499 black wampum (valued at twice that of white wampum), and 24,100 white wampum. In addition, there was reserved for the chiefs ruffled shirts and silk handkerchiefs, with one scarlet vest laced with silver reserved for Pontiac. Nor did the order omit Jews' harps of which the Indians were fond, 19 dozen being sent.

Jews' harps were the only musical instrument ever mentioned in the western traders' invoices. Shaped like a harp, but so small that it fitted into the palm of one's hand, the little lyre-shaped instrument was placed between the teeth and a bent metal tongue struck by the finger. The Indians like to play these harps as they were simple to pluck and the sound fascinated them.

Why they were called Jews' harps is no longer known. Perhaps Simon, Levy & Franks were the first to trade with them on a large scale. In keeping with the wit of that day and age, it was asked: "Did you ever see a Jews' harp? "No," was the reply, "but I have frequently seen a Jew sharp."

In May of 1765, the Simon, Levy, Trent & Franks train shoved off from the banks of Pittsburgh, guarded by a protective party of soldiers and friendly Delaware who accompanied the transport down the Ohio River.

On June 8, at the mouth of the Wabash, Kickapoo fired from the riverbank, killing six of the Delaware, then suddenly discontinued their shooting. The Kickapoo approached in apologetic humbleness. The Delaware, they explained, resembled the Cherokee, their deadliest enemy. The Kickapoo then insisted upon conveying the party to Fort de Vincennes, over which still flew an old French flag. Lowered by the British, the fort was renamed Fort Sackville.

The gifts of the Jewish and Quaker firms had accomplished what the British army could not effect. On October 9, 1765, after Pontiac smoked the peace pipe, troops from Fort Pitt arrived in Fort du Chartres and raised the Union Jack over what they called Fort Chartres. The British was the new power in the West from the Appalachians to the Mississippi.

When Indiana Was South of the Ohio

A new era of trade was begun in the West. It was the beginning of a short but peaceful period leading up to the Revolutionary War. Jewish merchants were in the forefront of the Indian trade, competing with the powerful Quaker firm. Simon, Levy & Franks moved fast into the

Illinois Country, but even faster—and first to open an outpost on the Mississippi—was Baynton, Wharton & Morgan. The latter member of the Quaker firm, George Morgan, left for Kaskaskia and opened western headquarters for his firm on the Mississippi.

Kaskaskia, the largest of the far western settlements, was founded by the French in 1700 and boasted a population of 3,000. Though set in picturesque surroundings, Kaskaskia was a drab place, its two or three long narrow unpaved streets often knee-deep with mud; its residences were shacks of wood with thatched roofs.

The townspeople maintained large vegetable gardens enclosed with crude picket fences. The produce grown in the rich bottomlands of the Kaskaskia River at its junction with the Mississippi provided the needs of the 300 army troops stationed at nearby Fort Chartres to the north.

On the heels of George Morgan, there followed agents of the Simon, Levy, Trent & Co., whose first shipment left Pittsburgh below the Ohio River under the charge of Captain Henry Prather and George Gibson. Arrived at Kaskaskia, the two men entered the riverbank trading post of their rival Quaker firm. They examined a fine array of deer, bear, raccoon, silver fox, and wildcat skins. A deal was made and the consignment bought by Gibson.

As Prather was carrying the furs out of the post, George Morgan discovered that the purchase had been made by his company's bitterest rivals, the Jewish firm. He flew into a rage and attacked Gibson. Prather came to his aid and pinned Morgan to the ground. Morgan yielded and conceded ". . . that his strength was much superior to mine as mine to a fly."

The sparring Jewish and Quaker firms gave no quarter. In an attempt to divert the flow of furs pouring into the Simon outposts in Pittsburgh—Simon & Levy, Simon & (James) Milligan, Simon & (Abraham) Mitchell (expanded about 1765 to Simon, Mitchell & McClure and contracted by 1773 to that of Simon & Campbell)—the Philadelphia based Baynton, Wharton & Morgan set up a trading post on the Scioto River. Situated in the heart of Shawnee country, midway between Kaskaskia and Pittsburgh, the Quaker firm would intercept pelts bound for the Joseph Simon trading partnerships in Pittsburgh.

The Quaker firm, however, failed to make any impressive gains as the tribes, even the hostile Shawnee, remained loyal to their old friend, Joseph Simon.

But the fur trade was a hazardous trade. After bringing the peltries to Philadelphia, they had to be shipped to London and the Indian goods transported from London to Philadelphia warehouses. Marine insurance was expensive and not always easy to secure. Once the trade supplies arrived and were shipped by wagon from Philadelphia to Lancaster and Fort Pitt, the canoes where loaded and sent down the Ohio. Frequently the Indians had to be "carried on the books" for a year before the furs came in. And when they finally reached the eastern and transatlantic market, there was question if the buyers could afford the luxury at the time.

There was only one hope on which the future of western commerce could be secured—Indian land to which the Jewish and Quaker firms had rightful claim. Both sought compensation for their losses at Bloody Run near Fort Detroit, suffered during the Pontiac Uprising in 1763. Though fierce competition divided the two major western firms in the Ohio, they united to seek joint compensation.

Simon, Levy & Franks, in concert with Baynton, Wharton & Morgan, claimed their despoiled goods totaled an astronomical 86,000 pounds. Referring to themselves as "suffering traders," the merchant-princes of the western trade consolidated to form a land company by which they attempted to gain compensation in Indian land. They called their proposed colony "The Indiana Company," seeking Indian territory south of the Ohio, in western Virginia, the region then known as "Indiana."

After four years of agitation, they seemed about to achieve their goal. On November 5, 1768, 3,000 braves from the Iroquois Six Nations—the Mohawk, Oneida, Onondaga, Cayuga, Seneca and Tuscarora—assembled at Fort Stanwix (present Rome, New York), a few miles east of Lake Oneida. Captain William Trent, Jr., an associate of Simon, Levy & Franks, sat at the head of the white delegation along with Sir William Johnson, Superintendent of Indian Affairs.

The Six Nations bartered for trinkets and goods an immense expanse of territory stretching from western New York to eastern Kentucky. Of this cession the Jewish and Quaker "Indiana Company" would receive 2,500,000 acres as soon as the Crown affixed its seal of approval.

The Six Nations, friendly to the British ever since the French killed two of their chiefs, in 1609, a year after Samuel de Champlain founded Quebec, were now forced by their allies to yield their hunting grounds to the white invaders from the colonies. A portion of these lands would pay the trading firms for attacks upon supply trains perpetrated by their tributaries, the Ottawa, Ojibwa, and Hurons—always friendly to the French.

The traders, particularly those of Simon, Levy, Trent & Company were dissatisfied for they had never been compensated for their massive losses suffered in 1754 when Shawnee and Delaware and other tribes destroyed their supply train consigned for General Braddock. That claim was again denied even though these tribes were tributaries of the Six Nations, for that occurred before the defeat of the French. Only the French could be held responsible, for they controlled those tribes before their defeat in 1760. The trading firms would have to resign themselves to compensation for the 1763 Indian depradations.

The Crown also refused to approve an Indian grant of land to the "suffering traders" whose losses in the Pontiac Uprising were at the hands of the Indians alone, the French having been defeated three years earlier. The English again claimed that the French had been the culprits. The western firms concentrated again on Illinois trade.

The following year, 1769, Simon, Levy & Franks managed to secure the highly profitable Fort Chartres provisions contract to supply the English troops stationed there. Baynton, Wharton & Morgan having lost that contract retreated from the western trade. The Quaker firm sold their Kaskaskia headquarters and secondary posts at Cahokia, Fort Sackville, and on the Scioto with all its supplies and goods for 10,000 pounds to Simon, Levy & Franks. The Jewish firm retained the services of George Morgan at the Kaskaskia headquarters.

But the Simon-led firm benefited little from the Fort Chartres deal. The following year the fort was flooded by the Mississippi on a rampage. The swampy stagnant pools left by the receding waters bred swarms of mosquitos that spread disease. Soldiers were prostrated and many died. General Thomas Gage ordered Fort Chartres abandoned and dismantled.

Joseph Simon, at the height of his power and position, retreated from the western fur trade. Whatever partnership dissolutions with western Indian agents were required they progressed as smoothly and amicably as could be for Simon's honesty was legendary. Among his partnership dissolutions was that, at a later date, of his relationship with Indian trader, Colonel Alexander Lowrey, a forty-year association. They never kept contracts, papers or books. Simon merely summoned arbitrators in whose presence he reminded Lowrey of payments made at a certain spring in distant Indian country. Lowrey then asked Simon to state the exact sum, which Simon precisely rendered. It was now Colonel Alexander Lowrey who reminded Joseph Simon that he paid him a quantity of wampum while the two sat on a log along a certain riverbank in the land of the Shawnee. Thus did the two old Indian traders barter over transactions of almost half-a-century and in short order they made a final, amicably concluded, settlement.

As Simon retired from his western trading posts he firmly believed that the day would soon dawn when the feuding colonies, Pennsylvania and Virginia, would settle their dispute as to who owned the west and either colony would then validate their grants.

Back at his Lancaster store, as he prepared to turn over his western trading posts to his new son-in-law Michael Gratz and his brother Barnard Gratz, who was distantly related through marriage, Joseph Simon firmly believed that though the Crown did not affix his seal of approval, the day would not be distant when his firm's claim for compensation in land for trade goods lost in the Pontiac War would be recognized. Both his firm and the Quaker firm united in the "Indiana Company" would achieve its just aim and their dreams of a colonial empire in the West would be realized.

Trading "Sundries" for the Illinois Country

Upon the dissolution of Simon, Levy & Franks' far western enterprises and the return of Levy Andrew Levy to Lancaster, Joseph Simon sent to Pittsburgh an ambitious son-in-law to manage with his brother and acquire the firm's frontier trading posts. He was Michael Gratz, who in 1769 married Simon's daughter Miriam.

After the French and Indian War, the brothers formed B. & M. Gratz Co. Having been apprenticed in the counting house of tycoon David Franks and schooled by Joseph Simon in the Indian trade, the brothers made many trips into the West.

Neither Barnard nor Michael remotely resembled the general image of the wilderness frontier trader. Barnard was stocky, short-necked, and shrewd. He seemed to belong on a high stool behind the desk in a counting house. Michael, rotund of body with small pudgy hands, had the look of a benevolent Mr. Pickwick. Yet neither hesitated, at any time since they first set foot in the West, to cast aside their counting-house garb for fringe jacket, breeches, boots, and rifles. Of the two brothers, Michael had proven himself the greater adventurer. On the high seas, he had traveled to India and the South Seas and on land journeyed deep into the Indian country of the West.

The religious scruples of the brothers were constantly in evidence. When Michael, once on his way to Curacao, survived a shipwreck in the Caribbean and was rescued a short while before the Jewish Sabbath, he scribbled a brief note to his brother. Curtly advising Barnard of his safety, he explained its brevity: "Being just Shabat—it being forbidden to write on a holy day."

Barnard was strictly observant and as a ritual slaughterer enjoyed meats even in the western wilderness. He was so adept that he issued a *kabalah* (a certificate to perform this sacred act) to 18-year-old Solomon Etting, his future son-in-law, in 1768 so that Lancaster's Jews would be provided with kosher meats. Solomon's father, Elijah Etting, was a pioneer Indian trader at York, Pennsylvania.

The entry of the Gratz brothers into the Far West came about when William Murray, a Scotch-Irish Indian trader, left Philadelphia to establish an outpost at Cahokia. He turned over his trading house to the brothers in Philadelphia and arranged that they supply his Cahokian outpost—William Murray & Co.—on the Mississippi.

William Murray, like George Morgan, loved the Illinois Country. He was not disappointed by the shabbiness of Cahokia, the oldest French settlement in the Mississippi Valley, having been founded in 1699, a year before Kaskaskia.

Cahokia's huge, grass-covered earthen mounds puzzled Murray as they had the early settlers. Certainly the majestic earthen pyramids could not have been built by the savage Indians. But as archaeologists would one day discover, Indians laboriously built at Cahokia 120 ceremonial burial mounds, covering about six-and-a-half miles. Cahokia flourished as a great city five centuries before the discovery of America by Columbus, boasting streets, warehouses, man-made lakes, and docks, crude but correct astronomical observatories and sun calendars, walled fortifications. The only known Indian city north of the Aztec metropolis that became Mexico City, Cahokia seems to have been the center of an empire that dominated the American Bottoms, a fertile 175-square-mile valley near the confluence of the Mississippi, Illinois, and Missouri rivers.

By the time the first Frenchmen arrived, the Indian city had vanished, only the mounds were evident to the fur traders but they remained to them a mystery.

Murray had no trouble finding living quarters because Catholic Cahokia had been depopulated five years earlier when many French families departed upon the raising of the British flag on the west bank, five miles upriver at Saint Louis in French Louisiana. Those French families were dismayed to learn that St. Louis and the west Louisiana were turned over to the Spanish but it was still better to be under the Spanish than the hated British.

Murray sent for his wife and children. They were shocked at the drab appearance of the town. He humored them with his mellow Scotch-Irish wit, which gained for him the friendship of villagers, *voyageurs,* and Indians alike. The light-hearted trader teased and humored even his boss: "Pray don't my friend forget the Little Ones [Baynton, Wharton & Morgan] down the river [at Kaskaskia on the Mississippi]. I wish they were bound to some honest tradesmen in town or country."

Murray found that his greatest adversary was not rival firms but the elements. When the Mississippi overflooded its banks, disease spread. Stricken with malarial fever for the sixth time in a single season, Murray scolded the Gratz brothers for being remiss in their shipments: "A plague! Why did you not send some good spirits, sugar, tea, court wine if possible, and some little etceteras for my own use. I must go to bed and sweat. God bless you." It was his way of chastising his bosses.

But there was no wine to send. The Gratzes were among the merchants who were then boycotting English goods in protest of Parliament's passage of taxes on a variety of goods shipped to them from the Mother Country. Michael replied apologetically: "I was sorry I could not assist my dear friend this time with a little good red port with which I tried hard for between Philadelphia and New York but it was not to be had at either place. So you must make the best of the cask of Madeira wine this time till by next Batteau if any is to be had you may depend on having some."

As they boycotted British imports, the Gratz brothers came to the conclusion that their western trade, though profitable, was resting on precarious foundations. Ofttimes the Indians had to be "carried on the books" for a season or two before the furs came in. So, too, the Gratz western agents, particularly George Croghan, who became exclusively identified with the Gratz brothers: he was perennially indebted to them for thousands of pounds. On one occasion the brothers accepted in payment of debts amounting to almost 12,000 pounds a section of land Croghan acquired in the Mohawk Valley of New York as his personal share in the settlement made with the tribes at Fort Stanwix. On this land they founded Gratzburg, an important supply point for pioneers since it was on the road winding through the only great break in the Appalachian Mountains that led into the West.

Until Croghan's death, the brothers were to remain his trusted bankers and faithful legal agents. On request, they lent him money at a reasonable rate of interest; they drew up and kept safe his documents; they received and forwarded much of his mail; through them his bills and debts were incurred and paid. To satisfy Croghan's personal wants on the frontier, the brothers shipped to their valued Ohio Valley agent everything from sugar and spices to fine liquors, clothing, and bridles. Above and beyond business relationships they were fast and firm friends.

Little wonder that the Gratz brothers, who risked so much in the fur trade, became convinced that the true wealth lay in land—virgin, western land.

The Gratz brothers set their sights beyond the boundaries set by the Treaty of Fort Stanwix, determined to barter for raw Indian Territory in the far western Illinois Country. They could monopolize the entire far western fur trade, by acquiring two huge triangular wedges of terrain, each comprised of millions of acres. One pointed southward to the confluence of the Ohio and Mississippi Rivers, the other was pointed northward along the Illinois River towards where the Checagou (later spelled Chicago) Creek emptied into Lake Michigan.

To achieve their objective, the Gratzes called upon William Murray to escort a batteau from Pittsburgh loaded with gifts and goods for the Illini tribes. They were convinced that the western chiefs would in return for the many "Sundries" cede those two choice Illinois parcels by appending their signature symbols upon a treaty.

The brothers undertook a fantastic gamble. They selected land in approximately the same location that the Quaker firm of Baynton, Wharton & Morgan had chosen in 1765 to establish the (First) Illinois Company, a venture that failed because the Crown refused to confirm.

But the Gratzes were playing for high stakes and believed that by acquiring the land directly from the tribes it would be theirs. They dared dangerous risks against all odds. It seems they planned to bypass the Crown's approval when they received new information from their western agent, William Murray. He informed them that during Croghan's visit to London on behalf of other western land companies seeking the Crown's confirmation, Lord Charles Pratt (later Earl of Camden) and Lord Charles Yorke, two eminent jurists, opined that certain East Indian grants and titles required no royal letters patent. Reasoned the Gratzes: Why not likewise in the Far West Indian grants in Illinois?

With twenty others, including David Franks and his son Moses Franks, his brother and nephew Moses and Jacob Franks of London,

Joseph Simon and his partner John Campbell, Levy Andrew Levy, the Gratz brothers' partner William Murray, was formed the Second Illinois Company. This powerful organization would finance the tremendous shipment of gifts to acquire from the Illini Nations huge chunks of Illinois Country. The order was dispatched by B. & M. Gratz Co., their first large consignment to the Far West. William Murray would lead the flatboats to the site he would arrange for the powwow.

Arrived at Pittsburgh to outfit and escort the "Sundries for the Indians" to rendezvous with the Illini tribes, the light-hearted Murray, unable to get bacon and eggs for breakfast that clear morning of May 15, 1773, wrote the Gratzes: "I arrived here last Monday and am in hopes to leave this wretched place tomorrow or Monday at farthest. I cannot have it in my palate to transgress Mosaic Law by eating swine's flesh here. Not an ounce of it can be had in this beggarly place nor indeed of anything else."

Murray also jibed about not having been able to discuss with his employers the giant shipment in preparation nor any business whatsoever as it was the Pentecost festival. "Now as the devil may have it, you must be informed forsooth that Moses was upon the top of a mount in the month of May, consequently his followers must for a certain number of days (two) cease to provide for their families though perhaps he may be promoted to such high rank above that he may think it beneath his dignity to associate with his countrymen."

As promised, Murray poled off the riverbank as fast as he could load the Gratz shipment of goods and trinkets on flatboats, reaching Kaskaskia after a month on the waterways, July 5, 1773. In a circle of Kaskaskia, Cahokia, and Peoria, tribes of the Illini Confederacy's tribal chieftains, with the exchange of goods and gifts valued at almost 40,000 pounds, Murray successfully negotiated and accomplished his mission. The Illinois Company, with treaty in hand, decided in favor of applying to the Crown for confirmation of title, doubtlessly over the Gratz brothers' objections.

Half a year passed and shareholder David Franks petitioned Virginia's governor, John Murray, Lord of Dunmore, to take the Illinois Company under his authority. Franks set forth in his petition that his company would bring fair and honest dealing with the Indians instead of the malcontent among the natives instigated by encroaching emigrants and lawless traders.

The shareholders of the Illinois Company felt that if they would be recognized by Virginia, if not the Crown, they would then dominate all the trade along the Illinois River bordering their northern Illinois segment by intercepting furs intended for the Canadian forts around the Great Lakes, even tap the furs of Indian trappers far beyond the "Father of All Rivers" in the Shining Mountains (later called Rocky Mountains).

Though David Franks, Joseph Simon, and the Gratz brothers were Pennsylvanians, they did not hesitate to switch their loyalties to the Virginia Colony, to become loyal supporters of the Virginian claim to the disputed Fort Pitt and Ohio Valley. They saw in Virginia a more aggressive attitude, for it was Virginia and not Pennsylvania that recognized in 1748 the founders of the Ohio Company, a group which included the brothers of the then teen-age surveyor George Washington. The Ohio Colony's object was to build roads into their colony where they would found settlements, farms, and cities. It was Virginia that sent agents into the "Land of the Forks" to stake their claim and build a fort there. In 1754, Virginia Colony sent Washington to demand that the French depart from the entire Ohio Valley.

Franks and Simon felt that Virginia would eventually gain control of the Fort Pitt and the Ohio Valley. As Franks predicted, news from the West hinted that an Indian uprising was brewing. Barnard Gratz received a hastily scribbled note from William Murray dated May 16, 1774: ". . . that 38 or 48 Indians have been killed by white people on the Ohio. . . . If this intelligence be true, it would be much against us and greatly endanger my scalp. . . ." Michael Gratz received a similar report from John Campbell at the Pittsburgh outpost. The frontier was ablaze.

The killings were initiated by white men, the "lawless emigrants" referred to earlier by Franks. A party of Mingo camped at the mouth of Yellow Creek. A group of them—five men, a woman, and a baby—canoed over to the white camp in peace. The white men gave them rum until they were drunk, then killed them. Other Indians across the stream, hearing the shots, started toward the scene when they too were killed. Among the dead were the father, brother, and sister of the kindly Mingo Chief Logan, a friend to the white man. He now turned into a savage avenger. In hot blood he led a small band to a trading post at Yellow Creek, a short distance from the scene of the murders, leaving with the scalps of seven adults and six children.

Virginia's governor, Lord Dunmore, interpreting his colony's charter to include the Fort Pitt region and all the Ohio Valley, was determined to negate by force Pennsylvania's claim which interpreted its charter to include the entire valley north of the Ohio River and west of the Alleghenies. Lord Dunmore took advantage of the disorders in the Upper Ohio to send troops into the ruins of abandoned Fort Pitt. Dr. John Connolly, Virginia's vice-regent and Captain of the Militia, turned to Simon & Campbell Co., whose trading post was one of about twenty built on the ashes of the former Pittsburgh, to repair the ruins of Fort Pitt and to build on the Ohio, fifty miles by the flight of the crow, Fort Fincastle (the future Wheeling in Western Virginia). As security, Connolly gave Simon & Campbell a mortgage on several thousand acres by the Falls of the Ohio. Simon & Campbell planned to build a city at that site, but they turned over their interests to others who would build a settlement there, the future Louisville, Kentucky (then in Western Virginia).

Virginia, bent on the military conquest of the West, felt that she would thereby be recognized as the dominant power in the Ohio, the protector of its settlers in what she claimed as her domain—the vast region from the Appalachians to the Mississippi and from the Great Lakes to the Tennessee River.

On October 10, 1774, one of the fiercest battles in frontier history was fought at Point Pleasant, on the Ohio River in western Virginia. A thousand Virginia troops battled a thousand Shawnee/Mingo warriors. The Indians defeated, the chiefs agreed to allow the white man's entry into the lands south of the Ohio, not to attack any flatboats on the Ohio, nor to hunt or fish in western Virginia. The sulking braves returned to their villages on the Scioto in the Upper Ohio.

At that moment of triumph for Virginia, in a strange turn of events, His Majesty approved the Quebec Act whereby the Indian country north of the Ohio River and south of the Great Lakes as far west as the Mississippi was restored to royal control. To the dismay and consternation of Virginia, the Crown had in the Quebec Act attached the Upper Ohio to Canada! The loyal and submissive fur-trading Canadians who wanted to leave the West as an Indian reserve were rewarded.

The colonists viewed Parliament's passage of the Quebec Act, which also guaranteed the French-Catholic Church in Canada its vast properties and freedom of worship, as a move to retain French loyalty to the Union Jack and prevent Canada from joining the thirteen colonies in their mounting opposition to the motherland.

Benjamin Franklin was nonplussed by the handing over of the West to Canada in the Quebec Act. In 1768, he had traveled to England to press the grant of western colonies. In 1769, he had proposed to Samuel Wharton, then en route to London, a plan to combine various land grants under one management.

Assessing the conflicting claims of the land colonies versus the Crown (Virginia Colony claiming in addition to western Virginia the Upper Ohio claimed by Pennsylvania Colony) and the Crown's answer by turning over the contested Indian country to Canada, he observed: "The affair of the grant goes on but slowly. I do not clearly see land. I begin to be a little of the sailor's mind when they were handling a cable out of a store into a ship, and one of 'em said: "'Tis a long, heavy cable. I wish we could see the end.' 'D-n me,' says another, 'if I believe it has any end; somebody has cut it off.'"

Virginia, Pennsylvania, the Gratzes, the western men, and the colonists were rankled by the Quebec Act almost as much as the other acts imposed by the Mother Country, which hastened the impending revolution. Virginia, in particular, was deeply aggrieved over the loss of the Upper Ohio to Canada, a land described by its illustrious son, George Washington, as the "Pearl of the western forest sea."

2

American and Hebrew Revolutions

The Seashore Aflame, the Frontier Ablaze

Confrontation between the colonists and the Mother Country had been coming ever since she had taxed Americans for troops stationed along the Appalachian passes and western forts. After driving the French out of the West, England, intent on keeping the peace and the profitable fur trade, planned to maintain the Ohio Valley as a vast Indian reserve.

Jewish merchants, nine in all, joined Christian businessmen in signing the non-importation agreement; among them the merchant prince David Franks and the Gratz brothers. Though they were interested in the fur trade and should have welcomed British policy, they were even more desirous to establish land colonies in the West—which the British plan precluded. These and many other colonial merchants agreed not to import many taxed products from the Mother Country until she would relent.

Clandestinely, British tea was smuggled into America to satisfy the colonials demand. Since it was impossible to sell this tea in eastern cities without being detected, it was offered for sale in the Fort Pitt store of Simon & Campbell.

But in that distant outpost, though undetected by the British, super-patriots decided to put a stop to tea trade:

> On the night of August 24, 1775, more than a score of Westmorelanders headed by Colonel Archibald Lochry rode into town . . . the next morning John Campbell was summoned to appear before the combined West Augusta and Westmoreland committees. He acknowledged that he had tea and delivered up all that remained unsold—two ten gallon kegs, one box and one bag—and this was carried to the liberty pole and there burned.

Indian tribes in the Fort Pitt area and the West, angered by the establishment of West Augusta and Westmoreland and other white settlements, and stirred by the British, began to take to the warpath against the Americans. They had not forgotten the bitter Shawnee/Mingo defeat and the loss of the Lower Ohio Valley, their Meadowland Ken-tu-cky.

Barnard Gratz's Pittsburgh agent, Robert Campbell, wrote him in July 1775 regarding bartering with the tribes for land: "No part of it is yet disposed of, notwithstanding our treaty is this day ended with the Mingo and Delaware Indians. The Shawanese did not come in according to appointment, which causes some uneasiness here; however, hope all will yet be well."

The following year, western men seeking to found colonies in the Ohio negotiated with Virginians on their way to the Continental Congress in Philadelphia, where it was hoped the new government would favor their land proposals. At this time Barnard Gratz left Philadelphia for Pittsburgh. The once bustling town of over 300 now was deserted, save for about twenty tradesmen whose future in that forsaken place was doubtful at best. Levy Andrew Levy and most other traders had headed east of the mountains earlier that year.

Barnard Gratz hoped to negotiate a new treaty with the Indians. On April 10, Captain John Neville was appointed by the Continental Congress to settle in friendly fashion a sum in dispute between the Gratz Brothers and Delaware Chief, Coquataginta, whom they called "White-Eyes."

But it was the Shawnee that had to be appeased. That spring, unsettled by the war against the British and yet unsure which side to favor, the tribe remained aloof. Unable to return home for Passover, brother Michael wrote to him from Philadelphia of conditions at home. At the end of July, 1776, Michael again wrote of the unchanged situation in the West: "I should have sent more b(ead) wampum which I have by me, but as you don't say if they will answer or not, must defer it at present. . . . No doubt you will stay now till after the treaty with the Indians is over, which I hope will be before Rosh Hashono (Hebrew New Year), so that you can be with us for the Holidays."

In the region east of the mountains, Michael continued to deal with the Indians. On August 10, 1776 the Committee of the Treasury of the Congress reported:

> there is due to Michael Gratz for Indian Goods provided by him in May and June last, and delivered to the commissioners for Indian affairs in the northern department, 653 dollars and $^{87}/_{90}$ths . . .

The tribes in the west however remained unsettled. Barnard realized he would have to remain in Pittsburgh for the Hebrew New Year. With Major Richard Butler he sent a message to Michael requesting high holy day prayer books be sent west by the next post-rider.

On that solemn day, alone, in the ghost town where hardly a soul stirred, in a boarding room of an empty house, facing east, he recited in his silent devotion words that had a personal meaning as never before: ". . . removed far from our country, so that we are unable to perform our duty in the habitation which thou hast chosen. . . ."

While Barnard represented the interests of Pennsylvania, Michael became deeply involved in those of Virginia. Whichever colony won the west, a Gratz Brother would be on the winning side. As early as March 26, 1776, the *Journal of the Committee of Safety of Virginia,* issued at Williamsburg, its capital, an order for 2800 pounds to Michael Gratz for sundry goods purchased from him. Month after month, the *Journal* notes warrants to Michael Gratz. And in the following year, it mentions a balance due Gratz of about 1270 pounds by Carter Braxton, signer of the Declaration of Independence for Virginia. Michael Gratz, with Carter Braxton, had shares in privateer ships that were licensed to attack British shipping and run the blockade. All loot, including enemy ships, captured by these armed vessels was the prize of Braxton and Gratz as privateers.

During the war, Michael Gratz moved to Virginia and took its oath of allegiance. Virginia employed him as a purchasing and shipping agent, particularly in the export of tobacco.

While their loyalties were divided between Pennsylvania and Virginia, both Gratz Brothers were patriots to the rebel cause—to establish true freedom for all.

They prayed for peace, but war had erupted. Indian trade and western expansion was again at an end. Throughout the seaboard colonies, men took up arms. The battle lines drawn, Daniel Gomez, the aged Jewish Indian trader and frontiersman, told the Continental Congress that he would organize and lead a rifle company against the redcoats and pick them off like red-breasted robins on a fence. When gently advised that at age 81 he was too far along to become involved in combat, Gomez retorted that he could stop a bullet as well as a younger man.

In the western wilds of Carolina, a younger man, a Jew, stopped a bullet to give his life for the rebel cause—the first of his people to die for the cause of Independence.

He was Francis Salvador, a prominent South Carolinian plantationer. Salvador owned 6,000 acres on Coronaca Creek near the Georgia border, planted with indigo by over 30 slaves. Educated in England, he traveled the European continent in the manner of an English gentleman. At 18 he inherited 60,000 pounds and a promise of marriage to his cousin, daughter of Joseph Salvador, his uncle giving him a 13,000-pound dowry.

Rich and carefree, Francis attended the stock exchange, frequented coffee houses and theaters attired in powdered wig, velvet clothing, embroidered linen shirts, silk stockings, and silver buckles on low-cut shoes.

In 1774 Francis's uncle and father-in-law, Joseph Salvador, sent him to America to study the possibilities of his South Carolina land holdings, amounting to 100,000 acres. Inspired by sun-browned planters and their black slaves toiling in the sun, Francis, the former London dandy, discarded his fine clothes for the homespun shirt and leather jerkin of the Carolinian men of the soil.

In this wilderness cultivated in part by plantationers and their slaves, Francis Salvador was elected to the South Carolina Assembly and the Provincial Congress of South Carolina by men who loved the soil, and admired Salvador's industry and sobriety. He became the first Jew to serve in any such august bodies outside of ancient Israel.

With Revolution brewing in the Colonies, two papers were circulated in July, 1775, for citizens to sign. One for those who favored the King, the other for those who would join the rebels. Francis Salvador and Richard Rapely his Jewish overseer, made speeches in favor of rebellion, and at times barely escaped with their lives.

Of greatest concern to them were the Cherokees who were incited by the Tories to fight off the white colonists influx into their lands. The restless Indians were angered that powder and trade goods had not been received as promised. Indian Agent of the South, John Stuart, sided with the British. He sent the Indians provisions and arms and told them to wait until the redcoats appeared. In July, 1776, the Cherokee heard reports that the British fleet was off the Carolina coast and went on the war path with the cry, "Kill the Long Knives!"

They killed all whites without regard for women or children or whether the men were Tories or Rebels. On July 24, William Henry Drayton, then chairman of the South Carolina Provincial Congress, ordered a punitive expedition "to cut up every Indian cornfield and burn every Indian town. . . ."

Salvador learned of the fierce fighting that the Cherokee demonstrated during the French and Indian War, when in 1760–61 they, especially the Cherokee farmers in the southern Appalachians, attacked the white intruders under their powerful chiefs Oconostota and Attakullaculla. It was in those battles that the Jewish officer, Joseph Levy, commissioned lieutenant in the South Carolina Regiment of Foot in 1757, saw action in Colonel Middleton's South Carolina Regiment. He lived to tell the tale when he returned to Charleston, South Carolina, to resume life as a merchant.

Once again the Cherokee were on the warpath, this time incited by the British to join in their battle against the white men who would move into their lands. The Cherokee gleefully joined forces with the redcoats, and ruthlessly despoiled pioneer farmlands and mercilessly attacked and scalped young and old, women and children—none were spared.

On the day he would die, Salvador rode 28 miles to the Keowee River to warn Major Andrew Williamson that on the western frontier Indians allied with the British (who they felt would keep the intruding colonists out of the West). The "Jewish Paul Revere" reported that they were dancing together following a massacre of settlers in the Appalachian foothills.

Major Williamson's force of 330 men selected from 1,200 volunteers, including the just arrived Salvador, crossed the Keowee River to challenge the enemy. At a South Carolinian Cherokee village, Essenecca—reportedly abandoned—the major's horse went down under him as he and his men were trapped in a crossfire of arrows and bullets. Shot three times, Salvador fell from his mount but crawled into bushes skirting the riverbank. There he was jumped upon and scalped.

However, he remained alive throughout the skirmish. Finally, he was found by Major Williamson and learned, while he was dying, that the enemy had been beaten.

At daybreak, a fellow officer told that he had seen the Indian who scalped Salvador hurrying towards him but in the darkness and confusion thought he was Salvador's servant going to help his master. Francis Salvador was buried at Essenecca with two others of the wounded who died that morning.

In September, Williamson began a march into far western Carolina that "scalped living Indians, killed women, even lame or fleeing, and destroyed every means of sustaining life with a savagery equaling and thoroughness surpassing their enemies."

As soon as the hostilities subsided and it was safe to travel on Atlantic waters, Francis' uncle arrived to oversee his plantation.

A description of the inland regions of South Carolina was sent by Joseph Salvador from "Coroneka 22 Jan(uar)y 1785" to his learned cousin in London, Emanuel Mendes da Costa, of his impressions:

> ... I am now in a wild country ... it is all woods with brooks and some fine rivers, but, strange to tell, you have woods without shade, brooks without water or fish, few birds but some beautiful, as the red nightingale and a green and gold small bird. The wild beasts are wolves, panthers, a wild cat, foxes, the hideous pole cats, deer and some buffaloes. We have oxen, sheep and goats, sufficient tame fowl, wild turkeys, partridge and doves and larks and blackbirds which are good, few hares or other game.... Our swamps are something particular.... In the bogs, cedars, cypress, firs of all kinds, form the tops; the bottoms are full of myrtle, evergreen, privets, the sensitive plant, magnolias, and a variety that would adorn the most curious garden of exoticks in Europe ...

The country beyond the mountain barrier was even more majestic. Of all the lush lands that lay west of the mountains, none were as coveted by the tribes as the Lower Ohio Valley. Nestled between the "Beautiful River"—the Ohio—to the north, and the sweeping bend of the Tennessee to the south, the rolling forests that gave way to open prairies—"bluegrass country" it would be called—were paradise on earth. Spring and fall, wild fowl flew overhead; elk, wolf, and bear were as numerous as deer. Buffalo ranged in such large herds that their tracks created roadways wide enough to accommodate the largest wagon. Here the tribes fought over the right to hunt and fish.

The white man, the Transylvanian, was attracted to its productive earth where nut-growing trees flourished, the best a farmer could find.

Such rich soil did this "Meadowland" possess that green leafy cane was said to rise to heights of 30 feet with stalks the width of a strong brave's arm. Grapevines a foot thick spread lofty tendrils through the dense canopy of forest leaves. Horses trampling through the wild strawberries were stained with juice to their knees. In abundance, wild flowers colored the landscape. In this veritable Garden of Eden, flocks of red, green, and gold parakeets flitted amidst flourishing saplings.

This was an unspoiled Indian domain, the hunting ground of the many Ohio tribes.

This land of Ken-tu-cky, which in Cherokee meant "Meadowland," also was the hunting grounds of the tribes of the Upper Ohio and came to mean "Dark and Bloody Ground."

The three Hart brothers of Kentucky had in 1775 joined the North Carolinian judge, Richard Henderson, in forming the Transylvania Company. They negotiated a treaty with the Cherokee, bartering 10,000 pounds of guns and goods at Watauga for all of Kentucky south of the Kentucky River—a 20,000,000-acre crescent of land between the Kentucky and Tennessee rivers.

The Transylvanians engaged frontiersman Daniel Boone to hack a path that settlers could follow and at the end of the trail build a settlement. Boone knew the Meadowland well. He easily recruited adventurous men to blaze a trail he had mapped through a gap in the Cumberland mountains that opened the mountain wall. It linked various Indian trails with the Warriors' Path trodden by the warring tribes to the Kentucky River where he would build Boonesborough.

Among the 30 woodsmen adventurers who cut the Wilderness Trail was the Jewish lad, Samuel Sanders. Despite protestations of innocence, Sanders had been convicted in a London court of "clipping coins," and had been ordered deported to Virginia Colony for seven years' servitude—the minimum term for involuntary indenture.

Samuel had no one to turn to for help in the colonies as did another Jewish teenager who, like himself, was sent to the colonies as a bond servant. That lad's concerned father pleaded with his relation, Meyer Josephson, an Indian trader at Reading, Pennsylvania, to ransom the youth.

That juvenile delinquent was Feibel Fibemann, sentenced in 1771 to servitude in the North American colonies for a pickpocketing offense in London. The boy's father, a recent immigrant from Germany, had just been elected *Hazan* and *Shochet* in Dover, England.

In being transported through Virginia, Samuel Sanders escaped and made his way through the Blue Ridge Mountains to the Watauga River in North Carolina, where Boone was about to begin his Wilderness Trail.

Boone took a liking to the Jewish teenager who in a sense took the place of his own son, killed two years earlier by Indians just short of the Cumberland Gap. To Samuel, Daniel Boone was a hero whom he imitated in his manner and garb. The boy wore a fringed hunting shirt that fell almost to his knees, deerskin leggings and moccasins, and a coonskin cap. In his belt he carried a knife and axe. From leather straps over his shoulder was slung a long rifle. A powder horn hung alongside, and a pouch filled with bullets—all provided by the Transylvania Company.

Samuel Sanders was one of the most active and well-liked of Boone's frontiersmen who labored to build at the end of the trail, on the Kentucky River, Fort Boonesborough.

The building of this fort aroused the tribes. Shawnee and Delaware raiding parties crossed the Ohio from the north with tomahawk and scalping knife in hand. Settlers were forced to flee eastward or take refuge in one of Kentucky's three forts: Harrodsburg, St. Asaph's, or Boonesborough. By the winter of 1777-1778 these palisaded posts were under almost constant siege, with life within them unbearable.

One day when Boone and Sanders were busily engaged in crystalizing salt at a spring just beyond the fort, Shawnee abruptly appeared and took them captive to their camp north of the Ohio River, exhibiting them proudly in different tepee villages. Their hair was plucked except for a scalp lock, a tuft of hair on the crown. Their "white blood" was washed away and their bodies painted to complete the initiation ceremony. The Jewish lad and the trailblazer were then adopted into the tribe.

Boone, however, escaped several months later in time to help save Fort Boonesborough under attack by 400 Shawnee led by Chief Blackfish. Thirty men and 20 boys fought off the first attack, when the Shawnee began to burrow under the fort walls. A second attack struck with flaming arrows setting the log buildings afire as Indians emerged from the tunnels into the fort.

Rain suddenly fell, putting out the fire and caving in the tunnels. Chief Blackfish withdrew and Fort Boonesborough was providentially spared.

Sanders, who could have fled with Boone from Shawnee captivity, chose to remain. He preferred the safety and freedom among the Indians to being in Fort Boonesborough, a ready trap for any bond-servant. Moreover, he was blissfully happy with a young Shawnee beauty who shared his tepee as his wife. There was no question in Samuel's mind, Indian civilization was superior to Caucasian culture.

Repeatedly, the Shawnee returned to the Kentucky forts to besiege and massacre. Continental troops fighting the redcoats could not be sent west of the mountains to subdue the Indians. Settlers began to flee from Kentucky, western Virginia, and Pennsylvania, when frontiersman George Rogers Clark prevailed upon Virginia's governor, Patrick Henry, to commission him to lead a band of recruits to break the British power in the Great Lakes forts, particularly Fort Detroit, where they armed and incited the Ohio Valley tribes.

Militia officer George Rogers Clark set forth in 1777 to win the West for the Americans. His major objective was Fort Detroit, where British Governor Henry Hamilton armed the Ohio tribes. But to protect his flanks, Clark would first have to seize Kaskaskia and Cahokia on the Mississippi and Fort Sackville (formerly Fort du Vincennes) on the Wabash.

One of the frontiersmen who joined Clark was 30-year-old Isaac Levy (Levi), a Hungarian-born Jew who had earlier enlisted at Lexington, Virginia, under Captain Benjamin Harrison. A medical doctor and tradesman, he proved to be invaluable to the expedition.

On the night of July 4, 1778, Levy, along with 175 sharpshooter Virginians and Kentuckians led by Clark, surprised British troops at Kaskaskia and took the French village. Clark proceeded northward along the bank of the Mississippi past the ruins of dismantled Fort Chartres to take the village of Cahokia. The Britishers now had good reason to regret General Gage's decision five years earlier to abandon the stone fortress between the two settlements because of the recurrent floods, which left waters in the swampy marshlands that bred deadly mosquitoes. Clark's lightning raid proved deadlier.

At Cahokia, Levy joined the French firm Gratiot & La Croix as its manager. In addition to supplying the troops, he engaged in Indian trade and was granted exclusive power of trade and free traffic from Cahokia northward to the mouth of the Illinois River "... in order to empower them better to carry out their patriotic design ... to furnish the states with provisions and other necessary things which are at present difficult to obtain." Levy settled down and married a French Catholic woman.

More than his goods, Levy's medical services were in constant demand. Only one complaint about his professional practice is recorded in the court records and Dr. Isaac Levy did not scruple to take an oath on the Holy Gospels.

A French trapper by the name of Buteau, suffering from a venereal disease, refused to pay an agreed 400 livres, insisting he had never been cured. The Court ordered Levy "to continue attending the defendant on condition that the defendant act according to orders and does nothing to counteract the medicines of the plaintiff."

Dr. Levy continued treatment, prescribing 67 pills to be taken by the trapper over a seven-day period. In a second judgment the trapper testified that he was still not cured. Upon being questioned he told the Judge that he had downed the 67 pills in two days so that he would be made well in less time. Dr. Levy then advised His Honor that such a massive does of medication ingested in two days would have been fatal and he secured a judgment against Buteau.

Clark and his frontiersmen prepared to march on Fort Sackville. It is doubtful if Levy accompanied them but he fulfilled his responsibilities of supply and treating the men.

For his outlays, Virginia later paid Levy in practically worthless currency. Clark did, however, pay for as much of his supplies as he could with English notes—which was much appreciated by Dr. Isaac Levy, now one of Cahokia's most notable citizens.

As Clark planned his conquest of Fort Sackville, the British Commander at Fort Detroit, Colonel Henry Hamilton, ordered additional troops to reinforce Fort Sackville, that garrison situated on the Wabash midway between Cahokia and Fort Detroit. When winter set in, Hamilton assumed no attack would be forthcoming until the snows melted and the waters receded. He recalled most of his troops to Fort Detroit.

As in a chess game, calculating the British colonel's actions, Clark planned to attack Fort Sackville in mid-winter but lacked additional funds to clothe and feed his men for the long march. Clark felt certain that a surprise attack upon Fort Sackville would assure an easy victory.

As Clark pondered his dilemma, aid came from a totally unexpected source. Simon Nathan, a Jewish businessman of Jamaica in the British West Indies. To the Continentals he shipped desperately needed powder, cordage, and canvas from his trading house in British Jamaica by way of Cape Nicola Mole, a free port in Santo Domingo. There gunrunning privateers smuggled materials past the British blockade to Continental shores.

When the British agents uncovered Simon's clandestine activities, the Jew fled with his cash assets, but left all his property to be forfeited to the Crown. He sailed to Spanish Cuba, then to Spanish New Orleans, where he learned of Colonel Clark's victories and present frustration. Inspired by the freedom-fighting frontiersmen battling seasoned troops, he purchased 52,000 dollars of drafts earmarked for the George Rogers Clark expedition. He then sailed to Virginia where he contributed 53,406 pounds to arm friendly Cherokee fighting alongside the Americans. This together with other advances totalled 323,000 dollars, leaving him with but one asset—himself. He joined the militia.

In December of 1778, Clark and his band set forth to take Fort Sackville. In the coldest, wettest weeks of winter they struggled through marshes, waded streams, and crossed swollen rivers until they surprised the unsuspecting Fort Sackville garrison late in February. The astounded British troops, together with their commander, were taken prisoner by the 175 stalwart men led by George Rogers Clark.

The power of the British throughout the Ohio Valley was shaken and the Mississippi Valley's key settlements were claimed by the rebels. The West had been won for the Continentals, save for Fort Detroit. Lacking enough manpower needed to subdue the powerful Great Lakes fort, Clark had accomplished his major goal, to secure the West for Washington.

On December 21, 1778, when George Rogers Clark and his band were on their way to Fort Sackville on the Wabash River, General Washington was en route from Valley Forge to an army base at Middlebrook, New Jersey, pausing that day at Easton by the forks of the Delaware, 30 miles north of the capital. His intinerary allowed for luncheon. He was welcomed at the home of Corporal Michael Hart, the peacetime Indian trader, now agent of David Franks, who was supplying British prisoners held nearby.

Hart's house was a two-story stone building on the southeast corner of the public square, directly opposite the courthouse. His general store was on the first floor, his residence on the second. Michael Hart's wife, Leah, prepared a kosher meal, probably complete with *latkes* (pancakes) in honor of the *Hanukah* festival, it being the sixth day of the holiday. Stepdaughter Louisa Hart would proudly record in her diary:

> Let it be remembered that Michael Hart was a Jew, pious; a Jew reverencing and strictly observant of the Sabbath and festivals, dietary laws were also adhered to although he was compelled to be his own Shochet

[ritual slaughterer]. Mark well that he, Washington, was then honored as first in peace, first in war and first in the hearts of his countrymen. Even during a short sojourn he became, for the hour, the guest of the worthy Jew.

Michael wished the general well in his future campaigns, expressing the hope that he, like the Maccabeans of old, would hammer and level the enemy as symbolized in the flattened pancakes enjoyed on the holiday. He also told of the custom of distributing coins to children to play games of chance. This custom is in remembrance of the Jewish students of Maccabean days, who used the game-playing as a ruse to circumvent the Hellenist enemy's prohibition of Torah study. The commander-in-chief presented the three young Hart sons, the eldest but four years old, with silver coins. These became treasured mementos to the Harts, even as the chair occupied by George Washington became an honored piece of furniture.

General Washington told the Harts how the *Hanukah* festival had inspired him during the previous year, when encamped at Valley Forge morale had sunk to its lowest ebb. The winter was cold, even colder to men lacking warm clothing, half of them without boots, all quartered in shabby huts eating rations.

It was at that period of gloom and despair that a young Jewish private tendered the General a ray of hope.

The soldier had emigrated from Poland, where he and his people suffered misery and degradation, to the new strange America. Now he was hungry and frozen, but proud to be a soldier for freedom and liberty.

It was the night of December 25, 1777. Christmas Day had been observed glumly and after eating their rations the men were bedded down for the night—all except the Jew. In a corner of the drafty wooden shack that served as their barracks, as quietly as possible, he lit his *menorah,* an eight-branched candelabrum that he had carried with him from overseas in his knapsack ever since the war had begun.

It was the night of the 25th day of *Kislev* on his Hebrew calendar, the first night of *Hanukah.* In the candle glow the Polish Jew was reminded of his humble faraway home, of the deep humiliation to which his parents and people were subjected by the so-called nobility, and of the cold his people endured in their hovels throughout every winter of their lives. The thought of their utter helplessness caused him to cry uncontrollably.

Suddenly, a hand touched his shoulder and a voice asked, "Why do you cry, son?"

Looking up, the soldier saw General Washington himself making the rounds that evening—for it was also Christmas—an aide in the background.

"Actually, I am not crying," the soldier replied. "I'm praying with tears for your victory."

"And what is this strange lamp?" asked his commander.

"This is my *Hanukah* lamp," and the young man related briefly the ancient story—how long ago a small bedraggled but patriotic army routed a huge and powerful foe.

"You are a Jew, a son of the Prophets and you say we will be victorious?" the general declared, his eyes fixed on the flickering flames of the menorah.

"Yes," the soldier unhesitatingly replied. "The God of Israel who helped the Maccabeans will help to build here a land of freedom for the oppressed."

To the Harts, General Washington recalled on his luncheon visit when *Hanukah* was again celebrated, that the warmth of the glowing candlelight and the words of optimism and courage on that darkest night at Valley Forge uplifted him and gave him the fortitude to fight against all odds for victory.

Neither Washington in the East nor Clark in the West would compromise with the idea of victory. In 1781, when victory appeared imminent in the East, Clark again was determined to complete his conquest of the West by occupying Fort Detroit and Fort Mackinac in Michigan. A more immediate and impelling reason was to again protect the Virginia frontier along the western Kentucky River from a threatened raid by British and Indians descending from the Michigan forts. With Michigan in the hands of the Continentals they might even conquer Canada, the fourteenth British colony.

The Gratz brothers had a personal as well as patriotic motive, for the Crown had withheld recognition of their claim to western lands; their interest in the Second Illinois Company was strengthened by its merger with the neighboring Wabash Company, the latter seeking to gain confirmation of two large land sectors along the Wabash River. And their close associates, Joseph Simon, David Franks, Levy Andrew Levy, and friends were the "Suffering Traders of 1763" who never received their compensation from the Crown to their Indiana Company founded in 1765.

An idea of the powerful combination of forces in the Illinois-Wabash merger can be gained when it becomes clear that they were attempting to acquire 60,000,000 acres—the entire southern half of what later became the states of Illinois and Indiana.

Along with the Gratz Brothers, General Washington and Virginia's governor, Thomas Jefferson, were anxious for Clark's success to add new domains to the "Empire of Liberty" and divert the coveted western fur trade from Canada and England.

Virginia had not however authorized any expenditures, so Gratz & (John) Gibson, the Gratz Brothers branch at Fort Pitt, accepted the personal bond of General Clark and his adjutant, Colonel Dorsey Pentecost, as a guarantee of payment. While the Gratzes looked upon their outfitting the Clark expedition with 1,500 pounds of supplies as an act of patriotism, they regarded its collection as an act of faith. Perhaps, they mused, they would be paid in Virginia tobacco which they would process at their snuff mill.

Awaiting orders for the expedition to start in June, General Clark was to learn that—Virginia, fearful of the British invaders on the coast and of Tories on the frontier borders in the back country—he was to march south of the Ohio. There was to be no march against Detroit.

General Clark and Pentecost kept their word. After the war they repaid their debt—in tobacco. Though the Gratzes lost money on the deal they were delighted that they contributed with their fellow Jews toward the cause of liberty upon the economic as well as the military battlefield.

The Ohio tribes with British backing, attacked mercilessly and relentlessly. In Kentucky, Captain Nathaniel Hart reinforced his fort, White Oak Spring, and its hundred residents.

Captain Nathaniel Hart had arrived in Fort Boonesborough in April, 1775, with the vanguard of the Transylvania Company, and in 1779 built his own fort at White Oak Spring, about one mile north of Boonesborough. In the summer of 1782, over a year after the British surrendered in the East, at Yorktown, Virginia, the Indians were besieging the forts in western Virginia which included Kentucky. For weeks the Hart family at White Oak Spring slept in their clothes, never ate their meals together, but whenever it was possible and wherever arrows ceased to fly. That July, Captain Nathaniel Hart bravely slipped out of the fort to ride to Fort Boonesborough but was slain on the trail. Fortunately, his wife, Sarah Simpson Hart survived with nine children to care for, as did a score of other women. They cherished a Hebrew

Bible passed on from their father, and kept by their sister Lucretia Hart, which inspired them to surmount the hardships of the frontier.

The "Hebrew Spirit of '76" may best be represented by Captain Abraham Simons, a Jewish veteran honored by the Daughters of the American Revolution. To this day, Captain Simons stands erect, dressed in his uniform of regimental blue buttoned in brass, his fingers encircling his trusty long-barrelled musket at his side. In accordance with his last will and testament, his widow Nancy Mills Simons, of an aristocratic Christian family, had the grave of her husband dug twice the usual depth and his casket placed upright. His grave lies in the woods off the Old Augusta Road near Thomson, Georgia.

Revolt in the Jewish Community

The early indications of a revolution can be seemingly insignificant. Sometimes even amusing—a tea party in Boston or a shave in Baltimore.

In September 1782 Ezekiel Levy visited the village of Baltimore on business relating to his dry goods store in Philadelphia. Isaac Abraham, a plantationer from Upper Merion, Pennsylvania, was shocked to see Ezekiel, son of a religious teacher, 'shaving there on the Jewish Sabbath. He reported the infraction to Philadelphia's Reverend Mordecai Moses Mordecai. However, for lack of corroborating witnesses no action was taken by the *Kehillah* (Jewish Community).

Throughout the Colonial period the *Kehillah* controlled all institutions of Jewish life: the synagogue, ritual pool, Passover baking utensils, mortuary, cemetery, even the hearse. *Kehillah* officers controlled every stage of Jewish life from the cradle to the grave. They imposed fines, expelled, excommunicated, and refused burial rites to those who violated Jewish precept, as in the case of the intermarried.

Upon the heels of the political revolution followed a religious revolution. Headed by the Reverend Mordecai Moses Mordecai, actually a pseudo-scholar, with his followers, they revolted against the authority of the *Kehillah*.

What manner of person was this man who could defy the ruling powers of the *Kahal Kadosh Mikveh Israel* (Holy Community Hope of Israel) in the nation's capital, which was then the leading Jewish congregation in the land; in its leadership Simon Nathan, Barnard and Michael Gratz, Haym Salomon, Jonas Phillips, and others of high standing. And how was he able to effect a breach in the all-powerful

Kehillah system that ruled the life of the individual and community?

His countenance, benign and serene, belied an inner restlessness and insecurity that possessed Mordecai Moses Mordecai. His father was rabbi in the renowned Talmudic center of Tels, Lithuania. Mordecai had studied Jewish law and lore but was never ordained. What motivated him to emigrate must have been his inability to succeed in his native Russia. He was determined to better his lot.

Upon his arrival in America during the French and Indian War, he lived in Lancaster, no doubt with an assist by Joseph Simon. Following the Indian treaty that opened up virgin territory beyond the mountains for settlement, Mordecai in 1769 joined the throngs of pioneers who stormed the land office to acquire raw acreage. His claim near Pittsburgh was approved and Mordecai Moses Mordecai became the first Jew to farm in the West.

Mordecai had never farmed before. Although a native of Russia, he married a Portuguese, Zipporah, daughter of Abraham de Lyon and Esther Nunez, who lived at the Forks of the Delaware River at Easton, Pennsylvania. De Lyon, an oenologist, had cultivated porto and malaga grapes on his Georgia plantation since his arrival in 1733 but fled in 1742 at the approach of Spanish troops from Florida. Abraham de Lyon convinced his perennially unsuccessful son-in-law to forget trading and try his hand at farming the West's rich virgin soil.

Mordecai set forth in the spring with his wife and 16-year-old daughter, Esther, beside him on a cushion-covered wagon seat. Cowbells rang in the valley at the approach to Pittsburgh, whose main street they would learn was often blocked by cows and hogs. The dusty roadways of the lawless, raucous frontier town accepted, among the hard-working, honest pioneers, many crass and crude characters—male and female—and the silent Indian.

The Mordecai family was given a hearty reception by their old friends the Levy Andrew Levys. Crude as their cabin appeared from the outside, the Mordecais were certainly surprised within. The interior was like a fashionable Philadelphia residence. The culture-conscious Mordecai glanced at almanacs, spelling books, English and Hebrew books, and copies of "Gentleman's Magazine." Zipporah's fancy was caught by Susannah's gold lockets and hair powder, as well as gold and silver thread. All the Mordecais admired the newly planted pear and cherry trees brought over the mountains from the East for transplanting.

Andrew Levy assisted Moses Mordecai to stake out his claim and provided him from the Simon & Levy outlet a variety of implements for seeding and cultivating. The oxen that had drawn Mordecai's covered wagon across the mountains now drew the plow. The grain he grew he used not only to ferment bread but to malt liquor in a still he acquired from the Simon & Henry Forge.

As he worked his land and sold his whiskey, Mordecai, the son of a rabbi, continued zealously to practice his religion. In his log hut he instructed his daughter in Judaism. Neighbors and townspeople titled him the "Reverend Rabbi." He prayed in his home fervently at the advent of each New Moon for the upcoming month's blessing replete with good fortune and prosperity but these petitions remained unanswered.

In 1770 the Mordecais revisited Easton and Philadelphia, making a stop in budding Baltimore. After they returned west they often talked about the possibilities of Baltimore, its growth as a commercial center, stores opening there, warehouses building there. Perhaps a still would do well there, though the town was peopled with Catholics. In 1772 Moses Mordecai returned to that port city. Though he found no newspaper yet in Baltimore, the town possessed the nucleus of a large city: a two-story courthouse, a jail, a whipping post, a pillory, and stocks. New roads now connected Baltimore with Pennsylvania towns and faraway metropolitan Philadelphia.

On January 9, 1773, Mordecai took a 99-year lease on a parcel of Baltimore property "on the West side of Jones' Falls" (present Fallsway), the Pittsburgher recording his occupation as "distiller." Here he erected a still. For a year and a half he dispensed his spirits, which were well received by the Catholic community; but even though he managed to pay off his mortgage, he had no funds left to manage his still. He returned to Pittsburgh to raise another crop and produce a brew that could not match that of his Scotch-Irish rivals. Perhaps his firewater had too much water and too little fire.

Needing funds to finance his venture, Mordecai mortgaged to Joseph Simon under a deed executed at Lancaster on July 19, 1775:

> One plantation and improvement, situate lying and being on Sucks Run near Pittsburg(h), and all houses buildings and appurtenances thereunto belonging and also two copper stills with all utensils thereunto belonging and all the household furniture now in my possession or belonging to me. . . .

Simon had owned by legal grant since 1768 (after the Indian cession at Fort Stanwix), 10,580 acres on Racoon Creek near Logstown (the future Legionville), to the northwest of Pittsburgh, a few miles from Sucks Run. Simon would also acquire waterfront lots along the Allegheny and Monogahela rivers, not to mention his vast land holdings east of the mountains.

Two months after Mordecai mortgaged his properties to Simon, on September 20, he was granted a license to distill hard liquor and operate a tavern.

But no sooner had he opened his saloon when it was feared that Indian hostilities were about to erupt. Mordecai promptly abandoned his holdings, packed their few belongings and returned East with the few other Pittsburghers.

Fearing for the safety of his family from Indian attack, Mordecai moved them to the secure settlement of Lancaster and joined the rebels. Suffering battle wounds, Mordecai settled in Baltimore in 1780, there to distill spirits and marry off his daughter, Esther, to another incapacitated Jewish war veteran, Philip Moses Russell. A surgeon's mate at Valley Forge, Russell contracted "campfever" there. His sight and hearing impaired, he was compelled to resign in 1780.

In 1782 the peace of the tiny port, Baltimore, was disturbed by British raiding vessels. Mordecai fled with rebels for the American stronghold of Philadelphia. There, with 35 other heads of families, he joined in raising funds for a synagogue edifice. The learned Mordecai composed a Hebrew letter of appeal, which he sent to Jewish communities in Dutch Surinam. Privateer Isaac Moses wrote English letters of appeal to English-Jewish communities at Cape François, Saint Thomas, Saint Croix in the West Indies; also to nearby *Kahal Kadosh Lancaster* (Holy Community of Lancaster), which organized with the influx of patriot refugees at the beginning of the Revolution and which would dissolve later that year, 1782.

Their letters of appeal read as follows:

> A small number of brethren, who, during this calamitous war, fled from different parts to find a refuge, in conjunction with those in this city, undertook to build a place of worship, that they might meet together to offer up prayers to the Holy God of Israel. . . .

Benjamin Franklin headed the list of contributors.

No sooner was the synagogue erected (in time for the High Holy Days, 1782) than Mordecai Moses Mordecai brought to the attention of the officers Ezekiel Levy's violation of the Sabbath. To the leaders of the Jewish community what may seem minor—shaving on a holy day—constituted a dire danger signal, for the ancient rabbis had admonished: "Be as careful with a light commandment as with a weighty one. . . ."

How right they were! Ezekiel Levy after the war moved to Fredericksburg, Virginia. There, in 1787, he married a Christian, Frances Sydnor, and joined the Episcopal Church.

Indifference towards what appeared to be a minor ruling was like the breaking of a picket in a fence protecting a garden. Jewish youth were being cut off from their ancestral roots and people by the spread of intermarriage. Marriages between Jew and Christian were reaching epidemic proportions, which if not checked would lead to the ultimate disappearance of American Jewry.

Precedent was first set by a Hebrew Pilgrim, Moses Simonson, who originated "from the Jewish settlement at Amsterdam." He arrived on the *Fortune,* which in 1621 followed the *Mayflower* to Plymouth Rock. His daughter Rebecca married John, the son of George Soule, and their son married Sarah Standish, granddaughter of John Alden and Myles Standish, Puritans who arrived aboard the *Mayflower.*

Ever since Solomon Pietersen's arrival at New Amsterdam in 1654 and that Dutch Jew's marriage to a Christian, attended later by the baptism of their daughter in the local Reformed Dutch Church, followed two years later by the marriage of "ye Jew Doctor" Jacob Lumbrozo at Baltimore to a Christian, the problem of intermarriage concerned the few Hebrew congregations that formed in the major seaport cities.

Wherever individual Jews settled, singly or in groups too small to form a religious community, intermarriage and assimilation resulted. A classic and typical example is that of the Franks family. When the future merchant tycoon of Philadelphia, David Franks, arrived in 1738 only two Jews resided there, his uncles Nathan and Isaac Levy. David was a fifth-generation American, a descendant of the Asser Levy family whose first member had landed at New Amsterdam with a contingent of 23 Jews shortly after Pietersen had settled there.

In 1742 David Franks' sister Phila came to Philadelphia with the socially prominent Oliver De Lancey of New York, with whom she eloped that year. David, one of a handful of Jews amidst 13,000 Philadelphians, married in the following year Margaret Evans, an Episcopalian. She was the daughter of Peter Evans, Registrar of Wills. All five of David Franks' children were baptized at Christ Church.

Uncle Isaac Levy ended his bachelorhood by taking Elizabeth Pue as his common-law wife. He was reluctant to marry a Christian woman—as would his brother, Samson, who upon his arrival in the City of Brotherly Love wed Martha Lampley Thompson. But Samson resisted Martha's attempts to baptize their children and in fact had his first son circumcised as a sign of entrance into the Jewish nation. Martha's charms would in time seduce the colonial Samson, who succumbed in 1780 and baptized 16-year-old Samson, Jr., 12-year-old Henrietta, and nine-year-old Rachel at Christ Church.

Samson Levy's changed attitude was shared by fellow Jews, symbolized in the spirit of the times by Reverend Jacob Raphael Cohen, spiritual leader of Philadelphia's *Mikveh Israel,* who marched in a victory parade held in the nation's capital, his arms interlinked with fellow Christian ministers who flanked him.

An impartial observer, Johann Conrad Dohla, a German mercenary who arrived June 2, 1777, in New York to aid in the British suppression of the American rebellion, wrote the following day in his diary:

> There are many Jews now resident in America, who carry on wholesale trade and business, and who are not easily distinguishable from Christians. . . .
>
> The Jews, however, are not like the ones we have in Europe and Germany, who are recognizable by their beards and their clothes, for these are dressed like other citizens, get shaved regularly, and also eat pork, although that is forbidden in their Law. Also Jews and Christians intermarry without scruple. The women also go about with curled hair and in French finery such as is worn by the ladies of the other religions. . . .

Dohla depicted American Jews as he had seen them at New Port, New York, and Philadelphia, where he saw service during the Revolution. His observations were accurate. Intermarriage was regarded by some colonial Jews as a form of socialization, no different from wearing the same style wig or dress.

In the first year following the American victory at Yorktown (October, 1781), one such case of intermarriage came to be a *cause célèbre* in the new land of liberty.

It all began innocently enough at a ball tendered at the courthouse in the village of Easton, Pennsylvania, to honor the country's hero, General George Washington, on July 26, 1782. The lavishness of the affair was such as had never been envisioned in that frontier settlement by the forks of the Delaware; over its public square and dirt main streets cattle and swine ran at large.

Among the most distinguished townspeople was Myer Hart, one of Easton's founders in 1752. He began his career as an Indian trader, became the town's first shopkeeper, innkeeper, liquor dealer, shipper of grain and sailing masts, and now the wealthiest Jew in Northampton County. A business associate of such pioneers as Joseph Simon and the Philadelphia Gratzes, and other Jewish as well as Christian merchants, he had amassed two houses, several slaves, a bond servant, six lots, a horse, a cow, and his stock in trade.

Myer Hart's wife Rachel de Lyon and her sister Rebecca de Lyon, the latter escorted by her husband Barnett Lazarus Levy, also exchanged pleasantries with the guest of honor. A third sister arrived from Philadelphia, Zipporah de Lyon with her husband Mordecai Moses Mordecai. Myer and Rachel Hart proudly presented their young adult family members, including daughter Judith, not only to the General but also to a number of soldiers and civilian guests.

A romance flared between the 20-year-old Judith and James Pettigrew, a Christian and a dashing officer who had served on General Washington's staff. A few months later, when it became obvious that Judith was pregnant, her Orthodox father's fury knew no bounds—not only at the fact of her pregnancy, but at the rumor that Judith had surreptitiously married Pettigrew during the ball by an Army Chaplain officiant, a Protestant.

The girl's distressed mother was torn between love for her husband and her daughter. She appealed to brother-in-law Mordecai Moses Mordecai to come to Easton to restore peace in her family. The irrepressible Mordecai promptly arrived, reconciled father and daughter that evening, and returned to Philadelphia the following day. Friends and relatives alike agreed it was a most dramatic achievement.

According to a secret agreement, as it would later be revealed, the young couple agreed to rear any girls born to them as Jews and any boys as Christians. Of their seven children, their three daughters married Jews. Apparently, it was this arrangement that appeased the distraught father.

One day, soon after Mordecai's successful mission, his brother-in-law, Barnard Levy (familiarly called Barnard or Baer) arrived from Easton in Philadelphia on a business trip. In a chance meeting with Simon Nathan, newly elected President of *Mikveh Israel* and other officers, Levy disclosed that when last in Easton, Mordecai united in

Jewish wedlock Judith Hart and her lover James Pettigrew, "according to the laws of Moses and of Israel."

To the astounded, unbelieving leaders of Philadelphia's Hebrew congregation, Levy proffered incontrovertible evidence that Mordecai married a Jewish woman to a Christian. He himself, as a witness, had signed the marriage contract together with Mordecai who performed the ceremony. (Jewish law requires the signatures in Hebrew of two male witnesses over 13 years of age.)

Since Jewish law permitted the marriage performer as a witness there seemed to be no question in the minds of the *Mikveh Israel* officers that Mordecai had indeed performed the illegal ceremony acting also as witness.

President Nathan summoned Levy to appear before a communal tribunal—a *beth din* (literally "House of Judgment") comprised of three learned laymen to act as judges. They took Barnard Levy's deposition.

Confronted with the evidence, Mordecai, who himself had on previous occasions served as a member of a *beth din* of *Mikveh Israel*, ranted that Barnard Levy was an ignoramus who violated every law of the Bible, and his testimony was therefore inadmissible. Furthermore, he angrily countered that the tribunal had acted illegally by taking the deposition in secret. Why had not he, Mordecai the aggrieved, been summoned to be present? Mordecai insisted also that the purpose of his visit to Easton had been to meet with his friend Joseph Simon on a business matter and not to become involved in a family dispute.

The tribunal weighed the facts and pronounced Mordecai guilty as charged—of having performed a marriage ceremony in contravention of Judaic law.

In a rage, Mordecai turned to Barnard Gratz, then *Parnas Residente* (Vice-President—during the second half of the Hebrew year from Passover to Rosh Hashanah, having served as *Parnas Presidente* [President] during the first half). In his letter he called Barnard his "good friend" and asked him to intervene on his behalf, to reconsider his case "for the sake of our friendship since youth (1750s)." He repeated his charge that the tribunal was incompetent to render judgement:

> I am surprised that the three judges, for even if they are not scholars they have manners and common sense, where then did they find this law . . . that a written deposition is accepted when the defendant is available . . . I can only think that they brought this practice from Spain and Portugal and that they act according to the practice of the Inquisition in hearing witnesses in secret. . . . I was sick all winter and now my wife is sick and

members of my family are suffering and distressed. . . . I think they properly observed the Rabbinic Dictum: "When the ox has fallen, sharpen the knife."

Parnas Presidente Simon Nathan, *Parnas Residente* Barnard Gratz, *Kehillah* officers and *beth din* appointees, were perplexed at the vehement declarations of innocence by Mordecai Moses Mordecai. He was, after all, a former rabbinic student and reputed to be as pious as Isaac de Costa, Joseph Wolf Carpeles, or Manuel Josephson, Pennsylvanians regarded as exemplary in conduct and in knowledge of the Jewish codes.

At the same time there was the deposition of Barnard Levy, alleging his having united in wedlock a Jewish woman and a Christian. They rationalized that possibly Mordecai had been swayed by his wife Zipporah, a descendant of Portuguese Jews, whose prolonged exposure under duress to Catholicism in the lands of the Inquisition predisposed them to laxity in lands of freedom.

At an impasse, there being no ordained rabbi settled in the United States, the dilemma was tabled, only to be recalled three years later when Mordecai led an open revolt against the authority of the *Kehillah,* again in a case involving intermarriage.

Benjamin Moses Clava, a one-time Lancaster resident, died in Philadelphia in the spring of 1785. He had been married to a Christian. Plagued with the growing number of intermarriages, *Mikveh Israel* officers suggested that he be denied Jewish burial rites. A *beth din* was appointed to decide the question. They ruled that since Benjamin Clava had been born a Jew, he be allowed interment in *Mikveh Israel* cemetery, but since he had not lived as a Jew none of the traditional Hebrew burial rites be granted. Accordingly, the corpse was neither to be ritually washed nor attired. Instead of covering the unwashed body with white linen, the corpse would be left uncovered and his shroud shredded, folded and placed in a corner of the deceased's coffin. As a further sign of dishonor, the *beth din* ruled that four teenaged lads (instead of men) serve as casket bearers, and after entombment no prayers be recited. Lastly, that the grave be dug in that remote corner of the cemetery reserved for suicides and undesirables.

Clava's wife appealed to Mordecai. Obligingly, he led a few of the community's malcontents into the "slumber room" and ritually washed the body, which they clothed with the only shroud available, the tattered linen covering him as best they could.

The angered officers, whose authority had been flouted, submitted a report of Mordecai's role in the Clava case as well as that of the earlier Pettigrew-Hart affair, both involving controversial issues relating to intermarriage, to the Chief Rabbi of Amsterdam, Holland, Saul Lowenstamm. Whatever his decision, it is regretfully not extant.

What is certain is that after the Revolution, the *Kehillah* lost its power and Mordecai Moses Mordecai continued to perform marriages with impunity while engaging as a distiller of spirits.

Barnard Gratz.

Michael Gratz.

Simon Nathan supported George Rogers Clark's 1778 conquest of the Upper Ohio.

Penn Square, Lancaster (*circa* 1800); Joseph Simon's house faced the square.

Torah scroll of Joseph Simon, Lancaster, Pennsylvania.

Gomez Trading House, built by Louis Gomez and son Daniel, *circa* 1719, north of Newburgh, New York.

An artist's rendering of Jewish New Year service at New Judean "Shul," founded 1724, Heidelberg, Pennsylvania.
Drawing by Kurt Friede

Trapdoor from pulpit of the Touro Synagogue, Newport, Rhode Island, which leads to an escape tunnel—a reminder of the Inquisition.
Photograph by John Hopf

Colonel David Salisbury Franks led the settlement of the Ohio Wilderness by French colonists in 1790. *Courtesy American Jewish Historical Society*

Levy Solomons, Canadian Jewish fur trader.
Courtesy American Jewish Archives

3

Jewish Settlers in Frontier Hinterlands

Virgin West Opens to Settlement (South of the Ohio)

The war ended, a new country began developing. Among its many founders was a husband and wife team, Aaron and Rachel Levy. They were building more than a house or group of houses. They were creating a town, one they hoped would grow into a city, its strategic location designating it as the capital of Pennsylvania.

Their dream occupied their thoughts in the early years of the Revolution. They lived at that time in Northumberland, a village deep in the hills of Indian country, at the confluence of the branches of the Susquehanna River. Of their many tracts of land they tried to guess which might be situated on the way west that was sure to open after the war for Ohio-bound pioneers.

In the summer of 1778 their daydreams were abruptly halted. A Mohawk massacre in neighboring Wyoming Valley (present-day Luzerne County), shocked the Northumberlanders. News reached them that as British-led Indians approached the Wyoming Valley, its 5,000 men, women and children converged upon the safety of palisaded Fronty Fort (near what is now Wilkes-Barre). Tories and Indian attackers, 1,000 strong, neared. Instead of preparing to defend themselves, 300 men and boys foolishly sallied out to rout the enemy.

The day after the Wyoming Valley Massacre, July 4, the Northumberlanders fled in all directions in what became known as "The Great Runaway"—the Levys reaching the safety of Lancaster.

Aaron Levy, an Indian trader for 20 years in Northumberland, also bartered with the farmers, exchanging goods for produce he shipped east. Now he engaged at Lancaster, as did fellow traders, in army supply. But he had more ambitious goals set for after the war. He planned to build a city that would bear his name. This city would serve as their own memorial, for the Levys were without children to carry on their name.

Anticipating a large movement west after the war, Aaron and his wife Rachel mapped out their dream town, to be built on a tract of several hundred acres called White Thorn Grove. It was located 30 miles from the confluence of the north and west branches of the Susquehanna River. There was good timberland roundabout and a fine rock quarry, offering wood and stone for construction. The region was fertile and excellent for farming.

The Levys chose this tract in preference to many others they owned in western Pennsylvania because it was located on an Indian trail they felt certain would be widened after the war into a roadway to accommodate westbound pioneers. Their dream town, Aaronsburg, 180 miles northwest of Philadelphia, would prove a perfect stopping place on the way to Pittsburgh—"Gateway to the West." In time, the Levys hoped that their town would become the future capital of Pennsylvania.

Accordingly, they laid out streets 50 feet wide that intersected at right angles. The main street, Aarons Square, running north and south, was 150 feet wide and so too was Rachels Way, running east and west, to enable Conestogas and other large carriages to maneuver with ease.

Lots were priced at 20 Spanish silver milled dollars, the Levys preferring that coin to Continental or English mint. The purchasers were Scotch, Irish, or Germans, with one exception. Simon Gratz, upon his *bar mitzvah*, purchased a parcel, offering the 20 Spanish silver milled dollars he had received in gifts.

Aaronsburg a reality, the Levys retired at the end of the century. A decade later the rival town built on the bank of the Susquehanna by John Harris south of Aaronsburg, a hundred miles northwest of Philadelphia, became the key stopping place for westbound settlers and after the turn of the century the capital of Pennsylvania.

Levy was in trouble, for the land boom collapsed and he was land rich and money poor. So he made an arrangement with Simon Gratz to turn over his holdings in return for an annuity.

It was more than a business arrangement. When the Levys first came to Lancaster, in 1778, they had become especially fond of Miriam Gratz's five-year-old son, Simon, and his younger brother, three-year-old Hyman, both Lancaster-born.

The childless Levys lavished affection upon their favorite adopted son, Simon. For the token of "one eagle" they deeded to the young man about 10,000 acres they owned around Aaronsburg and an additional 625 acres in Fishing Creek Township; also 625 in West Buffalo Township, which contained a grist and sawmill.

Simon and his brothers founded depot-towns on two of these tracts in Pennsylvania.

The Gratzes established their trading supply centers on the road west. Twenty miles northwest of Lancaster, by the Susquehanna River, they founded Gratz, Pennsylvania, in Dauphin County. And further west, 20 miles southeast of Pittsburgh, they founded Gratztown, Pennsylvania, in Westmoreland County. There, Simon laid out on Wildcat Hill, a former Aaron Levy tract, a last-chance resupply depot before settlers proceeded into the Ohio Valley.

The Gratz family envisioned a day not distant that the entire virgin Ohio Valley, including the "Indian side" north of the beautiful river, from the Land of the Forks to the Falls of the Ohio, even to the Mississippi, filled with settlers planting cornfields and vegetable gardens, raising poultry and herding cattle. Someday the bluegrass country of Kentucky, an Indian no-man's-land, would sprout villages, towns, and cities; so, too, the warring Shawnee and Delaware and Miami would be subdued and their forests cleared.

Their foresight was remarkable.

While attempting to found western empires on both sides of the Ohio, the Gratzes, both during and after the Revolution, invested heavily in tracts they bought directly from the state and federal governments, which gave them clear and uncontested legal titles.

In undeveloped western Pennsylvania and New York they (like Joseph Simon) purchased tracts of 10 to 50,000 acres. And across the mountains, within the strip ceded by the Six Nations, the brothers purchased such tracts as 321,000 acres on the Guyandotte, Little and Big Sandy Rivers just west of the Ohio River tract owned by the then Virginian justice of the peace, George Washington.

Much Kentucky land was acquired by Michael Gratz during the

Revolution when he was living in Richmond, engaged in privateering and army supply. His wife Miriam and young son then stayed with his in-laws, Joseph and Rose Simon, in Lancaster. Michael acquired prime bluegrass land offered for sale by Virginia.

At the war's end, he acquired from land speculator John Harvie, in an agreement dated July 23, 1783, 81,135 acres. In another deal with William du Vale, 162,607 acres. To Robert Morris, a leading merchant and minister of finance in the Continental Congress, the Gratzes sold 47,325 acres of virgin Kentucky bluegrass.

The Gratzes were among eight men who held a quarter million acres each of Kentucky land; next to them were about 240 men whose holdings ranged from 10,000 to 90,000 acres. The Gratz brothers also sought out Daniel Boone to survey lands for them to purchase in Kentucky but those records have been lost.

On a lesser scale, were the transactions of Jacob I. Cohen and Isaiah Isaacs, partners in the "Bird in Hand" Tavern, the oldest in Richmond, and traders in tobacco operating out of their silversmith house—Cohen & Isaacs. The duo had fought in the "Jew Company" under Captain Richard Lushington. They joined that predominantly Christian company at Charles Town, South Carolina; a third of its enrolled troops were Jews, and so it gained that unique title.

Isaiah Isaacs, the first Jew in Richmond (having settled there before the Revolution), was not the first in Virginia. In the capital of Williamsburg there had lived since 1745 the London-born Dr. John de Sequeyra whom Thomas Jefferson credited with introducing the tomato into the colonies as an edible fruit. (Europeans regarded the American fruit as poisonous and raised it for decoration. A superstition arose that the tomato's appearance stimulated love and it was called the "love apple.")

Isaacs in Richmond would marry twice, once to a Christian, Mary (Molly), and later to a Jewish woman, Hetty, the daughter of David and Esther Hays.

His business partner, Jacob I. Cohen, an Indian trader at Lancaster before the war, sojourned briefly at Philadelphia at the war's end, where his intended marriage became the focal point of an intense religious controversy.

Jacob I. Cohen requested the leaders of Mikveh Israel congregation in Philadelphia to wed him to the widow Esther Mordecai, the former Elizabeth Whitlock who had become a proselyte to Judaism. The *beth din* was appointed to decide whether a descendant of Aaron, ancient High Priest of Israel, as Jacob I. Cohen was deemed to be, could marry a widow, who was also a convert. They decided that while he could marry a widow, he could not marry a convert and vetoed the marriage. The congregation's *Adjunta* (Board of Directors) forbade its minister, Reverend Gershom Mendes Seixas, from performing it.

Despite the prohibition, two friends of Jacob Cohen, Haym Salomon, and Mordecai Sheftall, witnessed the ceremony performed by Israel Jacobs on August 28, 1782. Cohen took his bride to Richmond, there to live as an honored Jew in the community.

The partnership with Isaiah Isaacs prospered and they invested their profits in land speculation. Joined by Jacob Mordecai, son of Mrs. Cohen and her deceased husband Moses Mordecai, they acquired from Governor Patrick Henry, 12,396 acres in the Great Dismal Swamp near Norfolk. Looking westward, Cohen and Isaacs engaged Daniel Boone to search out for them prime property across the mountains in Kentucky. In his correspondence with Boone, Isaacs signed his name in Hebrew, not because he expected the woodsman to read that ancient script taught at Yale College, but because like many a colonial Jew he took great pride in his ability to read and cipher the revered characters. Boone was advanced six pounds specie toward payment.

Far less adept at wielding the pen than the axe, sitting at a simple desk in the first log cabin built in Fort Boonesborough, Boone wrote to the Jewish speculators:

> Received of Jacub Cohan 12 warrants consisting of 5000 akers of land and the same for Iasiah Isec, and six pounds specia, for which I promise to locate the said lands on as good as the cuntry will admit of.
>
> Gevn under my hand this 24 day of Desember, 1781.
>
> Daniel Boone.

Isaacs scrawled on the back of Boone's letter in Yiddish:

> Resit fun Kornel Bon far 10,000 agir lanit (Receipt of Colonel Boone for ten thousand acres land).

An amiable relationship continued between the Jewish partners and their land agent. Satisfied with the first selection of land in the heart of the bluegrass country, Cohen and Isaacs commissioned the pathfinder to survey adjacent Kentucky lands for them.

Before undertaking the survey, Boone insisted on cash:

Aprael the 28, 1784

No doubt you are desireous your land bisniss should be dunn but that is a thing imposible without money, and yours and Mr. Isaacs' will amount to a smart sum. . . .

Mr. Samuel Grant, my sister's sun will lykly hand you this later (letter). If so, he will be a good hand to send by, and I will be acountable for any money put into his hands inless kild by the Indins. The hole (whole) a mount, I think is 22. 10s. 8d. 2/s.

Your land lyes on Lickeng Rivere, on the south side, a bout 50 milds from the Ohigho (River) by water, and a bout 20 by land. Large bouts (boats) may come up to your doore.

I am, sir, your most obedent, omble sarvent,

Daniel Boone

The Cohen and Isaacs parcel proved to be an excellent investment as settlers by the hundreds and later by the thousands poured through the Cumberland Gap and boated down the Ohio into Kentucky.

And it was the Gratz Brothers who launched the first passenger boats and cargo laden batteaux down the Ohio and onto its tributaries into the Lower Ohio Valley. On the Kentucky River, twenty miles south of the Ohio, in Owen County, they established Gratz, Kentucky, as their supply base, centrally situated near Lexington, leading town of the Central Ohio West.

Virgin West Opens to Settlement (North of the Ohio)

North of the Ohio, on the Indian side, hostile tribes of Shawnee and Delaware and Miami deterred would-be settlers. The Upper Ohio was an endless, immense black forest where Indians tracked. Bears, wolves, and mountain lions padded through its thick woodlands; there were streams with a myriad of fish; there were deer, wild turkey, and an infinite variety of game. These tempting lures taunting white intruders were offset by lurking hostile Indians, including Ottawa, Illini, Wyandotte, and other Iroquoian Nations.

This forbidding land of 12 nations was a dark land because of its thickly forested woodland, stretching for hundreds of miles from the Alleghenies to the Miami River, then thinning to open grassy country beyond the Wabash to the Mississippi; bordered on the east by the mountains, on the west by the "Great River," on the south by the Ohio, and on the north by the Great Lakes.

In 1787 the United States Congress approved for this Northwest Territory the Northwest Ordinance. It provided for orderly settlement and division of Indian lands as they would become acquired by treaty and subsequent admission of that region for statehood.

In 1788, a year after the government approved the Northwest Ordinance, Rufus Putnam, the general who had driven the British out of Boston, led 48 daring pioneers to the bank of the Muskingum on the north bank of the Ohio. In Delaware country, 200 miles west of Pittsburgh, they hacked a clearing, built log cabins, and named their settlement Marietta.

Later that year, Judge John Cleves Symmes led sixty men poling their flatboats past Marietta to the Miami-inhabited woods at the high arching of the Ohio, there to found Columbia. Kentuckians crossed the river to found their town site nearby. A schoolmaster among them composed its ingenious name: Losantiville—*L* for Licking, *os* for mouth, *anti* for opposite, which put together meant "the town opposite the mouth of the Licking."

This scholarly composition was soon scrapped by Northwest Territory Governor Arthur St. Clair, who renamed the town Cincinnati—after the Roman general and statesman, Cincinnatus.

In 1790, a third settlement was founded in the Upper Ohio. Under the leadership of Lieutenant Colonel David Salisbury Franks, a charter member of the Society of the Cincinnati, 500 men, women, and children, emigrants from France established Gallipolis, meaning "City of France."

David Salisbury Franks, president of *Shearith Israel,* in Montreal when the Revolution broke, left Canada with the patriots, rising in rank to serve as aide-de-camp to two generals, Benedict Arnold and Benjamin Lincoln; also serving with George Washington at Valley Forge. After the war, the English- and French-speaking Jewish lieutenant colonel was on his way to France as the bearer of one of three copies of the treaty of peace ratified by Congress.

David Franks, a close friend of Secretary of State Thomas Jefferson and other high officials, was appointed to a Commission on Indian Affairs in 1789. They went to Creek country to negotiate a treaty. The mission failed, but the commission, including Franks, upon its return dined with President Washington, a memorable and rewarding experience recalling meager rations at the general's marquee headquarters in Valley Forge.

Especially rewarding to David Salisbury Franks was Congress's grant to him of a warrant for 400 acres of land located at the confluence of Raccoon Creek and the Ohio River. Having heard of his desire to travel west to clear his land, Congress named him to lead to lands near his grant 500 emigrants stranded at Alexandria, Virginia.

Franks accepted for he felt a kinship to these upper-class Parisian noblemen and courtiers, professionals and artisans, with whom he socialized. They had suffered following the revolution when mobs stormed the Bastille on July 14 of the previous year. They had no idea when they bought western land in the Upper Ohio that it was wild Indian country. The prospectus they read of the proposed settlement, at the confluence of the Scioto and Ohio, described that region as "the garden of the universe, the center of wealth, a place destined to be the heart of a great Empire" and predicted that the town they founded would probably become the capital of the United States.

Upon landing in Virginia's port of Alexandria, they learned to their dismay that they held worthless titles, for the Scioto Company never bought a single acre from its owner, the Federal Government. They thereupon appealed to President Washington and were granted that land on liberal terms. Congress promptly dispatched 50 farmers to clear the Scioto woods and build a village. David Salisbury Franks was appointed to lead them to their destination.

Franks, on horseback, started out at the head of a motley caravan that sultry month of July. Over the dusty roadway followed women and children in light wagons, a file of saddle horses, hogs and cattle, high-wheeled canvas-topped freight wagons loaded with log chains, mattocks, axes, burlaped seedlings and crates of chickens, along with valued possessions brought from France—chests and portmanteaus, silver teapots, chafing dishes, chess sets, and musical instruments.

They rested at the town of Winchester, then at the signal followed Franks's lead, climbing through the mountainous winding roads northwestward to the Monongahela River. Wagons converted into flatboats, they were borne down the current to Pittsburgh. The gateway to the West was at their midway point—200 miles having been traversed in two weeks. Franks assured them that the remainder of their journey was comparatively comfortable.

They poled off from Pittsburgh down what Franks called *La Belle Rivière*. Wildlife was everywhere in the waters below, in the skies overhead, and along the riverbanks. Occasionally deer swam with the current. They passed Fort Wheeling and scattered cabins on the south bank but saw none on the north side until they reached Marietta, which Salisbury told them was named for their own Marie Antoinette. Here they were heartened by the Upper Ohio's first pioneers, who gave them fresh meat and corn meal, hay and grain, and fresh water. They learned that 36 men of Marietta were on their way northward up the Muskingum to found another settlement on the fertile Big Bottom.

Poling deeper into the Ohio, they reached a second clearing on the Upper Ohio on October 19, 1790. Opposite the mouth of the Great Kanawha they sighted, upon a high steep bank, a stockade with two-story blockhouses at each corner, all framed by thick forest and the riverbank. Fifty men carrying rifles and axes who built their village were on hand to greet them, escorting them to 80 cabins built within the high walls.

Unpacking their belongings, including ivory dominoes, flutes and fiddles, they took in their soft white hands picks and shovels to plant fruit and nut trees and vegetable gardens and, like the Indians, fished in the Ohio and hunted in the Scioto woods where the Shawnee roamed. Franks left to visit his land warrant on the Raccoon Creek but soon returned to Gallipolis to help secure that community.

In the summer of 1791 swarms of mosquitoes swooped from over the walls to infect settlers with malaria. Some shook with ague, others burned with fever.

There was an even greater danger ever present. The Indians, deep in the forest, who following the trails of the buffalo and watching the soaring eagles to find passes through the mountains, could tell that the white man was near. He knew from the swarms of honeybees, a European importation that the Indian called "English flies," that the white man was encroaching upon his domain. Having been forced out of the Lower Ohio, his best hunting grounds and fishing waters, he was infuriated by the oncoming white settlers in his Upper Ohio.

As winter neared, news reached Gallipolis of the Indian massacre at Big Bottom and that the governor and his troops were on the way to avenge the Big Bottom pioneers.

Half a dozen other settlements were hacked out of the forest that year. The Indians, deprived of their hunting grounds by the fenced farms of the intruders, resented and fired upon by the white man for no apparent reason, took to the warpath with a vengeance.

On January 2, 1791, Delaware and Wyandotte struck at Big Bottom, a settlement about thirty miles north of Marietta up the Muskingum. A few days after the massacre the half-burnt bodies of twelve persons were found in a log cabin at Big Bottom. Though the hut had been set on fire, the green logs did not burn well and the victims' charred faces were identified.

Governor Arthur St. Clair dispatched troops to punish the responsible tribes, but they were defeated. The braves boasted that "there should not remain a Smoak on the Ohio by the time the Leaves put out."

St. Clair took up the challenge and led a thousand troops; one of his captains was Nathaniel G. S. Hart, son of Colonel Thomas Hart. Again St. Clair met disaster at the hands of Little Turtle and Blue Jacket and 2,000 braves.

As the jubilant Indians retired to their tepees and loved ones, David Salisbury Franks returned to Philadelphia to assume the post of assistant cashier of the Bank of North America. Upon his arrival, he startled his friends, who had heard that he had been among the massacred. Surviving the wilds, David Salisbury succumbed in civilization, to a yellow fever epidemic that in 1793 claimed this American patriot and pioneer.

The Ohio tribes, incited by the British, hoped to drive out the American intruders and regain the entire valley. They attacked settlers, stole their horses and cattle, and took captives. Finally, in the summer of 1794, President Washington sent General Anthony Wayne to secure the Upper Ohio Valley.

Instead of rushing headlong into Indian country unprepared, Wayne spent months training his men. Then he marched into the tribal land and burned their corn fields to deprive them of food. Arriving at Maumee Rapids, they found 2,000 Indians awaited them. Outnumbered two to one, Wayne delayed battle for three days to starve the Indian braves, who were hidden behind protective fallen trees felled by a tornado that had cut through the forest.

The sign to attack was given at last. In the front line was Infantry Sergeant Simon Magruder Levy, son of Levy Andrew Levy, the pioneer western trader of Fort Pitt, now moved to Baltimore. Simon Levy, a member of Captain Lockwood's company, advanced with trained rifle to rouse the Indians from their coverts at bayonet point. He charged in the face of Chippewa and Iroquois who also rose with rifles poised. However, Levy and the troops fired and charged so rapidly that the Indians did not have time to reload. Within 40 minutes the battle was over. Five hundred Indian warriors lay lifeless amidst the stumps and fallen trees by Maumee Falls. Simon Levy, who in 1802 would be one of two Marylanders in the first graduating class at West Point Military Academy, became known as "The Hero of the Battle of Fallen Timbers."

Having toppled Chief Little Turtle among the "fallen timbers," Indian fighting ended in the Upper Ohio, and the peace pipe smoked on August 3, 1795. Frontiersmen, settlers, peddlers, farmers poured into the region that would soon become the state of Ohio.

A flood of westbound pioneers made their way on foot, horseback, and covered wagon over the Alleghenies to Pittsburgh, gateway to the West. There they removed the wagon wheels to transform their schooners into flatboats. On these rectangular rivercraft, some equipped with huts, they brought aboard their families. Some brought their servants and slaves, their cattle, hogs, horses, sheep, fowl. These veritable "Noah's Arks" moved comfortably with the downriver current, poled away from obstacles and banks by able-bodied men who were always on guard. They constantly watched the north bank, "the Indian side," as they directed their craft to a sight on the southern bank or to continue down a tributary. After the Shawnee and Delaware were decisively defeated and new settlers had their choice of either side, many preferred the unpopulated virgin Upper Ohio in the Northwest Territory.

German Jews Migrate to the Ohio Valley

Welcoming immigrants to the land of liberty, where freedom was guaranteed and equal rights assured to all, attracted the attention of one German Jew in particular—the one believed to be the famed emancipator of the Jews of Germany, banker Moses Mendelssohn. As the West became populated, he looked to America as the haven of refuge for his oppressed German brethren. Upon the election of General George Washington to the Presidency of the United States, he wrote to the new head of state:

> You would be astonished most mighty president, at the perseverence of the German Jew if you could witness it. The great, nay, perhaps the greatest part of them, spent almost their whole life on the highway in

> pursuit of retail business, and the trader consumed for his own person nothing but a herring and a penny loaf; the nearest brook or well has to supply his drink. . . .
>
> Granted that a Jew has at last become possessor of a capital that would suffice to support a family, still he will not be able to marry the woman he loves . . . he is obliged to acquire protection money . . . and then seeks permission to marry. If he obtains it ,. . . he has to pay dearly for this permission.

The German Jew could not engage in a trade or profession unless he obtained a "Letter of Protection" from the government. Because of the strict quota system, one might have to wait years: only upon the death or emigration of a holder of this document would a new one be issued.

In Bavaria, a province in southern Germany, in addition to horse and goose and numerous other taxes, a Jewish youth faced a most severe hardship. If he sought to marry and was not the first-born son, he could not wed unless he obtained what was called a *matrikel*—this registration certificate costing as much as 1,000 gulden, or 1,000 florins. In addition, the holder of a *matrikel* had to prove that he had a "respectable" trade or profession. But the occupations followed by most Bavarian Jewish young men were peddling or cattle dealing, both declared "disreputable." And if a Jew could prove his profession or trade respectable, the community where he wished to reside had a right to oppose the newcomer as unwelcome.

Some young men remained bachelors throughout their twenties, thirties, and even forties, before they could amass a thousand coins. For this reason, Bavarian Jewish youths in their late teens and early twenties were attracted to America, which offered them both the opportunity to marry and settle and to work in freedom and dignity.

To the young Bavarian Jews, the newly opened western Ohio country was to their liking, for it was depicted as being a land of infinite beauty in its rivers, valleys, and hills, much like their native rural homeland. They could pursue there an occupation that they knew best and that required little or no capital—peddling.

One by one, these lads made their way from Bavaria to Germany's port of embarkation in the north, Bremen, or Holland's Rotterdam. They purchased the cheapest accommodations offered aboard tiny sailing vessels, which was steerage. Some could not even afford steerage and indentured themselves for from two to seven years, to a master who would buy them upon arrival in an American port to repay them for their passage across the Atlantic. Little did they realize that their status would not merely be that of a servant, but rather like that of a slave; the only difference being that after serving their time of indenture they would be free.

Since colonial times many a traveler to America had done so to reach the promised land. They generally had no idea of what was in store for them when they would arrive as an indentured servant in America, the land of freedom.

Some made their way to Strasbourg in Alsace. In Alsace, they boarded empty cotton wagons for the trip to Paris, and on to the seaport of Le Havre. Prussian Jews (those from Posen, a Polish appendage to Prussia in northern Germany) and those from central Germany generally followed the river routes along the Elbe or the Weser to Hamburg.

At Le Havre, Bremen, Hamburg, as at the ports of Amsterdam or London to which many penniless German youths had come with intentions of remaining, local dispensers of charity, as well as relatives or employers in those cities, persuaded them to embark for America. Many needed no prompting. They were determined to reach the land of promise no matter what the hardship.

The journey to America took from two to five months and steerage accommodations meant being crowded into a cramped wooden sleeping bunk. For the Jewish young man the trip posed an even greater sacrifice. On the verge of starvation from his refusal to eat non-kosher foods, he finally surrendered his religious conformity in order to survive; salted pork was the staple on board. Not until the mass migration of Bavarian Jews began in 1836 was kosher food to be had for the entire transoceanic voyage.

But throughout the early years, hunger and sickness were the lot of lone Jewish travelers. Those who survived the ocean voyage in those small slimy sailing vessels—some having spent the entire journey in the hole in the deck reached by a ladder, called steerage, and not having seen sunlight for months—upon their emergence were capable of any accomplishment.

After such a grueling trip, an indentured person was kept on board upon anchoring in an American port. The ship's captain advertised his bond-servants and described their age, sex, nationality, and services for which best suited.

One such bond-servant was fortuitously discovered by Aaron Levy, founder of Aaronsburg. When he was a young man, an Indian trader in

Northumberland County, he would return to Philadelphia to resupply. During one of those visits he passed on a Sabbath morning the residence of a wealthy Christian merchant, Samuel Chew. A young girl scrubbing the outside stoop to the Chew residence was weeping. Aaron asked what troubled her. The girl replied between sobs that she was Rachel Phillips and had been sold as a bond-servant to the Chews. There was little she would eat and now she was required to labor on the holy day. Levy arranged with Chew to pay the amount owing for her redemption, but instead of setting her free, married her.

Probably upon Rachel's urging, Aaron arranged to obtain a Jewish bond-servant who of course did not labor on holy days and was free to observe Judaism. Aaron Levy, a Dutchman, a native of Amsterdam, accepted the indenture of a fellow Dutch Jew, Isaac Salimen (Solomon), who overseas bound himself to Levy for a period of four years in payment for his "Freight" from Rotterdam. He was a commodity, fortunately to be well cared for by his Jewish owner upon his arrival, provided for in his indenture:

> Philadelphia SS.
>
> This indenture witnesseth that Isaac Solomon, of his own free will, hath put himself servant to Aaron Levy, for the consideration of nineteen pounds 10s., paid to E. Duthil & Co., for his freight from Rotterdam; as also for other good causes, he, the said Isaac Solomon, hath bound and put himself, and by these presents doth bind and put himself servant to the said Aaron Levy, to serve him, his executors and assigns, from the day of the date hereof, for and during the full term of four years from thence next ensuing, during all which term the said servant his said master, his executors, or assigns faithfully shall serve, and that honestly and obediently in all things, as a good and dutiful servant ought to do.
>
> And the said Aaron Levy, his executors and assigns, during the said term, shall find and provide for the said servant sufficient meat, drink, apparel, washing, and lodging, and at the expiration of his term, he shall give said servant two complete suits of cloaths, one whereof to be new.
>
> And for the true performance hereof, both the said parties bind themselves firmly unto each other by these present(s). In witness whereof, they have hereunto interchangeably set their hands and seals. Dated the fourth day of January, *Annoque Domini,* 1788.
>
> Bound before me,
> Lewis Farmer,   Isaac Salimen
> register

Indentured servants, like the black slaves with whom they often labored, at times fled their masters. A mass break for freedom occurred at the outset of the American Revolution. Seven bonded servants, fired with the "Spirit of '76" made their escape from a farm in Harford County, Maryland. Master Purdue offered a reward for their capture. He described 28-year-old Abraham Peters as a German Jew who spoke Dutch, was black-bearded, and walked with a limp. Yet he outdistanced his pursuers.

The pitiful condition in which the youths arrived in the major American port of entry, Philadelphia, aroused the Jewish community. Their clothes were worn thin, in shreds after the months of ordeal on the high seas. They suffered from scurvy and other maladies due to a lack of fresh foods, particularly fruits and vegetables.

Philadelphia's *Mikveh Israel* congregation organized in 1783 (upon the very first arrival of the lone Jewish youths from southern Germany) the first Jewish immigrant aid society in the United States, *Ezrath Orechim* (assistance to the wayfarers).

The aid society outfitted these young men, some of them teenagers, with clothing after first caring for their health. They even supplied them for the occupation ahead—peddling. Wearing boots with pants legs tucked in, woolen jackets, berets, caps, or hats in various shapes and colors, and some dressed in long coats—invariably all had one thing in common, the pack on their back. As they made their way westward they would occasionally see a successful peddler riding on horseback, packs astride his mount, at times even a proud peddler at the reigns of his wagon. But in the hinterland, roads were rare and trails many. These would be their routes in the Ohio Valley, to be mapped out by their supplier.

In about a month after his arrival in America, the peddler had learned enough English words to make himself understood—also recognized, for he spoke with a heavy guttural accent, which to many recalled the Dutch. For this reason he was called either "Dutch Peddler" or "Jew Peddler."

It was told by a Jewish reverend traveling on a boat, that he saw a peddler walking around the boat, wringing his hands in agony. Asked if he had lost anything, the peddler responded in German: "Have I lost anything? . . . I have lost everything! I have lost my English language." The reverend could not understand. "You do not understand? Neither do I, and therein lies my misfortune. I arrived at New York, and after I had paid my debts I had 20 dollars and three shillings left. So they said to me, 'Cohen, you must buy a basket for six shillings, and 20 dollars' worth of kuddel muddel, what we call in German *meshowes* (notions), and then you must go peddling in the country.'

"I cry out, 'The country speaks English, and I do not. How in the world can I get along?' 'That makes no difference,' they told me; 'we will write everything down for you.' Well, they gave me the basket filled with kuddel muddel, and wrote down for me the English language on a piece of paper, and sent me to Hudson. Now I have lost the English language, and am perfectly helpless."

The sympathetic reverend comforted the distraught peddler, had him write in German the sentences he needed, and translated them into English. Even then the immigrant had his difficulties and persisted in saying, "You fant to puy somdink? Can I shtay mit you all nacht?"

The German-Jewish peddler's accent was captured for all time by John Howard Payne, the author of "Home Sweet Home," who was reputed to be the first outstanding American dramatist. In 1815 he wrote "Trial Without Jury," also titled "The Maid and the Magpie." John may well have had contact with the peddling Jews at his home in Long Island where his grandfather, Aaron Isaacs, had lived. Though Aaron married a Christian, his tombstone declared him to be "an Israelite in whom there was no guile." Nonetheless, in his play he expresses typical prejudices against the Jew.

The plot hinges on the theft by a magpie of a silver knife owned by the mistress of the house. A duplicate of this knife is also owned by the maid, Rosalie, who sells it to a Jewish peddler, Solomon Isaac. Rosalie is charged with theft of her mistress's knife and arrested together with Isaac, who had already sold the knife when loss of the mistress's was discovered. When the magpie's mischief is known, Rosalie is freed, but we hear nothing of Isaac's release.

Isaac is the conventional stage Jew. He is first heard offstage peddling his wares: "Knifes! Fine knifes! Chewels! Fine lace! Chentlemen and ladies, come puy! Come puy! Come puy!" He speaks throughout in dialect and bargains with Rosalie in the usual sharp manner of the stereotype. When he gives her six shillings for it, he adds in an aside, "I vas nigh do give sheven." A friend whom Rosalie tells of the sale exclaims, "I'll wager now he's got it for next to nothing. For they are so Jewish, those Jews!"

Peddling in the Pennsylvania hinterlands, Solomon Raffeld (Raphael) mastered the English language sufficiently by the fall of 1788 to write on October 13 a formal request to the president of Philadelphia's synagogue, requesting his marriage be solemnized by the *hazzan* or minister. His almost unintelligible English was deciphered by the leaders of the congregation as the secretary read:

> To the anerable, the presedent, and the genthelman jauntay (Junta or Board):
>
> Weer as I have pramis mie selleff in matteri mony whit o ne gall, the dogter of Mr. Barent Jacob, in the Norderen Libberthes (a suburb) in Philadelphia; and I would be werry happy that jour anerable budday would order to Mr. Jacob Kohon as gasan of the congragashis of Mikvy Israel to give mie goupa and kadousin agins Dousday. Ther for, genttelman, I pray one ansver of jour shentel man to mourow . . . the 12 day of Tisri at 11 o'clok and, by soo douing, your pertisnar will eiver pray.
>
> Froom jour omble sarwint,
>
> Salomon Raffeld
>
> To Mr. Levy Phillip, President of the K.K. Mikvy Israel, Philadelphia, Sonday, the 11 day of Tisri, 5549.

Solomon Raphael's request to the officers of *Mikveh Israel* congregation, Philadelphia, was promptly approved. On Tuesday, October 13, 1788 he was married according to the law of Moses and Israel.

His father-in-law was the highly respected Barnard Jacobs, in the 1760s and 1770s, the "Jew Rabbi" of western Pennsylvania.

Peddler Raphael was most fortunate in that he possessed two licenses envied by all his countrymen who went on to peddle beyond the mountains. To Solomon Raphael had been granted a Hebrew marriage certificate, approved by Levy Phillips, president of *Mikveh Israel,* and he had been issued a peddler's license signed by Benjamin Franklin, president of the Executive Council of Pennsylvania.

Solomon Raphael rapidly climbed the ladder from pack-carrier to merchant and auctioneer. In Philadelphia, he sympathized with more recent German-Jewish immigrants who left friends and family to build a new life. He assisted in outfitting them as they started on their way west; he gave them advice and directed them to other suppliers.

To novices concerned about Yankee peddler competition, Raphael explained that they represented no competition since Yankees dealt in novelties such as clocks, patent medicines, and housewares, whereas Jewish peddlers sold primarily thread, ribbons, buttons, lace, knives, and jewelry.

Any would-be peddler who contemplated walking and hawking in the Philadelphia area or any eastern region was quickly told that in cities where population was dense, and neighborhoods thickened, or in the countryside where the smoke from one man's chimney could be seen from another's front door, stores were patronized. Such city or country dwellers were no longer satisfied with transient or periodical supplies. They demanded that which was constant and regular, as available in the little neighborhood stores usually found at "crossroads" or next door to the blacksmith's shop. Neither would a peddler succeed in an area where there were too few farms.

Philadelphians directed doubting newcomers to take their advice and proceed into the rapidly developing Ohio Valley. The overwhelming majority of the immigrants heeded their advice.

After crossing the mountains they reached Pittsburgh. The region roundabout offered little opportunity as the farms were few and far between. But in the Ohio Valley, in Kentucky, there were many small farms along the riverways. They dotted the south bank of the Ohio from Wheeling in western Virginia to Louisville in western Kentucky. Tens of thousands of settlers had already built log cabins along the south side of the "Beautiful River" and its tributaries, generally navigable for about 70 miles. As they would discover, their suppliers would map out their route first on an upriver boat for about 70 miles, then to return by foot on a circuitous route from farm to farm. Towns, villages, and supply centers—as envisioned by the Gratz brothers, who became firmly entrenched in Kentucky—were springing into reality.

Pittsburgh, the springboard into the West, was described by one Jewish peddler-to-be as "a stirring and lively city." It was cosmopolitan, as recorded by the English actor, John Bernard, who performed there at the turn of the century: "natives of every State, besides English, Irish and Scotch, French, German, Dutch, Jews, and Indians."

The Bavarian immigrant Jew stopped in Pittsburgh just long enough to hop aboard a riverboat poling off down the Ohio.

The peddlers were supplied by special wholesale houses, such as those operated by the Gratz brothers, which (unlike the general stores that carried the necessities of life) were stocked with articles the pioneer settlers regarded as luxuries. Whatever they could not themselves make in the home, or obtain in the general store, the peddler carried. Into the pack were placed "notions," which included buttons and pins, needles and thread, combs, toothbrushes and toothpicks, and dry goods; consisting of ribbons, laces, bows, pillowcases and pillow shams, as well as ready-made clothing.

His supplier often helped select a stretch of country settled by farmers as well as villages as yet visited by few of his competing countrymen. Having extended credit, he often did not provide a license, which cost ten dollars. He could, however, peddle on the riverboats only to passengers on board or entering at the landings without a license.

In a conversation aboard a riverboat, a passenger asked a German Jewish peddler: "And did you make anything out of the deckers (the other passengers on the boat)?" and he replied: "Te Goots I solt on te bassage . . . gost me vorty tollar—dey prought me von huntret and tirty. My pusiness is to pe alvays at pusiness, everywhere. On te steampoats dey ton't make us bay licenze."

When the steamboats first appeared on the Ohio and its tributaries they were welcomed by all, especially by the peddlers, who benefited from the faster travel and the increased number of passengers. All but one, that is.

He was the Jewish peddler Hyman Lazarus, who supplied at Malta. In that village, Isaac Baker built the first mill in Ohio, its base on two flatboats. One day, Lazarus watched an apparition in the distance as it puffed up the Muskingum headed for the Malta riverbank. With eyes wide open, gazing with alarm and astonishment, he ran and gasped: "Mr. Baker! Mr. Baker! You mill haf got loose, und he is coomin oop the river a-grindin like the Devil!"

"Son of the Weary Foot" the peddler was named by the Philadelphia reverend, Isaac Leeser, spokesman for the American Jew and a man always concerned about the hardships and sufferings of the western Jew, alone and isolated from his people. That title had special meaning to Lewis A. Gratz (not related to the Gratzes of Pennsylvania and Kentucky). Eighteen when he arrived in America, he obtained a pack at Knoxville, Tennessee, filled with thimbles, shoelaces, and stockings. He peddled in the back country as the rains came. Soaked to the skin, his clothes and shoes drenched, he was seized with high fever and his leg became infected.

In mud knee-deep, pack on his back, he limped for 25 miles to return to Knoxville. Assigned a bed in a public hospital reserved for the poor, he left after six weeks, his leg improved, his fever at its peak. A kindly physician finally cured the insidious fever. Promptly he returned to the only occupation he knew, peddling.

Perhaps the peddler should have been more fittingly called Son of the Bitten Foot, for dogs were ever tearing at the legs of his trousers.

As he approached a farmhouse, his worst enemy, even worse than the farmer's dogs, was the hateful farmer who yelled to his mongrel: "Get him, Sultan; sic him, he is of the brood of Moses!" On the road, his greatest torment was the taunt of the anti-Semite. Pack-carrier Henry Seesel, as he trudged the lonely paths hunched under a heavy load, encountered a crude character who looked him over. The stranger with a curse punched the bearded youth, shouting "Damned Jew Dog!"

Few called him a swindler and a cheat. The one thing the Jewish peddlers in America were known for was their honesty and integrity. A rare exception was the German Emanuel Lyon and his Irish-Jewish partner Isaac Jacobs. After a lapse of six months, their creditors realized that they had absconded with their goods. They offered a reward, and the following notice was published on August 10, 1772, in the *Supplement to the Pennsylvania Packet and the General Advertiser:*

FIVE HUNDRED DOLLARS REWARD

> Any person or persons who shall apprehend and deliver to the sheriff of Philadelphia county, Isaac Jacobs and Emanuel Lyon, Jew pedlars, who left this city sometime in February last, shall be entitled to the above reward . . .
>
> Philip Francis   Edward Batchelor
> Thomas Asheton   Henry Kepple, Jun.
> Joseph Dean

Virtually every Jewish peddler worked hard to repay his creditors and saved his profits for the day he would no longer have to peddle on foot. He wanted to buy a horse and wagon. Those who did found that the ancient rabbis of the Talmudic era were right when they said "the more wealth, the more worry." Isaac Wolfe Bernheim discovered to his dismay that his profits were being eaten by his horse, for the expense of feeding, shoeing, and stabling far exceeded his gains. The happiest moment in his entire peddling career was the morning he found his horse had died. Thereafter, he progressed uphill rapidly.

Most peddlers took a chance and peddled on land without a license. After traveling aboard a riverboat for a distance of about 30 miles from their supply base, they made off on tiny boat landings with peddler's pack in circuitous route in the direction of the home supply base, hoping to return at the month's end with pack empty and purse full.

As Lewis Stix carried his pack from the landing, a merchant at that point named Johns demanded to see his peddler's license. Lewis, pretending to be a French Canadian, made signs that he did not comprehend. Johns called for his son, a student of the French language.

Perplexed but composed, Stix started to speak to the young man in his native Yiddish. The son, interpreting, informed his father that Stix spoke a French dialect not universally known.

Stix was lucky to be spared a fine or imprisonment had he been detected and unable to pay the penalty. He knew that the "Jew Peddler" would be sternly dealt with if caught without a license. Back East, where some Yankee peddlers made the rounds as well as German Jews, a peddler staggered into an inn at Easton, Pennsylvania, in deep snow and quite frozen. A number of guests were seated that evening about the glowing stove. They observed his pale face, as white as his snow-covered cap.

Complaining that he had not earned enough for a drink after tramping the entire day in the cold, the guests patronized him. Then one of the smiling men round the pot-bellied stove approached and took the stranger aside. He quietly asked to see his license.

The immigrant peddler admitted that he did not have one, whereupon the questioner asked, "Are you a Jew?"

The stranger replied in the negative and produced his passport. Aware that the young man, despite the ten-day-old beard, was indeed not a Jew, he sympathetically said, "Since I see that you are an honest Protestant Christian, I shall let you go although I am losing $25 through it. I have no kind feelings for the Jews and were you one of them I would not treat you so gently. If I wanted to arrest you, you would have to pay a $50 fine or until you were able to raise it you would have to go to jail and half the fine would be mine. Still, I shall forego that but you better give up your trade and look for another one. Sooner or later you will be caught and then you will be out of luck."

As he trudged the western valleys and hills, the terrain reminded the Jewish peddler of his native southern Germany. But he was surprised to find that the sport of the civilized white man was as cruel as that of the Indians. Boxing was properly called "gouging." These bouts allowed kicking, biting, kneeing, maiming. Contestants grew their thumbnails long to help in extracting an opponent's eye. One who fought such an opponent could readily be recognized by his eyepatch, or chewed-off nose, or bitten ears.

Somehow the Jew instinctively steered clear of these pastimes, but there were exceptions. Most notable was the bout in which not only the contestants were Jews but so too were the seconds, witnesses, and referee. The fight took place between Moses Silberstein and Isaac Salomon at Bergen Point in the East for a stake of 200 dollars. There were 26 rounds and finally Silberstein was declared the winner. The report tells: "The two men were woefully mauled and Salomon went through the last four rounds blinded. He immediately sent his victor a new challenge."

All Jews seemed to steer clear of sports that involved cruelty to animals. "Bear baiting" was popular in the Ohio. A bear would be chained in an outdoor enclosure and packs of six or seven dogs set loose on him. The recreation lasted until the bear was torn apart or the dogs killed.

But there would be moments of tranquillity and joy as well.

Once off the boat and on his route, the peddler began his arduous walk along cowpaths and trails and rutted roads, always in the direction of his supply base. At most farmhouses he was warmly welcomed. He was the "bearer of civilization" in the wilderness, bringing news of settlements and cities and other lands. He also brought manufactured luxuries of the latest designs.

Oddly enough, the peddler preferred to pursue his trade in the harsh wintry months, for despite the cold and snow, his chances for a sale were better for then the farmers were indoors on weekdays as well as weekends. In all seasons he could count on a free meal and a night's lodging.

After chatting about the latest events, he flung his pack across the wooden planked floor or rough-hewn table and opened the pack before the gawking wide-eyed cabin settlers. The housewife was most interested. "How fascinating the horn-combs painted like tortoise-shells sparkled when held by the peddler against the dark head of hair of the blushing daughter. In the drab surroundings, what splendor was revealed in the just-unpacked piece of calico, whose marvelous design with lightning-like zig-zags and countless moons and stars drew a loud 'Ah!' even from the elderly grandmother; and then at last the towels and ribbons, the mother-of-pearl buttons and hairpins with the small colored pearl glass-globes mounted on top, and the hairbows and bracelets, the chains and the fire-flashing earrings...."

Pack peddlers and wagon peddlers all suffered from bad debts incurred by those to whom they extended credit. Even the local courts favored the farmers and villagers, so the poor peddler had no recourse. But profits were generally high, as recounted by Theodor Griesinger:

The country is big and there are still places . . . where people are so good-natured or so simple that they allow themselves to be duped a little. Sam finds these places and the farmers are happy to see the peddler, for then they need not make the long journey to the city. But Sam is still happier, since he sells at 200 per cent profit and gets a night's lodging and evening meal free.

Eventually the day came when the peddler who succeeded in his sales purchased a lot in a settlement or a spot somewhere on his route that seemed favorable and set up a store. When Moses Tubal opened a place in one of the Ohio River landings, his Christian competitor next door raved and ranted about the "Jew Store." He was John Beauchamp Jones who for some reason wrote under the pseudonym Luke Shortfield that "The Shylocks prefer to be on the navigable streams," and poured forth his wrath on his new competitor:

He came on foot, but from what place no one knew. He was a young man somewhat older than myself, with a prominent nose, high cheek bones, and small sparkling eyes. Before the day was over, I began to suspect he might be one of those vendors of "tender" goods, a cunning Jew, in quest of a location to cheat his neighbors, and spoil the regular trader's business.

Despite his prejudice against Jews, Luke Shortfield left for his annual trip east to resupply at a Jewish wholesale house, which he called "Keen, Cunning & Company, of Philadelphia."

Luke asserted that the Jewish wholesaler did not trust any Jew of the West. In fact, stated Luke, the Philadelphia Jew told him that "he had supposed Moses (Tubal) was a Jew, although his language and dress were in exact imitation of the thorough-bred western merchant." Furthermore, upon putting the question to Moses directly, he had forced him to make an affirmative reply, and then the wholesaler declined selling him anything on credit. Luke added: "All this surprised me. Why had Moses attempted to conceal the fact of his being a true Israelite?"

Ignorance, Indifference, Intermarriage

Why did the western Jew conceal his identify as an Israelite?

For many a German Jewish youth, his first violation of the Judaic laws was aboard ship when in the course of his voyage he found himself compelled to partake of non-kosher food. But he reasoned this was in truth not against his faith, for in situations where survival was at stake, he was commanded to eat forbidden food to keep alive.

When he first began peddling, his pockets bulged with hard-boiled eggs and a pan was in his pack for cooking vegetables and other permitted foods he obtained at farms and settlements, such as fish and fruit. But his most distinguishing sign was the eggs that constituted his staple diet. No wonder the Cherokee called him *Jew-wedge-du-gish*, which in their tongue meant "egg-eater."

But not all could continue for long being "egg-eaters." When kindly farmers offered them cakes, breads, meats, and other home-cooked and baked foods, many succumbed and no longer kept the kosher diet. Neither could the peddler rest on the Sabbath day, but was compelled to be on his way after the night's lodging.

Even the staunch Abraham Kohn, who made every attempt to observe Judaism's laws while peddling in the Upper Ohio bartering wares for such foods as Indian maize (corn), vegetables, and eggs, in order to keep the kosher diet, complained:

> ... none of us is able to observe the smallest commandment. Thousands of peddlers wander about America: young, strong men, they waste their strength by carrying heavy loads in the summer's heat: they lose their health in the icy cold of winter. And thus they forget completely their Creator. They no longer put on the phylacteries; they pray neither on working day nor on the Sabbath. In truth, they have given up their religion for the pack which is on their backs. ...

Not only was the peddler unable to observe the holy day of the Sabbath biblically ordained from sunset Friday to sunset Saturday, but well-meaning farmers urged him to attend Church on Sunday. Kohn cried out in anguish:

> God in Heaven, Father of our ancestors, thou who hast protected the little band of Jews unto this day, thou knowest my thoughts. Thou alone knowest my grief when, on the Sabbath's eve, I must retire to my lodging and on Saturday morning carry my pack on my back, profaining the holy day, God's gift to his people Israel. I can't live as a Jew. How should I go to church and pray to the "hanged" Jesus? Better that I be baptized at once, forswear the God of Israel, and go to hell. ...
>
> No, by the God of Israel I swear that if I can't make my living in any other way in this blessed land of freedom and equality, I will return to my mother, brothers, and sisters, and God will help me and give me his aid and blessing in all my ways. ...

Here again, Kohn was one of the strong-willed Jewish peddlers who proved that one who peddled could resist all temptations, though admittedly strong. However, many Jewish peddlers became accustomed to visiting Christian churches as they became thoroughly assimilated.

Everywhere he went, the struggling peddler also found strong prejudices directed against him, against the Jew, carried over from the Old World and handed down in the remotest regions of the New World.

In her novel *Harrington,* Miss Maria Edgeworth relates how violent hatreds and fears against the "Jew Peddler" were transmitted; the story, published in London in 1817, proved so popular that an American edition appeared in New York that very year.

The subject, a six-year-old boy, one evening delayed his bedtime. Fascinated, he watched from the balcony of his upper room in his parents' house an old man with a long white beard and dark complexion approaching with a lantern. Holding a big bag slung over his shoulder he walked slowly down the street crying "Old Clothes! Old Clothes!"

"Time for you to come off to bed, Master Harrington," insisted the maid. The boy resisted. She threatened, "I'll call to Simon the Jew there," pointing to him, "and he shall come up and carry you away in his great bag."

After a restless night, the boy asked the next morning whether Simon the Jew was a good or a bad man. The maid replied: "Simon the Jew is a good man for naughty boys."

For some time afterwards she continued to warn the lad that "Simon the Jew" would come to get him, but when that threat wore off, she told the boy stories of Jews who kidnapped poor children for the purpose of crucifying, then sacrificing them at their secret feasts held at midnight. She cautioned the little boy to take care when walking in the streets that they do not catch him, adding that there was no knowing what they might do with him.

As a young man, Harrington recalled: "I shudder when I look back to all I suffered during the eighteen months I was under her tyranny. Every night, the moment she and her candle left the room, I lay in an indescribable agony of terror; my head under the bed-clothes, my knees drawn up, in a cold perspiration. I saw faces around me grinning, glaring, receding, advancing, all turning at last into the same face of the Jew with the long beard and the terrible eyes; and that bag, in which I fancied were mangled limbs of children—it opened to receive me. . . ."

Many a "Jew peddler" in the Ohio had the door slammed shut in his face by a farmer who in his childhood had heard fearful stories of the Jew. It never occurred to such that he who was crucified on the cross was likewise a Jew.

In this country, ignorance rather than prejudice prevailed. Tennessee folklore told of a Jewish peddler tramping down the trail who was accosted by a mountaineer who had just 'sperienced religion at a camp meeting. "Say," said the newly converted hillbilly, "ain't you a Jew? I never seed a Jew but I calkalate you is one."

The peddler modestly answered the question in the affirmative, ignorant of the results.

"Put your pack down," said the convert. "Now I am going to knock hell out of yer," and proceeded to punch the bewildered Jew.

"What you hit me for?" cried the peddler.

"What fer?" exclaimed his assailant, "What fer? Well that's a nice thing to ask a gentleman. You crucified our Lord, that's what you done."

Then the Jew explained that it had occurred nearly 2,000 years ago and he had absolutely nothing to do with it.

"Scuse me," said the mountaineer, "I'm sorry I beat you. I was told up there at the camp meeting, that the Jews had crucified the Lord, and I calkerlated you was one of the men that did it. I never heard of it before today."

Having fled Germany to escape the wrath of those who called him Christ-killer, he found human nature unchanged in the land of the free. This teaching even permeated the converted African slave who in some instances trembled at the thought of serving a Jewish master.

When the day came for a black servant to go to her new mistress the girl was nowhere to be found. After a thorough search she was discovered hiding beneath a bed. On being questioned as to her reason, her quivering lips were heard to utter: "I don't want to go to live with Miss Isaacs."

"But why don't you want to live with her? She is a good lady, and will make you a kind mistress; and besides you won't have any hard work to do."

Shaking like a leaf, the fearful girl revealed: "Ah!" but Mass F——, they tell me Miss Isaacs is a Jew; an' if the Jews kill the Lord and Master, what won't they do to a poor little nigger like me!"

The free black who bought from the Jewish peddler "gew-gaws"— cheap trinkets that attracted their fancy, or "notions"—never associated him with the "Children of Israel" whom the Almighty freed from

Egyptian bondage. One old "mammy," who had often heard the story of the exodus, expressed before her mistress the wish to see some of the Children of Israel, inasmuch as she could not visit the Land of Canaan. To satisfy her, the mistress, upon learning of the coming of a peddler to a nearby village, told her servant that she might pay a visit there, and view the "Child of Abraham."

The servant soon returned, and indignantly exclaimed: "Missus! dat's no Chillen o' Israel. Dat's de same ol' Jew peddler w'at sole me dem pisen, brass yearrings las' 'tracted meetin' time. Sich low down w'ite man as dat, he nevah b'long to no Lan' o' Cainyan."

In the towns, there was more prejudice toward than ignorance of the Jew. Thus it happened that in a northern Ohio town, Cleveland, a Madame Levy went to see the owner of a house she desired to rent. She inquired as to the price and upon reaching an agreement, the owner asked her, as he proceeded to fill out the form:

"Madame, and your name?"

"Madame Levy."

"Are you a Jewess?"

"Yes, Sir."

"I do not rent my house to Jews."

"Are you in earnest about this, Sir?" asked Madame Levy, astonished.

"I am in dead earnest."

"O, I feel sorry for you," replied Madame Levy, with rare presence of mind, "Now I know why the virgin Mary had to be delivered of her child in a stable!"

4

Hebrew Patriots, Pioneers, Pirates

First Jews West of the Mississippi

In 1803 America formally assumed possession of the Louisiana Territory at New Orleans. No one then knew its full extent—almost a million square miles of prairie from the Mississippi River west to the ridges of the Shining Mountains (the Rockies), and extending from the Mexican Gulf to the Canadian border.

Flag-raising ceremonies in the Upper Louisiana were held in 1804 at St. Louis, a rough-and-tumble town of a thousand French Catholics. The town was centrally situated, being midway between the gulfport of New Orleans and Innijiska at the confluence of the Mississippi and Minnesota rivers (today the site of the twin cities of St. Paul and Minneapolis).

In this vast Louisiana Territory neither the French nor the Spanish who first discovered the region allowed Jews upon its soil, the Spanish operating under the laws of the Inquisition and the French under the Black Code.

A change took place at the end of the eighteenth century that would allow Jews to settle in Spanish Louisiana. In 1787, when the United States government provided for the establishment of states in its Northwest Territory east of the Mississippi and north of the Ohio, dashing the aspirations of western men who worked for decades to found empires in that region, the Gratz brothers turned their sights to the lands beyond the Mississippi. They dispatched their western agent, George Morgan, from their Kaskaskia trading post to the western bank of the "Great River" into Spanish Louisiana.

The Gratzes dreamt of creating a land colony to be directed by Morgan from the site of their trading post in what was called New Madrid. George Morgan suggested to Spanish officials the establishment of a Spanish-American colony. The Lieutenant-Governor at St. Louis approved. He favored the idea of a buffer zone of about 15,000,000 acres for American settlers. Each settler would be offered a liberal grant of land, local self-government, and religious freedom.

Among the Americans attracted to New Madrid and its region was Andrew Block (Bloch). Little is known about him. He may well have been a relative of the Gratz brothers, Barnard and Michael, whose grandfather was Jonathan Bloch (Block).

An older son of Jonathan Bloch, Zevi Hirsch, removed to Langendorf in Bohemia and retained his father's surname. But Zevi Hirsch Bloch's sons, Jacob and Solomon, after they moved to England dropped Bloch in favor of Henry—the English equivalent of their original patronymic Zevi Hirsch.

Jacob Henry, in search of greener pastures, ventured to America and arrived in Philadelphia in 1751. He clerked in the firm of Simon & Franks, and it seems that his teenage cousin, Barnard Gratz, replaced him at the counting house of Solomon Henry in London. In 1754 Jacob Henry returned to England and Barnard Gratz crossed the ocean to clerk at the firm of David Franks in Philadelphia, followed three years later by his younger brother Michael. Henry remained but a short while in London, then returned to Philadelphia.

Relationships between the Gratzes and Henrys, cousins and grandsons of Jonathan Bloch, were warm and cordial, as evidenced by their correspondence. The Gratzes became a symbol of success to the Bloch family of Bohemia and Silesia and may well have attracted as early as 1787 one of them, Andrew Bloch, to settle in the Far West.

Andrew Block, opened his trading post on New Madrid's Main Street, the roadway beginning at a right angle from the riverfront, thus enabling the Jewish Indian trader and others to keep one eye on the Mississippi landing and the other on the hills to the west. From the vast unexplored Louisiana interior Indians came with their peltries, which they bartered in New Madrid, to be boated down the Mississippi to the Ohio and Eastern ports. Thus Bloch and Morgan tapped the rich furs that came from as far west as the Rocky Mountains to reach the Gratz brothers.

As for the Spanish-American colonization dream of Morgan and Gratz, it never materialized. Though approved by the lieutenant-governor of St. Louis, it was disapproved by the governor-general at his office in New Orleans.

Even as the Gratz brothers may well have influenced Andrew Block to come west, Andrew in turn may have drawn another of the Bohemian clan, Ezekiel Block, to Missouri. Ezekiel was living in Richmond, Virginia, at the turn of the century. Shortly before the Spanish cession of Louisiana, he left to settle in the proposed Spanish-American colony on the west side of the Mississippi. On a promontory near Cape Girardeau, 150 miles downstream from St. Louis, Ezekiel Block acquired a plantation, which was worked by nine black slaves (four male and five female) and two horses.

It was a gala event in November 1804 when Ezekiel and fellow plantationers gathered at Cape Girardeau to welcome De Lassus, the newly appointed lieutenant-governor of Louisiana. He was en route to New Orleans after having formally accepted at St. Louis the transfer of Upper Louisiana from Spain to the United States. Cape Girardeau's commandant, Louis Lorimier, saluted De Lassus's arrival with ten shots, which he fired, in lieu of a cannon, from a hole bored in a tree. Drinking, gambling, and cock-fights marked the memorable day.

Ezekiel Block wrote to family in Virginia and Bohemia of the vast opportunities in the virgin Missouri. Singly and in twos and threes they came to Missouri. Over the next 20 years more than 20 Blocks settled beyond the Mississippi.

In 1806 the Jew Samuel D. Solomon came to Missouri, the first of his people to settle in St. Louis, but he did not do so entirely of his own volition. He was literally run out of the East. Solomon came to America from Liverpool, England, where he claimed to have earned a medical degree from the University of Aberdeen in Aberdeen, Scotland, and a fellowship in the Royal Humane Society, a government-sponsored project founded in London in 1774 "for recovery of persons apparently drowned."

Actually he was a cure peddler who convinced the naive of the medical wonders wrought by his cordial balm of Gilead and other liquid remedies. "Doctor" Solomon next appeared in Philadelphia, where he remained for a while touting a cordial elixir from which it is reputed he amassed a fortune.

The quack doctor was uncloaked in 1805 and with charges pending he fled toward the most distant of all United States territories—Louisiana.

Making his way as unobtrusively as possible in the summer of that year, Samuel Solomon leaped from the boat as it touched the St. Louis dock. The escapee from the East found the town's streets unpaved. There were about 200 homes—many of them frame houses, others the original cabins and shacks put up by the original settlers 40 years earlier when they felled trees for logs. There was a good-sized warehouse and a church. Hundreds of boisterous *voyageurs* dominated the wild community. Horse thieves were hanged at Bloody Island; chained slaves were penned for auction nearby, awaiting inspection by plantation and farm owners as well as well-to-do townsmen seeking a house hand. A few Protestants had arrived.

The suave Samuel D. Solomon opened a shop visited by the French madames and mademoiselles who in addition to fancy lacy and racy outfits procured his youth balms.

Apparently, his balms failed to charm the male species of St. Louis. A bodily attack upon him by a *voyageur,* Joseph le Blond, provoked one of the town's original suits-at-law, Solomon vs. le Blond, seeking the sum of 500 dollars in damages for "trespass and vi et armis" (by force and armed power).

Trial was held early in 1808. Solomon was declared the loser. He became a double loser when at the end of the year, scarcely recovered from his court defeat, Solomon was again thoroughly beaten by three of le Blond's rowdies. Reeling Solomon wisely did not chance another lawsuit, having had his taste of western justice. He was further aware that whatever the verdict he would become the victim of a third beating.

Solomon's trade grew with the town. After he became a merchant of standing, a warden in the Catholic Church, influential and patronized by the leading families, he never forgot the beatings he suffered at the hands of the *voyageurs.* Fifteen years after those humiliating experiences, when he resided in the little town of Carondelet on the outskirts of St. Louis, he and resident Paul Robert petitioned for the appointment of a justice of the peace. The petition, signed by 33 townsmen, was addressed "To the Honorable County Court of the County of St. Louis." Therein the "Subscribers"

> Humbly sheweth that they have no peace officer in said town and are daily in want of a justice of the peace they being exposed to the rude insults of boat men and other malicious persons passing through said

town. They also meet with considerable inconvenience by going at a distance to seek redress for rongs which aught to bring the Culprits to immediate punishment by securing them from flying in the face of the law . . .

In the early days, among those "flying in the face of the law" was the Jewish mulatto Edward Rose. He arrived in St. Louis in 1807, a year after Samuel Solomon. Rose was an outlaw, a member of a river gang infesting the Mississippi River islands, plundering boats and sidewheelers making the 700-mile New Orleans-St. Louis trip. They preyed upon those who became stranded on a sandbar or docked at a traders' wharf along the riverbank, the attacks sometimes ending in murder.

Territorial Governor William Charles Cole Claiborne declared action against the river bandits but few were apprehended.

Rose—described by the famed writer Washington Irving as "a dogged, sullen, silent fellow of sinister aspects"—developed a sudden longing for the unknown lands beyond St. Louis.

A company of explorers and fur trappers under Captain Ezekiel Williams, resting in town, was due to travel into the Rocky Mountains in the unexplored West. Edward Rose joined them.

When the Williams party had thrust as far as the Big Horn Basin to the west of Yellowstone, the powerfully built and fearless Rose, far beyond reach of the white man's law, abandoned the expedition to become a blood brother of the savage Crow—the Upsarokas, as they were sometimes called.

The Jew helped the braves hunt elk, deer, and antelope, the plentiful game that flew overhead as well as the mountain sheep, buffalo, and beaver. He fought with the Crow against their deadly foe, the Blackfeet. In one attack the Blackfeet barricaded themselves within an entrenchment that could not be reached by Crow arrows.

"Who will lead?" was the demand.

"I," cried Rose, and placing himself at their head, rushed forward. At the appearance of the first of the Blackfeet, Rose shot him down with his rifle and snatched up the dead Indian's war club, swinging at four attackers whom he killed with powerful blows.

The Blackfeet turned and fled as Rose scalped his victims, returning a hero to camp. He placed the five Blackfeet scalps on poles before his lodge as trophies. The tribe named him *Che-ku-ka-tes* (the man who killed five) and looked upon him from that day on as their chief.

Ultimately, Chief Che-ku-ka-tes, the mighty man who killed five, was himself vanquished by an unseen enemy. He died in great anguish, said to have been felled by a venereal disease.

During 1807, the year Edward Rose sojourned briefly in St. Louis, there arrived in that westernmost fur trading outpost a Philadelphia Jew, Joseph Philipson (Phillipson). Thirty-four years old and the youngest of three brothers, Joseph came west at the urging of Zachary Mussina, brother-in-law of Simon, his oldest brother. Mussina was the company's western agent, bartering for furs and sending them east.

Joseph Philipson opened in December 1807 a store that numbered among his patrons such prominent Americans as Alexander McNair, first governor of the territory, and Meriwether Lewis, the famed commander of the expedition that first explored the Missouri and Columbia rivers and traversed the entire Northwest from the Mississippi to the Pacific. Lewis was at the time of Philipson's arrival governor of the Louisiana Territory.

Joseph's brother Jacob arrived the following year, 1808, to help manage Philipson & Brothers Company's western trading post. Furs were bought from various suppliers, including John Jacob Astor—on his way to becoming the fur king of the world. The St. Louis outpost of the Philipsons shipped bales of pelts to Simon at the company's Philadelphia headquarters. Next to beaver, buffalo hides were demanded by eastern tanners. Buffalo hunting had begun on a large scale on the western plains and in half a century the thundering herds of bison that covered the plains would be virtually extinct. A typical Philipson invoice noted a shipment of "Missouri beaver, dressed buffalo hides, raccoon, muskrat, bear and other skins shaved in the hair and Indian dressed deerskins."

Jacob preferred to keep a general store apart from the smelly fur outpost. Brother Simon shipped a variety of manufactured goods to him, and Jacob advertised on July 12, 1808, in the first issue of the *Missouri Gazette:*

> . . . opening at his new store opposite post office, a seasonal supply of drygoods and a general assortment of groceries, among which are blankets, shoes, madder and turkey red, linseed oil, tanner's dew, fresh teas, coffee, chocolate and sugar, shad, mackeral, a few German and English bibles, hymn books, etc., which he intends selling for cash at reasonable prices.

Jacob soon expanded and publicized that "In addition to his former stock he had just received and is now opening a handsome and general assortment of drygoods, hardware, groceries and queensware."

Jacob Philipson did considerable business with the firm of René Auguste Choteau. René had come in 1763 at the age of 14 to open a trading post with his father, Pierre Liguest Laclède, on that high bluff that fanned out on the west side of the Mississippi, which they named Saint Louis. Laclède, a New Orleans fur trader, had obtained from the French governor-general of the Louisiana Territory exclusive rights to the Indian trade throughout the Missouri Valley. He brought with him René, eldest son of his paramour, after whom was named Choteau's Pond, where Indians camped into the nineteenth century.

Among the transactions between Philipson and Choteau was that Philipson invoice dated October 10, 1809, which notes Choteau's purchase of a barge and rigging for 500 dollars. Another, dated July 8, 1811, indicates of the request to Philipson Co., by Bryan & Morrison Co., of Kaskaskia, to "Please pay Mr. Auguste Choteau the sum of $550.25 which will be in full for ten pounds figured calicos, two pounds light colored chintz (56 yards), four pounds blue shroud, six dozen butcher knives, two blankets, six vermillion."

Jacob Philipson moved his store in 1809 to Main Street in the heart of the business section where eleven other general stores were situated. But needing more space he moved again in 1810 to a building "next above Mr. Chas. Gratiot's house." And in 1811 he decided to move again, this time to Sainte Genevieve, Missouri's oldest settlement, south on the Mississippi River. Here he built a stone house, on the southeast corner of Second and Merchant Streets, which is to this day one of the show-places for visitors.

Remaining only three years in Ste. Genevieve, Jacob Philipson returned to Saint Louis to open a brewery. He fermented beer in a pirogue (canoe of hollowed tree trunk) and sales were good. He wholesaled his beer at the high price of eleven dollars a barrel, with one dollar refunded upon return of the barrel. He retailed his beer at twelve-and-a-half cents a quart. During 1814 and 1815 he built two two-story frame buildings on the West side of Main Street between Biddle and Carr Streets. The St. Louis Brewery, first brewery west of the Mississippi, was the first (in 1820) to distill whiskey and was accordingly renamed the St. Louis Brewery and Distillery. Jacob invested its profits in a sawmill he built; the St. Louis Sawmill was the second in the city.

Joseph Philipson was at the height of his career during the years 1817–1822 when he numbered among the leading stockholders in the

Bank of St. Louis, first in Missouri. He was one of nine on the Board of Directors, which included Thomas Hart Benton, a future Senator.

But disaster struck when financial panic gripped the country in 1821, the year the Missouri Territory became a state. The Bank of St. Louis failed; the brothers, Joseph and Jacob Philipson, closed their stores, brewery, and parted with all properties they acquired in town.

To help arrange their affairs, brother Simon Philipson came from the east. Liabilities met, Joseph, an accomplished musician, taught piano and other instruments; Jacob, an accomplished linguist, taught English, German, and French; Simon, having sold his Philadelphia store, bought a farm, raised poultry, and sold eggs. Simon's wife, Susanna Mussina, mother of six, apparently found farm life too strenuous and died later that year. She was buried in the City Cemetery. During Simon's lifetime, three of his children would die, all from unnatural causes.

Simon Philipson's children possessed a lust for adventure and a love of the natural beauty of the virgin west. Nine years after their mother's death, teen-age Philip Philipson set forth to trap in the distant Rockies. There he remained as a "Mountain Man" for four years. He endured the elements, battled beasts, befriended Indians, survived disease, only to succumb at Lexington, Missouri, on his way home.

Undeterred by Philip's untimely death, Louis, a younger brother, after two years passed ventured forth towards the Rockies in the party of author Edward Warren Steward. But he drowned in his attempted crossing of turbulent Lewis' Fork, his dream to become a "Mountain Man" unfulfilled.

Their sister Amanda, though remaining in civilization, lived a wild, carefree life. She gave birth to a son reputedly fathered by one John Fuller and died in the prime of life.

Her sister, Esther, lived to marry the distinguished Indian fighter, United States Army Lieutenant Robert Emmett Clary. That veteran of the campaign against the Sauk and Fox, forced to remove from Illinois to Iowa in 1831, negotiated the treaty with Chief Black Hawk in 1832. Best man at the wedding was Clary's West Point classmate, Jefferson Davis, later president of the Confederate States of America.

Esther and Robert's daughter, Marie Louise Clary, would marry Charles P. Stone, who was to gain immortal fame as the chief engineer for building the Statue of Liberty.

Esther, too, died young. She was buried in the City Cemetery alongside sister Amanda and brothers who died on the western trails, and mother.

Of the Philipson brothers—Joseph, Jacob, and Simon—only Jacob left instructions for a Jewish burial. Only he retained his religious identity on the far western frontier. But while his daughter Esther married Alexander Lewis and Rosa Adelaide married a Mayer, Lavinia married a Christian, Antonio Prietto.

The most important contribution of the Philipson brothers to St. Louis was cultural. Not only did they bring an appreciation for music, in which they excelled, but also for art. They brought to the wild frontier town three hundred and ninety paintings and a hundred prints valued at almost three thousand dollars. Simon owned one hundred and fifty of these works of art, valued at a thousand dollars. These oils of the great masters, laboriously collected in the East, had been carefully crated and transported by stage and barge. Among them were the works of Rembrandt, Colbert, and Da Vinci. Their most valuable pieces were "Hagar in the Desert" by Bartolome Esteban Murillo, and "The Savior and the Cross" by Peter Paul Rubens, each valued at four hundred dollars. Simon personally cared for them, and was often seen dusting the canvasses with ostrich plumes.

After the last of the Philipson brothers died, the paintings were stored in a room above the Post Office, until Simon Philipson's son-in-law Lieutenant Robert Clary removed them. What then happened to this earliest of art collections in the West remains to this day a mystery.

Hebrew War Hawks

Rivalry between the American and Canadian fur traders intensified as they clashed in the Great Lakes region. The Montreal fur traders never accepted the United States boundary drawn through the Great Lakes and along their canoe route from Lake Superior to the Lake of the Woods. The Union Jack continued to wave even after the Indian (and British) defeat at Maumee Falls in 1795, over trading posts and tepee villages in Wisconsin and west from Menominee to Mandan lands. Clashes occurred, too, south of the Lake of the Woods to the source of the Mississippi where the boundary was in question.

The Americans complained that the Canadian fur traders were moving freely on American soil and that they were inciting the Indians. The Canadians complained that the Americans were carrying away annually 150,000 pounds of peltries from their rendezvous sites.

It seemed that the Canadian fur traders were more powerful, for they were better organized and more unified in strong cooperatives established as early as 1775.

Until that year Abraham Chapman, Ezekiel Solomons, Levi Solomon, Benjamin Lyon, and Gerson Levy had chosen different locales from which to set forth to tap western furs. Now, they were aware that only by pooling their assets could they truly survive. When United States army officer Zebulon Montgomery Pike set out in 1806 to explore the Louisiana Territory he took note of their far-reaching trade into that wilderness and wrote of their beginnings: "In the year 1776 the trade was extended from Mackinac to the northwest by a few desperate adventurers whose mode of life on voyage and short residence in civilized society attained the name of Coureurs des Bois," (Forest Runners).

Pike was referring to such men as Ezekiel Solomons, one of the most distinguished *voyageurs*. Ezekiel, married to a French Catholic, Louise Dubois, spent much of the year away from his Mackinac trading post, taking with him his sons Ezekiel Solomons, Jr., and Lewis. In the wilds, Ezekiel Solomons, Jr.'s sons would live all their lives among the tribes as *coureurs des bois*. His son, Samuel, married an Indian girl, Marie, who carried their son, Alexis, in her papoose. Another son of Ezekiel Solomons, Jr., William, lived among the tribes with his Indian wife, Agibicocona.

In 1779, the Jewish traders, joined by about 25 Christian merchants representing fur-trading companies in the Upper Michigan peninsula, formed the Mackinac Company, a cooperative general store, one of the first department-store operations on the North American continent.

Boldly, after the American Revolution, the Mackinac Company founded in 1783 the North West Company to compete with the Hudson's Bay Company, who contemptuously labeled its founders the "Montreal peddlars."

Though Michigan had that year become part of the United States, the English did not evacuate Fort Mackinac. From that northern Michigan region, Ezekiel Solomons and fellow members of the North West Company canoed as before to the western Upper Country, trading at Grand Portage, located at the northwestern end of Lake Superior, about 30 miles west of the Kaministiquia River (present site of the town of Grand Portage, Minnesota).

There were lesser Canadian firms but equally ambitious that operated in the first American Northwest, in Wisconsin. One of these, Ogilvie, Gillespie & Co., based in Montreal, sent Jacob Franks, a Jew, to set up a branch post to trade for furs on the western shore of Lake Michigan in Wisconsin, there to barter for the plentiful and rich peltries of that country.

Jacob emulated his father, after whom he was named. Jacob (John) Franks, Sr., a seasoned fur trader of Fort Detroit, established trading posts in the Hudson Bay Territory, penetrating into the very heart of the wild, unsettled Northwest in his rendezvous with the Indians. He, too, sought to emulate his illustrious father, David Franks of Philadelphia.

It was the will of the recently deceased David Franks that sparked the interest of his son and grandson in the West. Therein he bequeathed to his son, Jacob ". . . my lands situate . . . in the Illinois Country." When this will was probated in 1794, Jacob Franks Jr., left for Wisconsin, then a part of the Illinois Country in the Northwest Territory.

Twenty-six-year-old Jacob Franks, Jr., canoed up the St. Lawrence and across the Great Lakes with a stock of sugar, tea, and rum. Rowing along the west shore of Lake Michigan into Green Bay, he set up his tent at the mouth of the Fox River, in Wisconsin's oldest settlement, Green Bay, then part of the Illinois Country. Though this was the American Northwest Territory, the region ceded to the United States in 1783, Franks raised the Union Jack as did others in the trading post—the British flag flying over Prairie du Chien near the confluence of the Wisconsin and Mississippi Rivers and in Indian villages in Wisconsin as in Michigan and the Great Lakes region.

The Indian tribes became friends with Jacob Franks. In 1794 they gave Jacob a 999-year land grant in a deed that declared:

> Know all Men by these presents that We the Undersigned Chiefs of the Falavoine (Menominee) Nation of Indians, acting for the Nation in general have Given, Granted and Confirmed, and by these presents do Give, Grant and Confirm unto Jacob Franks, his Heirs, Executors or Assigns and every of them, all our Title, Claim or demand on a Tinement or piece of land with all its Singular appurtances Containing Three Acres in front on One Hundred Acres in depth, situate at La Baye in Upper Canada bounded in front by the Riviere des Renards, on the North Side by a land Granted to Dominique Ducharme and on all other sides by Land unconceded, for the Term of Nine hundred and Ninety Nine years, free and clear of all former or Gifts or Grants, Rents, Rent

Charges, Titles, Troubles or incumbrances whatsoever for value received.

In Witness Whereof we have hereunto in the presince of the Undersigned Witnesses, set our hand & Seals at La Baye this Eighth day of August in the year of our Lord One Thousand Seven hundred & Ninety four. Also a piece of land situate on l'other side of the Riviere Containing Nine Acres in front on one Hundred in depth, clear of all incumbrances as the above mintioned tiniment on l'other side of the River

L. Fily

Witness Claude + Caron
Thomas + Caron

Witnesses
George Gillespie
Jean Ecuyer

witness Chiatche (a turtle) Angueman

Alex^r Kennedy
G^t Lagoterie

witness
Atawoinabie (an eagle)

The Jay Treaty having been ratified that year (1794), two years later the British relinquished their hold on their Michigan forts and trading stations, but not those in Wisconsin, where the American troops did not tread. Franks resigned the French firm to open his own and operate a blacksmith shop alongside. He prospered and opened a branch at Fond du Lac on the southern tip of Lake Winnebago and another at the confluence of the Menominee, Kinnickinnic, and Milwaukee Rivers (site of the future Milwaukee), there to barter for raw deerskins and other peltries.

In 1797, when Jacob Franks went to Canada to buy the outfit for his expanding trading post, he brought back with him his 16-year-old nephew, John Lawe, a native of Montreal. The lad could handle the brisk trade at the confluence of the three rivers. During an average summer season that post amassed over 10,000 pounds of deer tallows which Jacob Franks boated to Fort Mackinac. Travelers through Wisconsin spoke of the uncle-nephew duo as "Jews extensively embarked in the fur trade."

Expanding his enterprises, Franks erected in 1805 a grist- and sawmill on the Devil River, three miles south of Green Bay and as many miles east of De Pere, the first in this region. The feat made necessary the construction of a dam at nearby Rapides des Peres.

Franks and Lawe married Chippewa women. However, Jacob Franks ultimately yearned for the refinements of city life and the companionship of a lady of his own race and religion. One day in 1810 he left his Indian wife and family and extensive land holdings in the care of his nephew and departed for Canada, never to return. In Montreal, Jacob Franks married his cousin, Mary Solomons. Mary's mother, Rebecca Franks, was the sister of Lieutenant Colonel David Salisbury Franks, the American patriot. Jacob remained loyal to England and would serve as a lieutenant in the upcoming war with the United States.

So, too, did the members of the North West Company, loyal to England, ignore American claims.

These *voyageurs* extended their travels beyond the Grand Portage, carrying their canoes and supplies overland over the nine-mile portage past the falls and rapids of the Pigeon River to canoe westward to the villages of the Sioux, Fox, and Nadowessious in the land of the Menominee and Minnesota, acquired in 1803 by the United States.

During the first decade of the nineteenth century, the Canadian fur traders opened the Far West. They penetrated the plains of Manitoba and the undulating prairies of Saskatchewan, and they crossed over the magnificent snow-capped Rocky Mountains to the Pacific Coast. Their competitor, the American Fur Company (headquartered at Fort Mackinac and directed by John Jacob Astor), founded in 1811, at the mouth of the Columbia River in the land of Aragon (later Oregon), the trading post of Astoria, and the Hudson's Bay Company also made its thrusts in this distant land.

Jacob Franks, John Lawe, the Solomons brothers (Lewis, William, Samuel, and Ezekiel, Jr.), and other Canadian fur trading *voyageurs* stirred up the Indians to resist the Americans who were driving them and their animals from their ancestral grounds. A last great stand against the white man in the Ohio Valley was made in 1811 by the Shawnee Chief Tecumseh. He worked hard to unite all the western tribes against the common enemy. During his absence from his fortified settlement Tippecanoe (where the Tippecanoe Creek flowed into the Wabash River), General William Henry Harrison attacked and burned it to the ground.

The Indian aggression had been backed by the British, cried American westerners irked by the Canadian control of the Great Lakes/Upper Ohio fur trade that reached across the plains and Rocky Mountains to the Pacific. They demanded the conquest of Canada. A simple matter as they saw it—the mere fording of the Detroit, Niagara or St. Lawrence Rivers, a quick march on Quebec, capital of Lower Canada, and Toronto, capital of Upper Canada.

The westerners reasoned: Didn't 6,000,000 Americans outnumber 500,000 Canadians? Were not two-thirds of the Canadians of French descent unfriendly to the British? And how could a mere scattering of Canadian forts, standing isolated along a thousand-mile border that stretched from Fort Detroit to Quebec, expect to deter a determined force?

These bellicose war hawks found a leader in the western Senator, Henry Clay of Kentucky. Clay thundered to the Senate: "The conquest of Canada is in your power. I verily believe that the Militia of Kentucky alone are able to place Montreal and Canada at your feet."

America declared war on Canada, June 18, 1812.

Stalemate in the States

In the summer of 1812, during the early days of the war, the British Lion pounced upon the western war hawks before they even had a chance to take to flight. First to be conquered was Fort Mackinac. Its garrison of 60 men, unaware that war had been declared, fell prey to 600 Indians led by British officers. Second to fall was Fort Dearborn, near the small settlement of Chicago. Five hundred Potawatomi massacred 50 and captured 31, including women and children. Then the key Great Lakes fort of Detroit was taken by Shawnee, Ottawa, and Potawatomi who walked in without firing a shot. They found the fort had been abandoned by the Americans.

All the Michigan Territory with its few American settlers was in British hands. Pioneers shunned that barren, northern wilderness. A popular jingle warned them: "Don't go to Michigan, that land of ills; the word means fever, ague and chills."

British Lieutenant Jacob Franks, stationed at Fort Mackinac, cheered loudly when he received two letters dated September 8, 1812, telling of the surrender of Fort Detroit: "The place surrendered as soon as our forces reached town. . . ." Whether "surrendered" or "abandoned," the Union Jack waved over that important position.

Another correspondent writes: "Detroit was taken by Gen. Brock on the 16th of last month. Gen. Hull, with two thousand four hundred men, laid down their arms. The American regulars are all gone to Quebec.... Gen. Brock has acquired much glory, and the Americans, after their vain boasting are covered with disgrace...."

The writer of the second account, fur trader Robert Dickson, added that Lieutenant Lawe (nephew of Lieutenant Jacob Franks) of the Indian Department, had gone on a mission to the Mississippi, taking along on the expedition several *"mangeurs de lard."* The Britishers and Indians were carrying the Union Jack westward to Wisconsin and into Minnesota.

Along with the British takeover of the American Northwest was sounded an alarm from the Far West at St. Louis. There Samuel D. Solomon, a war hawk, chattered loud and clear to make known his concern and that of the city's citizens. His letter to William Rogers Clark, newly appointed governor of the Missouri Territory, dated February 8, 1813, read:

> Blondeau (interpretor for the Sac and Fox tribes) says that the British have landed at Chicago and that they are collecting all the Indians to make a descent on this place in the spring. Robert Dixon (Dickson), Canadian fur trader in the Red River Valley at Green Bay, also assembling the Puants and Follavoine for the same purpose, ten lodges of Sacs—nearly one hundred—have also joined our enemies.
>
> Part of the Sioux have accepted the British wampum and are preparing. Quasquamis Brothers have been killed by the rangers, being found inside the lines. Several others have been seen. Nothing doing here for the defense of this place. The winter has been very severe indeed. The Missouri and Mississippi have been frozen over....

The United States, having lost its key forts on the Great Lakes, prepared to invade Canada from Fort Niagara. This launching site was regarded as a crucial pivotal point, since the Niagara River linked Lake Ontario, the northeasternmost of the Great Lakes, to Lake Erie, which sprawled southwestward. This Niagara sector was bounded by New York to the east and Ontario to the west.

From the very outset of what America would call her Second War for Independence, munitions were in short supply. The second generation Gratz brothers, Simon and Hyman, in partnership with Charles Wilkins, came to the rescue. They supplied from Kentucky's Mammoth Cave (discovered 12 years earlier on land they acquired) great quantities of saltpeter for the manufacture of gunpowder. This cave, the largest single cave in the world, contained the only large supply of saltpeter known in the United States at that time. The chroniclers of the history of that natural wonder made a most interesting observation concerning the part it played in the war:

> Emphasis should be laid on the fact, not mentioned in any history of the United States, that our War with Great Britain, in 1812, would have ended in failure on our side had it not been for the resources so abundantly furnished by American caverns for the home manufacture of saltpeter at a time when by a general embargo we were wholly cut off from foreign sources of supply.

Hyman Gratz, while exploiting Mammoth Cave's natural resource, saltpeter, also found archaeological remains of interest. He sent specimens of artifacts and cloth to an eminent scientist, Dr. Samuel Latham Mitchill, with a note published five years later in the *Medical Repository,* which noted:

> We have, also, an Indian bowl, or cup, containing about a pint, cut out of weed, found also in the cave, and lately there has been dug out of it the skeleton of a human body, enveloped in a matting similar to that of the *kinniconecke* pouch.

At the time, Simon Gratz had an interest in an allied field; he was a director of the Pennsylvania Botanic Garden.

Simon and Hyman's brothers, Jacob and Joseph, enlisted with other members of their faith to bear arms for their country. Mordecai Myers, captain of the Thirteenth United States Pennsylvania Infantry, ordered to Fort Niagara, wrote: "I buckled on my sword to advance to my station to begin duty as one of the defenders of my country . . . we arrived at Charlotte on the east bank of Lake Champlain." Despite the impressive title of his Infantry, it was but a small company the Jew commanded. This prompted him to write somewhat apologetically to his friend Naphtali Phillips, editor of the *National Advocate* in New York, "A great man once said he would rather be the first in a small village than second in Rome."

Myers, though American-born, a native of Newport, Rhode Island, his command of written English could have been improved. In his inimitable English, he offered another bit of homespun wisdom. In praise of Phillips' war editorials, he advised, "Sum must spill their blud and others their ink. I expect to be among the former and hop you are amongst the latter."

On October 13, 1812, Myers led his detachment across the Niagara River to fight in the Battle of Queenstown. Lieutenant Colonel Winfield Scott and Captain John Wool, both destined subsequently to achieve fame as generals, led the assault.

Defeated in that engagement, the United States invasion of Canada was abandoned for the winter season.

During that fierce, bleak winter of 1812-13, encamped at Flint Hill, three miles from Buffalo at the mouth of the Niagara River, Captain Mordecai Myers and his infantrymen relived the trials of a previous generation of soldiers at Valley Forge as they awaited the spring.

Mordecai Myers noted how grave were his responsibilities: "I have the sick, the invalids and convalescents of three regiments to superintend, besides their protection and the general police of the whole, ordering of courts martial and approving of sentences. . . ."

In the spring of 1813 the invasion of Canada was resumed. Under orders of General Alexander Smyth, Myers led 150 of his infantrymen northward toward the river. They fought side by side with Lieutenant Colonel Scott's troops to ford the river and take Fort George and nearby Queenstown. American troops advanced to capture York, capital of Upper Canada.

The western war hawks cheered but the tide soon turned. The Canadians forced the Americans out of York and vowed to avenge the burning of their public buildings at York by burning the American capital. The following year British troops captured Washington, D.C., burned the government buildings then returned to their ships.

The war teetered and tottered with neither side gaining the advantage. Captain Mordecai Myers's remark at the beginning of the war became reality to him. It will be recalled that he had written to Naphtali Phillips that "Sum must spill their blud and others their ink," and that "I expect to be among the former and hop you are amongst the latter." In the ill-fated invasion of Canada, at a point midway between Montreal and Kingston, at Chrysler Field, Captain Myers, commanding 86 infantrymen, later reported:

> Got permission to take position in a field on the enemy's right flank where my *buck and ball* told well. . . . I was wounded by a musket ball passing through my left arm, two inches below the socket. I received the wound while advancing and no doubt from excitement believed it to be a chip that struck my arm.
>
> My wound being very painful on account of the pressure of my coat on the swelling arm, I gave the command of sixty-three men, twenty-three having been killed, to my first lieutenant.

The lost and killed and wounded on both sides was not less than 800, about equally divided. The result is as often called a defeat, a victory.

The wounded officer, during his convalescence, met romance. The daughter of Judge William Bailey of Plattsburgh was visiting her uncle and chanced to meet Myers. She cared for him, fell in love, and the 17-year-old Charlotte Bailey married the 38-year-old Jewish captain. Myers's life changed radically. He abandoned Judaism, substituted for his name Mordecai the initial "M," and no longer identified with Jews —including his own brother Benjamin, married into the proud Hays family.

Though his Jewish life was cut short, M. Myers lived to be 95 years of age, and to proudly tell of his role in the War of 1812 and the attempt to occupy Canada and oust the British from all North America.

Hebrew Pirates—Heroes of New Orleans

The Americans and Canadians at a stalemate, peace missions from the American states and British Isles sailed to Ghent in neutral Belgium to sign a treaty. The English, however, had no way of transmitting this news to the giant British army being transported aboard the fleet of His Majesty's Navy sailing somewhere in the Atlantic toward American shores.

The British fleet of warships and troops aboard were fast approaching the Florida peninsula to enter the Gulf of Mexico. Its secret mission was to capture the port city of New Orleans and seize control of the Mississippi Valley.

After Napoleon's defeat and abdication on April 11, 1814, Great Britain had prepared to concentrate its might against the Americans. She was determined to regain the Mississippi Valley, which she claimed rightfully belonged to Spain and which had been fraudulently sold by Bonaparte to Jefferson. In its conditions of peace, Britain demanded the return to Spain of Louisiana, and if she was too weak to take it—and powerless she was—England would take it on her behalf.

Half a year passed and all was in readiness. Great Britain dispatched across the Atlantic a mighty armada of 50 warships manned by the sailors who had fought so valorously at the Nile and Trafalgar to convey an equal number of vessels and a fleet carrying 8,000 soldiers, including the crack troops of the Duke of Wellington who commanded the British forces.

This formidable force was accompanied by a complete civil governmental staff to rule over "The Crown Colony of Louisiana," so convinced was the British Parliament of victory.

England's battle-seasoned troops, en route to the Gulf of Mexico, disembarked on the soil of their Spanish friends at Pensacola, Florida, drilled there, and prepared for the pending invasion of Louisiana.

Unnoticed by any American troops or sloops, an armed English brig sailed into Barataria Pass on the Louisiana Gulf Coast on September 2, 1814; upon its mast waved the Union Jack and a truce flag.

Herein lay the pirate lair of the Baratarian pirates led by the famed Jean Laffite, known to everyone as a pirate-chief, to few as a fiery Jew. The English brig was escorted by a vessel sporting the flag of Colombia through Barataria Pass, a waterway sufficiently deep and wide to accommodate seafaring vessels provided one knew the source of its channel.

On each side of Barataria Pass was one of the twin islands Grand Terre and Grand Isle, each appearing as a silent sentinel, each eight miles long and a mile wide. Their tall trees concealed the tallest masted vessels that sailed into 18-mile-long Barataria Bay having gained refuge from the shot of pursuing ships or the severity of hurricanes that lashed the Gulf Coast.

Dropping anchor at Grand Terre, situated about ninety miles south of New Orleans, two British officers, Captains Locker and McWilliams, came down the gangplank seeking an audience with Jean Laffite. Graciously the buccaneer chief received them, wined and dined them in grand style in his elegantly furnished mansion overlooking the bay.

The officers presented Laffite with a sealed packet. The chief split open the envelope marked "Highly Classified." It was from Lieutenant Colonel Edward Nicolls, Commander of His Brittanic Majesty's Forces in the Floridas and, dated from British Headquarters, Pensacola, August 31, 1814.

He read and reread the offer of 30,000 pounds sterling, a commission as captain in the British Navy, and enlistment for Baratarians in the English Armed Forces—if he guided the British troops from Barataria Bay through the maze of waterways leading to New Orleans.

No one knew the bayous and inlets between the gulf and New Orleans as did the pirate chief. Laffite had spent countless hours paddling his pirogue through the rising, gyrating bayous. He assiduously acquainted himself with the confusing array of stumps and swamps that wended amid cypress-shrouded streams and oak-topped mounds, mapping out the many courses and routes within the primitive unexplored 10,000 square miles of delta. His intimate knowledge meant the difference between victory or defeat at the coming Battle of New Orleans.

Laffite feigned to accept the British offer as soon as he could arrange affairs—in a fortnight—but by the time the Britishers departed Grand Terre to return to Pensacola, Laffite's trusted lieutenant, Rancher by name, was on his way to deliver a packet from his "Bos" to Jean Blanque, a highly respected New Orleanean.

Monsieur Blanque studied its contents, which revealed the British invasion of New Orleans was imminent and that its writer, Jean Laffite, in return for a governor's pardon (wanted posters offered $500 for his head), would serve with his buccaneers as American patriots in defending the city. Blanque immediately brought the communique to Governor William C. C. Claiborne.

Louisiana's governor reacted with a vengeance. He outfitted a formidable naval force not to combat any English invasion, but to destroy the pirate stronghold at Grand Terre.

Laffite ordered his gunners neither to give battle nor to set sail for Cartagena. All was to be left intact. Any buccaneer who wanted to go into hiding was allowed to do so. As for their property, Laffite promised he would recover them legally, for his men were not pirates but privateers under the protection of the Colombian tricolor.

Jean Laffite's brother, Pierre, ailing and weak, was brought to the mansion of a friendly plantationer south of New Orleans, where he recovered. Two other brothers, Alexandre Frederic(k)—alias Dominique You(x)—and Henry Elias—alias René Béluche, alias René Paul, alias Renato—remained at Grand Terre.

U.S. vessels, encountering no opposition, took all buccaneers they found on the island prisoners, seized all goods in the warehouses, and blasted them, the pirate huts, and Laffite's mansion to smithereens. They returned to New Orleans joyful and triumphant.

But the jubilant governor and elated officials soon assumed a more somber, sober outlook. They had earlier ridiculed and ignored Laffite's warning that a British fleet prepared to invade the city. Now reports reached them from "reliable" sources that a powerful British flotilla was sighted sailing toward the Louisiana coast.

At that moment, the United States General, Andrew Jackson, Commander of the Seventh Military District, was in Alabama punishing Creek Indians. He promptly replied to Governor Claiborne's cry, arriving in New Orleans on November 30, 1814. "Ole Hickory," as the Tennessean general was nicknamed by his riflemen, inspired the trembling inhabitants of the Creole City.

Ten days passed. The British Armada had arrived at the mouth of the Mississippi. Every able-bodied man was given arms. Though General Jackson despised the Indians, he accepted into his forces a hundred Choctaw braves. There was no way to receive help in time from any other troops for none knew of their plight.

Frantically the governor appealed to General Andrew Jackson, Commander in Chief of the New Orleans defenses, to free the imprisoned pirates so they could man the cannon and artillery.

Reluctantly Jackson ordered the release of those he called "Hellish Banditi." For the first time they would do battle on land instead of water. Chief Jean Laffite and his brother Pierre would guide the American forces through the marshland maze, which confused everyone except themselves. They would be among Old Hickory's closest advisors. Sending Jean with secret instructions to Major Michael Reynolds to fortify the pirates' stronghold at Barataria, and keep a sharp lookout to guard against a surprise attack from the rear, the Gulf, General Jackson concluded: "The bearer, Mr. Jean Laffite, has offered his services to go down and give you information. Dismiss him as soon as possible. I shall want him here."

During Jean's absence, Pierre Laffite remained in his shop on Royal Street, its shelves stocked with the finest of goods, all pirated, to be available to Old Hickory, who tactfully came to consult with him, giving the pirate the rank of liaison officer.

The oldest of the Laffite brothers, Capitaine Dominique, organized three artillery companies of buccaneers. For his own company, he selected the second oldest of the Laffite brothers (he being the oldest), René Béluche, to serve as his First Lieutenant. René Béluche was further entrusted to select the men to man the cannons.

These buccaneers were assigned by General Jackson to guard the old Spanish fort at the site where Bayou St. John emptied into Lake Pontchartrain at the rear approaches to the city. They knew that way well for often they smuggled "black ivory" (as they called slaves) into New Orleans from Barataria.

Thirteen more days passed but they remained alert at their posts. On the night of December 23, the English soldiers were sighted approaching by a direct frontal route, by way of Bayou Bienvenu and Lake Borgne, five miles southeast of Lake Pontchartrain.

Jackson ordered the pirate band to remain at the fort and Major J. B. Plauché to march at once his Battalion de Orleans towards the battle front.

Capitaine Dominique, anxious for action, watched unhappily as Major Plauché and his 372 troops assembled to depart. That battalion's youthful corps composed of the city's Creole aristocracy were roused by their band, energetically blaring battle hymns led by the Jewish Sergeant of Musicians Solomon F. de Jonce, Chief Musician of Plauché's battalion.

The slave-snatching and selling -pirates mused as the band played in that southern city "Yankee Doodle." Many of the buccaneers, including the Laffite's of French origin, cheered as the band switched to *"La Marseillaise"* and with the "Chant du Depart," the entire corps ran over six miles to the heart of the city, a run repeated annually to this day. Starting at the site of the Old Fort, it ended at the old Place d'Armés, which now bears the name of Andrew Jackson.

That night, Pierre Laffite played a most conspicuous role. In the pitch blackness he deftly guided General John Coffey and his rifle-bearing Tennesseans through the marshy lands to surprise and repel the invaders' flank. Old Hickory would later write Pierre a personal letter of commendation for his valiant behavior which turned the tide of the Battle of New Orleans.

The defenders of New Orleans that fateful battle day of December 23 and in subsequent fights included the few Jewish residents—Reuben Levin Rochelle and his partner in business Hart Moses Schiff. They served in Dejan's First Regiment, and Alexander Phillips for his role was commissioned Second Lieutenant. Samuel Kohn served in the Compagnie Gray des Carabiniers; Samuel Hermann in De Cloute's Regiment; Maurice Barnett in the Compagnie de Franks; Simon Cohen and Jacob Hart in the Compagnie de Dragons.

The British momentarily retreated to regroup their forces. Americans returned to their posts. It was December 24. Overseas, at Ghent, Belgium, a treaty of peace was being signed. The next day, the defenders of New Orleans awaited the next battleshot to be fired. It was the day when Christians the world over prayed for "Peace on Earth, Good Will to Men" that British General Edward M. Pakenham, brother-in-law of the Duke of Wellington, led an assault force upriver from the Mississippi delta and camped en route three days in final preparation for the attack.

On December 28, Pakenham's army marched in solid ranks against the Tennessee frontiersmen, Choctaw tribesmen, free blacks, Creoles and all New Orleans, and last but not least the pirates of the Gulf. As they approached, the defenders of the city nestled in the crescent of the Mississippi behind a trench they had dug called "Jackson's Ditch," and from which they poured forth with such a withering fire that the British ranks broke and the troops dispersed.

The British returned on New Year's Day, 1815, determined to blow the stubborn defenders out of their entrenchment. Again, pirate cannon outshot British cannon, strong fire directed from Number Three Battery, manned by Capitaine Dominique and his fighting buccaneers. Their twin 24-pounders churned up the enemy's position as told by a New Orleans cotton merchant on the scene, Vincent Nolte.

The largest British Battery directed its fire against the battery of pirates Dominique You and René Béluche. Dominique was studying the enemy through a telescopic glass when cannonshot wounded his arm. As it was being bound, he said, "I will pay them for that." He again eyed the enemy battery through his glass, directed a 24-pounder, gave the order to fire. The ball knocked an English gun carriage to pieces and six or seven men to kingdom come.

The battle ended and their positions unchanged, Capitaine Dominique, questioned about his armwound, retorted, "Only some scratch, by gar." A fellow Jew, Judah Touro, was seriously wounded. While carrying shot and shell from the magazine to Humphrey's Battery where the Louisiana Militia was situated, he was struck on the thigh by a 12-pound shot.

Found dying in an old building behind McClotey's plantation by his friend Rezin D. Shepherd, an aide to Commander Daniel Patterson in charge of the Naval Station, hurrying to deliver a message from General Jackson, chose to risk court-martial. He gently placed Touro in a cart, gave him brandy to ease his pain, pushed the vehicle and its patient aboard to a residence, and lodged him with some ladies to be nursed. Judah never forgot his benefactor, whom he made the residuary legatee of his large fortune, and the city from which he had drawn his wealth, to whom he donated a hospital that became known as the "Touro Infirmary."

New Year's Day ended with the defense of New Orleans intact. The British retreated to prepare for a final overwhelming attack.

A week passed. Pakenham's troops awaited the signal, the firing of two rockets to explode high in the sky. Jackson's forces spent the time digging deeper into the gumbo soil and lengthening their trenches.

In the predawn hours of Sunday, January 8, 1815, Old Hickory awakened from an uneasy sleep and made the rounds accompanied by his aides General William Butler, Edward Livingston, and Captain Hockfre, Chief of Artillery.

They received reports from all batteries of unusual activity all along the British front. The officers sensed sudden attack. It was now daybreak. Twenty yards before reaching Battery Number Three, the aroma of dripped coffee in an iron pot over a small fire made them forget the enemy for the moment.

"Hmm. That smells like better coffee than we can get," the General remarked.

Approaching Capitaine Dominique, Andrew Jackson inquired, "Where do you get such fine coffee? Maybe you smuggled it."

The Jewish pirate rejoined, "Maybe so, General." He grinned and offered him a small tin cupful from the pot. It was black as tar and the finest in quality, and Old Hickory drank it with gusto.

He thanked Dominique and commented as they were out of earshot of Battery Number Three: "I wish I had 50 guns on this line and 500 such devils as those fellows are at the butts."

A dense fog lifted within the hour after daylight. Two rockets exploded in the air. Column after column of British soldiers advanced, only to drop by the unerring rifle fire of the sharpshooting Tennesseans and buccaneers.

The battle lasted exactly 25 minutes. General Edward Pakenham and his commanders lay dead. Of 6,000 seasoned veterans of European and African battlegrounds, 2,600 lay dead or wounded. Mopping-up operations continued throughout the day. At evening only one pocket of resistance remained.

Commander-in-Chief Jackson issued the following order to General Morgan:

> Hqa. 7th Mil. Dist.
> 8 Jan. 1815.
>
> Sir,
>
> This will be handed to you by Mr. (Pierre) Lafitte whom I have sent to you as a man acquainted with the geography of the country on your side of the river and will be able to afford you any information by which the enemy will attempt to penetrate. . . . I rely upon you to accomplish it, they are not more than four hundred strong and your task not a diffi-

cult one. We have beat them here at all points with a loss on their side of at least a thousand men.

Brig-Gen. Morgan
right side of the river

ANDREW JACKSON
Maj-Gen. Comdg.

With Laffite's expertise in negotiating the labyrinth of bayous that writhed through the marshland, Morgan was able to position the forces to gain an upper hand. The enemy withdrew from the west bank of the Mississippi. Fighting ended on both sides of the river and at long last on both sides of the Atlantic.

The West had been saved. Andrew Jackson and Jean Laffite emerged as the new heroes of the Republic. Laffite's brothers, too, were credited with their role in defending New Orleans.

Thus wrote General Jackson in his dispatch dated January 21, 1815:

> Captains Dominique and Béluche, lately commanding privateers at Barataria, with part of their former crews and many brave citizens of New Orleans, were stationed at Batteries Three and Four. The general cannot avoid giving his warm approbation of the manner in which these gentlemen have uniformly conducted themselves while under his command, and of the gallantry with which they redeemed the pledge they gave at the opening of the campaign to defend the country. The brothers Lafitte have exhibited the same courage and fidelity, and the General promises that the government shall be duly apprised of their conduct.

James Madison was moved. On February 6, 1815, he issued a presidential pardon to the pirate chief Jean Laffite and the buccaneers under his command. Taking advantage of the amnesty, many of the fierce ruffians settled down to the peaceable lives of fishermen along the shores of Barataria Bay. Of all the Jews of the early West, obscure or well-known, famed or infamous, none remains more vividly remembered than Laffite, for whom a picturesque Louisiana fishing village has been named. It is a village of ramshackle little cabins strung along the shore of the bayou; its chief highway to this day is made up of the mud paths, two feet wide, directly at water's edge. Live oaks line the path, called Main Street, their moss-dripped limbs seeming to weep for something never quite attained. A pirogue bobs before nearly every little cabin wherein the inhabitant could be descended from one of the Baratarian buccaneers who sailed under Jean Laffite.

Laffite Learns of his Ancestry

Jean, youngest of seven Laffite children, was lovingly cared for during his childhood, along with his three-year-old brother Pierre, by grandmother Zora Nadrimal. Their mother, Dona Maria, died a year after Jean was born in 1782 on the island of Saint Domingue (the Spaniards called it Santo Domingo, originally Hispaniola) in the West Indies.

As soon as Jean and Pierre were old enough to understand, grandmother Maria Zora told them of her flight with their mother from Spain to France in 1765 to escape the Inquisition, which was responsible for the death of her husband (Jean and Pierre's grandfather), Abhorad.

Her ancestors, Zora explained, lived many centuries in Spain when it was in the hands of the Moors. Jews and Arabs together created one of the golden ages of culture. But in the late fourteenth century, in the Catholic-ruled region of Spain, Jews were given the choice to remain Jews and be treated as inferiors or convert to the Holy Roman Church and enjoy status as second-rate citizens.

Of those who converted, many continued to practice Judaism secretly. The Spaniards contemptuously called them *Marranos,* meaning "swine." Of those who became faithful Catholics, Tomas de Torquemada reached a high office in the Church. Appointed in 1481 First Inquisitor-General of the Holy Office, he set up a network of informers to spy upon and ferret out converted Jews who had not remained faithful. Suspects were tortured, their wealth sequestered, and punishment was harsh. Those apprehended a second time for Judaizing were garroted and their bodies burned at the stake. If they did not repent at the stake, they were burned alive.

In January 1492 the Moors were driven out of the Iberian Peninsula, and the Holy Office cast its sights upon the wealth of obstinate, unconverted Jews. These were ordered to depart Spain and forfeit their fortune, baptism being their only salvation.

Zora and Abhorad Nadrimal's ancestors elected to convert, but like many *Marranos* remained loyal to Judaism, married among themselves, and at the risk of their lives taught their faith to their children. They were aware that by Jewish law they were Jews even though they had undergone baptism, the principle being once a Jew, always a Jew.

The *Marranos* sadly watched over half a million of their brethren go into exile the very day that Columbus set sail toward the East Indies by going west.

Some of the hapless unconverted Jews found refuge in the port of Lisbon. But in 1497 they were dragged by their Portuguese hosts to baptismal fonts and forcibly converted. To their grief, their children were dispatched with criminals and the insane to the "Islas Perdidas"—uninhabited islands in the West Indies.

Many children died en route aboard ship from cold wind and foul food. Of those dropped off at St. Thomas some were devoured by crocodiles, others poisoned by serpents, a few raised by the cannibal Carib Indians. Upon reaching maturity, they innocently mated with their own brothers or sisters, one who somehow returned to Lisbon was unknowingly married to his own mother.

Parents who were able set out to the West Indies in search of their children. Others set out to flee the fires of the Inquisition. So many had come in a score of years that Spain established the Holy Office in Mexico, capital of New Spain, which included the West Indies, the Florida coast to Panama, and Calafia (California). And, continued grandmother Zora, the first victim of the Inquisition in New Spain was a blacksmith who lived on the very island where the Laffites lived—his name was Hernando Alonso.

Alonso, as the Holy Office of the Inquisition at Mexico recorded, had reached western shores no later than 1511, during which year he fought with Hernando Cortes (Cortez) in the conquest of Cuba. Along with other *Marranos,* he settled in the city of Santo Domingo, on the island then called Hispaniola, discovered along with St. Thomas by Columbus on his second voyage in 1493. The discoverer's brother Bartholomew established on the Ozuma River the city of Santo Domingo, first in the western hemisphere, in 1496.

So many Marranos were brazenly practicing Judaism in that city that in 1520 agent-priests of the Holy Office arrived to check heresy in Hispaniola. They promptly renamed the island after their order and many suspected Judaizers fled, among them Hernando Alonso. He made his way with his wife and young son to Vera Cruz, New Spain. There he rejoined, as Hernando Cortes' *conquistadores,* 500 strong, poised to invade the Aztec capital, the megalopolis they called Mexico-Tenochtitlán.

The spring of 1521 found Alonso fighting and conquering. It took another five years to quell sporadic Indian uprisings. Following battles in which Alonso served, at Panuco and Guanachuato north of Mexico, he was rewarded with a country estate at Actopan, 40 miles northwest of the capital, staffed with Indian slaves.

The conquistadore's landowner status explosively expired in the year 1528 when an agent of the Inquisition, Vicente de Maria, arrived in Mexico with authority to act in matters of faith. An informer, a former resident of Santo Domingo, came to De Maria's Holy Office, revealing that he had seen in Hernando Alonso's house a curious rite about the year 1519. A man named Palma was holding a naked two-year-old upright in a basin, and Alonso poured wine over the boy's head, then collected the drippings from the child's sexual parts into a cup. They drank the wine and danced about him singing *Dominum Deus Israel Egypto* (a hymn commemorating Israel's exodus from Egypt—a probable reference to Psalm 114).

Alonso was imprisoned, charged with Judaizing (though no such rite exists in Judaism). He was specifically accused of baptising his son "according to the ritual of the law of Moses" after the boy had been formally baptized in the Catholic Church.

His brother Francisco de Morales, also a conquistador, was also brought before the tribunal of priests and charged with disrespectful treatment of a crucifix.

Both were sentenced to be burned alive, though it was their first offense, to which they confessed under torture. As in Old Spain, Inquisition officials conceived the fateful day as a gala event, an *auto-da-fé*, thus making it an act of (Christian) faith to attend. The deep grief of the families of Hernando Alonso and Francisco de Morales, required by the Holy Office to behold the execution, contrasted starkly to the joyous holiday mood of the populace.

Leading clergymen and distinguished citizens—the Viceroy of New Spain, Alcalde of Mexico—ascended the platform in the stand erected in the center of the city's plaza—the Square of Santiago de Tlaltetolco, there to sit under an awning shading them from the blazing sun. The victims tightly bound to stakes, a lighted torch was touched to the brushwood near their feet.

Amidst the cheering men, women, and children were Indians who recalled that at this identical place that the flames rose to consume the two Jews, Aztec priests had torn the hearts out of their victims in sacrificial rites, for by this very spot where now loomed the Catholic Cathedral, had formerly stood the Aztec Temple of Tlaltetolco.

And, continued grandmother Zora, a century after their martyrdom, Hollanders wrested Brazil from the Portuguese. Jews and former *Marranos* openly worshipped the God of Israel and built synagogues in that Dutch-occupied land. They fled, however, when a quarter of a century passed and (in 1654) the Portuguese reconquered Brazil. Most returned to Amsterdam, but a few scattered in the West Indian islands and a handful reached the tip of Manhattan Island, to settle in New Amsterdam on the North American mainland. After the English gained the colony they renamed New York, Jews built there the Mill Street synagogue, the stones of the nearby mill used to grind flour into *Mazoth,* the very bread baked by the freed ancient Israelite slaves. Those millstones are to this day a treasured possession of that Portuguese Mill Street synagogue, *Shearith Israel.*

Almost a century passed before a second large number of Portuguese Jews to reach the North American mainland settled at Savannah in the newly founded thirteenth English colony, Georgia.

About 1730 the English decided to establish a buffer region between Spanish Florida and their own colony of Carolina. The Jewish community in London provided for the passage to this colony of a number of impoverished Portuguese Jews. Arriving in 1733, they settled alongside the first settlement of whites who arrived a few months earlier in Georgia, near Savannah. Their position was precarious: to the south, the Spaniards threatened, and to the west were the slightly less intolerant French.

These Jewish colonists of Georgia labored hard to make a success of their enterprise. Having brought a scroll of the Law with them, they organized upon their arrival a congregation called *Mickve Israel* (Gathering of Israel). Four years afterwards they even managed to build and dedicate a ritual pool, called a *Mickve* (where waters gathered).

Most influential among Georgia's Jews was Dr. Samuel Nunez Ribiero, the only man of means in their midst. One of the court physicians in Lisbon, he and his family had observed Judaic rites there in secrecy for generations. When it was learned that his profession of Christianity was a pretense, they were plunged into prison. The merits of his medical skill operated for his release—on the condition that two officials of the Holy Office should reside in his house.

Soon afterward a member of the doctor's family was discovered observing some Jewish rituals. He was given the choice of either immolation at the stake or public renunciation of his religion in the cathedral at Lisbon on Christmas morning. His courage failed. He consented to the second alternative but—facing the images of the Catholic creed at the altar—he decided to die rather than sacrifice his faith. Addressing the figure of the Virgin Mary, he made a scurrilous comment on the birth of Jesus Christ. This witticism cost him his life: he was immediately led to the stake and burned.

This circumstance convinced Nunez that it was time to leave Portugal. A man of great wealth, in the habit of entertaining the principal families of Lisbon, Nunez arranged a dinner party at his elegant mansion on the banks of the Tagus. He included the captain of an English brigantine anchored in the river. During the festivities, the captain of this vessel invited the Nunez family to accompany him on board, ostensibly to share a light lunch. The group, which included the dogged spies of the Inquisition and a number of the guests, went aboard. While they were eating in the cabin the anchor was weighed, the sails unfurled, and the brigantine suddenly shot out of the Tagus. It carried the whole protesting party to England.

All this had been previously arranged between Nunez and the captain at a price of one thousand *moidores* in gold. In addition the Nunez females had quilted all their diamonds and jewels into their dresses, and the doctor, who had changed all his assets into gold, had distributed the coins (concealed in leather belts) among his sons.

Once aboard, Nunez did not hesitate, but made up his mind to emigrate to the New World. Upon his arrival in Georgia, he used his wealth to acquire six large farms and settled·down with his fellows. All the Jewish colonists were required to clear ten acres within ten years and to plant at least 100 mulberry trees per person. Nunez's primary objective was silk culture, but he also sponsored Abraham de Lyon, a Portuguese enologist, who cultivated the Porto and Malaga grapes "to great perfection."

In 1742 there came a Spanish attack at Frederica. The English lines held, but mere rumors of Spanish conquest and the apparition of the Inquisition were sufficient to frighten away the Portuguese Jews. They scattered to the West Indies, or northward to Carolina and New York, De Lyon, as mentioned, having "Gone to Conestoga."

A short while after the dispersion of Georgia Jewry, a third contingent of Portuguese Jewry fleeing the Inquisition reached Newport, Rhode Island. An earthquake in 1755 devastated the Capital of Portugal and shattered the dungeon walls wherein had languished many *Marranos*. A few managed to escape and at Lisbon charter a ship that took them directly to their haven in the New World.

These thankful Jews erected *Yeshuat Israel* synagogue in Newport during the French and Indian War (1759-1763). The spectre of the Inquisition ever before them, though the Spaniard was in the distant

West Indies and Louisiana, they nonetheless built a secret escape passage. From the floor of the pulpit a trapdoor under a carpet near the reader's desk issued down a stairway into a small basement. There a tunnel led to an exit 100 feet beyond the south wall. It opened over where the hillside tapered off into a ravine shaded by chestnut trees.

Most honored at the dedication of the Newport synagogue was Jacob Rodrigues Rivera, who traced his ancestry to American martyrs of the Inquisition. Diego Lopez Rivera and his wife Dona Blanca de Rivera, who fled from Spain to New Spain, arrived in Mexico (City) about the time the Pilgrims arrived in Cape Cod aboard the *Mayflower,* and for even more compelling religious persecution than the suffering English refugees.

Unlike the Pilgrims, who made a new life for themselves to worship God according to the dictates of their conscience, the Riveras were among those who, convicted by the Holy Office of "Judaizing," were in 1648 martyred at the stake in Mexico.

Like the *Marrano* martyrs victimized for their faith, but even more for their wealth, so, too, were the Jewish traders and Christians killed by ruthless Spaniards. Such, recounted Zora, was the fate of Jacob Gomez. He, the brother of Daniel Gomez, an American-Indian trader, was a merchant and served as Spanish interpreter to the English Admiralty for twenty years. His career was cut short when, in 1723, Jacob put into a Cuban port with his cargo in the hold of the vessel *Greyhound.* Spaniard thugs jumped aboard, cutting up the defending Jew into quarters.

Even into the days of Laffite there were Portuguese Jews living whose limbs had been mangled by the rack or whose bodies exhibited the tortures and ordeals endured at the mercy of the Spanish Inquisition.

Visions of the dismembered Gomez; of the martyrdom of Don and Dona de Rivera, Hernando Alonso and many others; of hundreds burned at the stake in the Spanish Vice-royalties in the New World, at the plazas in Mexico (New Spain), Cartegena (Colombia), Lima (Peru); and of the thousands who languished in dungeons of the Holy Office—including his grandfather, Abhorad Nadrimal, who Zora recalled was an alchemist in Old Spain, there tortured to death in Zaragosa because he refused to embrace the "true faith": such tales of horror gave young Jean Laffite no rest.

Impressed in his mind was the stoical heroism, of Francisco Maldonado de Silva, whose martyrdom became enshrined in the heart of every Marrano and Jew. Francisco's father, Diego Nunez de Silva, had been reconciled by the Inquisition in Portugal in 1605. Diego, a skilled surgeon, in fear of his life and that of his family by those envious of his financial successes, sailed to the New World to settle in Callao on the Chilean coast.

Francisco, at age eighteen, studied medicine and while rummaging through a book shop came across a copy of *Scrutinium Scripturarum*, written in 1391 by Pablo de Santa Maria, a convert to Christianity.

The padre, the former Rabbi Solomon ha-Levi who became Bishop of Burgos and regent of Spain during the minority of Juan II, wrote his *magnum opus* to prove the truth of Christianity. This work became much favored as a basis upon which to influence Jews to convert.

But the more young Francisco read, the more he questioned the acceptability of Christian doctrine. His father finally revealed that he was a Marrano, always observing the Law of Moses in secrecy while outwardly acting as a Catholic. The father taught his son the commandments and belief of Judaism until his death in 1615. Francisco then revealed to his two sisters that they were all Jews and should promptly return to the faith of Moses and Israel. The sisters instead revealed to their father-confessor what they were told. He directed them to denounce their brother to the Holy Office of the Inquisition, which they promptly did.

Francisco was arrested on December 12, 1626. Because of his high standing in the community as a leading physician and his ingenuity in defending the religion of Judaism instead of immediate torture and confession, the priests reasoned with him. The polemics continued for 13 years. Then he took upon himself an 80 days' fast, during which time he wrote two books, each over a hundred pages, the scraps of paper pieced together with great ingenuity from the husks of maize. His ink he made of charcoal and his pens were cut out of egg shells by a knife he fashioned out of a nail. He grew his hair and beard as did the Nazarite and called himself Heli Hazares, "unworthy servant of God."

Convicted of apostasy, Heli Hazares was transported to the prison at Lima, to await execution with other condemned Judaizers.

The Lima prison was filled with fellow Jews facing the fearful fate of being burnt alive. Some sought to renounce their faith to escape such a fate. Francisco heard of this in his cell. He twisted maize-husks into a rope and starved himself until he could squeeze between the bars. He made a round of the cells urging the prisoners to be brave and not weaken in their faith. When guards were nearby, he wrote verses to pass to others to inspire them in their courage.

At last the great day for the *auto-da-fé* arrived, January 23, 1639. Of the 63 Jewish victims, 11 were to be burned, the others "reconciled" to the Church to suffer lesser penalties. As the procession proceeded to the central plaza, 62 of the prisoners carried green crosses as part of the pageantry. Francisco alone refused to do so.

As they stood around the scaffold, the "sermon of faith" was preached and the prisoners were turned over to the secular authorities who pronounced the dread sentence of burning. Fagots were piled about the victims, bound to their stakes, and the fires were about to be set when, records the Chronicler, "A strong wind arose that old inhabitants of this city affirm (that) they had never seen any wind so strong in many years. It tore away with great violence the awning which darkened the scaffold at the very spot where Francisco was standing, who, looking up towards heaven, said: 'The God of Israel has ordained this in order to see me face to face from Heaven.'"

After his grandmother passed away, Jean remembered her tales and hated the Spanish with a burning passion.

Vendetta with Spain

The teenaged youth, Jean Laffite, clerked in the store of his father, Marcus, at Port au Prince, Saint Domingue (present-day Haiti), until a slave insurrection erupted on the island at the turn of the century.

Most plantation owners regarded the Africans as sub-humans. Throughout the Caribbean islands and mainland they were cruelly subjugated. Chained in groups by means of long heavy chains called caufles, often weighted with iron collars around their necks, the males labored in the fields from dawn to dusk. They were clad in cottons during the summer and thin woolens during the winter, suffering heat and cold. Any attempt to escape or even to complain was punished by branding, whipping, or in extreme cases, hanging.

Slave revolts on a minor scale began during the 1790s, their inspiration to liberty fired by the American and French revolutions. Their drive for freedom was finally attained on the island of Saint Domingue in a great uprising in 1801. The slaves seized weapons, and gained control of the interior mountain passes. Greatly outnumbering their masters, they overran sugar and coffee plantations and massacred all whites they captured.

Awaiting execution at dawn was the captive French-Jewish plantation owner, Aaron Soria. The coffee and sugar he raised were stored in his warehouse in the capital city of Saint Domingue. Nearby was his retail outlet, both located on the public square. He was captured while on guard duty in the capital when on a very dark night he hailed a band he mistook to be on patrol. They were blacks who took him prisoner, derisively calling him "white monkey."

About midnight the door of the guardhouse suddenly opened. A tall, stalwart Negro dressed in full regimentals, with chapeau, plume, sword and epaulettes appeared. He was the general commander of the guard. Singling out Soria, he walked up to him, extended his hand, and exclaimed, "Why, citizen Soria, how came you here? Do you not know me?" "General," replied Soria, "your face is familiar to me, but I cannot recall your name." "Do you not remember *Pierre!*"

Soria recalled. This was the slave whose master gave permission to work a while on his own and requested of Aaron permission to place his table for the sale of beer and foods in front of his store. A gang of sailors ate and drank but refused to pay. Aaron rushed to his aid and compelled them to pay the amount due Pierre.

Pierre continued: "I have never forgotten your kindness. I will serve you if I can, but never divulge that I liberated you. Do not compromise me; when I next open your prison door and *raise my chapeau,* make your escape, fly down the mountains for your life."

Upon reaching the capital he found his wife, Rachel Mendes, and daughter Judith safe. He secured passage on a New York-bound schooner. About to board, French troops ordered him to remain and serve guard duty, as no white man could depart the island. At the same time, they forced the women to sail.

Aaron, determined to rejoin his family, hid on the next New York-bound vessel in the hold of a cargo of coffee. At New York he learned that his wife had left for Charleston, South Carolina. At Charleston he learned that his wife had set sail for Saint Domingue the moment she received news that the rebellion had been quelled.

Aaron booked passage on the next vessel bound for St. Domingue but, upon landing, learned that his wife had upon her arrival on the island been told of his secretive departure for New York to join her there.

Three successive tail chasing voyages up and down the Atlantic seacoast between the Caribbean Island and Manhattan Island ensued, husband and wife in search of each other. Half a year and about 12,000 nautical miles later husband and wife were finally reunited in New York City.

During the rebellion it was easier for those residing in the ports of

St. Domingue to escape the island. The Laffites residing at Port-au-Prince carried their goods aboard their own schooner, *La Soeur Chérie* (The Beloved Sister) and sailed off to French Martinique. There, the Laffite brothers purchased from the French government authorities a "Letter of Marque" authorizing them to seize enemy vessels (France's enemy then being Spain).

So the Laffite privateers flying the French tricolor set sail in search of Spanish vessels as lawful booty. In the port of St. Croix, Jean met a Danish Jewess, Cristiana Levine, and after a short courtship they were married. They soon received news that the insurrection at Saint Domingue had been quelled. Laffite's father returned to Port-au-Prince, as did the newlyweds. Through their father's store the brothers sold out quickly (at bargain prices) captured Spanish loot, including slaves.

As he set out to capture Spanish vessels, he was ever guided by the vision of his beloved grandmother, Zora. Jean Laffite penned on the flyleaf of his Bible: "I owe all my ingenuity to the great intuition of my grandmother, a Spanish Jewess, who was a witness at the time of the Inquisition."

After four profitable years of privateering he sailed with his wife, two sons and daughter, and all his wealth to reside as a gentleman in France. But they never reached the Atlantic waters, as he again wrote in his "Journal":

> She, Cristiana, was rich and beautiful. I determined to go to Europe and I wound up my affairs in the West Indies. I sold my property there, I bought a ship and loaded her, besides which I had on board a large amount of specie. All I was worth, in short. When the vessel I was aboard had been a week at sea we were overhauled by a Spanish Man of War. The Spaniards captured us. They took everything, goods, specie, even my wife's jewels.

> They set us on shore among a barren sand cay with just provisions enough to keep us alive a few days until an American schooner took us off and landed us in New Orleans. I did not care what became of me. I was a beggar. My wife took the fever from exposure and hardship and died in three weeks after my arrival.

Pierre too left Saint Domingue at about the same time as his brother, sailing aboard *La Soeur Chérie*. Upon anchoring in New Orleans, the newly arrived American governor of Louisiana, William Claiborne, ordered the vessel confiscated.

Privateer Pierre Laffite, whose vessel flew the French flag, told U.S.

customs agents that having weathered a storm, he put into port to repair the hull, reset masts, renovate sailing gear, and caulk the seams.

Customs agents were suspicious. Fourteen crewmen were aboard but 60 signed on at Saint Domingue. Missing were 28 white crewmen and 18 black crewmen; also seven of her 10 cannons and an entire cargo of coffee.

Pierre, the captain, explained that the missing crewmen jumped ship at Port Aux Cayes in Saint Domingue, that the 10 four-pounder cannons were shoved overboard during the storm, and that the beans were sold shipside as soon as his vessel docked.

Customs officials thought differently. Governor Claiborne charged Pierre with smuggling, as proved by the missing crewmen, cannon, and coffee.

Deprived of his vessel, penniless Pierre remained in New Orleans, where he was soon joined by his pauperized, widowed brother, Jean. With an audacity and boldness that would typify the Laffites, they resorted to the unexpected and enlisted as agents in the service of U.S. Customs. Even more astounding was the fact that they were not only accepted, but promptly elevated to the rank of deputy marshals. This was not, however, as surprising as it would seem, for who knew more than they about smuggling?

The brothers harbored the secret longing to someday avenge Spanish vessels—especially Jean, who sought to capture that vessel responsible for the death of his beloved Cristiana. The opportunity presented itself one day in 1806, as recorded by Jean: "I met some daring fellows who were as poor as I was. We bought a schooner and declared against Spain eternal war. So long as I live I am at war with Spain, but no other nation. I am at peace with the world except Spain."

That year the French islands of Martinique and Guadalupe were occupied by the British. So the Laffite brothers sailed to Colombia to obtain its "Letter of Marque." That South American country declared her independence from Spain and welcomed the participation of privateers in her struggle.

Issued the prized letter, the Laffites lowered the French tricolor and raised the Colombian tricolor. Their vessel may have been the two-masted, square-rigged *Misère* owned by Jean Laffite. He promptly sallied forth to capture and plunder Spanish ships wherever they could be found in Gulf waters.

Laffite's *Misère* soon captured *La Rosalia,* a copper-bottomed schooner, which he renamed for the golden dolphin *Dorade*. The armed schooner *Las Caridad* (The Charity) surrendered to the unerring Laffite fire. To honor Colombia and its hero, the South American patriot Simon Bolivar, he renamed this schooner *General Bolivar*. The sting of Laffite was felt by yet another Spanish vessel, the *Wasp;* also a large wide-bottomed schooner and another were taken, the former named *Last Prize,* the latter *Surprise.*

It came as no surprise that as Jean Laffite swept the Gulf he captured the very vessel that three years earlier had plundered his schooner and left him with his family to die upon a desolate reef.

Among the numerous Spanish vessels taken by Laffite's personally owned hermaphrodite brigs were the *Maria* and *Louisa Antonio.*

While Jean and Pierre worked as a team, their brothers captained their own vessels. The oldest Laffite brother, Alexandre Frederic, popularly called Capitaine Dominique or Dominique You (Dominique perhaps a reminder of his native Saint Domingue), outmaneuvered *The Fly* and overpowered *El Tigre.* Laffite's brother René or Renato Béluche (how or why René acquired or assumed that name is not known) captained the *Genny* and *El Esbion,* no doubt his prizes of capture.

It is not known which of the Laffite brothers should be credited with the capture of *Nuestra Senora del Carmen,* renamed *Esperanza; La Cometa,* which in turn captured the black-and-yellow-striped *Harlequin; Philanthrope; L'Aquila* (The Eagle), renamed *Petit Milan;* the armed schooner *Demi Lune* (Half Moon); *The Lady of the Gulf; Republican; Milita; La Flora Americana; Diligent; Cassadoré; Non Such; Panchita.*

These and many others were skillfully maneuvered into Barataria Bay, about 90 miles south of New Orleans, through dangerous Barataria Pass at the mouth of the Gulf.

The pirate hideaway at Barataria Bay was as safe and sound as could be, its location unexcelled. Sixty miles from New Orleans as the crow flies, they deposited their pirated goods at "The Temple," a mound where an ancient Indian tribe, the Showasha, buried their dead. Here, businessmen from New Orleans arrived under cover of night to purchase the auctioned rich loot of captured Spanish vessels.

Dominique You and René Beluché remained here between sailing trips, while Jean and Pierre settled in New Orleans. Jean opened a blacksmith shop at the corner of Bourbon and St. Philip Streets.

Behind its respectable facade, wild African blacks were tamed and slaves forged the links that made up the caufles for chaining their brothers and sisters in transit and on the plantations.

Pierre opened an exclusive classy shop on Royal Street from which he sold pirated silks, exotic laces, and a variety of fancy "imports."

Of the four Laffite brothers, Jean possessed the greatest charm and expressed himself fluently in any of four languages: French, Spanish, Italian, English. The olive-complexioned Jewish Creole stood almost six feet tall with black hair and flashing eyes, his appearance imposing. Sportily dressed, he entertained lavishly at his mansion over his blacksmith shop, his etiquette impeccable and his manners delightful.

His charisma enchanted the elite of society. Aboard his schooners on the Gulf and at Barataria, too, when among the unshaven, unkempt, unruly ruffian buccaneers, Jean's suave polish and natty dress made him an object of respect. The crudest and crassest of the pirates was aware that beneath his clean-shaven face and polished nails lay as devilish an outlaw as was Blackbeard, the pirate chief, who in 1718 found refuge in Barataria Bay.

Jean was deadly as an enemy, quick on the draw and cool as ice. But he was more than that. He was an analyst, shrewd and calculating. He studied the inherent weaknesses of the men and their associations at Barataria. He watched their depradations upon the very merchants who came to bid and buy. He watched the rival pirate captains feuding with each other as they competed in lowering prices to gain sales.

Jean Laffite observed a sharp increase in their rivalry after January 1, 1808, the deadline imposed by the U.S. Congress for importing Africans into the United States. This act legally ended the overseas trade in slaves, but opened a feverish activity in Barataria. The reason was obvious. The price for a black male sold in Havana for $300 after January 1 soared to $1,000 in New Orleans, where plantation owners from all along the Mississippi River and its tributaries arrived to purchase more and more slaves.

But Jean Laffite noted that instead of taking advantage of the principle of supply and demand, the buccaneer captains were in rivalry, stole each other's blacks, and offered prime males for sale at a mere dollar a pound. Accusations and arguments between them would soon result in open warfare that threatened the very existence of Barataria. It was then that the fighting captains agreed to unite under Jean Laffite.

Standing on a hillside before a motley assemblage of almost 500 sabre-rattling sea robbers and cut-throats, knife-and-gun-brandishing felons and desperados, the Jewish Creole dandy stood firm, yet relaxed, speaking in his gentlemanly fashion.

He told the men that henceforth they would act only under his orders, not as lawless pirates but as lawful privateers flying the flag of Cartagena (Colombia). But all the pirates knew that Jean Laffite was no privateer. Instead of his complying with maritime law, which required that a captured ship and cargo could be kept only after it was first brought into the port where the "Letter of Marque" was issued—Cartagena—and there the seizure formally approved by an Admiralty Court, he brought his prizes directly to Barataria.

Some of the pirates knew that Laffite the Jew had loot as a secondary motive, that his main objective was to destroy the Spanish shipping as fast as possible with as much a semblance of legality as possible.

A follower of pirate leader Gambino or Granbo, himself a savage grim character, stepped forward into the clearing before Laffite to challenge him. Gruffly he jeered Laffite for calling himself a privateer. He guffawed at the idea that the baby face standing before them could qualify as a pirate. Laffite calmly drew his pistol and shot the dissident through the heart. A spontaneous outburst of cheers issued from the throats of hundreds of pirates assembled. They shouted to Laffite, Bos and Chief. Never thereafter did any buccaneer similarly challenge their leader.

Laffite set the men to work transforming Grand Terre into an island fortress. They built his mansion on a hillock overlooking the entire island and Gulf. This he outfitted and furnished with the finest of draperies, rugs, figurines, lamps, the richest of loot that was en route on Spanish ships somewhere in the Gulf.

Sturdy thatched hut abodes were built by and for the buccaneers. Huge warehouses and a new barracks were built to replace the shabby storehouses and dilapidated slave quarters. Goods and "black ivory" could now be better stored until sold.

African slaves could no longer be imported, yet sales of the blacks did not diminish and none questioned their sources of origin. It was assumed by many that Barataria had become the major source of imported "black ivory." From far and near the slave traders flocked to "The Temple"; the prices controlled by Laffite gave both the pirate sellers and plantation and city buyers a handsome profit. Safe escort was assured for all by order of Jean Laffite. No Baratarian dared disobey.

New Orleans businessman David G. Seixas, who owned a few slaves, acquired a schooner and possibly arranged for their shipment and transport. His uncle, Abraham Mendes Seixas, who had engaged in the slave trade at Charleston, composed the following doggerel published in the *South Carolina State Gazette:*

> Abraham Seixas
> Also gracious
> Once again does offer
> His services pure
> For to secure
> Money in the coffer.
>
> He has for sale,
> Some Negroes, male,
> Will suit full well grooms,
> He has likewise
> Some of their wives
> Can make clean, dirty rooms.
>
> For planting, too
> He has a few
> To sell, all for the cash,
> Of various price,
> To work the rice
> Or bring them to the lash.
>
> The young ones true,
> If that will do,
> May some be had of him
> To learn your trade
> They may be made,
> Or bring them to your trim.
>
> The boatmen great,
> Will you elate
> They are so brisk and free;
> What e'er you say,
> They will obey,
> If you buy them of me.

Competing with the leading slave traders, Franklin & Framfield of Richmond and Charleston, a Christian company, was the Jewish company, Ansley, Benjamin, George, Solomon Davis Co. Based in Richmond and Petersburg, Virginia, the four brothers' firm did not hesitate to go at lengths to obtain slaves, advertising their supply throughout the south. Thus, they announced in the Columbus, Georgia *Enquirer*:

"Sixty likely Virginia Negroes—house servants, field hands, blow boys (buglers), cooks, washers, ironers and three first rate seamstresses."

The Davis Co., like Franklin & Framfield, kept their source of supply secret. They assured everyone that they would continue to receive slave shipments by every arrival in Columbus.

The slave-trading Davis family was singled out by Harriet Beecher Stowe in her commentary, *A Key to Uncle Tom's Cabin,* noting that "The Davis' in Petersburg are the great slave traders. They are Jews, came to that place many years ago as poor peddlers. These men are always in the market, giving highest price for slaves. During the summer and fall they buy them at low prices, trim, shave and wash them, fatten them so that they may look sleek, and sell them to great profit."

Scornful of the Davis brothers, Stowe praised the Friedman brothers, whom she may have known personally while she lived in Cincinnati. Joseph and Isaac Friedman, after they first arrived in Ohio, moved south to Tuscumbia, Alabama, to open a store in that town. One day the slave Peter Still, hired out by his master John Hogun to a bookseller in town, approached Joseph Friedman, in whom he discerned a man of compassion.

Still told Friedman that he had been kidnapped in his early childhood from the doorstep of his home in New Jersey and taken as a slave to Kentucky. There he appealed to Henry Clay but was unsuccessful in gaining his freedom. He labored as a slave in Alabama for over 40 years and longed for freedom.

Joseph, who had labored with a pack on his back for seven years, sympathized. He agreed on a plan to free "Uncle Peter," as Still was called. But it was frought with danger. The Jew, small in stature, with black hair and keen dark eyes, upon his arrival was regarded with suspicion and dislike by the people of Tuscumbia. Now he had gained the confidence of everyone by integrity and neither he nor his brother were treated with rudeness or disrespect. But an aroused public could change that hard won sentiment, and they could suffer being tarred and feathered or worse.

Perhaps their isolation, their not mingling freely in society, attracted Peter. Whenever he was in their presence, although no word was uttered respecting himself, he felt that he was regarded as a man.

Peter Still influenced his master to let him live with the Friedman brothers and work for them and keep his pay. The arrangement was against the law, but his young master assented, and the secret kept.

After Peter accumulated over $200, he asked Joseph to buy him from his master. Hogun, however, said that he could get $1,000 for him any day.

Joseph then bid Peter farewell as he left to trade across the Mississippi in the Red River country, and Isaac continued as his boss.

Young John Hogun's aversion to selling Peter was suddenly removed when an auction held in town included two choice 16-year-old boys. Wanting to own them, he offered Peter to Isaac if the Jew would buy for him those lads. Isaac talked it over with Peter, who told him: "You are not used to dealing in slaves, and you'd best not buy the boy. There'll be some game about it. If young master wants to buy him, he'll come round, I reckon."

Hogun again met with Friedman, who told him that he would not buy the boys, but would give him for Peter his top price of $500. Hogun went to the auction. The boys were put up on the block. The sale was going on. Hogun grew desperate. The boys he wanted would not wait for bidders, for they were choice fellows.

"Well," said he, as he walked towards Friedman's store, "you may have him for $500; but it's a shame to sell him so."

The deal consummated, Hogun hurried back to the auction. One boy had become the property of a planter near town, the other he managed to purchase for $750.

Peter, that night, brought to Friedman a bag containing all the money he had earned during the years he had been out for hire, $300. He trusted Isaac, but had known many defrauded by their benefactors. Isaac Friedman wrote a receipt for the silver. Peter could not read it but believed it genuine.

Townspeople heard of the sale. "Poor Uncle Peter sold to a Jew. Jews will sell their own children for money. Friedman will probably send him off to the rice swamps. Poor Uncle Peter."

Men and women of Tuscumbia, who bought and sold, beat and oppressed the black man, considered it their right to do so, but to give a Jew—a foreigner, too—such a right was unthinkable.

Friedman, despised and suspected, arranged with Peter that as soon as he should have earned another $200, he would give him his free papers.

Within two years, Peter earned his freedom, the papers given to him by Joseph Friedman, who returned from his stay in the Arkansas territory.

Joseph left again and Isaac decided to remove to Cincinnati, where his brother Levi resided. He took Peter with him on the boat for Louisville and Cincinnati. Peter continued on to Pittsburgh and Philadelphia to seek out his brother. He found his way to the office of the Underground Railroad, where he told his story to a young black attendant. It was his own younger brother, William Still. At last, Peter was reunited with his mother, brothers, and sisters.

Peter returned to Cincinnati to the Friedmans and sought their advice on helping his wife, Vina, escape. Friedman gave Peter a "pass" to a "Mr. Alexander," requesting that he serve as Peter's guardian, and the duo left for Tuscumbia, Alabama. To all who inquired he kept his freedom a secret and said that Friedman would be returning to Tuscumbia.

Fortunately, an abolitionist, Seth Concklin, helped Peter Still in his attempt to save his wife from slavery. Guided by Concklin, Peter and Vina made their escape, but when the runaways reached Vincennes, Indiana, they were detected, arrested, and returned. Seth could have escaped but refused to leave them. On the boat trip to Alabama, Seth Concklin, chained and shackled, "accidentally" fell overboard and drowned in the Cumberland River.

Levi Friedman prepared to risk a visit to Tuscumbia to help Peter Still and his family but was warned not to undertake such a futile and hazardous mission. One of his friends wrote him from Alabama that the Tuscumbia townspeople blamed the Friedman brothers as instigators of the entire affair.

This case became a cause célèbre with Harriet Beecher Stowe and others who espoused the cause of freedom for all people. Eventually enough money was raised to pay for the freedom of Vina Still and her husband and family.

There were many Jews who agreed with the Friedman brothers, an overwhelming majority in the deep South as in the North.

Cotton Commission Agent and New Orleans banker Julius Weis(s) could never reconcile himself to the institution of slavery. He came south as a peddler, trudging through Mississippi from plantation to plantation. At first he watched aghast as he beheld Negroes stripped naked, bound to a post, and whipped on their bare backs by an overseer. "I afterwards got somewhat accustomed to it, but I always felt pity for the poor slaves." But he never forgot the fate of a runaway slave, and recorded what to him was a nightmare.

"One night I stopped at the house of Mr. Jefferies—during the night 12 of his slaves ran away. The next morning he sent for a man named Ridel who had 12 bloodhounds and who made a business of catching runaway slaves. There were several in the party who were going in pursuit and when they started off they asked me if I would go along and as the sight was new to me I concluded to go.

"The dogs got on the trail of the Negroes and we followed them for about five miles and finally çame upon them in a thick growth of brush where they were huddled together. Some of them had climbed up into the trees and the rest were on the ground where the dogs jumped them and tore them in such a manner that I was disgusted at the sight. I started back to the house.

"When I had nearly reached the house, one of the Negro women in the party who had gotten away from the rest and was trying to make her way back home, came up to me and asked me to protect her from the dogs. I told her that I would if I could, but before we got to the house the dogs overtook her and as I had no weapon with which to defend her, they jumped on her and before the men arrived they had torn almost every thread of her clothing and bitten her severely."

"Disagreeable and repulsive," wrote Weis, "was the tactics used by southerners in capturing the slaves."

At the commission brokerage house in New Orleans, operated by the Jewish merchants Ruben Levin Rochelle and Hart Moses Shiff, a slave working there (but owned by a Louisiana judge) escaped. His Honor demanded the lad's return. Rochelle & Shiff placed the following notice in the *Louisiana Gazette* of January 18, 1812:

20 DOLLARS REWARD

> Absconded from the house of the subscribers, on the night of the 16th inst. a mulatto boy, named Ovid, (the property of Judge A. Trouard, of the German Coast,) about 17 years of age, about five feet high, he had on a grey coloured coatee, with a black velvet collar and plated buttons, a grey waistcoat, white nankeen pantaloons, and short boots. Whoever will deliver him to the subscribers, or to his owner, or secure him in any Jail, shall receive a reward of twenty dollars, besides all reasonable charges. Masters of vessels are forewarned from harboring or carrying off said boy at their peril.

Slaves, always in increasing demand in New Orleans, were smuggled from Barataria past such men as Antonio Mendez, "Civil Commandant of a district about six leagues (18 miles) below New Orleans." He had been appointed to this position by Governor Claiborne, who so informed James Madison, Secretary of State, forwarding Mendez' limpieza.

Mendez, a *Marrano,* attempted to conceal his Jewish identity during the period Louisiana was under Spanish rule. He acquired in 1784 from the Spanish Court a *limpieza*—a certificate usually awarded to "Old Christians" that attested to their purity of blood, free "of all taint of bad races of Moors, Jews, Mulattos and Indians." This was his pass into Catholic society.

In 1790 he married French Catholic Felicité Ducre in New Orleans' St. Louis Cathedral. Nonetheless, Antonio Mendez was harassed by the Catholic inhabitants of his district. Madison read his *limpieza* and dolefully commented: "Mr. Mendez, although a Catholic, is said to be of Jewish extraction and on this account is by no means a favorite with his neighbors and manifests disquietude." In 1808 Mendez was transferred by appointment of Governor Claiborne, Justice of the Peace for St. Bernard's Parish (the Louisiana equivalent of county). Ignoring the Laffite smugglers he maintained peace in his parish.

Once a week and sometimes oftener, slave auctions were held at "The Temple" in Barataria. Laffite kept his "privateers" constantly on the move. Within an amazingly short time the organizing genius of Jean Laffite manifested itself. He systematized a dispatch of 50 ships to sweep the Gulf for Spanish prizes, thus assuring a constant flow of loot into "The Temple" and an ample supply of slaves in Barataria's baracoons.

Plantationers and slave traders were generally satisfied with the quality of Laffite's slaves. His Africans were sturdy and healthy, for only the hardiest blacks survived confinement in the deep dark stuffy hulls of the slave ships, not to mention the contagious diseases and brutal treatment that marked their months-long journey.

Among the Jewish merchants of New Orleans who became closely associated with Jean Laffite were such leading auction houses as Jacobs & Asbridge and M. Barnett, which was operated by hot-tempered Maurice Barnett who was married to Marie Céleste Trahan. It was rumored that the high cost of supporting his wife's many relatives was responsible for his ill disposition. Continually he received bills they incurred when they dined in elegant inns at his expense: "For pancakes with Senor Trahan," another "For Young Trahan," and another for "Dinner for Louis"; "For account of David," "For Joseph and Louis" or for "oranges . . . (and) apples given to your father (in-law)." These were petty as compared to the statement "For the ball of his mother-in-law," not to mention the times they all came to him for cash.

To support them, if for no other reason, he needed to associate with Laffite.

One of the leading auctioneer houses of New Orleans parading blacks on the slave block was that operated by Levy Jacobs and his Christian partner, George Asbridge. Since January 1, 1808, they, like all auction houses, sold many domestic slaves, inferior to Laffite's imports. At times, as when they auctioned off about a hundred "prime Virginia slaves selected expressly for this market," Levy and Asbridge were accused of selling inferior Kentucky slaves. Angrily, auctioneer Jacobs publicly demanded his accuser to step forward and substantiate his charge if he could, or forever hold his peace. There was no response. He again invited buyers to come forward and see for themselves.

Prospective plantationers came forward. They carefully looked over various parts of the anatomy, particularly the teeth, which enabled them to determine the age. Experts could tell at a glance a slave's point of origin. They were satisfied that these were "Virginia slaves."

Why Kentucky slaves were regarded as inferior in Louisiana was a riddle to the nephew of plantationer Sam Fechheimer of Rogersville, Kentucky. On his large estate there were many log cabins side by side, in which his slaves lived. Sam's young nephew, Alfred Seasongood, visiting from Cincinnati, went to the slave quarters, "watching the little pickaninnies play and their mammies comb and wash them." He particularly enjoyed their singing. One handsome young "darkey," who was his uncle's valet, sang and played "most divinely." In his log cabin hung banjos, guitars and other stringed instruments along the wall.

The mammies called "aunts" were quite musical and some had excellent voices. One was especially endearing to young Alfred. She was Aunt Tobithy, "very black and fleshy, but the dearest, most affectionate woman." She would sing the oddest little songs while he sat on her knee and taught him many melodies. The one he liked best was "Buzza Buzza Sitting on a Yoe . . . "

But to Sam Fechheimer and other Kentuckian plantationers, while their slaves performed well in the house, they were not as adept as those in Virginia who toiled at hard labor in the fields. For this reason, Kentucky slaves were considered inferior.

And Virginia's native slaves did not compare to imported African "Black Ivory" offered at Laffite's "Temple." Slaves from Africa's Gold Coast, pitch black and ferocious, brought the lowest prices. Preferred were those from French Dahomey, tobacco-colored and gentle.

Males in their twenties brought higher prices than females of that age, and children lesser prices.

Most desired were the females from French Senegal. They were priced even higher than prized males. These possessed fine figures with silky black hair that flowed to their waists and knees. French and Spanish plantation owners in Santo Domingo, by selective breeding, had produced an exotic type they called "Les Sirenes." These, whom Southerners called "Serpent Women," had remarkably exquisite facial features, lithe bodies, small hands and feet. These above all were sought as mistresses.

Laffite maintained a number of tantalizing "Serpent Women" at Grand Isle, across Barataria Pass from Grand Terre. He turned Grand Isle into an island of pleasure—saloons for drinking and gambling and bordellos lavishly outfitted. "Les Sirenes" were among as many as two hundred alluring females of all nations. These beauties offered guests a combination of Laffite's Lucullan delights and the orgies of the renowned New Orleans Swamp.

Virtually all honest businessmen of the Crescent City, Jew and Christian alike, began to deal exclusively in highly profitable pirated Spanish goods. One of these, the first Jew to arrive in New Orleans under the Stars and Stripes, in 1804, the 23-year-old Jacob Hart of Philadelphia, aided by his father Jacob Naphtali Hart, sold great quantities of varied imports, from logwood and mahogany to olives and raisins. He became the owner of a number of vessels, including the schooner *Celestine*. Confiscation of the latter, on a voyage to the Yucatán in New Spain, gave him good cause to join in trade with Laffite. Spanish authorities kept its super-cargo and arrested the *Celestine's* captain, Jean Robert, and the entire crew.

Captain Robert was charged in 1809 with being an American spy and his crew a vanguard unit of a planned invasion. Rebellion was brewing at that time throughout Mexico. Though the charges were unfounded and unproved, captain and crew languished in a Mexican prison, released only by intervention of Louisiana's governor.

Upon Robert's return to New Orleans, Hart rewarded him by making him a full partner. Sharing their hatred of Spain, together the Jew and Christian dealt in contraband obtained at "The Temple." But they were in good company—most New Orleans merchants.

Laffite increased his merciless, relentless attacks on Spanish shipping, emboldened even further by news that the Mexican Revolution for Independence was being waged by the rag-tag army of Reverend

Miguel Hidalgo, hailed as the George Washington of Mexico.

Armed with only machetes and spears, they were routed outside Mexico City and the revolt crushed. The church decreed that since a rebellion against Spain was a rebellion against God, 58-year-old Father Hidalgo was excommunicated for being a Lutheran and a heretic, a Judaizer and an atheist. He was executed by a firing squad in Chihuahua and beheaded; his head taken to Guanajuato, there hung in a granary as a warning to those who would dare revolt against Spain.

Laffite sought vengeance. He intensified his pursuit of Spanish shipping and became known everywhere as the "Pirate of the Gulf." The United States, involved in a dispute with Spain over the Louisiana/New Spain boundary, warned Laffite to desist from further acts or suffer severe punishment. Louisiana's Governor Claiborne ordered the chief of the pirates to close his Baratarian trade mart and disperse his pirates, but for another reason.

"The Temple" was doing a trade of such magnitude that it wreaked havoc with the entire economy of the Gulf and far inland regions. As many as 400 blacks were sold in a single day and smuggled into New Orleans and out of Louisiana by their new owners or Laffite agents. New Orleans banking declined and it was apparent that Laffite was monopolizing Louisiana's import trade and the commerce of the entire Mississippi Valley. Jean Laffite had become the greatest trader in all the West.

Even the national government felt the loss of revenues. Laffite had no intention of dissolving his thriving empire. The order to disperse ignored, Louisiana's governor posted a $500 reward for the head of Jean Laffite. The "Bos" countered with a reward of $1,500 which he posted throughout New Orleans for the head of Governor Claiborne.

The United States government had become embroiled in the War of 1812 and turned its attention away from the pirates of the Gulf towards the redcoats of Canada. But Governor Claiborne acted, as we have seen, to annihilate Barataria.

The "wanted" Laffite became the "most wanted" in all the West when General Jackson sought his services in defense of the city and again after the war when pirate-chief and general stood side by side in sharing the limelight as the "Heroes of New Orleans."

However, Jean Laffite's greatest pride was his share in smashing the fleet of Spain, avenging the might of those who were responsible for his wife's death, his grandfather's murder, along with the murder of thousands of other Marrano martyrs, and for the exile of all Spanish Jewry.

By the SUPREME EXECUTIVE COUNCIL

of the Commonwealth of *Pennsylvania*.

WHEREAS Solomon Raphael _____ the Bearer hereof, intending to follow the Business of a Pedlar within the Commonwealth of *Pennsylvania*, hath been recommended to Us as a proper Person for that Employment, and requesting a Licence for the same: WE DO hereby licence and allow the said Solomon Raphael _____ to employ himself as a Pedlar and Hawker within the said Commonwealth, to travel with one Horse and to carry &c and divers goods, merchandize until the twenty first Day of March next; Provided he shall, during the said Term, observe and keep all Laws and Ordinances of the said Commonwealth to the same Employment relating.

GIVEN under the Seal of the Commonwealth, at Philadelphia, the twenty third Day of March _____ in the Year of our LORD One Thousand Seven Hundred and eighty seven.

ATTEST:
Samu Bryble
for John Armstrong junr Secy

B Franklin Presd

Peddler's license, which was issued to Solomon Raphael (1787), was signed by Benjamin Franklin.
Courtesy American Jewish Historical Society

In 1786 Aaron Levy founded Aaronsburg, Pennsylvania.
Courtesy American Jewish Historical Society

An Aaronsburg's lottery ticket, signed by Aaron Levy. *Courtesy American Jewish Historical Society*

Jacob de Silva Solis and his wife, Charity Hays, early Jewish pioneers in New Orleans.

Log cabin courthouse of John Hays, sheriff (1798-1818), Cahokia, Illinois.
Courtesy Illinois State Historical Library

Benjamin Gratz.

Joseph Jonas was one of Cincinnati earliest Jewish settlers.
Courtesy American Jewish Archive

Abraham Kohn, a founder of Chicago.
Courtesy American Jewish Archives

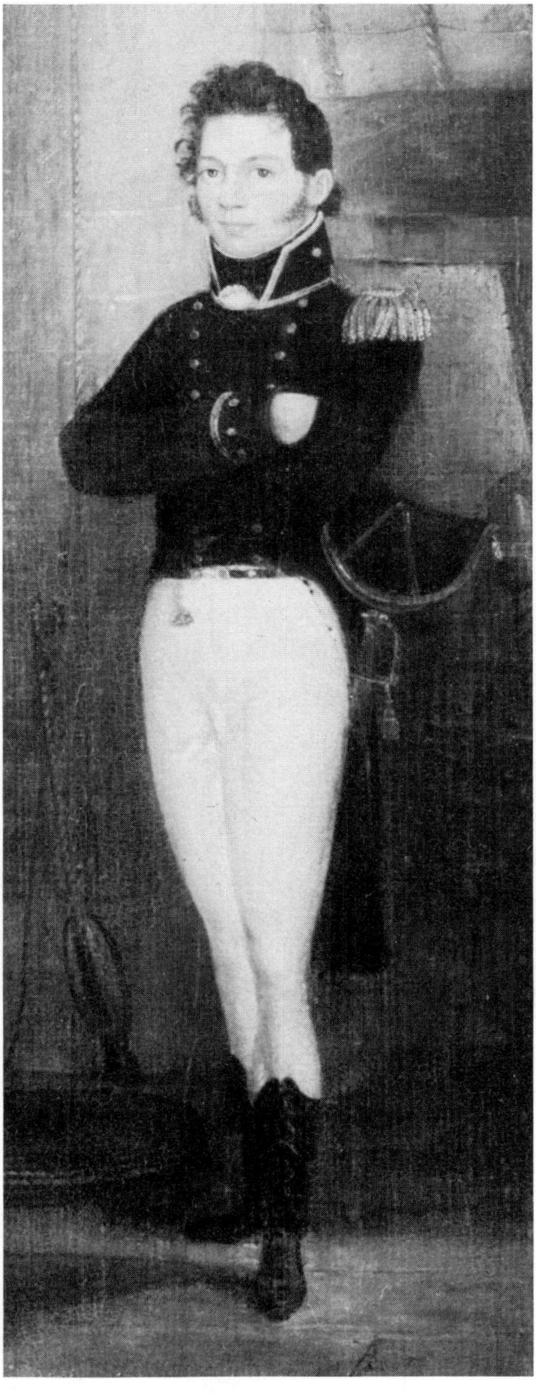

Major Mordecai Myers, War of 1812 hero.
Courtesy American Jewish Historical Society

Commodore Uriah Phillips Levy.
Courtesy American Jewish Historical Society

Portrait of Jean Laffite (1804).

5

Judaism Takes Root in Western Wilderness

Hebrews in Bondage

Overseas, the Napoleonic era brought to the Jews on the Rhine citizenship in the French Empire. The German Jew gained equality in the newly created Kingdom of Westphalia; Frankfurt granted Jews civil rights; so too did the Hanseatic cities. The Grand Duchy of Baden in southern Germany, also a member of the Confederation of the Rhine, declared Jews free hereditary citizens. Bavaria stood alone in her refusal to accord Jews any semblance of equality.

But the overthrow of Napoleon was accompanied by the restoration of the old "legitimate" regimes, and whatever civil rights had been granted Jews then were cancelled. The newly postulated concept of a Christian-Germanic state provided no role for the Jew; either he could enter via baptism or he could exit by emigration.

Bavaria continued to enforce the cruelest of all regulations, requiring the *matrikel* of prohibitive cost, for all Jewish young men except the first born, and other restrictions that made it almost impossible for them to marry. New oppressive measures were enacted.

The Bavarian Diet, in its determination to force the Jew to abandon his faith and be baptized, censored his sacred books, enacted special taxes for Sabbath and Festival candles. But the Jew refused to yield. Few—very few—converted to Christianity. To the young, America was the place that offered both religious and economic freedom; only in that land could they enjoy the Napoleonic ideals of liberty, equality, and fraternity—these essentials withdrawn and withheld from them by the reactionary government bent on stamping out what they deemed "the disease of liberalism."

Anti-Jewish legislation infected universities with virulent anti-Semitism. Frenzied Wurzburg University students led the attack, physically attacking Jews with the blood-curdling cry, "HEP! HEP!"—the initials signifying the Latin phrase *Hierosolyma est Perdita* (Jerusalem is lost). Riots spread from Wurzburg to the cities of Bayreuth, Bamberg, Hamburg, Frankfurt, Darmstadt, Danzig. Everywhere mobs looted Jewish stores and ransacked their homes.

America beckoned to these hounded Jewish youths to come to its hospitable shores. In such a typical community as Middletown on the Connecticut River, the *Middlesex Gazette,* quoted in its issue of April 1, 1819 from the Philadelphia *Franklin Gazette:*

> What! still reject the fated race
> Thus long denied repose—
> What—madly striving to efface
> The rights that heaven bestows?
>
> Say, flows not in each Jewish vein,
> Uncheck'd—without control;
> A tide as pure—as free from stain—
> As warms the Christian's soul!
>
> Do ye not yet the times discern
> That these shall cease to roam—
> That Shiloh, pledg' for their return
> Will bring his ransom'd home!

Hundreds of Middletown-like communities in the Ohio Valley as well as in the East, though they may have been without a press, had able spokesmen through the letters of German Jews already settled in the West. Their enticing accounts coupled with the driving barbarism of the Germans meant that many a Jewish youth was westward bound.

Poor but desperate German Jewish youths indentured themselves to reach America. One, who told of his arrival and treatment in letters that never reached his parents, was Wolf Samuel.

When his ship, *Vrouw Elizabeth,* docked at its destination after seven months on the high seas, Samuel wrote from Baltimore: "I myself was completely bereft of clothes. You can imagine that when a ship is at sea for seven months everything is worn out and in pieces. This is what I brought off the ship—one pair of corduroy trousers, which were not good, two shirts, an overcoat and a black coat which was old. In short, my belongings were not worth four dollars."

The ship's captain sold Samuel at the auction market to Stephen Boyd, a wealthy farmer, for the price of passage—$76, plus $2.50 for interpreter and indenture fees. The farmer incurred an additional $5.45 for having Samuel transported to his farm at Peach Bottom, York County, Pennsylvania.

In another letter Wolf Samuel described life on the plantation. Its owner, he wrote, was a Dutch Jew who after being in the United States only 17 years had become a millionaire. The owner made him supervisor of 94 blacks. Daily he studied English for one hour, and his kind master, who was paying for the teacher, provided him with good clothing, and a special pair of shoes for the Sabbath. He was given food and tobacco of excellent quality. During his servitude which would last two years, he would be able to save a substantial sum of money. All in all, Wolf concluded, he could not wish for anything better for himself.

With the exception of his master's name, there was not a word of truth in the entire letter. His period of bondage was three years and two months. He received no wages, for toiling along with three slaves to construct a fish reservoir on his master's land on the Susquehanna River. He lacked decent clothing and food. Overworked and underfed the lad fell ill. When he complained and refused to work until his health improved, Boyd vowed: "By heaven, I'll have you up before the judge in York (Pennsylvania)."

"I wish you would take me there," Samuel retorted.

"You will go before the judge, Goddam your blood."

Samuel defiantly retorted that he wanted to go to court. Boyd angrily shouted, "Shut up or I'll thrash you and I'm the right man to do it."

Boyd continued to curse Wolf, warning him that if he did not watch his tongue he would be consigned to a local jailhouse to be beaten.

Wolf Samuel bore his servitude for a year and a half. Conditions worsened until, unable to endure his captivity any longer, he ran away.

Boyd placed the following announcement in the *York Recorder:*

FIVE DOLLARS REWARD

Runaway from the subscriber in Peach Bottom Township, on the 7th instant, a servant man, who while he was with me, went by the name of William Samuel Verrend. He had on when he went away a pair of Nankin pantaloons, green cloth coat, brown surtout coat, a wool hat, and coarse leather shoes; he is about twenty-three years of age, five feet seven or eight inches high; stout made, and fair complexion. The above reward will be given to any persons for securing the said runaway in any jail so that I get him again, or for delivering him to the subscriber. All persons are warned against harbouring him.

STEPHEN BOYD

Stephen Boyd certainly thought well of his runaway bond servant in offering that reward when compared to that offered by Naphtali, the elder son of Michael Hart of Easton in Northampton County, Pennsylvania. When his bond servant, a female, fled his service, Naphtali Hart placed the following advertisement in the *Easton Sentinel,* July 17, 1818:

ONE CENT REWARD

Absconded from my service last Wednesday night a bound servant girl named Sarah Kennedy about 17 years old with a small scar under one of her eyes. She took with her a variety of clothing, not all recollected, and a few yards of Irish linnen, part of which was made up. Whoever brings home said runaway shall be entitled to above reward, but no expenses paid by

NAPHTALI HART

As for Wolf Samuel, he fled into the western wilderness, probably to peddle in the Ohio Valley. At last he was a free man in a free country where no one asked a person's past. At last his letters reached his grieving parents. All his previous communications were never sent by Boyd, who stashed them away in his attic. Had Boyd been able to read the contents of Samuel's letters written in Yiddish he would most assuredly have sent them. Instead of presenting his bondage as the nightmare that it was, he sought to allay the concern of his parents. And like many an indentured servant who left his master, with or without his blessings, Wolf Samuel found independence in the American West.

The desperate plight of the assaulted German Jew gave rise to the idea of founding for them a place of refuge in America. At Philadelphia, the port city which served as the entranceway to many, merchant William David Robinson, a concerned Christian, offered Jews a solution to their plight. He published a pamphlet entitled *The Plan for Establishing a Jewish Settlement in the United States.*

The plan urged well-to-do Jews to purchase a large tract of land in the Upper Mississippi and Missouri region, northwest of the Ohio Valley. Here, Robinson contended, in this unspoiled wilderness, persecuted German Jews not only could live in peace, but could engage in that enterprise forbidden to them in Europe—agriculture—and thereby further the development of the young nation.

That Philadelphia merchant knew the Far West, having traveled to the Louisiana Territory as well as Spanish America (Mexico, Venezuela and Colombia). Robinson, one of the earliest Americans to advocate an interocean canal from the Atlantic to the Pacific through Nicaragua, wrote a booklet entitled *The Route to the Pacific*. In this early guidebook for travel into the undeveloped West, he described various possible routes from the Mississippi River to the Pacific. Robinson published this guide 10 years after the epic Lewis and Clark expedition from the confluence of the Mississippi and Missouri Rivers to the mouth of the Columbia River at the Pacific.

Robinson's plan for German and other oppressed European Jews said, "Several large tracts embracing several millions of acres adjacent to the Mississippi and Missouri Rivers," were being offered for sale at extremely low prices. It should be recalled that the United States acquired this land as part of the Louisiana Purchase at less than four cents an acre. He went on to state that the climate of this area was well adapted for Europeans, and that its soil, once cleared of forests, would prove fertile and productive.

This land, Robinson insisted, inevitably would become the most populous and flourishing region in the New World. A Jewish colony therein would ultimately prove highly profitable not only to the settlers, but to the struggling young nation.

> We should behold Jewish agriculture spreading through the American forests. Jewish towns and villages adorning the banks of the Mississippi and Missouri and the arts, commerce and manufactures would advance with the same rapidity in this new settlement as has been exemplified in all the other agricultural regions of the United States.

His premise failed to effect the loosening of purse strings by those to whom the message was primarily directed.

Individual Jewish Indian traders and peddlers would come to the wooded wedge between the Missouri and Mississippi Rivers when the Upper Missouri, Iowa, and Minnesota regions were still Indian lands. They came with other pioneers, farmers, lumberman, after the old Northwest Territory became populated. Never would they establish their own state in that territory as would Mormons in the middle of the century, between the Wasatch and Sierra ranges in the mountains in the Far West.

Even where Jews concentrated, they would live as Americans assimilating in the melting pot that was the frontier. Few of the western Hebrews would see themselves as a separate entity in the multiethnic society that was America.

English Jews' Synagogue Adorns "Queen City"

English Jews enjoyed freedom of economic enterprise. Few emigrated to America. Those who did sought to better their fortune. Arriving as men of means and occupations, they settled in urban centers in the East. They mingled in the social circles of the native American Jews. After Great Britain was reconciled to her rebellious offspring only one of the American-bound English Israelites set his sights on settling in the West.

Family and friends tried to dissuade him. They argued that "in the wilds of America and entirely amongst Gentiles, you will forget your religion and your God." They offered as evidence the fact that there was not even one synagogue in the entire American West.

Hoping that he might be "a nucleus" around which the first synagogue might be built, Joseph Jonas resolutely boarded a transatlantic vessel in 1816, America-bound.

Jonas, a native of Exeter, elected to settle in the Ohio Valley. A mechanic by trade, specializing in watch repair, he decided upon Cincinnati. Having gained most of the Ohio River commerce, Cincinnati had become the West's largest city, and its enthralling beauty awarded her the title "Queen City of the West."

Arriving in Philadelphia on January 2, 1817, Jonas rode the stage past Aaronsburg to Pittsburgh. There he was forced to remain until the ice in the Ohio broke. Upon the breaking of the ice, Joseph boarded the first boat down the Ohio to the city that lay between the Little Miami and Big Miami Rivers. It was exactly as others described it—set amidst romantic hills with terraces rising high above the beautiful river's north bank.

Jonas's first act upon acquiring a building wherein he combined home and silversmith-watch repair shop was to hammer a *mezuzah* upon his doorpost.

Almost immediately he and his *mezuzah* became the center of intense interest. Everyone in the vicinity wanted to have a look at the entrance to his quarters. The kindly Jew responded to their queries explaining that within that little case was a roll of parchment upon which were inscribed in Hebrew passages from the Bible that reminded the Jew to love God and obey His laws. Jonas added that the rabbis believed it to bring blessings to one who touched it but because of its sacred character must only be touched with clean hands.

Word that a descendant of the people of the Bible had settled in Cincinnati spread far and wide. Somewhat against his will, Jonas became an exotic exhibit in his chosen city. One elderly lady, a Quaker who traveled a great distance to see this *rara avis* asked, "Is thee truly a Jew? Is thee an Israelite? One of God's own people? Will thee let me examine thee?"

Jonas admitted the distinction and gave his permission for the survey. The old lady turned him round and round, inspecting him closely and finally exclaimed: "Why thee is no different than any other man!"

Jonas not only revealed this incident to his parents at home in Exeter, England, but more importantly he told them of the respect extended him by the entire community. He presented Cincinnati as a city of excellent business potential and described the enchanting beauty of the surrounding country.

Over the next year his many letters persuaded his brother Abraham Jonas, brother-in-law Morris Moses and their friend Jonas Levy to brave the ocean-land-river journey to Cincinnati. The arrival of this first conspicuous contingent of observant Jews stirred considerable attention throughout the region, and Jonas wrote home:

> ... Many persons of the Nazarene faith residing from fifty to one hundred miles from this city, came into town for the special purpose of viewing and conversing with some of the Children of Israel "The Holy people of God," as they termed us.

They looked with reverence upon their fringed prayer shawls, phylacteries donned upon forearm and forehead, and other ritual objects: wine goblet, spice box, and eight-branched candellabrum. Frontiersmen were drawn to the knives used in ritual slaughtering. One of the Jewish settlers explained that the slaughtering knives were honed smooth and sharp so that not the slightest nick could be felt. He pointed out that he inspected the lungs of cattle, buffalo or deer to ascertain not only that the animal is healthy at the time it was slaughtered but that it could have lived as a healthy animal for at least a year. All visitors left impressed at the scholarship and piety of these Jews.

These "Children of Israel" were continually called upon to explain the Bible and Judaism. One day in 1821 they were asked by a Christian woman to visit the home of a dying man, her husband, who requested they be summoned to his bedside. Standing by him, the man revealed to them that he had been born a Jew but had not lived as one. He pleaded that they give him a Jewish burial and recalled his Hebrew name, Binyamin Leib. They promised, and with the *Shema*, Israel's affirmation of faith, he died in peace.

But there was no hallowed Jewish ground in all the West save the Saloon and Bar, so advertised by Henry Hyman, who came to Louisville, Kentucky, about 1814.

> WESTERN COFFEE-HOUSE
> AND HYMAN'S ALTAR
>
> South side of the Market House,
> between 4th and 5th Streets.
>
> Since Hyman's torch e'er now is beaming,
> Shedding its refulgent light around;
> Since golden rays from it are streaming,
> Prepare to tread the hallowed ground.

In fact, until the coming of the English Jews to Cincinnati, the only place hallowed to Jews and many non-Jews too, was the Saloon where strong drink had taken the place of sacramental wine drunk on holy days. Wealth was worshipped; little else mattered. Judaism was ignored and if a Jew died, he was buried in any burial ground, be it a church cemetery or a potter's field.

There being no Jewish burial ground in Cincinnati or anywhere else in the West, the few men led by Jonas purchased for $75 a small plot "... in the western part of the town on the west side of Western Row, adjoining the farm of W. Betts," (presently the north side of Chestnut Street, near Central Avenue). They buried Binyamin Leib, most probably in the far corner by the fence—the spot traditionally set aside for the intermarried, suicides or criminals.

One wonders if Binyamin Leib, whose name translated to Benjamin Lyon, may have been the renowned Canadian-Jewish Indian trader who escaped the Indian massacre at Fort William Henry and at Fort Mackinac during the French and Indian War, to join after the war with fellow *voyageurs* in canoeing to the far northern Rupert's Land and southward down the Mississippi to Cahokia in the Illinois Country.

Over the next three years Cincinnati Jews interred in their consecrated burial ground three who died across the river in Kentucky and paid all costs to bring a fourth from Louisville, 200 miles away. Joseph Jonas recorded ". . . we have already interred four persons who, but for us, would have lain among Christians . . ."

How many Jews were in the West was anyone's guess. Cincinnati Jews were even unaware of the presence of Binyamin Leib who had settled in their community many years before the arrival of the Queen City's "first" Jew, Joseph Jonas. How many such "Binyamin Leibs" were scattered throughout the Ohio Valley no one knew. There must have been hundreds, perhaps 500 or more. Even after the Queen City became the major supply center for Jewish peddlers the Jewish census was pure conjecture.

With the establishment of consecrated burial ground, Cincinnati's Jews undertook the establishment of a congregation which they believed would serve as a barrier against intermarriage. So many, like Binyamin Leib, had married out of faith and their children had been lost forever to Israel.

Some Jews married Indians. Near the falls of the Ohio, one, surnamed Levi, reared three children in their Indian mother's faith. That these and other children of Jewish fathers and non-Jewish mothers were lost to Judaism was recorded in a London publication in 1844, entitled *Uncle Sam's Peculiarities*. It tells of "Frame Winnerbag . . . son of an Indian squaw and his father a Dutch Jew . . ."

Asked, "You call yourself Winnerbag?" the young man replied: "No, stranger, I don't. I call myself Gray Bear, when I am at home, somewhere between the Blue Mountains and the Pacific Ocean. My father was a Jew cheat, and I don't know *his* name, but I know who my grandfather was, the fine old *Indine,* and that's more than some of these white robbers do. . . . It is the blood of the Gray Bears, and was in it before that old Jew blackguard, my father, came to this country and entered into our family . . ."

This tale told with the prejudices of the day endured by many a Jewish peddler in the Ohio Valley prompted them to deny and obliterate all memories and signs of Hebraic ancestry.

Typical was John I. Jacob (Jacobs, also recorded as Thomas P.), residing in Louisville. He was probably the son of Moses Jacobs of Baltimore. Upon his father's death in 1802, 25-year-old John left for

Shepherdsville, Kentucky, and from there went to nearby Louisville. Twice he married the daughters of well-to-do Christians, and became the richest citizen in town. He had 11 sons and daughters, one of whom married James Clay, son of Kentucky's political leader, Henry Clay, and another of his sons gained distinction in the Episcopal Church—all members of this large family lost to Judaism.

Among the best known of Kentucky's Jews was Benjamin Gratz. Admitted to the Philadelphia bar in 1817, he chose instead to go west and represent the family's extensive land holdings. In Vincennes, Indiana Territory, he was concerned with his father, Michael's, and grandfather, Joseph Simon's, colonial land claims in Indiana and Illinois. After a half a century, these were still in litigation with the federal government. His sister Rebecca Gratz wrote to him:

> The Illinois & Wabash claim, of which I have all my life heard of so much, seemed like a romance—I never expected to see anything but maps & pamphlets of the subject, or that it would cost us your society, for so long a time—but since it has proceeded so far—I catch a little of the mania and frame wishes for its success . . .

Five years later, in 1823, the Supreme Court would rule that the West belonged to the federal government.

After a year in Vincennes, Benjamin Gratz left for Kentucky, where the family's great land holdings obtained during the days of the Revolution by their father, Michael, were not based on Indian treaties as those north of the Ohio were, but on acquisitions approved by state and federal governments. While taking charge of the Gratz acreage, he accepted a position as clerk in the Lexington branch of the Bank of the United States, arranged for him by Ezekiel Salomon. Ezekiel was the eldest son of Haym Salomon, the patriot broker of the Continental Congress during the Revolution.

Ezekiel Salomon had come to Kentucky around 1808, at age 30. He engaged in banking at Harrodsburg, Kentucky's first settlement. Though single, he built a fine stone mansion (still the prettiest house in the town). During the War of 1812 he joined the Navy and was assigned to the post of purser. In 1816 he returned to Lexington, as cashier of that branch of the Bank of the United States. In three years he was elevated to manager.

Working at the bank, Benjamin Gratz encountered a problem that, for an observant Jew, was a major one. The bank opened its doors on Saturday, the Jewish Sabbath. His father had never conducted any business on the holy day. Never was coin, wampum or bill handled on sacred days; no travel or transactions allowed. On the eve of the Sabbath, Benjamin's mother, Miriam, lit candles and all worldly labors ceased as it had been in her parents' home, the home of Benjamin's grandparents, Joseph and Rose Simon.

In a quandary, Benjamin turned to Salomon. He, too, had come from a home where Judaism was strictly observed by his mother; his father was an orthodox Polish Jew who died before he was born. But orphaned of his father, he missed an important religious catalyst and the single young man settled in the far western frontier land of Kentucky was far removed from the traditions of his people.

So Salomon ridiculed Benjamin's scruples and advised him to throw the velvet bag containing his prayer shawl and phylacteries over his shoulder behind him, and report on time Saturday morning.

Benjamin considered. He no longer kept kosher. Why keep the Sabbath? Even in the East, in Philadelphia, his older brother, Simon, married Mary Smith, a Christian. And his deceased Aunt Shinah had married Dr. Nicholas Schuyler, back in 1782, defying her father, Joseph Simon, who reacted to the marriage by rending his clothes as in mourning for the dead.

In his last illness, in 1804, 92-year-old Joseph Simon was tenderly nursed by Benjamin Gratz's sister, Rebecca. Calling her to him one day, he asked what he could do to repay her devotion. Her eyes brimming over with tears, young Rebecca answered, "Grandfather, forgive Aunt Shinah." Touched, the old man pressed her hand, and in a broken voice said, "Send for her." And the staunch orthodox patriarch forgave his estranged daughter, gave her his blessing, and died in her arms.

Benjamin Gratz thought of his cousin, Levy Andrew Levy, now 85 (1819) who was contemplating conversion to Christianity under the urging of his daughter who bore her deceased mother's name, Susannah. Her converted mother and Christian husband lay buried since 1807 in St. Paul's Episcopalian Cemetery in Baltimore, Maryland. Levy Andrew's son, Simon (Simeon) Magruder Levy, born and entered into the Covenant of Abraham at Lancaster in 1774, a West Point cadet in 1802 and ordered to Georgia's Fort Jackson in 1804, died there in the same year of his mother's death. Christiana Magruder, believed to be Levy Andrew Levy's sister-in-law, was interred in the Levy family plot at St. Paul's. The entire Levy Andrew Levy family had intermarried. Levy Andrew Levy was himself baptized in

1827 at St. Paul's Parish and two years afterwards was interred in his family plot in the Episcopalian Cemetery.

Benjamin, youngest of Michael Gratz's 12 children, having seen so many of his own family married to Christians, needed little convincing. He had fallen in love during his stay in Vincennes with Maria Cecil Gist, daughter of Colonel Nathaniel Gist, a Revolutionary Army veteran, and granddaughter of Colonel Christopher Gist who accompanied George Washington into the West in 1753 and fought in the disastrous battle led by Braddock. For his military service Christopher Gist received a grant of 1,200 acres of land in Kentucky, and soon became acquainted with the Gratz brothers. Christopher was the first to survey and map for the Ohio Company of Virginia (then western Virginia, its westernmost portion was Kentucky). As the Gratz brothers continued to acquire Kentucky land, their numerous holdings were such that they reflected upon every new map drawn by Christopher Gist of the Ohio Valley. The Gratz and Gist families were intertwined in the development of Kentucky.

Benjamin and Maria Gratz had five sons. Maria was described as a woman of rare charm and culture, a lovely Gentile. Upon her death in 1841, Benjamin was remarried to Mrs. Anna Maria Boswell (Ann Boswell Shelby), a niece of his deceased wife. To Benjamin and Anna were born two daughters and a son who died in infancy.

Benjamin's talented and most sought after sister, Rebecca, did not approve of his marriages. Writing to a Christian friend, she remarked:

> My most cherished friends and the companions of my choice have generally been worshippers of a different faith from mine—and I have not loved them less on that account. But in a family connection I have always thought conformity of religious opinions essential, and therefore could not approve my brother's election . . .

Rebecca Gratz chose spinsterhood over marriage to a Gentile she loved. Her beauty was captivating, her charm irresistible. Her dark, sparkling eyes, soft, sensitive lips and her buxom and shapely figure were captured in a portrait by painter Thomas Sully.

Many a Jewish suitor would have fallen to her feet, but she loved a Christian and could not bring herself to give her hand in marriage to anyone, least of all her lover, Samuel Ewing, son of the Provost of the University of Philadelphia, and a budding lawyer of great promise.

Ewing married another, became a father, then died tragically before he was 30. Rebecca Gratz quietly entered the room where his body lay in the coffin, placed three white roses on his breast, put a miniature of herself next to his heart and left as silently as she entered.

Rebecca's lofty spiritual qualities so captivated Washington Irving, the first American author to gain international renown, that she would be destined to live forever in the pages of one of the great novels of all time. Irving's fiancée, 18-year-old Sarah Matilda Hoffman, when afflicted with tuberculosis was said to have been attended by her. Disregarding all danger of contagion, Rebecca Gratz nursed her during the most difficult period of her suffering until she died April 26, 1809.

Traveling abroad to assuage his grief after his fiancée died, Irving called upon Sir Walter Scott at his residence in Abbotsford, England. The Scottish novelist who reputedly had never met a Jew, expressed surprise at Irving's high esteem of the Gratz family. Scott was particularly impressed by Irving's description of the self-sacrificing Rebecca Gratz whom he envisioned as one no less than the Biblical matriarch whose name she carried.

Later, as Sir Walter Scott mulled over his next novel, its medieval setting—castles and moats, monks and nuns, knights in shining armor and swords clashing over an alluring damsel charged with witchcraft—he seized upon Irving's fascinating Jewess for his heroine.

Published in 1820, Scott sent the first copy of the novel, *Ivanhoe,* to Washington Irving with a note, "How do you like your Rebecca? Does the Rebecca I have pictured here compare with the pattern given?" When Miss Gratz was asked whether she was the original of Scott's Rebecca, she answered, "They say so."

Rebecca Gratz was well aware of the dangers intermarriage posed to the continuity of Judaism. Her brother Benjamin's children were reared as Christians and like many Jewish children attended Christian Sunday School. Rebecca founded in Philadelphia the first Hebrew Sunday School in America.

Rebecca Gratz lived to be 80, and was interred in the family plot of *Mikveh Israel* Cemetery. When her younger brother Benjamin reached the ripe old age of 90 he applied for interment space in the Gratz family plot, but was refused. He then turned to Dr. Isaac Mayer Wise, Reform leader at the German congregation of Cincinnati, and was assured Hebrew funeral rites.

Two years passed and 92-year-old Benjamin Gratz died (1884) at his homestead on Mill Street, facing Gratz Park in Lexington, Kentucky. His record had been most impressive. As early as 1827 he was elected a trustee of Transylvania University, the leading institution of learning in the region. Even as his father and uncle opened the West to settlement and brought goods west, Benjamin too helped speed western development. He served as director and second president of the Lexington and Ohio Railroad—the first railroad west of the Alleghenies. When Lexington was incorporated as a city in 1832, Benjamin Gratz became a member of the first city council; he was named a member of the first Board of Directors when a branch of the Bank of Kentucky was established in Lexington in 1834, and when the Northern Bank of Kentucky was founded in 1835, he was chosen as a member of the Board of Directors. Benjamin Gratz was also concerned for the less fortunate; he was one of the incorporators of the Orphan Asylum in 1833.

When Henry Clay died in 1852, Gratz accompanied Clay's remains from Washington to Lexington; he was a pallbearer at the funeral and a member of the Clay Monumental Association that erected the Henry Clay monument in the Lexington cemetery.

When Benjamin Gratz died 32 years later, the descendants of Henry Clay were among those who assembled to pay their respects. Among the family members assembled was daughter Anna and her husband Thomas Hart Clay. He was named after Colonel Thomas Hart, a founder of the Transylvania Company and one of the earliest citizens of Lexington. Colonel Thomas Hart's daughter, Lucretia, was married to Henry Clay.

Another family member who bore the name of Colonel Thomas Hart was Senator Henry Clay's contemporary, Senator Thomas Hart Benton of Missouri, a great-nephew of Thomas Hart.

The Clay's most treasured possession was an old Hebrew Bible, in its cover inscribed the name of its original owner: HART.

The descendants of Benjamin's first love, Maria Gist, were present to pay their respects. Their son, Henry Howard, arrived with his wife, Minerva Campbell Anderson, and family: daughter Mary Cecil with her husband, Judge Jeremiah Rogers Morton; daughter Hermine Cary with her husband, John Johnstone; son Benjamin III with his wife, Caroline C. Bryand; and son Anderson with his wife, Laura Cary Bodlye.

Other grandchildren included Alexander, married to Birdie Virginia Ogden, he being the son of deceased Hyman Cecil Gratz and Laura J. Hamilton.

There also came the grandchildren of Benjamin's brother Simon: Ella married to Henry Clay Marshall, Sarah Campbell married to Colonel Lucius Rogers, Cora and her husband, Alexander K. McClure, and Charles Cunningham from Michigan.

Descendants of Benjamin's sister Frances and Reuben Etting included their son Horatio with his wife, Frances Marx, and family: Samuel and his wife, Sarah E. Smyth, and Edward Johnson II and his wife, Maria Newbold.

Reuben Etting's brother, Solomon, was a director and promoter of the Baltimore and Ohio Railroad. Solomon was a son-in-law of Joseph Simon who had close ties with Solomon and Reuben's father, Elijah Etting, pioneer Indian trader in York, Pennsylvania.

The lineage to ancient Israel of Benjamin Gratz's grandfather Joseph Simon was supposedly unbroken. More recently, the family line included the famed Jewish historian Heinrich Gratz. But Jewish ancestry was hardly in evidence at the funeral.

The large gathering of mourners paraded past the open casket to view the remains, a ceremony borrowed from the Indians. Flowers were heaped upon the bier in the custom of Christians. The *Kaddish,* an Aramaic memorial prayer, hinted at the Jewish roots of the deceased.

Upon returning home, the rabbi, Isaac Mayer Wise, quipped: Only two Jews were present in the funeral parlor—himself and the corpse.

Every American Jew who intermarried and assimilated, who did not live as a Jew during his lifetime, wished to be reunited in death with his people—all except one, chemist Charles Clemens Coleman Cohen, an avowed atheist whose scientific studies led him to discard "the idea of an immaterial mind and the existence of a soul distinct from our laws and affections of matter."

London born Cohen, married in 1829, emigrated to the United States and earned his living as a druggist. He avidly studied Hume, Voltaire and other philosophers and religiously attended the lectures of Johann Gaspar Spurzheim, the founder of phrenology.

The 27-year-old Cohen published an article in the *Free Enquirer,* New York City, Saturday, February 16, 1834, expounding his godless doctrine and ridiculing those atheists who upon their deathbeds would turn to their respective deities. "For my part," Charles Cohen emphatically declared, "I would say I can attach no idea to the word God and cannot consequently believe in him."

No one ever would be able to relate how C. C. C. Cohen might have reacted on his own deathbed. A week later the *Free Enquirer* reported that on the Jewish Sabbath of the publication of his article, while working in his laboratory "seven pounds of fulminating mercury exploded while he was preparing it, blowing off an arm that was never recovered. His body had gone one way, his head another, given to the Society for Phrenological Studies."

Charles Cohen, who neither believed in a supreme being, an afterlife, nor in the resurrection, might have changed his mind had he seen the plot of Levi Solomon, an English Jew of an earlier generation. Thrice married to Jewish women, that peddler who made his home before the Revolution near Freehold, New Jersey, arranged for his wives to be buried one on either side of his grave and one at his feet. Solomon certainly would enjoy a glorious afterlife.

While few Jews turned to atheism, many like Cohen became estranged from Judaism through intermarriage. There was hardly a Jewish family in America that could claim to have resisted the charms of Christian daughters.

At Cincinnati, David Israel and his bride Eliza, arrived from England in 1818. Eliza was the first Jewish woman to settle in the Upper Ohio. The couple did not remain in the Queen City but boated downriver 26 miles to the Whitewater and proceeded upriver 40 miles to Brookville, Indiana Territory. At Brookville, a ridge between the forks of the Whitewater, David canoed his boat, laden with Indian goods, veering it upriver the West Fork of the Whitewater 18 miles to Connersville. Here was located the trading post of David's brother, Phineas Israel, who for some reason no longer known had been dubbed at this settlement, Johnson. David too adopted that surname. Phineas, possessed with a roving spirit, moved on to St. Louis.

The Johnson brothers, David Israel and Phineas Israel, proud descendants of the famed English D'Israeli family, found adjustment to the American frontier from the British metropolis difficult. After two years of primitive living, David and Eliza took their year-old son, Edward Isaac, and removed to Cincinnati. The Jonas brothers and other Hebrew townspeople heartily welcomed David and Eliza—the only Jewish couple in the Queen City. In 1821 they attended the ritual circumcision of eight-day-old Frederick A(braham?) as the second born was initiated into the Jewish fold. Two years later they all welcomed the arrival of yet another Johnson, a daughter, Selena.

Israel Johnson was saddened to learn that Phineas married in St. Louis to a Gentile, Miss Clarissa Clark. Though she was a grandniece of Abraham Clark, a signer of the Declaration of Independence, Israel noted that Clarissa descended from Abraham Clark, not Abraham the Jew.

A son (it is not known if he was of the Ohioan or Missourian Johnsons) settled in Oklahoma. Whatever his given name, he was known everywhere by his nickname "Boggy." He had opened a trading post at Boggy, located about a mile east of the Clear Boggy Creek, which flowed southeastward to conjoin with the Muddy Boggy Creek, to pour the mingling miry, murky waters into the Red River. In that wilderness, he married a young Chickasaw maiden and cast his lot with the Indian tribes.

Likewise, Simon Block was concerned over intermarriages in his family of Missouri settlers. Simon Block had come from Schwihou, Bohemia, in 1798, possibly with his brother, Jonas, and his wife, Resna. After a few years in Baltimore, trader Simon moved to Richmond, Virginia, where other Bohemian Block family members had settled.

About 1820, Simon Block's cousin, also named Simon, arrived from Bohemia with another cousin Wolf. Wolf Block was making his second trip to St. Louis, having established a trading post there in 1816, amassed enough funds to return for his wife. She, however, refused to leave Schwihou for the American West. Wolf divorced her and was returning to the country he loved.

Wolfe's companion was a newcomer to America; his given name, like the Block of Cincinnati, was Simon. He settled at Sainte Genevieve, oldest settlement in Missouri. There he established the firm of "Block & Philipson." His partner was Jacob Philipson, formerly of St. Louis, who was married to a daughter of Simon Block of Cincinnati. Not only did Jacob Philipson marry a Jew, so unusual for a western Israelite, but her father was pious and learned, acting as *Shochet* for the Jews of Cincinnati and also as *Mohel*; his ritual circumcisions, first in the West, he performed for the sons of David Israel Johnson.

Like Simon Block of Cincinnati, Simon Block of Missouri was an observant Jew; so, too, his brother Phineas who came from Bohemia with another brother, Jacob, to settle at Cape Girardeau, Missouri. Phineas opened a grocery, then acquired a steam floating mill. He also owned and managed the Northern Mississippi Steamship Company, in partnership, under the name of Block & McCune. Phineas was a *Shochet* and kept a kosher household. For this reason, Missourians called him "rabbi."

But Phineas Block's daughter Annie was not a "chip off the old Block." She married John Leach and justified her marriage by pointing to Uncle Jacob, Phineas' brother, who married Catherine Adams.

Another Jacob Block was the son of Simon Block of Cincinnati. When they lived in Virginia, before moving to Cincinnati, Jacob Block served in the Richmond Light Infantry Blues and after the War, served in 1817 as president of Richmond's Congregation *Beth Shalom* (house of peace). That year, the congregation acquired a new burial ground on Shockoe Hill. Benjamin Wolfe successfully negotiated with the city for its acquisition, for he was a member of the Common Hall. Laughingly Benjamin remarked to Jacob that courtesy demanded that as "in all new grounds the parnass (president) should be the first person interred." To this Jacob Block quoted Scripture to the effect that "he who digs a pit for another should be first to fall in it." First to be interred in the new ground was Benjamin Wolfe.

Unlike Jacob who piously followed the tenets of Judaism and was overjoyed to learn of his father's presidency of a new congregation formed in the Queen City, Jacob's brother, Levi, settled at Troy, Missouri and married Miss Massey of Massey Iron Works, a Catholic. Levi Block abandoned his faith.

Probably influenced by Levi Block, his cousin Eliezer, was married in Troy to Lucretià Parker. After her death, Eliezer moved to St. Louis where he married Sarah Kittredge. When he lay upon his deathbed, Eliezer Block, a member of the Presbyterian Church, declared that he had never given up his Jewish faith. He asked to be buried as a Jew. His minister, the Reverend Dr. Post, did his best to oblige. The good man omitted all Christian references from the burial services.

Like all other western Jews, the brothers, Joseph and Abraham Jonas, had found no one to marry and no one to pray with. Though there was no quorum for public worship until the early 1820s, they held private prayers in their homes. But for their wives they traveled East in 1823. At New York they courted the daughters of Reverend Gershom Mendes Seixas, patriot rabbi during the American Revolution. There they were gratified to meet not only merchants but also peddlers who had married Jewish women.

The Jonas brothers thoroughly enjoyed the popular ditty "Pretty Sally Solomons," which extolled in song the praises of such a love. Its verse and attendant commentary were on the lips of many a Jew with a pack on his back:

> Though every place I rove,
> A peddler by my trade,
> And soon I fell in love
> With a very pretty maid...

> . . . one day, instead of calling my shoestrings
> I cried "Sally Solomons, all a penny a pair;"
> so de people laughed, and I looked like a fool—
>
>> And 'twas all for Sally Solomons,
>> Pretty Sally Solomons,
>> Oh, listen, love, to me;
>> Would you be Mistress Ab'rams,
>> How happy should I be . . .
>
>> No girl in Duke's Place should compare
>> Bid her to buy and sell:
>> She made such bargains you would stare,
>> And so in love I fell.
>
> . . . she got de tings more as twenty per cent,
> cheaper den her old father Shadriack, who kept
> a closhs shop and two counters in it . . .

The Jonas brothers married the Seixas sisters: Joseph to 22-year-old Rachel Agnes and the younger, Abraham, to 18-year-old Lucy Orah. The sisters met untimely deaths, Lucy being fatally stricken two years after her marriage and Rachel four years after hers. Abraham was remarried in the later 1820s to Louisa Block of St. Louis, Eliezer Block's sister. Louisa's sister, Elinor, wedded Cincinnatian Phineas Moses whose brother Morris was married to Sarah, a sister of the Jonas brothers. Joseph Jonas left for his native England to remarry and tell his bride and family of the Jewish community he founded in the Ohio Valley.

Led by Joseph Jonas, who returned from his native England with his bride, joined with his brothers, brother-in-law, fellow English Jews and others who had come to Cincinnati on January 4, 1824, 24 men in all, at the residence of Morris Moses, to organize a congregation. Named *B'nai Israel* (Sons of Israel), they assembled in the fall for High Holy Day worship. Their first public house of worship was a frame building on the west side of Main Street, between Third and Fourth. Within their ark they placed two scrolls of the law. Little did they realize that their prayers for a synagogue edifice to adorn the "Queen City" would be achieved only after a decade of energetic effort.

After the autumnal holiday season, president-elect Joseph Jonas drafted an appeal for funds to erect a synagogue edifice. Printed as a "circular," it was sent to old established congregations dotting the Atlantic seaboard and Caribbean. He wrote:

> ... (that) separated as we are and scattered through the wilds of America as children of the same family and faith, we consider it as our duty to apply to you for assistance in the erection of a House to worship the God of our forefathers. ... We have congregated where a few years before nothing was heard but the howling of wild Beasts, and the more hideous cry of savage man. We are well assured that many Jews are lost in this country from not being in the neighborhood of a congregation, they often marry with Christians, and their posterity lose the true worship of God forever ...

Jonas gave further impact to his appeal by citing the religiously disadvantaged co-religionists of the southwesternmost city in the land:

> It is also worthy of remark that there is not a congregation within 500 miles of this city and we presume it is well known how easy of access we are to New Orleans, and we are well informed that had we a synagogue here, hundreds from that City who now know and see nothing of their religion would frequently attend here during holidays ...

That Cincinnati is within easy access to New Orleans seems inconsistent even by jet-age standards yet in Jonas's day river travel by steamboat was regarded fast and comfortable. It took less than a month to journey between the Queen City and Crescent City.

Steamboating to the "Crescent City"

In the spring of 1827, Jacob da Silva Solomon Solis, his wife Charity Hays and their seven children had taken the Ohio River steamboat bound for New Orleans. They took advantage of the few hours' pause at the Cincinnati Landing to visit the Queen City. As at most river landings, businesses were concentrated along the waterfront. At Cincinnati as elsewhere, Jewish-owned stores were heavily concentrated on the street facing the river.

Jacob Solis, a merchant who had served in the east as a religious teacher and ritual slaughterer, was profoundly disappointed to learn that no synagogue had yet been built in the Queen City of the West. Donations received from eastern cities and the West Indies in response to their circular had fallen far too short of the required sum.

They reboarded the steamer, the Ohio waterway winding southwestward. Thrilling was the ride past the Falls of the Ohio at Louisville, Kentucky. The melted snows had raised the river sufficiently high for the steamboat to safely negotiate the rapids. Excitement over, there was time to chat.

Charity recalled to her husband that her cousin Samuel Hays was married to Richea Gratz, Benjamin Gratz's sister. Her younger sister, Hannah Hays, was in the previous century among the Tennessee pioneers, married to Benjamin Myers of Nashborough (later Nashville). In 1795 Hannah gave birth to a daughter, Sarah, who edged the population of Nashborough a notch closer to the 300 mark. Sarah was a fifth-generation American.

First of the Hays clan to come to America was Charity's great-grandfather, Michael Hays, who sailed his own vessel manned by his six sons and crew from Holland across the Atlantic. Charity's grandfather, Jacob, was a leader in the Portuguese *Shearith Israel* synagogue of New York City. So highly regarded was he for his Jewish knowledge, that the congregation titled him "Reverend."

And there were next in line, Charity's parents, David and Esther, patriotic as any blueblooded American. David Hays enrolled in the Virginia Militia to serve under Colonel George Washington in the ill-fated Braddock march on Fort Duquesne in 1755 and during the Revolution at great risk to their lives, he and his brother Benjamin herded their livestock from their Westchester County farm in Bedford, northeast of New York City, through English lines to reach the Continentals. How they accomplished this feat they never recorded, but it must however be considered one of the most adroit non-combat strategies of the Revolutionary War.

When the brothers returned to Bedford, they found a heap of ashes and charred wood where their homes had stood, burned to the ground by vengeful Tory neighbors. Much less concerned about the loss of his house than the fate of his wife, Esther, and new-born son, Benjamin Etting, David heaved a sigh of relief when he located them safe and sound at a neighboring farmer's house. Their faithful Negro slaves, Darby and his wife, had helped mother and child from the flaming farmhouse.

David then struck from his prayerbook the invocation for the welfare of "Our most Sovereign Lord King George the Third, Our most gracious Queen Charlotte, the Royal Highness, George, Prince of Wales and all the Royal Family . . ."

And when talking about her family, Charity always bragged about her brother, Jacob, Chief of Police of New York City and much respected for his sleuthing. It was said his steel-like stare could make a criminal confess to crimes that a third-degree could not. Yet, it was also observed that Hays had a soft heart when it came to women criminals. We can only guess at the reasons.

As the steamboat glided downriver the Ohio past Cairo, Illinois, where the beautiful river flowed into the Mississippi, Charity also recalled a member of the Hays family who had settled to the north in Cahokia and became most prominent in the Illinois country. He was Sheriff, Postmaster, Collector of Internal Revenue, Indian Agent, Indian trader and merchant John Jacob Hays. In 1827, he had already served five years as agent to the Potawatomi and Miami by appointment of his dear friend, John C. Calhoun, then Secretary of War.

Charity loved to tell of John's youth and how he made his way West and of his many and varied attainments. He was the roving son of Revolutionary Army Lieutenant Barrack (Baruch) Hays who switched his loyalties to be appointed a British "officer of guides" (chief of scouts). After the war, he fled to Canada with his bride Rachel da Costa, and 13-year-old son by a previous marriage, John Jacob. The teenager tired of city life and had no desire to follow the occupation of his father, auctioneering.

Entering the Indian trade, he bartered for a fur firm in Montreal, canoeing to Fort Mackinac, and from there he set forth in 1790 for a life of primitive adventure in the Far West, to the Lake of the Woods. In that Indian country southwest of Lake Nipigon at the headwaters of the Red River in Canada, he and a companion came to trade with the Indians. But instead they were engulfed in a freak snowstorm, trapped in the midst of a raging blizzard.

The swirling flakes blinded their vision, the shifting drifts and icy blasts prevented them from seeking shelter. They wrapped themselves in thin blankets, and snuggled against each other for warmth, dropped off to sleep from sheer exhaustion. Upon awakening they found themselves submerged in snow. They fashioned an igloo-like cave in which they remained for a few days until the storm subsided. They survived on a plentiful supply of dried meat, but suffered from lack of water for they had no way to melt the snow in the near zero temperature.

Returned safe and sound to Montreal, John Hays was sated with excitement and adventure. His cousin, 24-year-old Solomon Hays, thirsting for thrills, in 1794 indentured himself to work for Grant, Campion & Co., for three years in the Upper Country (Ontario) Indian trade. Solomon's youthful years had paralleled those of John and his parents, for his father Michael Solomon Hays, a Loyalist, fled from

New York after the Revolution to Montreal with his mother, Abigail Hays. The western drive was strong within young Solomon for mother and father were first cousins, both of the Hays clan, all of whom possessed pioneering spirit.

Solomon Hays's departure fired the adventuresome zeal within his cousin, John. He arranged with Todd & Hay Co., to represent that Montreal fur firm in warmer climes south of the Upper Country, in the American Northwest Territory. Reaching Cahokia, word soon came that Todd died and his partner Hay closed the company. Resourceful John Hays opened his own trading post. Annually he led his own fleet of canoes northward into the land of the Winnebago, Wisconsin, and Menominee, bartering for rich peltries and prospered.

Cahokian townspeople liked Hays as did the Indians and *voyageurs*. Appointed postmaster, he was re-elected for so many years that no one could remember another holding that post before him. In 1798, Governor St. Clair approved Hays for the post of Sheriff of St. Clair County, Northwest Territory. In 1809, when the Illinois Territory was carved out of the Northwest Territory, President James Madison confirmed for the gun-toting Jewish Sheriff, the post of Collector of Internal Revenue. Ten years later he resigned for a more important post.

His public service was recognized when in 1820 he was appointed Indian Agent for the tribes in Indiana at a generous salary of $1,200 a year. So he was informed by the Secretary of War, John C. Calhoun.

Cahokia's zenith having passed, the slack river town noted only for the roistering weekly balls of the French-Canadian *voyageurs,* Hays left his wife and family and set forth for Fort Wayne, that lone outpost in the wilderness of Indiana abandoned by the army the previous year. John arrived in the rude little stockaded village at the junction of the St. Mary's, St. Joseph's, and Maumee Rivers to find about 20 cabins and a boat landing in the busy fur center. Indian traders and Indians came and went; only a few traders were settled in the former garrison.

Upon opening the Indian Agency, the Baptist preacher Isaac McCoy and his wife came to request permission to continue their school within the fort. Hays, having been impressed by the interest of the 26 young Miami and Potawatomi, also a few Shawnee, Chippewa and Mohegan, granted his request cheerfully—an approval he soon regretted. Within the year the number of students doubled; in their free time they raced about the stockade like trapped wild animals, to Hays's dismay, causing much damage. This was in addition to the already poor condition of the buildings, which were unable to resist the assaults of pelting rains and swirling snows. The outer walls of the fort, hewn logs 35 feet high, looked deceivingly substantial.

The greatest responsibility of Indian Agent John Hays was disbursing government money to the Indians in payment for lands they had ceded. The Miamis received $18,000 annually, the Potawatomi nearly as much. But they still held much land. Hays had to gain their confidence too so that the government could acquire their land peaceably. To achieve this end, Hays initiated a new method of disbursing the money to the Indians whose lands had been ceded. The money was disbursed, one silver dollar at a time, to each member of the watching circle of tribesmen. All felt they had been fairly treated.

Many of these silver dollars found their way into the hands of traders who supplied them with great quantities of liquor. The temper of the Indians flared and usually ended in tomahawkings.

As if to compensate, Hays felt a measure of satisfaction when he succeeded in interesting a band of Miami in farming. They agreed to pay for plows, tools, harness and fence rails out of their annuity.

About every six months, John made the 18-day journey home to Cahokia. Returning to Fort Wayne in May 1821 he collapsed after the first 15 miles. Several weeks later he started out again with one of his daughters to care for him. Intending to resign his post as Indian Agent, new orders arrived from Washington. He was to proceed to Vincennes to take the deeds of lands ceded by the Wea and Kickapoo Indians on the Wabash above Vincennes. The transfer not completed, Hays in ill health returned to Cahokia, there to be bedridden all winter.

In May, 1822, Hays returned to Vincennes to accomplish the hopeless task given him by Secretary Calhoun, to cajole stubborn remnants of the Wea and Kickapoo into going west of the Mississippi.

Returning to Fort Wayne, problems had multiplied. The government was six months behind in its allowance for the Indians. Six murders had been reported. Some funds finally came and Hays juggled and manipulated payment as best he could. He pointed to the Miami farms that succeeded. A few villages had been built—Turtle Town on the Eel River and the Forks of the Wabash and White Racoon's Village. Hays said that at White Raccoon's Village the Miami "have 20 head of Cattle, and some Hogs, and they raise corn sufficient to accommodate Travellers that may pass the road. they can give a good breakfast or Dinner. they make butter &c. and raise numbers of chickens . . ." But most Miami and Potawatomi longed to continue their unfettered life in unfenced country.

After the winter of 1823, Indian Agent John Hays, suffering rheumatism and fever sent in his resignation, emphasizing that he could no longer endure the fatiguing trip between Fort Wayne and Cahokia. Secretary Calhoun reluctantly accepted.

At home, John Jacob Hays decorated his office wall with a large collection of warrants that he received over the years attesting to various offices he held.

But, lamented pious Charity Hays as she told of her distinguished relation, the prize John Hays cherished the most above all his certificates was his marriage license to a French Catholic, Mary Louise Brouillet. It had been personally presented to him in 1801 by his old friend, William Henry Harrison, then governor of the Indiana Territory, present at the wedding.

Leisure time on board the Mississippi steamboat was spent on deck with many of the passengers performing their skills—singing, dancing, acting. An amazing feat of memory was displayed by two Jewish peddlers. One was blindfolded, the other would call out numbers that he wrote in chalk on the deck. After hundreds of numbers circled the deck, his blindfolded friend would repeat the numbers in their correct order.

To the astounded passengers, Charity and Jacob Solis later revealed that the letters of the Hebrew alphabet also represented numbers. By taking the Hebrew Psalms, for instance, which the peddlers knew by heart, word for word and letter for letter, they simply substituted numbers in place of the corresponding Hebrew letters.

As the steamboat chugged southward, making countless landings to let off passengers and take on others, deposit cargo and load new shipments, Charity told Jacob that she wished they could step off at an Arkansas landing and travel across the territory to Washington. Her niece, Frances Isaiah Isaacs, had recently moved to the village of Washington, the first Jewish woman in that wilderness. Frances, daughter of Hetty Hays, was married to Captain Abraham Block, a veteran of the War of 1812. Frances's mother, long deceased, had married a pioneer, Isaiah Isaacs, said to be the first Jewish settler in Richmond, Virginia.

When Captain Abraham received a letter from his cousin Eliezer Block in St. Louis the previous year telling him of the booming trade with Mexico, of caravans moving in strength over the newly opened 1,000 mile trail to Santa Fe in New Mexico and to its destination, Chihuahua in Old Mexico, the Blocks made their move.

A touch of humor occurred at their leaving. Charity mentioned that when Frances and Abraham prepared to vacate their home in Charlottesville, Virginia, that previous year in September of 1826, a theft was noted. Their slave, Matilda Drew, absconded with two pounds of cheese and two of sugar, and a bottle of cordial. Caught by the sheriff and taken to court, she was found not guilty. For defending her from the charge of stealing property valued at $1.62, the court allowed her counsel $10.

The Blocks made their way to New Orleans and after a brief stay in the Upper Red River country settled at the tiny village of Washington, recently founded. There Abraham set up his trading post to supply caravans on their journey over the Chihuahua Trail as well as plantationers and Indians.

But with seven mouths to feed and children constantly impatient to reach their new home, there was no time for detouring and visiting.

A month on the steamboat from the time they left Pittsburgh, Charity and Jacob Solis finally disembarked at the New Orleans landing. Jacob opened in the Crescent City an auction house and learned that he, too, may have had a pioneer ancestor in the West. Almost half-a-century earlier one Joseph Solis together with the Marrano, Antonio Mendez, introduced the sugar cane into Louisiana, now grown at many plantations. Jacob knew that his family tree was rooted in Solomon and Isabel who escaped the Inquisition from Lisbon to remarry at Amsterdam according to Jewish rites in 1670. None in New Orleans could say if Joseph Solis, his predecessor, had stemmed from these progenitors of Jacob's lineage.

But Charity was to have the last word on relations. In New Orleans too, she learned of a family member residing in the city, who was one of its most prominent citizens—the renowned Judah Touro. His mother was Reyna Hays, wife of Judah's father, Reverend Isaac Touro, who ministered at Newport, Rhode Island, during the colonial period.

Charity and Judah were second cousins to each other; the Solises often visited with Judah. Despite his wealth, he lived with a minimum of comfort. He was a frugal man, different from his New Orleans coreligionists, who once acquiring fortune lived lavishly as did most of the wealthy. Judah was possessed with a heart of gold that balanced his gold-filled chests. He spoke seldom, as though words were golden coins, each counted and weighed. But to the Solises he revealed much.

Judah came to New Orleans when the Spanish flag yet waved over it. Having been robbed during his voyage from Boston of $100, he had not even a copper cent in his pocket upon landing. This did not affect him as strongly as his deep depression at having arrived alone, without his beloved whom he left behind.

After his father had died, his mother brought him to Boston to live with her brother, Moses Michael Hays. She died soon afterward.

In his uncle's home Judah was raised with his cousin Catherine. They fell deeply in love with each other and planned to marry. While Moses the Lawgiver permitted the intermarrying of cousins, Moses, the father, forbade Catherine to contemplate marriage to her cousin. He ordered Judah to leave, never to return.

Grieving inwardly, Judah traveled to what New Englanders regarded the end of the earth—New Orleans, in Spanish Louisiana. There were in 1802 in the Crescent City about 4,000 Creoles (white persons of French or Spanish descent), as many Negroes, a polyglot mixture of seafarers, pirates of all nations, Indians, and a few Marranos.

Though his uncle refused to accept Judah as his son-in-law, he did respect his integrity and honesty, and sent him a consignment of goods on credit. From this modest beginning the penniless Touro established a wholesale house, selling to storekeepers and plantationers.

Plantation owners from along the Mississippi and Gulf came to New Orleans to buy, sell, trade slaves, consign cotton, purchase supplies. They bought large quantities to provide for their slaves, the small plantations like that owned by Jewess Abigail Minis, worked by 17 blacks, larger plantations like that owned by the Jew Jacob Ottoleungui, worked by 1,000. At Touro's emporium they found a vast variety at little markup. Judah's principle was high volume, not high price.

At times Judah sold his cargo directly at the dock, advertising in such instances in the *Louisiana Gazette,* as on February 19, 1805:

> Now Landing From on board the Schooner *William,* Abraham Waters Master, from Boston, lying opposite the old Custom House, the following articles:
>
> 130 Boxes Cod Fish, 28 half barrels of 1st quality beef, 2 do [ditto] Neats Tongues, 10 Casks Cheese, 19 do Potatoes, 2 do French Hair Powder, 70 Boxes Mould Candles, 18 do Castile Soap, 60 do American brown Soap, 4 do Chocolate, 5 Cases Britannias, 2 do Platillas, 6 Kegs Butter, 2 Pipes Holland Gin, 6 Barrels Nuts, and a quantity of Pickled Fish in Kegs, in excellent order, consisting of Salmon, Mackerel, Herring, Tongues and Sounds, Soused Lobsters, &c.—ALSO—A few thousand Joice [joists] and Boards, which will be sold reasonable for cash . . .
>
> J. Touro

Solis, pleased over Touro's success, was uneasy over his business being open on Jewish holy days. Solis's was the only store in the city closed, as in Wilmington, Delaware, where he had operated a wholesale drygoods store and manufactured quilt patterns, his advertisements advised, "No business transacted on the seventh day."

Jacob told Judah that they had moved from Wilmington to Mount Pleasant, New York, home of Charity's parents. There they became deeply involved in the care of homeless Jewish youths. He hoped to amass a quick fortune in order to finance his pet project, an orphan asylum and trade school for Jewish youth.

A few months before steamboating to New Orleans the *Intelligensia* of Patterson, New Jersey, dated June 7, 1826, announced:

> Jacob S. Solis of Mount Pleasant, Westchester County, is forming an institution for educating Jewish youths and for teaching them trades and mechanical arts, agriculture, etc. He intends to erect factories under his own immediate inspection to be located in the same place. Also to be an asylum for orphans of Israel.

The Hays farm would house, if Jacob Solis could raise the funds, a unique institution in American Jewish life.

Judah, who could easily have subscribed the necessary sum, was withdrawn at this time from contributing to Jewish causes. He did not donate a Jewish house of worship to the Jews of New Orleans for he was not impressed by his coreligionists, most of whom were intermarried and indifferent.

But he did own a house of worship. In 1822, when the First Presbyterian Church was deep in debt, its building and land auctioned to pay its debts, Touro offered the highest bid—$20,000. Everyone in the crowd assembled whispered that the skinflint of a Jew would tear the old church down to build a row of stores. Judah came forward to accept its key and deed and announced: "I am a friend to religion, and I will not pull down the church to increase my means," and handed the key to its pastor, the Reverend Theodore Clapp, whose eyes welled with more tears, tears of joy replacing those of sorrow. Judah told the minister that he would allow the membership its continued use rent free. Touro expended thousands of dollars for its repair, even contributed to the pastor's salary. Judah Touro became distinguished as the first and only Jew in history to own a church.

But Touro remained an enigma to his coreligionists, especially those at Cincinnati. Why did he not respond to their request for funds to build a synagogue. His cousin Charity, however, felt that she understood her introverted cousin. He loved his people, his faith, his country. There would come the time when at a propitious moment he would open his heart to them openly and publicly.

Jacob Solis had hardly enough time to set his shop and house in order for the coming Passover festival. He asked fellow Jews where *matzah* (unleavened cakes) could be obtained and was appalled to learn that none was to be had anywhere, though there were over 100 Jews in the city.

In his home, Solis ground his own meal, kneaded the dough, careful that it not remain unattended for 18 minutes or more (as leavening would set in), hastening the flat round cakes into the oven. With each *matzah* he kneaded and baked, Jacob became more determined to organize a congregation that would in the year to come arrange for *matzah* to be prepared in a communal bakery so that all New Orleans Jewry could fulfill observance of the festival of freedom.

After Passover 1827, Solis led in organizing a High Holy Day worship for the fall. Under his leadership 34 men assembled December 20 of that year to found Congregation *Shanarai Chasset* (Gates of Mercy) and elect officers. Manis Jacobs, the only Jew to have identified himself with his faith in the Crescent City in the early days prior to the War of 1812, was elected president.

The Hebrew Godfather

February 2, 1828 saw the new Jewish community of New Orleans publishing its constitution and by-laws; acquisition of a burial ground was now of primary consideration. There being no funds as yet in the treasury, President Manis Jacobs personally outlayed the sum of $361.25 for a section of land to be consecrated as a final resting place.

Upon official incorporation of the congregation, March 25, 1828, Jacobs was reimbursed.

In the late spring, after celebrating Passover with *matzah* enjoyed by all who cared to purchase them, many ignoring the festival, Solis boarded a northern bound steamer, pausing at Cincinnati on his way to New York. He received there a message from President Jacobs dated June 4, 1828. Manis Jacobs's letter told of the passing of Hyam Harris who owned a small store in New Orleans and had contributed to, but not as yet joined, the congregation.

Manis wrote that Hyam had been interred in the recently acquired burial ground and that:

> ... Since you been gone I had hard work, to do, that is to Say, to Say prayers every Evening in the house of the mourners, and you know that I do not know much about the portuguaise minhag (rite) Still we come on pretty well. I have been yesterday in the afternoon on horse back to the burial ground and the Sons of the demise have made already a tombstone over the grave; when you will write me from New York inquire how a corpse must lay. For Some think yet that the feet ought to lay in the East, write me also how you came on at Natchez, and write another letter from Louisville and one from Cincinaty . . .

Upon inquiring, Solis learned that there were a variety of recommended and accepted practices for positioning the corpse in a Jewish burial ground. One suggested "That the feet are to lay in the East," another urged to the South, and a third preferring that the feet lay in the direction of the entrance to the cemetery. There was no set law.

Solis also received copies of the *Shanarai Chasset* constitution and by-laws that he helped frame. They had just been received from the printer. Jacob was stunned, as would be any faithful Jew, when he read a stipulation in the by-laws that:

> No Israelite child shall be excluded either from the schools, from the temple or the burial ground on account of the religion of the mother.

That the child of a non-Jewish mother could be accepted as a Jew completely contradicted the biblical and rabbinical dicta recognized by Hebrews in all lands since they became constituted as a nation at Sinai. From the day they received the Decalogue and Code of Laws and throughout all their generations, to be a Jew one must be born of a Jewish mother.

But Manis Jacobs effected that stipulation unbeknownst to Jacob Solis because he wanted his children, Felix and Thérèsa, accepted as full-fledged Jews though their mother, his wife, was a Catholic.

Virtually every Jew in the Crescent City who took a wife had intermarried with a French Catholic.

In 1807 young Joseph Gratz arrived in New Orleans on business—to trade bagging manufactured by the Gratzes in Lexington, or whiskey, hemp, tobacco, raised on their Kentucky acreage, for bales of cotton to be added to the cargo of ships sailing for Philadelphia, and ultimately for the Gratz warehouse on Market Street. His concerned sister, Rebecca, alerted him in her letter that "In New Orleans there are many who call themselves Jews, or at least whose parentage is such, but who neglect those duties which would make that title honorable and then respected—among such, my dear Joe, I hope you will never make one . . ."

Of all the urban centers in the land, why were New Orleans Jews least concerned and most lax in their Judaism?

Perhaps it was the climate, the country, the sub-tropics, as one Jewish traveler nearing New Orleans wrote:

> . . . as soon as one crosses the Mississippi, one is so to say, in another world . . . Until then one saw well-cultivated stretches of land. But now primitive woods and swamps broke the serenity. The nearer one approaches New Orleans, the more numerous the swamps seemed to the traveler and the greater in extent until one finally sees only swamps . . .

The glare of the intense sun, dispelled by a fine haze, the heavy air seeming about to liquify, and the soft, subtle light of opalescent tint gave New Orleans an appearance different from any other community in the country.

The Spanish siesta, female slaves, lively bars and taverns, the French Quarter, the Swamp, moved New Orleans citizenry in a relentless, restless, quest for a life of "wine, women, and segars," in that open port city, the Crescent City Emporium, to which came the men of all nations.

A testament to its citizens' emphasis on pleasure was made by a group of the city's churchmen who dispatched this censorious report to Rome:

> . . . There is rife in the city of New Orleans, a spirit of unbelief, or rather of godlessness which is gradually corrupting the whole mass. This plague is to be attributed to the coming of a great number of free-masons and hucksters of every description, to the spread of French maxims, to infrequent preaching of the Gospel, to love of lucre and pleasure, so much intensified by the climate and the number of female slaves . . .

New Orleans was a city of mixed and hot blood. The Mississippian/Gulf port bustled with Spanish, French, Portuguese, English, German, Negro, Indian, and Creole half-breeds. There were over 2,000 free colored crowded within half a dozen blocks on each of three sides surrounding the Place D'Arms.

Since the American takeover of the Louisiana Territory and New

Orleans, the blacks were given greater freedom on Sunday. Red wine flowed, slaves roamed freely to play for themselves, stores were open. Everywhere cards, music, billiards, dancing, attended by gaiety and revelry in a carefree existence where money and whiskey flowed until the dawn's early light and a new work week began.

Crescent City Jews blended into their environment to become morally and religiously adrift. Samuel Kohn found the city's carefree life to his liking. Overseas, in his native Bohemia, Kohn was known all over the countryside as a good-hearted, harebrained ne'er-do-well, fond of the tavern and a game of cards and fonder still of the women.

There he lost both his fortune and self-respect.

Soon after his arrival in New Orleans, Kohn became co-owner of an inn at Bayou St. John. In his "House of Entertainment" was served "the best of liquors, several rooms for private parties" and a promise "that every care and attention will be observed to render the house agreeable to those that may visit it."

He loaned his profits at interest, became a banker, investor, real estate promoter, and one of the city's leading financiers.

There being no Jewish women in the gulf port city, marriage did not concern him. His "housekeeper" Delphine Blanchard Marchegay arrived as a slave from Santo Domingo, served him well by day and by night.

Since interracial cohabitation was illegal though quite common, "housekeeper" was actually a euphemism for "concubine." Some of the most prominent New Orleanians preferred to mate with their "housekeepers" rather than legally marry according to civil if not religious law. Among these men was the Jew Daniel Warburg.

The irrepressible bon vivant Warburg, first member of that distinguished German-Jewish clan of bankers, scientists and philanthropists to come to the United States, found New Orlean's "wine, women and segars" costly. He tried to acquire instant riches by demanding $10 million from the United States government—approximately the same sum paid for the Louisiana Purchase—for "revelation of a secret to . . . what is termed the quadrature of the circle."

His cryptic demand ignored, Daniel successfully engaged in real estate, a commission business, a development firm, and became a director of the Levee Steam Cotton Press, as well as board member of the Citizen's Bank.

There were not only color distinctions between black and white, but in the degree of black, a qualitative as well as quantitative difference.

The full-blooded Negro slave had no social status. When a white man cohabited with a black slave, their mulatto offspring was elevated on the social ladder. The offspring of a white and a mulatto was a quadroon (one-fourth Negro blood), and the offspring of a white and a quadroon was an octaroon (one-eighth Negro blood)—the more white blood the higher the rung on the social ladder.

Wealthy whites were therefore especially desirous to take octaroon or quadroon girls as mistresses. Under Louisiana law, they could never live as man and wife, nor could they cohabit. Nonetheless "Quadroon Balls" were openly and publicly held in New Orleans.

One of the better known of these meeting places was the Washington Ballroom operated by Simon Sacerdote (Latin for "priest"), his surname originally Kohn (Hebrew for "priest"). He was the brother of Samuel Kohn.

Together with his French Catholic wife, Aime Dauqueminil de Morand, and Antoine Jonau, a wealthy f.m.c. (free man of color), Simon managed the Washington Ballroom.

The "Serpent Women"—quadroons and octaroons—dressed differently than white women. Their petticoats ornamented at the bottom with gold lace or fringe, richly tasseled, their slippers of gold embroidery and so their stockings. Tight-fitting velvet jackets were buttoned or laced in front, trimmed with pearl tassels, occasionally fastened to the side with clasps of jewels. The common headdress was of gold gauze braided with diamonds or of chains of gold and pearls twisted in and out of a fullness of fine black hair.

Following investigation of an interested gentleman's references, including his financial status, the mother, satisfied, would give permission for her daughter to serve as his mistress. The gentleman in turn made provisions for adequate security for both mother and daughter.

There were also generous men who made provisions for their beloved slave women with whom they mated and bore children. Jacob Monsanto, son of Isaac Rodrigues Monsanto, one of the very first known Jews to settle in New Orleans, owner of a several-hundred-acre plantation at Manchac, fell in love with his slave, Mamy or Maimi William. He baptised and made her his mistress. Their daughter Sophia, grew up to be a lovely quadroon. Jacob set Maimi in residence at 64 Bienville Street and their daughter Sophia in her own residence at 61 Bienville. One wonders if Jacob's sister, Angelica, married to her second husband, a Presbyterian minister, Dr. Robert Dow, while out strolling ever smiled to her niece quadroon Sophia Monsanto.

In his will, Jacob Monsanto remembered his mulatto mistress and quadroon daughter. "Fifty pesos to the quadroon named Sophia, daughter of the mulattress Mamy. Another 50 to said Mamy."

Jacob's daughter and his wife were Christians. So, too, were the children of fellow New Orleanian Jews and their French Catholic wives. Samuel Kohn witnessed the baptism of Edward, son of Hart Moses Shiff and his wife Margarite Basilique Chessé. Broker Asher Moses Nathan who had gone broke but regained his fortune, married to Margarite Dalton, witnessed the baptism that followed Edward's. It was his sister, Marie Virginie. Hart Moses and Margarite had both immersed in the same day. Margarite Shiff was the honored godmother at the baptism of Samuel Arthur, son of Joachin Kohn, brother of Samuel Kohn, and his wife, Marie Thalie Martin—the child named after his uncle.

And the honored godfather at the baptism of Hart and Margarite Shiff's daughter, Louisa, was Ruben L. Rochelle, a peppery Jew. His hot-blooded fierce temperament was often displayed, as that one night in 1810 when he heard two ruffians abusing a fine family on the street. Ruben ordered them away. But returning to his house, Ruben met up with them at his door, both armed with dirks and swords, demanding admittance. They threatened him with death. They forced open the door as the Jew armed himself with a sword. He held them at bay until neighbors rushed to even the sides. In his honor, the Shiffs named their daughter after his middle name, though Levin was also called Louis or Luis.

Ruben Levin Rochelle was well liked in his role as godfather at the Shiff baptism, and he was again so honored by finance wizard Samuel Hermann. Frequently when Rochelle's business partner, Hart Moses Shiff, was away from the city, it was Samuel Hermann who managed his affairs. But now was the joyous moment for Samuel and his wife, Marie Emeronthe Becnel Brou, celebrating the baptism of their second son, Louis Florian, with Rochelle as godfather. Their older son, had been baptised Samuel Edmond Hermann but later became known as Samuel Hermann, Jr.

Whereas Portuguese Jews named their children in honor of relatives or friends and the German Jews in memory of departed relations or friends, the assimilated Jews of New Orleans in the manner of their Christian counterparts named their offspring after themselves, if they so chose. The son of Maurice Barnett and his wife, Marie Céleste Trahan, was named Maurice, Jr. In attendance at the baptism was Maurice's brother Edward and his wife, Modeste Ledoux.

Last but not least, Sol Audler, secretary of *Shanarai Chasset* congregation, in the presence of proud grandparents Maurice and Marie Barnett, celebrated with his wife, Hélène (like her mother, Marie, a non-Jew) the immersion rites of their children.

Whatever names these children bore was of no significance to Jacob Solis, founder of *Shanarai Chasset* congregation. He was appalled that the baptised children of Christian mothers who remained unconverted to Judaism should be accepted as Jews. He had no regard for his predecessor-namesake Joseph Solis who had married Felecite Ducre at St. Louis Cathedral, the only place in New Orleans where weddings and baptisms were solemnized.

New Orleans attorney, Judah Benjamin, who would become famed as a brilliant jurist, eloquent orator, spokesman for the Southern way of life, married a beautiful Creole Catholic, Natalie Saint Martin. He purchased for his bride a plantation in the Louisiana bayous, six miles south of his office in the city. For her he restored and embellished the mansion called "Bellechasse."

Its graceful elegance was seen in its great double-level porches almost 15 feet across, a parade of massive rectangular pillars, curving stairways of mahogany, impressive carved decorations, silverplated door knobs, extensive rose gardens between the house and the levee and an enormous bell into which Benjamin dropped 500 silver dollars when it was being molded to sweeten the tone. Natalie, however, became bored with plantation life and left for France to permanently reside in Paris.

Despite his marriage to a Catholic and remaining apart from a Jewish community, he took pride in his ancestry. General Henry Gray, his opponent for election to the United States Senate in January, 1859, said of Benjamin: "His forefathers have crucified the Savior of the world."

Benjamin rose to the occasion and proudly replied: "It is true that I am a Jew, and when my ancestors were receiving the Ten Commandments from the immediate hand of Deity, midst the thunderings and lightnings of Mount Sinai, the ancestors of my opponent were herding swine in the forest of Great Britain."

In the Senate, too, Benjamin would be subjected to slurs about his Jewish ancestry. The Jewish Senator supported the institution of slavery—contending that it was more humane to whip and brand the black man than to imprison or transport him. Ohio's abolitionist Senator, Benjamin F. Wade, denounced Louisiana's Senator Benjamin as "An Israelite with the principles of an Egyptian."

Another Senator slurred Judah for being a Jew, which prompted Benjamin to extol his people, with whom he had never before identified, and boasted as had D'Israeli in the parliament of England: "The German will please remember that when his half-civilized ancestors were hunting wild boar in the forests of Silesia, mine were the princes of the earth."

It has been said that his relations with Jefferson Davis began as a result of some objectionable remarks about his people on the floor of the Senate in June 1858. This led to Benjamin's challenging Davis to a duel. But Davis withdrew the remarks, and mutual respect and esteem followed.

Never having studied Judaism, Judah Benjamin was unaware that according to his religion, a Jew who owned a slave was expected to convert him if he was to keep him, though he could not compel his conversion. If a slave refused to convert, Judaic law required the Hebrew master to sell him.

After being taught the Hebrew beliefs and observances, the male slave who agreed to undergo voluntary circumcision and immersion for formal induction into Judaism, and the female slave upon being immersed for her voluntary induction into Judaism, were raised above the level of the slave in such a society. The purpose was not missionary.

Conversion of a slave had a basic human goal—to grant the servant (Hebrew term for slave) a degree of freedom—that amount of free time a Jew takes to observe Sabbaths and Festivals and other holy days when rest was enjoined. Male slaves who converted were only required to observe the lesser number of biblical commandments that were observed by Jewish women and children. Thereby, every human was reminded that each individual has an inherent right to be free.

Benjamin remained to the end a brilliant defender and exponent of slavery. On his death he was interred in the Catholic Pére Lachaise Cemetery in Paris, where his selfish but devoutly Catholic wife, Natalie, lived in luxury provided by his liberal allowance.

Benjamin was a Jew who lived as a Southerner, rather than a Southerner who lived as a Jew. That intermarriage was a form of assimilation that could even lead to apostasy was fully demonstrated by one

New Orleanian Jew. Victor Souza underwent baptism 19 days before his wedding date to Rose Bourdeaux in order to marry her. But Christianity meant as little to him as did Judaism.

Soon after the honeymoon, scoundrel Souza absconded leaving his wife and creditors beyond reach. Circulars were posted throughout the territory:

WANTED

Victor Souza, a Jew, is about 4 feet 11 inches high, has a large face, large nose and a small mouth; his face is red, and his beard strong and black . . .

The reference in the wanted poster to Victor Souza, the apostate as a Jew, constituted a factual counterpart referred to in a parable of that day.

A Jewish convert, respected and honored by everyone and believed to be very wealthy, lived in a modest manner. He died at a ripe old age and was survived by many who had anticipated considerable gain through his bequests.

His will, however, bequeathed substantial property to his servants, to the poor and to good friends, but to his relatives a great iron chest found in the basement was the coveted prize. A fortune in gold was rumored to be contained therein.

When opened, the chest revealed only a painting of a cat and a mouse, beneath which was inscribed: "As this cat is too large for a mouse to eat, so Christian from Jew is an impossible feat."

"Acting Rabbis" at "Gates of Mercy"

Manis Jacobs, president of *Shanarai Chasset*, aspired to the title of "Rabbi." Though unordained, he felt his ability to recite Hebrew prayers qualified him. He proudly signed his name in Hebrew on bills of sale, as a cachet or seal—some on his transactions involving the purchase of slaves still exist.

Jacobs was the first New Orleans Jew who refused to be wedded in St. Louis Cathedral, even though he was marrying a Christian. His became distinguished as the first marriage in Louisiana Territory not performed in a church. Since there was no rabbi in that region, nor in the entire country for that matter throughout the 1830s, Manis Jacobs assumed the revered title, "Rabbi."

He led the first Crescent City High Holy Day worship in a structure at the corner of St. Louis and Franklin Streets, across the street from the St. Louis Cemetery where many early Jews slept eternally with their Catholic wives and children. In attendance was his wife, Angelique Charlotte Jacinthe Pernauille, with their son and daughter. They felt at home with other Catholic women and children, worshipping today the Father, tomorrow also the Son.

After the conclusion of the service, their Jewish husbands and other single men removed their prayer shawls, congratulated their "rabbi" and perhaps even bestowed the title of "rebbetzin" upon his wife Angelique as they extended their good wishes for a Happy New Year.

After the High Holy Day season ended, the congregation's founder, Jacob Solis, returned to the city from New York, bringing new stock to his auction house. As he prospered and became a property owner, purchasing within the year two blocks of land bounded by Josephine and St. Andrews Streets, Jacob and Solis Streets, in the heart of the city, he contributed liberally and raised funds for the acquisition of a synagogue edifice.

But as with the Cincinnati group, the sum total fell far short of the requisite amount. The one man who could have single-handedly purchased for his fellow Jews an edifice for use as a synagogue was Solis's cousin Judah Touro, the wealthiest Jew in town. But Touro, who had a reputation as an eccentric, turned down Solis's plea. Solis then turned to Harmon Hendricks, the leading Jewish merchant in New York City. Hendricks, deeply committed to Judaism, had served as President of the Portuguese congregation *Shearith Israel* since 1824. And the following year he helped launch New York City's second congregation, the Dutch German-Polish-English *B'nai Jeshurun*.

Industrialist Harmon Hendricks was the first iron monger in America. From rolling cigars he turned to rolling copper, the poor man's metal. In 1812 he opened a vast copper rolling plant—the first in the country—at Soho, near Belleville, New Jersey.

Probably his largest account was the Bostonian firm, Paul Revere & Son. The father, best known for his famous midnight ride at the outbreak of the American Revolution, was an inventor, gunmaker, gunpowder manufacturer, caster of bells and cannon, skillful engraver, artist, gold and silversmith (his *kiddush* wine goblets were a work of art). It was the Hendricks Co. that supplied the young inventor Robert Fulton with copper boilers for his first steamwasher filter.

For 30 years he would supply Fulton with copper boilers for all steamboats (the inventor had a monopoly on their manufacturer for over three decades). Thus Harmon Hendricks helped launch a new era in water travel.

The magnate, Harmon Hendricks, who owned 30 choice acres of Manhattan Island from 20th to 22nd Streets, between Sixth and Seventh Avenues, and along Broadway, contributed nearly $5,000 of the $8,000 to purchase the elegant edifice of the African Church at 119 Elm Street for the new German-rite congregation of New York City.

When Solis left for New York in the summer of 1829, he gave Manis Jacobs the name of Harmon Hendricks as a possible contributor. On August 26, Manis dispatched the exciting news in a letter to Solis that the congregation had acquired at an auction a 70 by 80 foot lot at the corner of St. Louis and Franklin Streets, for only $205. For the construction of a synagogue edifice, around $5,000 was needed, but Jacobs couldn't remember the name of the *Shearith Israel* president-philanthropist. Again from Solis he obtained the name: H. Hendricks, Esqr./New York.

On August 27, 1829, President Manis Jacobs wrote the following letter to Harmon Hendricks:

> Having heard of your Noble action and your magnanimity, towards our brethren, therefore, we the officers of the Israelite Congregation, Sharei Shisset of New Orleans, take the liberty to address ourselves to you, hoping that you will not reject our request. New Orleans had always the reputation by Israelites, Gentiles, &. to be the last place in the union for religious Societies, it is but 17 months ago that there was not here, the least iot of an Ysraelite Congregation. Since that the time they have a place of interment a Metaher House (at the cemetery for the ritual washing and dressing of the dead for burial) and a lot to build a temple on, and all that through your worthy fellow Citizen Mr. Jacob S. Solis, we now pray you to advance the Said Society the Sum of Six Thousand Dollars, with a Small Interest and Mortgage on the property till final payment for which we have authorized Mr. Jacob S. Solis to make arrangements with you . . .

Everything looked promising. New Orleans, sin city of the West, would be the first to have a synagogue; Cincinnati, second. But Jacob Solis took ill. At the Hays home in Mount Pleasant, at age 49, he suddenly died on December 29, lamented by his widow and children in New Orleans along with the membership of *Shanarai Chasset*. The congregation's officers wore crepe on their left arms during the *shloshim,* the 30 days of mourning following interment, a period of deep grief.

Three years later the New Orleans Jewish congregation finally prepared to purchase a scroll of the law, essential for public worship. Prior to that time, a printed Pentateuch had been substituted. "Rabbi" Manis Jacobs wrote to Solomon I. Isaacs, the president of *Shearith Israel,* in New York, on May 31, 1833:

> Having now commenced in a Country where no more than 33 years ago the name of an Israelite was an abomination to establish a small place to Worship the God of our Fathers and Wishing to read in the holy written Book his command every Saturday We therefore have accepted the offer of Mr. Jacob Luria and are willing to pay you what he may owe you on it you will be so kind and have it sealed with your Seal, and send it by the first Packet with his Bill in the hands of the Captain, which will be paid to him on delivering the Sephar (Torah Scroll)...

The High Holy Days nearing, Manis Jacobs additionally requested that a ram's horn be sent along with the scroll. At last a complete worship would be held.

Only in a polyglot Jewish community as existed in New Orleans could public worship have been maintained for years with neither a Torah or ram's horn to usher in the New Year. And only in the Crescent City would interments in the Jewish cemetery take place in water, for one could not dig more than a few inches beneath the surface into the swampy marshland without encountering moist and soggy soil.

In this setting, the "Rabbi" performed one of the most bizarre burial services ever. There lived two Jews outside of the city, possibly in St. John or St. Charles. Their names were unrecorded, but for the sake of clarity they will be called Michael and Israel.

The pair was engaged in business. Leah, sister to Michael, had become the wife of his partner Israel. When she was stricken with a fatal malady, Leah made her husband promise to bury her in the Jewish cemetery in New Orleans. After her passing, however, the level of the waterway had dropped so low that it was impossible to transfer her body by boat or pirogue to the city. It was too dangerous to transport the corpse by land, through soggy marshes infested with crocodiles and other reptiles.

Her body was placed in a barrel of alcohol while the mourning husband, Israel, and brother, Michael, awaited the rains to come and the water to rise, so that river travel be resumed. But the dry spell persisted. Day after day they waited, until the 30 day mourning period which usually followed interment was over, yet no final honors had been provided to the deceased.

Then the rains came, but only enough to support one man in a canoe. Summoned to the gulf port on urgent business, Israel, traveling alone, managed to reach his destination. While there, he became engaged to another woman. When he returned home it was possible to boat by water again and Michael and Israel brought the corpse to the Jewish cemetery.

Israel, attired in a black suit, was accompanied by his new bride, dressed in white. Manis Jacobs officiated over the burial.

The all-wooden casket with holes bored in its bottom as well as in its sides was lowered a foot below the moist soil to float on a pool of water. Then, two Negro gravediggers jumped onto each end of the casket, which filled with water, to sink it to the bottom of the tomb. They scrambled out, Jacobs concluded the burial prayers, and the grave was covered with a mound of mud.

As the years passed, "Rabbi" Manis Jacobs became lax in the observances of Jewish practices he formerly kept. As in years past, in 1839 he led the congregation in worship on *Yom Kippur,* the holiest day in the Jewish calendar and a day of fasting. He intoned from the High Holy Day prayer book: "On New Year's Day the decree is inscribed and on the Day of Atonement it is revealed: Who shall live and who shall die; Who shall attain the measure of advanced days and who shall not attain it; . . ."

In the afternoon of the Day of Atonement he did not remain at the synagogue but left to enjoy a hearty meal. A number of the members were shocked. Upon his return they demanded an explanation. "Rabbi" Jacobs replied that to fast was "execrable nonsense" and advised them to eat heartily.

At the close of that most holy day of Judgment, the Divine Judge, whose words were read from *Leviticus* 23:29 at New Orleans as throughout the world, sealed the fate of Manis Jacobs: "Whatsoever soul it be that shall not be afflicted (fasting included) that same day (of Atonement), he shall be cut off from his people."

The Heavenly Ruler decreed that Jacobs should not attain the measure of advanced age. Forty-seven year old Manis Jacobs died six days after *Yom Kippur.*

With interment held in *Shanarai Chasset* cemetery, controversy continued through his funeral and graveside service. Only with difficulty was Jacobs's widow restrained from placing a crucifix in his coffin.

The mantle of spiritual leadership fell upon the shoulders of Albert J. Marks. Like his predecessor he could read Hebrew, but it is not known if he could write its sacred characters.

That Rabbi Marks neither observed the Sabbath or dietary laws distressed no one, least of all Dr. Samuel Harby who was married to 15-year-old Marie Ulalie Pouillot, a Catholic. Dr. Harby was 21. His father, Isaac Harby, a playwright, was determined to strengthen Judaism by breaking with tradition and reforming the worship service, authoring an English-Hebrew prayer book with hymns adapted from Christian sources. His reformed prayer book was published in 1830. It is not known if Dr. Samuel Harby introduced his father's prayer book at *Shanarai Chasset*; to most New Orleans Jews it would not have made any difference for they did not attend.

The synagogue on St. Louis Street was visited as infrequently as the Catholic cemetery across the street. A visitor in 1842 wrote that the scroll acquired in 1833 was "so shot through with holes that even ten years ago no one would have ventured to read it." The Jewish law prohibits reading a defective scroll in public worship.

After playing Old Rowley in *The School for Scandal,* the only character for which Albert Marks received recognition in the press, he inherited the nickname "Roley." That name suited him for he was short, pudgy, round-faced, and happy-go-lucky.

Roley received meager earnings for his various duties, which included officiating at worship, secretarial services, maintaining minutes and correspondence. Rarely did he receive compensation for performing funeral rites. His dependable income was that received as captain and secretary of the Washington Fire Engine Company.

His popularity heightened as director of the Firemen's Charitable Association. To raise funds he put on a burlesque show and composed a ditty called "The Firemen's Song." For that highly acclaimed literary composition the city of New Orleans proclaimed Roley "poet laureate" of the Crescent City Firemen.

On weekdays he donned his fireman's cap, on Saturdays his rabbinical cap. In the summer he put both away to tour as an actor with theatrical appearances as far north as Kentucky. When he appeared at Louisville, theatrical producer George Washington Harby and his Kentuckian wife, Mary Olivia, applauded his character portrayals. Harby's nephew, Samuel Harby, a physician, moved from their native Charleston, South Carolina, and settled in New Orleans. He was a firm supporter of Rabbi Marks. Upon his return to New Orleans he rollicked on the stage of the American Theatre, where he probably drew a larger Jewish gathering than at the synagogue.

Rabbi-captain-actor, Albert Marks gave priority to all engagements over that of the ministry. It should not have come as any surprise, then, that on Purim eve, he was absent from the synagogue as the worshippers sat in their places to hear Roley read the scroll of Esther. That night Captain Marks was busy directing his engine company in a fire fight. His congregation never forgave. Discontent rose to a high pitch on the Jewish New Year the next fall.

Leading the opposition to Marks was Gershom (Gershon) Kursheedt, son of Israel Baer and Sarah Abigail Mendes Seixas. His father had come to America as a German immigrant in the latter part of the eighteenth century; his mother was the daughter of Gershom Mendes Seixas, "Patriot-Rabbi" during the American Revolution and of Spanish stock.

As the reverend Roley Marks ascended the pulpit on *Rosh Hashanah,* Kursheedt stood before him demanding that he step down. Roley's smile changed to a frown, and asked "Why?" Kursheedt replied in the presence of the assembled worshippers with a series of charges: that he "eats whatever comes before his maw, never keeps the Feast of Passover"; "had none of his boys circumcised" (though he performed the act for others for a fee); and for becoming beastly drunk "on the day his two sons died"—an allusion to the biblical report of the death of the two sons of the high priest Aaron who were consumed by fire on the Day of Atonement for violating their sacred trust.

In a fit of rage, Roley Marks furiously pounded the prayer desk, screaming: "By Jesus Christ! As your rabbi, I have a right to *daven* (Yiddish "to pray"), and no one will stop me!"

Statue in a Synagogue Courtyard

Upon his arrival in New Orleans in 1840, Gershom Kursheedt became the acknowledged leader of the Orthodox in the community. Many were newly arrived German Jews, immigrants who were among the first wave of the mass migration of Bavarian and Posen Jews begun in 1836. Gershom's father, Israel Baer Kursheedt, was regarded as the most learned Jew in the United States since his arrival before the turn of the century until 1840 when the pioneer rabbi Abraham Joseph Rice arrived from Bavaria and settled in Baltimore.

On September 3, 1837, Israel Baer Kursheedt, joined by prominent New Yorker Jews, published a "circular" appealing for funds to assist the large waves of needy immigrant German Jews, observing: "The number already arrived is at least 3 or 400, and the probability that an equal number are now on their way to this country, and mostly bound to the port of New York."

Little did they realize that the ripples would crest into a tidal wave that would rise in a geometric rather than an arithmetic progression. The plague of anti-Semitic legislation and special taxes were then aggravated by an economic depression that impelled not only single Jewish youths but entire families and communities to emigrate.

By 1840, 10,000 German Jews, mostly Bavarian, had reached the United States to outnumber the 5,000 native Jews, 2 to 1. Perhaps a few hundred reached New Orleans. Fifty of them, led by Gershom Kursheedt, in 1841 signed a new *Shanarai Chasset* by-laws, which barred the intermarried from membership and changed the order of prayers established in the 1828 by-laws from the Portuguese rite to the German rite.

The differences between them were minor as both were Orthodox; but while the basic prayers remained essentially the same, the selection of liturgical poetry varied a great deal. In 1845 Kursheedt led a secession and founded a new congregation named *Nefutzoth Yehudah* (Dispersed of Judah), choosing the Portuguese rite for worship and all the congregants, German Jews, agreed with the selection.

The reason for the agreement to form a Portuguese congregation was that it was named in honor of Judah Touro whose father, Reverend Isaac Touro, had ministered to the Portuguese-rite synagogue of Newport, Rhode Island, originally named *Nefutzoth Israel*. Certainly, Kursheedt and his followers thought, this would move Judah Touro to provide the congregation bearing his name with an edifice.

Kursheedt approached Touro with the dramatic news, that a congregation had been named after him. He then told of the dedication of the *B'nai Israel* synagogue edifice in Cincinnati, in 1836, the fruits of the labors of one man, Joseph Jonas. He told of how five large brass chandeliers had been received from the Portuguese congregation *Shearith Israel,* in New York, that adorned its first synagogue built in 1728. These candlestick chandeliers were shipped to New Orleans and then boated up the Mississippi and Ohio Rivers.

On the day of the dedication of *B'nai Israel,* so many Christian friends came that not all could be admitted. Joseph Jonas, president of the congregation, recalled in good humor that six years earlier a member of the building committee in reviewing plans for the structure objected vehemently: "What is the use of putting up so large a structure?" he argued. "You will have to get the *shammas* (sexton) a horse to go around and hunt up enough members to fill it. I am for building one half the size."

So great was the influx of German Jews since 1836 that by 1840 they seceded from *B'nai Israel,* founded by English Jews, which followed the Polish rite to organize *B'nai Jeshurun* (Sons of Jeshurun) and worship according to the German rite.

Joseph Jonas's dedication address was lost but its words he preserved in a *Memoir* he wrote in 1843:

> Having passed this great epoch in our history, and established our congregation on a firm basis, and having returned thanks to the Giver of all good for the protection afforded us, and for the prosperity, with His assistance, to which we have arrived at this period, let us now rest awhile, and view the Jewish horizon around us. Alas, it is a bleak and dreary view. In the whole Mississippi Valley, from the Alleghany Mountains to the city of New Orleans included, excepting Cincinnati, not a single community of Israelites is to be descried. Numerous families and individuals were located in all directions; but not another attempt at union, and the worship of our God appeared to be dead in their hearts . . .

In the early 1840s there were in New Orleans only two Jews who observed the Sabbath, and two others who maintained a kosher household; and but a third of the Jewish community circumcised their sons. Perhaps the other two thirds were of mixed marriage: Jewish fathers, Christian mothers. Little wonder that many of the fifty seats in their rented synagogue quarters were vacant even on the high holidays.

But the leadership of Gershom Kursheedt sparked new hope for the revitalization of Judaism in the Crescent City. His sincerity impressed Judah Touro, who was deeply moved. Touro had great respect for Kursheedt, a successful broker and publisher of the *New Orleans Commercial Times*. Touro abhorred the antics of "Rabbi Roley" and admired Kursheedt's stance. He therefore accepted Kursheedt's proposal to finance a synagogue named in his honor. A modest man, Touro was nonetheless deeply impressed by the honor of having a role in the founding of the Congregation *Nefutzoth Yehudah* (Dispersed of Judah). After half a century of isolation from the Jewish community, Judah Touro emerged to accept the responsibility of establishing a house of worship for these earnest men and their families.

In his unobtrusive, reserved manner, Judah Touro in 1847 exchanged a lot he owned at the corner of Canal and Dauphine with the Episcopalian Society for its lot on the corner of Canal and Bourbon, upon which stood the deteriorating frame sanctuary of their Christ Church. Judah spent many thousands of dollars to restore that edifice and effect its conversion into the *Nefutzoth Yehudah* synagogue. Its restoration took three years.

On May 14, 1850, a quiet dedication service was held in the morning. Judah Touro sealed a commemorative stone in the portal in the presence of Gershom Kursheedt and a few select persons. In the afternoon the edifice was thronged with Jews and non-Jews, with Reverend Isaac Leeser, American Jewry's spokesman, arrived from Philadelphia along with other notables. Touro was absent but the day was his.

Many of the Jews who attended the dedication absented themselves thereafter save on the High Holy Days. Touro, who was absent at the dedication, attended regularly thereafter—for Sabbath worship the year round as well as on the High Holy Days. He was as punctual in his religious attendance as he was in going to his emporium. In fact, New Orleanians began to set their watches to Touro's steps, as he went to store or synagogue. Judah Touro built a schoolhouse next to the synagogue and provided an apartment within for Kursheedt, its superintendent. But not only did Touro pay and pray, he closed his wholesale house and became a Sabbath observer. In his will he bequeathed his fortune to American, Christian, humanitarian, as well as to Jewish causes.

Neither would anyone ever know the full measure of his beneficences. Only because of public clamor to know the name of the contributor of $10,000 that was required to complete the Bunker Hill Monument was the name of that first great American-Jewish philanthropist revealed. Judah Touro additionally endowed hospitals, synagogues, churches, and orphan homes. In his will, he provided a fund to help the destitute Oriental Jews of China; he also supported the construction of almshouses outside the walls of Jerusalem, and he helped found the new city of Jerusalem. But many of his great benefactions would never be known even by his own community.

Many mourned the loss of the man interred in "The Jewish Cemetery at Newport," who was immortalized in a poem of that name by Henry Wadsworth Longfellow. Among them was the old Christian lady whose story was one of the very few preserved for posterity:

> ... on one occasion a poor widow called Mr. Touro and offered to him a moving budget of grief. She had several children, the rent was due and

her landlord threatened to eject her. She had not a cent with which to buy food or clothes. Long before she completed her affecting jeremiad, Mr. Touro filled out a check and directed her to go and draw it at once.

The poor woman proceeded to the bank accordingly and eagerly presented the check at the counter. The teller carefully examined the check and then surveying the poor, woe-begone, poorly dressed woman, shook his head and informed her that the check could not be paid. With a heavy heart and a sense of mingled shame and indignation that she should have been thus cruelly trifled with, she returned to Mr. Touro's store and handed him the check, remarked that it ill-became a rich man to subject a poor widow to insult and mockery. "The bank officer refused to give me anything for it," she said.

"Oh, yes. I see it all," exclaimed Touro. "He required proof of your identity. Here," he said, turning to his clerk, "go down to the bank with this lady and tell them to pay that check."

No wonder the teller had hesitated to pay the check for $1500 to such a poor and forlorn looking woman.

After Touro's death, his executor and trusted confidant Gershom Kursheedt was puzzled by two recipients of his benefactions. A note in the amount of $4,100 was found, made payable to Ellen Wilson, f.w.c. (free woman of color). This note led to his discovery that Judah Touro had purchased a house for her, and the deed was in her name.

But Ellen Wilson never stepped forward to claim her inheritance. It was thought that she might have been his mistress, a conjecture that was given credence when Kursheedt recalled that Touro had also appointed as executor of his will Pierre André Destrac Cazenave, a mulatto, to whom was bequeathed the sum of $10,000. Everyone knew that 29-year-old Cazenave had been Touro's confidential clerk, and his favored pet. Everyone wondered if mulatto Pierre had been his son—the son of Ellen Wilson, whom Judah may well have freed from slavery.

The answers to these questions about the extent of his benefactions and business dealings could undoubtedly have been discerned in his personal correspondence, business records, donation receipts, and other notes, but by order of Judah Touro, all were burned upon his death. For over two full days, wagonloads of record books, letters, papers, were burned in an old brick well.

At the end of a year of mourning, Hebrew congregations throughout the land, beneficiaries of his munificence, recited memorial prayers and a monument was dedicated to honor the most reverenced Jew of the century. The monument was but a simple shaft, humble as the man it recalled. It bore the well chosen words:

> The last of his name
> He inscribed it in the Book of
> Philanthropy
> To be remembered forever

But in New Orleans, the congregation *Nefutzoth Yehudah,* which bore his name, proposed a more suitable monument to honor the memory of the nation's most illustrious citizen, and the Jews' most distinguished son. Acting on their recommendation, its minister, Reverend James Koppel Gutheim, announced that a fund had been established for the purpose of erecting a life-size bronze statue of Judah Touro to stand in the *Nefutzoth Yehudah* courtyard.

A committee began actively seeking contributions for the Touro Monument Fund when there arrived in the city an exotic Turkish-born globe-trotting Jew, who introduced himself as Benjamin the Second.

His full name was Israel Joseph Benjamin. Already he had traveled five years in the Orient and North Africa. Now he planned to spend three years in the North American continent.

Invited to attend a meeting at *Shanarai Chasset,* under the ministry of the Reverend Solomon Jacobs, he was stunned to hear that funds were being requested for the erection of a statue to honor a Jew. The former rabbinical student raised a solitary, vehement voice of protest, denouncing such a tribute as forbidden in the Ten Commandments. Supported by Reverend Jacobs, the request for funds by *Nefutzoth Yehudah* was turned down.

Reverend James Gutheim decried the stranger's interference, pointing out that the renowned U.S. Naval commodore, Uriah Phillips Levy, had provided in his will that a life-size statue of himself be erected after his death and not a solitary protest was heard.

An angered Benjamin Da Silva, son of the beadle and sexton of *Nefutzoth Yehudah,* openly threatened to shoot "the meddling traveler whenever the two might meet that evening."

That this was a dire threat was recognized by any Southerner. Oscar Solomon Straus, who later became the first Jew to occupy a post in the cabinet of an American President, was then a boy living in the South. In his memoirs, recalling his boyhood, he recorded the differences between Southerners and Northerners:

In the North, when boys got to fighting, they used their fists; in the South, they used, besides their fists, sticks and stones, and consequently it was a more serious and dangerous affair. If in the North one boy cursed another or called him a liar, it would not necessarily lead to a fist fight; in fact, it usually stopped at recrimination. In the South, that kind of quarreling meant a serious fight.

Oscar Straus believed the reason Southerners took an insult more seriously was because they were accustomed to being much more polite to each other in their speech and therefore were more sensitive. Straus wrote:

> I recall one fight between two of the leading men . . . both deacons in the same church. One took out his pocket knife and cut the other's throat, and he died. After considerable delay, the murderer was tried, but because of his high standing in the community he was acquitted, doubtless on the plea of self-defense, and he got off scot-free.

Reverend Jacobs called upon Benjamin the Second to warn him of the danger to his life. He explained that in America a threat to shoot was generally executed and urged the learned traveler to notify the police.

The Jewish minister of New Orleans pointed out that duels were fought over trifles and Benjamin would well have to defend his honor according to the code of Southerners. As an example, Reverend Jacobs cited the challenge between two Jews, New Orleans merchant Solomon Audler and L. A. Levy, Jr. (probably the son of Simon Magruder Levy, a West Point cadet who died during service in Georgia, and grandson of Levy Andrew Levy, pioneer Indian trader in the Ohio Valley).

Levy's challenge was over the billing of a coat. It happened that auctioneer Asser Phillips promised Levy a linen coat at the same price as those he auctioned off in lots. When the garment did not fit, Levy exchanged it for one in the lot bought by Audler, who billed him. Since he had already paid Phillips for the coat, Levy told Audler to collect from Phillips.

Audler maintained that his was a direct dealing with Levy. The case came to court and Audler lost. Refusing to accept the verdict, he called Levy a thief. Levy, in turn, challenged Audler to a duel.

When Audler refused, Levy branded him a coward. Audler thereupon published in the press his account of the dispute and asked the public to decide whether an individual guilty of such conduct as exhibited by Levy should be entitled to a duel which satisfaction was only due to a gentleman.

"I have been required to give gentlemanly satisfaction," declared Solomon Audler. "To whom, I would ask—to a man? a gentleman? No! it is to one who cannot prove himself a gentleman, for the act with which he stands charged by me cannot be termed the act of a gentleman. A man he is not, it needs but a glance to perceive it; he was well aware at the time he wrote the challenge that he could not obtain a gentlemanly satisfaction from me, otherwise he would not have demanded it . . ."

Unable to bring Audler to take sword or pistol in hand, Levy continued to taunt him, to duel him with words, apparently in the belief that the pen is sharper than the sword. Levy's denunciation of the one he depicted as a coward was a masterpiece of invective:

> This self same Audler—this vendor of worn out harness—this wash-tub dealer has with the impudence and characteristic daring, inherent in triflers called me that which in the hearing of our most respectable citizens and in a most public place (New Exchange) he himself was called—"a Thief" Audler! Ay Audler! Sol Audler!!! and who does not shrink at the very letters of his name. He *has* been *is* and *ever will be* the detestation of the honest man, the land mark for the Coward, the beacon for the Insolvent debtor, the light house for the smuggler—he dares to speak of intrusion on the public! well may he do so. Oznaburgs, Italian silk cottonades, old swords and belts, &c. &c. groan loudly a requiem for the ledger of his poor creditors—As to an enlightened public to which he thrice appeals I will but say that it is too 'enlightened' ever again to trust this blackened lump of infamy . . . the public must condemn him for calling *me* a Thief when he himself is so notoriously known as an adept in the business . . .

Reverend Jacobs continued his account of the Code Duello amongst Jews by pointing out that if Audler was a coward, as accused by Levy, at least he remained a live one. He did not want to chance being like the hero Matthias Gomez, a great-nephew of Daniel Gomez, America's earliest Jewish fur trader to live amongst the Indians. Matthias accepted a call to a duel by one Bosqui over the correct wording of a stanza in a poem. The weapons were muskets; the distance forty paces.

Bosqui had previously killed his cousin in a duel, but Gomez had no fear. Upon the count, Gomez and Bosqui wheeled and fired four times. Bosqui, wounded in both legs, fired a fifth shot and Gomez fell dead.

Karl Cohen was among the witnesses and wrote to his uncle, Samuel Kohn, then in Paris: "The physicians thought it incumbent upon them to have one of his (Bosqui's) legs amputated, but he, fluttering as he was between life & death, preferred rather to die than to be maimed, & would not permit his limb to be amputated—now he is almost able to walk again to the great disappointment of every orderly & quiet townsman—."

Reverend Jacobs stopped with this duel, telling Benjamin the Second that these were but a few of the many duels fought between adversaries who sought gentlemanly satisfaction to any affront.

Fearlessly, the intrepid traveler who would prove his dexterity in handling six-shooters against attacking stagecoach bandits, visited the various quarters of the Creole City. "Luckily for both of us," Israel Joseph Benjamin wrote in his diary, "we did not meet. Indeed, I was not afraid of being overpowered by him, for I had been lucky enough to ward off many an attack. However, I had never yet had to fight against a fellow Jew."

Jewishness of the American Indian

In the year 1836 when the exodus of German Jews was set into motion and they reached western shores, the last of the Indian tribes inhabiting those shores were driven from their ancestral lands. These were the civilized Creek Nation, forced by the federal government to flee Georgia and Alabama by land and river routes that were called the "Trail of Tears," then to cross the "Great River"—the Mississippi—and resettle along the Red and Arkansas Rivers in the Arkansas Territory.

A few years earlier, the civilized Choctaw Nation of Mississippi had been driven to the Arkansas Territory. In 1866 they appropriately named the land to which they had been exiled Okla-homa, meaning in their language, "people-red," recalling that they were robbed of their hunting grounds and fishing waters because of the color of their skin.

Unlike the tribes north of the Ohio that the white man accused of being "savages," the southern tribes were civilized by European standards. Unlike the northern Iroquois, Illinois, Delaware, Potawatomi, Sauk, Miami, Shawnee, forced west because they were regarded as subhuman, the Lower Ohio tribes—the dominant Cherokee, Catawba, Chickasaw, Choctaw, Creek—were cultured, assimilated into the dress, habits, and civilization of the white man.

The "Five Civilized Nations," as they were called, adopted the ways of the white man. The Seminole dressed like gentlemen and frontiersmen; the Chickasaw built houses and courthouses and towns; the Cherokee raised crops on their fenced farms; the Choctaw owned cotton plantations and black slaves, and published a newspaper in their language; the Creek produced a Bible in their tongue.

But the "civilized" American white man, driven by greed for land, began to classify the "Five Civilized Nations" as savage wolves in sheep's clothing who must be driven into the wilds beyond the Great River. The land in the Red River country would be the Indians' reserve "as long as the grass shall grow and the rivers shall flow."

Thus were the dispossessed five nations forcibly moved by trails past Nashville and western Kentucky and by the Tennessee River across the Mississippi to the Arkansas River and Territory.

Sad indeed was the parting at Coosada Bluff, Alabama, between 86-year-old Abraham M. Mordecai and his lovely Creek wife, married almost half a century. Tears streamed from his deep hazel eyes, as the puckish old man, short in stature, watched his beloved exiled with her people, the Upper Creek, fade in the distance as she took the infamous "Trail of Tears" to the Far West.

Who was this unusual Jew living isolated in the wilds of Indian country, away from family and community? Very little has been recorded about him.

It seems that Abraham M. Mordecai was born out of wedlock, fathered by Moses Mordecai, in 1755. Virile for his age, the 49-year-old Englishman, Moses Mordecai, fell in love with teenaged Elizabeth Whitlock, a Christian, and five years later they came to America. In Philadelphia she converted to Judaism, married Moses Mordecai under the Hebrew name Esther. She gave birth to a son, Isaac, and when she was 18 to another son, Jacob. A fourth son was born when she was 22 and Mordecai almost 60. Since Moses Mordecai had already given his sons the name of the patriarchs, to his newborn infant, was assigned Joseph.

As for Abraham, a stigma must have been attached to his being born out of wedlock, though Judaism would not regard him illegitimate, the general community may well have whispered him to be a bastard. Such a stigma no doubt moved him to remove as far from Philadelphia and the eastern seaboard as possible, away from the white man's civilization.

Pennsylvania-born Abraham M. Mordecai, a veteran of the American Revolution settled in 1783 at a place called Buzzard Roost on the Flint River in southwestern Georgia. There he built a cabin and adjoining storehouse. He traded with the Kashita tribe in whose midst he lived, and he set out on trips into the wilderness to barter with other tribes.

In many a settlement he came upon white women and children taken captive by the Shawnee during their incursions into Kentucky and Tennessee. He bartered for food or wampum with the southern tribes.

Mordecai's friendly relations with the chieftains as well as his knowledge of all the trails and villages deep in Indian country gained him an appointment by Indian Agent James Seagrove to seek out captured whites and arrange for their redemption. On his mission the Jew penetrated into the very heart of the Chickasaw, passed the Falls of the Black Warrior to arrange for the release of hapless wives and children of frontiersmen.

About 1790 Mordecai moved his stock westward to the mouth of Line Creek in Alabama (where the city of Montgomery would rise). He occupied one of the few buildings of mortar and frame in that country that had been built by the Spanish during the Colonial Period. Settled amidst the Curvalla tribe of the Creek Nation, Mordecai bartered manufactured goods for peltries, pink-root and hickory nut.

Squaws cracked the hickory nuts, brewed their oil for baking Indian cakes. These were considered a delicacy by the Spaniards living along the Gulf Coast who spiced the cakes with condiments.

The oil of hickory nuts was much in demand. Obtained from boiling the broken nuts in pots of water and skimming the oil as it floated to the top, it was then put into barrels for shipment. Mordecai had the barrels of hickory oil transported by the Curvalla tribesmen over the Pensacola Trail to the gulf city of that name and to coastal Mobile, even to far off New Orleans in large canoes. On one occasion the governor of New Orleans requested 30 gallons of the brewed hickory oil extract.

Other Mordecai pack trains carried many bales of peltries to Augusta, the leading center for Indian furs in the South.

Learning of the cotton gin (invented by Eli Whitney in 1793) Abraham became convinced of its potentialities. He arranged with the Koasati Chief of the Hickory Creek for property rights to erect a gin house on their land, at the eastern river bluff below the confluence of the Coosa and the Tallapoosa.

Koasati meant "cane," a prophetic word, as Mordecai's destiny would prove. Mordecai's cotton gin, the first in Alabama, was built in 1802 by the Jewish draftsmen, Lyons & Barnett of Augusta. They brought their tools, gin saws and other work materials on horseback to that beautiful bluff overlooking the two riverways. From the very first year he operated the cotton gin it proved its worth. It was easy for squaws to paddle canoes laden with raw cotton to the site.

The cleaned cotton subsequently brought a high price at the New Orleans Cotton Market, and with his portion of the profits, Mordecai bought a $400 riverboat. Three years after building of the gin house, catastrophe struck. Two of Mordecai's horses wandered into a tribal field and ate the young corn. The Chief of the Koasati, Isaak Towerculla, increasingly jealous of the trader's influence with his people, mustered 16 braves whom he armed with long hickory canes.

Confronted by the warriors, Abraham offered to pay for the loss. The Chief struck him. As Abraham struggled with Isaak, the braves beat him to the ground with their staves.

Regaining consciousness, the Jew found his gin house, barge and cotton bales in smouldering ruins. His left ear was almost totally severed from his head and his body covered with bruises. His wife nursed him back to health.

Married to an Indian girl, Mordecai rationalized—as had other Jews—that the Indians were descendants of the Lost Ten Tribes of Israel. As evidence of this descendence, Abraham who learned to speak the Creek tongue fluently and became integrated into their customs and manners, declared that during the performance of the Creek's "Green Corn Dance" he heard them uttering the expression "Yavoyaha, Yavoyaha," which they told him meant Great Spirit, their term for God. To Mordecai it sounded like Jehovah, Jehovah, to whom they gave thanks for their harvest.

To his wife he owed his recovery and his life. She was the woman who helped him lay the foundation of a great city. When she was removed from him in old age, life lost all meaning to him. Thereafter Mordecai lived in a small Indian hut, where he constructed his own coffin, off which he ate until he died at the age of exactly 100 years.

Abraham Mordecai never learned if his wife reached the land to which she was exiled—Oklahoma. He sadly watched as she and her people were forced to leave their native land, Alabama, while the marauding whites plundered their vacated homes. On the "Trail of Tears" she and her people suffered worse deprivations and miseries. Stalked by the troops who kept them constantly on the move, many moccasins worn through, they walked barefoot and nearly naked; many of the once proud people were so weakened by hunger and disease that they dropped and died in their tracks. The survivors struggled for life in their exiled Oklahoma reservation.

Their plight and that of all Indians driven across the Mississippi into the Far West deeply concerned the American-Jewish leader, Mordecai Manuel Noah.

Mordecai Noah, son of a revolutionary soldier who served as aide de camp to General Washington, was one of the most versatile and admired men of his day. A publisher, duelist, dramatist, politician, consul, sheriff, he became grand sachem of Tammany Hall, surveyor of the Port of New York, and judge of the Court of General Sessions of New York.

When Noah was appointed sheriff of New York County, a political opponent declared that it would be a pity to have a Jew hang a Christian. Noah retorted that he would be a fine Christian to have to be hanged.

Sheriff Noah was as quick on the draw as he was quick-witted. This was the lesson learned by the Southern Jew, John Canter, who for some trifling, refused to accept from Noah either explanation or apology, but summoned him to a duel.

Noah's close friend, John Getty, speaker of the house and later governor of South Carolina, lent him horses and carriage and a case of fine hair triggers.

On a delightful June morning Noah rode into a green valley outside Charleston, with a surgeon engaged alongside him. A few carriages dotted the meadow, as did men in gigs, on horseback, others who had walked, a cluster of Negroes, groups of neighbors already assembled, some betting on the outcome.

Soon Canter and his suite appeared.

Noah, as the challenged, had the choice of weapons, position, and distance. He chose pistols, back to back, to wheel and fire at ten paces apart, at the word.

"Gentlemen, are you ready?"

"Ready," responded two resolute clear voices.

"Wheel and fire!"

They turned, fired; the challenger reeled and fell. Noah stood apprehensive as spectators dashed forward to crowd about Canter's body. To Noah's relief, he heard Canter shout vindictively, "I'll have another shot!" But he was unable to rise. Noah's bullet had penetrated the calf of his left leg, below the knee, and it was bleeding profusely. Noah's surgeon dug out the bullet and lifted Canter aboard Speaker Getty's carriage.

On June 15, 1812, Noah wrote to his uncle, Naphtali Phillips, editor of the *National Advocate,* "In order to prevent any uneasiness, I state to you that a puppy by the name of John Canter had the insolence to send me a challenge to fight him. I accordingly met him on Sunday last and pumped him the first shot in the leg, to the joy of all Charleston ... I was very cool and comfortable on the occasion."

During his stay in Charleston, he was awarded the title "major" but not because of his standing in the Militia of New York State. Challenged to a duel by one Joshua W. Toomer, Mordecai Noah winged his challenger. Two South Carolinian militia officers present bestowed upon the declared winner, Mordecai Manuel Noah, the title of major. Afterward he told with glee that the militia officers were the only persons present to witness the duel, the duo serving as "seconds."

Mordecai Noah stood up for the defense of the rights of others as for himself. After the War of 1812 he was appointed consul to Tunis, there seeking the freedom of American sailors seized by the pirate vessels of that nation and its neighboring Barbary States. Soon after his return to America he dreamt of a western haven for oppressed European Jews and downtrodden American Indians.

A leading exponent of the ten-tribes theory was Elias Boudinot, one-time president of the Continental Congress and later president of the Board of Directors of The American Society for Meliorating the Condition of the Jews. Dr. Boudinot published at Trenton, New Jersey, in 1816 a booklet entitled "A Star in the West; or, A Humble Attempt to Discover the Long Lost Ten Tribes of Israel." He, too, was interested in identifying the natives as Jews ripe for conversion.

But Boudinot was not satisfied with the proofs advanced by those who preceded him. He expressed the wish that absolute evidence be presented to prove that the American Indians were descended from the ancient Israelites so that they may share in the restoration of Jewry to Zion and Jerusalem.

Such proof was brought to Boudinot's attention two years later. An account by Elkanah Watson, a pioneer of the village of Pittsfield in the Berkshire Hills of Massachusetts, dated November 10, 1815, told of the discovery of a Hebrew phylactery on the outskirts of the settlement. It was found by Captain Joseph Merrick on his farm, on a hill at the south end of Lake Onata.

Boudinot learned that Pittsfield's first settlers were incorporated by the Great and General Court of Massachusetts in 1753 as "The Proprietors of the Settling lots in the Township of Poonstoosuck." With the French and Indians on the warpath, they built a fort "Indian Hill" (where the Mohegans once worshipped), which became known as "Fort Hill." While ploughing that ground, Merrick found, a few inches below the surface, the Hebrew phylactery. It was then that Elkanah Watson rushed over to Merrick's house, finding several clergymen there. One of these was probably Reverend William Allen of Pittsfield. They opined that the ancient relic found its way into the area by means of the lost descendants of Israel—the Indians. Watson surmised that after the Ten Tribes crossed the Bering Strait and peopled the continent from pole to pole, "those in the extreme north and south, becoming the most savage, as in the milder regions they have been found the most civilized, and in possession of arts and sciences, especially in the City of Mexico and Peru."

When in 1823 Reverend Ethan Smith, Pastor of the Congregational Church of Poultney, Vermont, published his "View of the Hebrews" supporting the contention that the Indians were the Ten Lost Tribes, President Griffin of Williams College called his attention to the discovery of the phylactery in Pittsfield. Reverend Smith immediately traveled to Pittsfield to behold the find and interview settlers. He learned that townsman Sylvester Larned, anxious that the relic not be lost, had brought the phylactery to the American Antiquarian Society at Worcester, Massachusetts, of which he was a member. But upon the Society's failure to honor a condition that a description of the phylactery be published in its annual report that year, Larned presented the historic find to the Honorable Elias Boudinot of New Jersey.

Dr. Boudinot was satisfied that proof positive at last had been discovered, not only in the relic itself but in the confirmation of Reverend Smith, who was told by the townspeople that "no Jew was ever known in Pittsfield." Neither Smith nor Boudinot was aware that the name of Isaac Isaacs appeared on the Pittsfield military rolls in 1780-1781, nor that Jewish traders traveled the Mohawk Trail, the main colonial thoroughfare of western Massachusetts, less than two days' travel from the trading center of Albany, New York. As far as they were concerned they possessed irrefutable evidence that the Indians and Israelites were blood-brothers of common ancestry.

M. M. Noah, playright and publisher of *The New York Inquirer,* the *Commercial Advertiser, The Times and Messenger,* and two New York daily newspapers, the *National Advocate* and *Evening Star* (though not all concurrently), was a friend of publisher Solomon H. Jackson (whose niece he would marry). Jackson in 1824 edited the first American-Jewish magazine published in the United States.

The Jew: Being a Defense of Judaism Against All Adversaries and Particularly Against the Insidious Attacks of Israel's Advocate, was a polemic against Christian missionary activity (Israel's advocate), which preached conversion of the Jews.

The Jew had few readers, and was discontinued within a year. At that time, Mordecai Manuel Noah launched a project to combat a missionary plan proposed by the American Society for Meliorating the Condition of the Jews. Founded in 1820 by the Honorable Elias Boudinot, the Society was seeking 20,000 acres to accommodate 200 Jewish families to be converted. Noah's countermeasure was to establish a colony for all needy Jews, for those persecuted in other lands, and for the exiled tribes of the American Indians.

Noah was convinced that a Jewish haven in the American wilderness was feasible, for such an all-Jewish colony thrived for a century and a half in the wilds of the Surinam jungles. Jewish plantationers cultivated cane fields and built sugar refineries along the Paramaribo River in Dutch Guiana. Upon a hillock by the river, deep inland, they cleared jungleland and built a city, Die Joden-Savannah (the Jewish-Savannah), complete with synagogue, court, school, fire department, and stores. Their own Jewish Militia protected their plantations and city. What was achieved in South America could be repeated in North America on a grander scale, thought Noah.

Together with a Christian friend, Samuel Leggett, Noah purchased 2,555 acres in thickly wooded Grand Island opposite Tonawanda where the newly completed Erie Canal met the Niagara River.

At dawn on September 15, 1825, the day after the Hebrew New Year, Buffalo's inhabitants were awakened by a thundering blast of cannon. At this unannounced salute, 2,500 astounded villagers rose to look out of their windows and rush into the street to the sight of parading Military and Masonic companies.

First came the marching soldiers, led by Grand Marshal Colonel John Potter. Then followed the ranks of national, state, and municipal officers. Next in step were the militia in full uniform, followed by Masons in their ceremonial regalia, accompanied by Indians bedecked with feathered war bonnets.

Marching directly behind the grand marshal and before the troops was Mordecai Manuel Noah, attired in black drape covered with a cloak of crimson silk, trimmed in white ermine.

The procession advanced solemnly to the shore of Lake Erie where there were not enough boats to transport the paraders to Grand Island. After hasty evaluation of the situation, all were led by the grand marshal back to town, to St. Paul's Episcopal Church, the only building large enough to accommodate the paraders and villagers.

Referring to himself as governor of Israel, Noah announced that he had come to lay the cornerstone of a New Zion for his oppressed people. The cornerstone, taken from its cart, was placed on the communion table. The band struck up the grand march from *Judas Maccabeus*. After appropriate biblical readings, Noah issued a proclamation, announcing the restoration of a Jewish nation to an American Zion. The self-proclaimed governor commanded that a global census of dues be taken from all Jews and a tax of three shekels in silver be levied annually. Jewish soldiers in European armies were to stay in service "until further orders." Magnanimously he allowed those Jews who wished to remain in their adopted countries to do so, but he demanded full cooperation from all.

In his call to Grand Island's Ararat, Noah particularly directed his invitation to the American Indians. He conjectured that they were of the nine and a half tribes captured by the Assyrian King, the tribes that, owing to their earlier suffering in Egyptian bondage, had wandered in a northwest direction, which brought them into the American continent.

As proofs of their Hebrew origin, Noah observed that they worship one Supreme Being, are divided into tribes as were the ancient Israelites, and that "Some of these tribes it is said are named after the Cherubimical figures that were carried on the four principal standards of Israel." Furthermore, they deemed themselves the select and beloved people of God. Their words, sonorous and bold, as their language evidenced Hebraic origin. They computed time like the Jews, dividing the year into four seasons and the months by the new Moons which commenced like "the eccelesiastical year of Moses, the first Moon after the vernal equinox." Their High Priests and prophets, towns of refuge, sacrificial cult, marriage and mourning customs, all resembled those of the Jews.

Asked Noah: "How came they on this continent, and if indigenous, when did they acquire the principles and essential forms of the Jews?"

Noah insisted that "The Indians are not Savages, they are wild and savage in their habits, but possess great vigour of intellect and native talent—they are a brave and eloquent people, with an Asiatic complexion, and Jewish features.

Eloquently, Noah pleaded: "If the tribes could be brought together, could be made sensible of their origin, could be civilized, and restored to their long-lost brethren, what joy to our people, what glory to our God, how clearly have the prophecies been fulfilled, how certain our dispersion, how miraculous our preservation, how providential our deliverance."

This dramatic address was reprinted in full by the New York *Evening Post,* on Saturday, September 24, 1825. Despite its impact, Noah found himself with few supporters.

To Erasmus H. Simon, Esq., of Utica, New York, Noah wrote a month after the Ararat dedication in a letter dated New York, 22 October 1825:

> Your favour from Utica has been duly received,—and for the obligding terms in which you are pleased to approve my recent measures towards our proscribed & unhappy bretheren I pray you accept my thanks. . . . I feel happy to perceive that you concur with me in opinion, that the aborigines of America, are the descendants of our lost tribes. You may not be apprised of the fact, that Manasseh ben Israel wrote a work 200 years ago, attempting to shew that they are the remnant of the lost tribes, relying upon facts produced to him by the first voyagers to Mexico.—[James] Adair & [Elias] Budinot have both written interesting works on the subject, & Sir Alexander McKenzie in his travels on the North West Coast affirms, that the Indians near the Copper Islands preserve the right of Circumcision. Your intentions of residing amongst them and endeavouring to soften & humanise them, in honorable to your feelings & creditable to your principles.—I shall not fail in the project I have undertaken, & shall settle a small congregation on Grand Island, from which tender plant may in time spring up a goodly & flourishing tree . . .

Two years passed when a New Orleans newspaper reported that "Two German Jews and their families, living in Jeffersonville, Indiana, of the names of Young and Fishley are preparing to proceed to Grand Island, on the Niagara River, to inhabit the new town laid off there, by M. M. Noah, prince of Israel, called the city of refuge."

A decade passed and neither Young, Fishley, nor any other Jew had come to settle in the modern Noah's Ararat. Convinced that only the ancient homeland of Israel could become the New Zion, for only that holy and promised land possessed the mystique to attract the descendants of the twelve tribes, Noah turned his attention to Palestine, which once again would become the Land of Israel, the homeland for all oppressed Jews, including Indians. The land of the Patriarchs, Noah believed, could be acquired by purchase and most assuredly by divine intervention. But to include the return of the native Americans, he would prove that they were the lost ten tribes and as such rejoin the two tribes in their ancient hunting grounds and fishing waters.

In 1837, a year after the Creek Nation was exiled with their kin southern tribes beyond the "Great River," Mordecai Manuel Noah addressed the Mercantile Library Association of New York on "Evidences of the American Indians being the descendants of the Lost Ten Tribes of Israel."

Noah affirmed that the Indians believed in the Unity of God. To the One they called the ".Great Spirit" they dedicated temples and altars modeled after the Holy Temple of Jerusalem.

They set aside a day of atonement, when they dressed in white doeskin and moccasins. In the spring they celebrated the Feast of Flowers, reminiscent of the Festival of Passover; at the beginning of summer, the Feast of First Fruits, their Pentecost; and in the fall, the Feast of Booths, like the Jewish Festival of Tabernacles.

And at the very time Noah prepared his address from the Oklahoma exile of the southern tribes came reports that the Yuchi Tribe, formerly of Carolina, were seen by travelers perambulating with plants during the autumnal full moon and dwelling in huts as did Jews the world over during that time.

Noah asked rhetorically:

> Weren't the Indians organized into tribal units with the land belonging to the tribe, rather than the individual as in ancient Israel? Also, like the ancient Israelites, each tribe recognized a Chief as their head. True, many Indian tribes no longer practice circumcision, yet hadn't the Jews in their forty years of journeying into the desert set aside the rite because of dangers from the elements.

Furthermore, the Indians manifested the Jewish traits of friendliness and kindliness described in a letter from Christopher Columbus to Ferdinand and Isabella, and Noah quoted in part:

> I swear to your majesties that there is not a better people in the world than these, more affectionate or mild. They love their neighbors as themselves. Their language is the sweetest, the softest and most cheerful, for they always speak smilingly.

From the writings of early adventurers and missionaries Noah adduced that the American Indians, like the Jews, kept some sort of kosher diet. They abominated the flesh of the swine, abstained from ingesting the blood of an animal, and even refused scaleless fish. Noah concluded that the natives "neither in mind, manner nor religion, bear any affinity to the Tartar Race." Asked Noah, "If they were not of the lost tribes of Israel, then who were they?"

In the mid-16th century, Bishop Diego de Landa was in the Yucatán, New Spain. He heard elderly Mayan tribesmen repeat folklore transmitted to them from their ancestors which was Hebraic in essence. One of these seemed to be a page taken directly out of the *Midrash,* the sacred Hebrew tome which preserves early legends. The Maya told that "his land was occupied by a race of people who came from the East and whom God had delivered by opening twelve paths through the sea."

Bishop de Landa concluded that "if this were true, it necessarily follows that all inhabitants of the Indies are the descendants of the Jews."

The Maya of the Yucatán were a highly cultured people. By the time of Columbus's discovery of the New World, they had achieved a civilization of superb architecture, sculpture, painting, astronomy, and a calendrical and counting system superior to their European counterparts.

The Maya, who invented the first written language in the Western Hemisphere, a system of hieroglyphics inscribed upon bark cloth paper and etched in stone, left a number of Hebraic representations upon them. An intricate carving upon a six-foot stone stela found at Campeche in the Yucatán depicted a Mayan dignitary wearing earrings upon which are engraved the Star of David. Across the lower half of the hexagonal star, wavy lines indicate an ocean crossing, and three waves carved beneath an anchor clutched in his left hand, indicate arrival.

The shape of the dignitary's hat resembled a boat, much like a rock carving uncovered among the ruins of the Jewish necropolis of *Beth She'arim* in the Holy Land. Part of the anchor held by the Maya appeared in a similar form upon ancient Judean coins. The Star of David upon his earrings was like that drawn upon a Hebrew merchant ship found in the *Beth She'arim* ruins. Most striking of the hexagonal stars was that giant Star of David etched on the 62nd step leading to the top of the Great Pyramid of Maya, identical to that etched in the Caperneum Synagogue of ancient Israel.

Much of their civilization went up in smoke when Bishop Diego de Landa ordered the Spanish to burn as many of the Mayan bark-cloth books as they could find, because they "contained nothing but superstitions and falsehoods of the Devil."

The Mayas were all but forgotten when in the mid-17th century there appeared one Antonio (Antony) de Montezinos in Amsterdam, Holland, before the famed Rabbi Manasseh ben Israel. Antonio repeated under oath that in 1639, he was traveling from Honda in the West Indies (now Colombia) to Popayan (province of Quito) Ecuador in the Viceroyalty of Peru, on mules with Indians led by Francisco "Cacique" (Chief).

During their crossing of the Cordillera mountain range, a violent storm struck. The Indians cursed their hard life, but Francisco calmed them and told them they would soon have a day of rest. They replied that they did not deserve it for they had so ill treated a holy people, and they deserved the Spanish cruelties. Francisco remarked to Antonio that an unknown people would avenge the Spanish cruelty.

Upon his return to Colombia, Antonio de Montezinos was imprisoned by the Inquisition at Cartagena. There he determined that upon his release, he would seek out Francisco and learn more about the "unknown people." Indeed he proceeded to the port of Honda, found Francisco, and the Indian agreed to once again accompany Montezinos on a journey inland. The *Marrano* revealed himself to be a Hebrew of the tribe of Levy. "What were the names of your ancestors?" asked Francisco. Montezinos answered "they were called Abraham, Isaac and Jacob." The Indian then asked, "Have you no other father?" "Yes," replied Montezinos, "his name was Luis de Montezinos." Again, the Indian repeated his query and after many others, said to him: "Are you not a son of Israel?" "Yes," replied the *Marrano*. Then the Indian rather angrily said, "So say so right away, instead of confusing me to death . . ."

Francisco then agreed to take Antonio de Montezinos to the "unknown people." They came to a river after two days travel, when three men and a woman met them in a canoe. After conversing with Francisco and Montezinos, to whom his guide served as translator, the three men and a woman disclosed that they were descendants of the tribe of Reuben and recited the Hebrew declaration of faith: *Shemah Israel Adonoy Elohenu Adonay Ehad* ("Hear O Israel the Lord Our God the Lord is One"). Montezinos was not allowed to cross into their land, but was visited by other Reubenites.

On their return journey, Francisco told Montezinos that the Indians had sought to slay these Reubenites but were defeated. From the latter the former learned that they were of the children of Israel whose God is the true God.

To the Dutch rabbi, Montezinos described them as tanned by the sun, their hair reached to the knees, though some wore it shorter; their heads covered with cloth. They were of good height, comely, and well proportioned.

Rabbi Manasseh ben Israel published this account in Amsterdam in 1650, entitled *Esperanca de Israel*. It was republished two years later in London under its English title, *Hope of Israel*.

The famed rabbi, whose books contained some illustrations drawn by his neighbor, one Rembrandt, noted in his *Hope of Israel* that "He (Montezinos) made the same oath on his death bed, which is where time most obliges man not to incur such a sin as perjury. All this being the case, why should I not give credit to a virtuous man, an enemy of self-interest? . . ."

Rabbi Manasseh added weight to Montezinos's account by recalling that he had seen illuminating Hebrew inscriptions in the Azores upon which were depicted synagogues, two of them identified as located in the Viceroyalty of Peru, at Guamanga and Tiahuancau. He noted that they appeared similar to synagogues erected in China. Rabbi Manasseh ben Israel concluded that the exiled ten tribes traveled from Palestine to the Orient, some continuing on to America.

Manasseh ben Israel further bolstered the ten tribes theory by the observation that the Indians of Mexico (Aztec), the Yucatán (Maya), and Peru (Inca), kept perpetual fires burning upon their altars as did the ancient Israelites in the Temple of Jerusalem.

This similarity was taken up by the Britisher, Viscount Kingsborough, who devoted his life and fortune to prove the thesis that the Indians were descended from the tribes of Israel. He noted that both the Mexicans and Israelites believed in miracles, in angels and devils, and in offering sacrifices poured the blood upon the ground. Moreover, the High Priest of Peru was the only one allowed to enter the innermost sacred section of the Temple as did the ancient High Priest of Jerusalem.

And in the region between Mexico to the north and Peru to the south, Father Joseph Gumilla declared: "I have found that the nations of Orinocco and its streams observe many Hebrew ceremonies handed down from father to son, without being able to assign any reason for the practice of them."

The reports of missionary priests and the rabbi, particularly the latter's *Esperanca de Israel,* stirred deep interests among the clergy in Protestant England. The very year 1650 that Manasseh ben Israel published his report of the Reubenites, a lost tribe of Israel, being discovered in America, Reverend Thomas Thorowgood of Norfolk, England, followed up with his *Jews in America, or Probabilities that the Americans are of that Race,* and an adjunct: "An Epistolicall Discourse of Mr. John Dury to Mr. Thorowgood. Concerning his conjecture that the Americans are descended from the Israelites. With the History of a Portugall Jew Antonie Monterinos, attested by Manasseh Ben Israel, to the same effect."

Thorowgood further announced his sensational discovery that all the Indians were descended from the lost tribes of Israel. Actually his rediscovery had already been published by Father Diego Duran in 1585 in his *History of the Indies and New Spain.* Duran alluded to the Indian/Israelite theory when he stated: "My opinion and supposition is confirmed that these natives are of the Ten Tribes of Israel that Salmanasser, King of Assyrians, made prisoners and carried to Assyria in the time of Hosea, King of Israel."

Thorowgood, troubled by the cannibalistic practices of certain Indian tribes, found an answer in Scripture: "And ye shall eat the flesh of your sons, and the flesh of your daughters, shall ye eat." This was in fulfillment of the divinely decreed malediction for the children of Israel who did not remain true to His commandments.

But that biblical source did not satisfy those who questioned such a rite as the Aztec, leading captive children to the summit of their temple-pyramid, there to stretch them upon the altar stone, slash their tender breasts with an obsidian knife, and tear out their palpitating hearts to appease their pantheistic god of nature. Nonetheless, Scripture continued to be the source of clergymen seeking to substantiate their ten tribes theory.

At a later date when questions were raised regarding the circumcised Chippewa who did not hesitate to scalp his captives, the Reverend Charles Crawford, Esq., quoted Scripture in his document, "An Essay Upon the Propagation of the Gospel," published in Philadelphia in 1799. "God shall wound the head of his enemies and the hairy scalp of such a one as goeth on still in his trespasses." Such tortuous practices were punishment for sin.

There was probably a good deal of speculation as to whether the good reverend was related to Colonel William Crawford, captured in 1782 while fighting Indians in the Upper Sandusky, in Ohio. Five other prisoners were tomahawked and scalped by squaws and boys who dangled the bloody scalps in Crawford's face. Crawford was stripped, tied to a stake, shot 70 loads of gunpowder into his body, cut off his ears, jabbed the hot ends of burning sticks into his skin while the women threw live coals they gathered up in bark upon his bare flesh. Two hours had passed when an Indian scalped him and another put live coals where his scalp had been. Slowly they roasted Colonel William Crawford to death.

How was it possible to maintain that the Indians who practiced such cruelties were related to the Israelites? The answer is to be found in Puritan theology having its beginnings in England with such clergymen as the Reverend Thomas Thorowgood and was promptly espoused in the Puritan settlements of Cape Cod, America.

In 1626, Puritans in Massachusetts came upon the Indian village of Nahum Keike which the Reverend John White revealed to be a Hebrew name. In his tract, "The Planter's Plea," London, 1630, White disclosed that those words meant "The Bosom of Consolation." The Puritans unknowingly had replaced that "Hebrew" named Indian village with Salem, also a Hebrew word, meaning Peace.

Certainly, opined John Eliot, this pointed to a Jewish origin for the Indian, and he taught that the 37th chapter of Ezekiel principally applied "to the Indians as such Jews."

Eliot further taught to Puritans the widespread belief among Christians of their day that the millenium would come when Jews would be scattered throughout every corner of the earth and then "called" for conversion to Christianity. He disregarded the arguments against the Indians being of Jewish descent as those advanced by Sir Hamon L'Estrange, a well-known theologian, who in 1652 published those arguments in his book: *Americans no Jewes, or Improbabilities that the Americans are of that Race.*

To Eliot it was only logical to identify the American Indians as Jews by seeking biblical sources. At the same time, he and the Puritans of his day, classed Jews along with unwanted Papists and heathens. The Indian was a different kind of Jew, to be looked upon with sentimental piety for these were living descendants of biblical Jews, ripe for conversion.

Reverend John Eliot preached from his pulpit in Roxbury, a Boston suburb, the gospel to the Indians. He converted 24 who in turn he sent out as missionaries, to convert not heathens but the progeny of the Hebrew patriarchs, to Christianity.

So, too, Roger Williams, the clergyman who fled Puritan Massachusetts because he advocated religious freedom for all men and founded Rhode Island, like Eliot developed intimate friendships with the tribes of his colony. In seeking to convert them, he discerned their beliefs to be akin to those of the Hebrews: "They hold that Nanawitnawit (God Above) made the heaven and the earth and some taste of affinity with the Hebrews, I have found," wrote Reverend Williams.

Another preacher of the time was the Quaker William Penn, founder of Pennsylvania, a colony where religious freedom would be enjoyed by men of all faiths. Shortly after Penn arrived in 1682, he sailed upriver on the Delaware to make a treaty with the tribes of his region, exchanging wampum belts with Chief Tamenend of the Delaware under the Shackamaxon elm near Philadelphia. During his visit he learned that they believed in the divinity of God and fundamental Hebrew belief in immortality. Penn wrote: "For their origin I am ready to believe them of the Jewish race, I mean of the stock of the Ten Tribes."

Penn's view had earlier been stated by Sir Charles Beatty who published in London in 1678 his "Journal of a Two-Months' Tour." Of his visit to the region, he noted that the Delaware Indians retained traces of Jewish origin.

Penn and Beatty's assumptions were strengthened by one Gabriel Thomas who in 1698 published at London a promotional pamphlet seeking to attract settlers to the new province. The booklet, entitled "An Historical and Geographical Account of Pennsylvania," included his observations of the Indians and their religious practices:

> The Natives, or first Inhabitants of this Country in their Original, are suppos'd by most People to have been of the Ten Scattered Tribes, for they resemble the Jews very much in the Make of their Persons, and Tincture of their Complexions; they observe New Moons, they offer their first Fruits to a Maneto, or suppos'd Deity·... and have a kind of Feast of Tabernacles, laying their Altars upon Twelve Stones, observe a sort of Mourning twelve Months, Customs of Women, and many other Rites...

At the turn of the century, in 1701, Antoine Cadillac established a fort on the Great Lakes (Detroit), and identified the Indians as being of the Israelite tribes. He detected a remarkable similarity in the customs of the Great Lakes tribes with those of the Jews. Cadillac noted "the Indians' concern about pollution and purification and the separation of married couples during the woman's menstrual period, the women living in separate tepees. Not only did this accord with the Hebrew precept but so too did their custom that the brother of a brave whose widow remained childless was to marry his bereft sister-in-law in order to perpetuate the brothers' name among the clansmen." Rabbi Manasseh ben Israel had likewise noted that the Indians of Guatemala and Peru observed the biblical law of the Levirate, unchanged since ancient days among the native Americans.

Half a century later Indian agent to the Cherokee, James Adair, published a monumental *History of the American Indians*. Living among the tribes south of the Ohio River, amongst the Cherokee, Catawba, Chickasaw, for over thirty years, Adair became fully conversant in their languages, customs and practices. Convinced of their Hebrew origins, he advanced in his history 23 arguments as certain proof that the American Indians descended from the Jews.

Before the American Revolution, when Daniel Boone and a few other daring adventurers penetrated deep into the Blue Grass Country toward the Ohio River, news of the discovery of "Naphtalites" deep in the Ohio Valley was reported. Two letters that told the story were published in a leaflet printed overseas at Frankfurt and Leipzig in 1774. It was entitled: "Thoughts of a Country Clergyman about a certain Jewish Settlement discovered on the Ohio River, written for reflection especially by reasonable Israelites."

The first of the two letters, dated December 3, 1773, opens as follows:

> Some time ago I read in the public newspaper (issue of November 30th), under the heading "London," a report saying that on the Ohio River there is a settlement of Jews who pretend that they are descendants *of the tribe of Naphtali,* and (that they came there as far back in time as when the Temple) of Solomon was still standing . . .

A few years passed when two Scotch Virginia settlers described their capture and escape from Hebrew speaking Indians. Their pamphlet, published in 1786 in Bennington, Vermont, was entitled: "A Surprising Account of the Captivity and Escape of Philip M'Donald & Alexander M'Leod of Virginia From the Chickkemoggs Indians and of their Great Discoveries in the Western World From June 1779 to January 1786 when they returned in health to their friends, after an absence of six years and a half years Written by Themselves."

The two men described their captivity and escape from Indians in 1779, and their wanderings and adventures in unknown western wildernesses. By October, the duo reached "a large river, or sea" which might have been Lake Michigan. Navigating this body of water in an Indian canoe, they were driven by a great storm for two weeks until they reached a shore of great trees and scant underbrush. Finally, after journeying afoot westward again, they reached "a large plain kind of tract free from every sort of vegetation." So vague and general is this description that it makes geographical identification impossible. M'Donald, who studied Hebrew at the University of Edinburgh, continues the narrative, relating that they "... were suddenly surprised by a human figure who with amazing agility jumped from a rock into the road, and walked towards us in seeming astonishment ... his aspect open, and free from that savage fierceness so conspicuous in the American Indians in general ... on his nearer approach he exclaimed in the Hebrew language—What creatures can these be? On hearing him speak, though imperfectly a language which we understood, who can express our joy? ... He was pleased beyond measure to hear us speak, and told us to apprehend no danger from him, for he belonged to a race of beings that never intentionally did harm to any creature ..."

Their fantastic tale met with such interest and popular acceptance that their little pamphlet was republished in Keene, New Hampshire in 1794, in Haverhill, New Hampshire in 1796 and in Rutland, Vermont in 1797.

They described the Great Lakes Indians as living in "a large regular built city ... houses were beautiful and lofty, tho' consisting of but two stories, and the people appeared to be exceedingly kind and tractable ... prohibited by their religion from war ..." While any Canadian *voyageur* would have scoffed at such a yarn, the country folk of the White Mountains of New Hampshire and those of the Green Mountains of Vermont believed it all.

One Jew, his name unrecorded, was curious enough to learn the truth about the Jewish origins of the Indian that he learned their language, probably in trading with them, and settled amongst them in 1837, somewhere in the vicinity of the Great Lakes. His view, recorded by French missionaries, was in opposition to the possibility of such a common origin:

> Originally possessed of a small fortune, he had exhausted it in travelling for the sake of his brethren, having gone to North America to investigate the question whether or not the Indians there were really the descendants of the ten tribes. He had lived a year among the Winnebagos and Micmacs, learned the Cherokee [Chippewa] and Oneida languages, conformed to their manner, often living almost naked in order to ascertain that question which he did not hesitate to decide in the negative.

As the question of the origin of the American Indian puzzled layman and scholar alike, what seemed to be proof positive was announced by David Wyrick, a printer of Newark, Ohio, who dabbled in ancient languages.

In the summer of 1860 he was digging in a mound, the type that had been laboriously raised by early tribes who carried and graded countless baskets of earth to create hillocks as holy sites for worship and burial. When the first white men entered into the Ohio Valley, for reasons known only to themselves, they ceased to form these sacred sites.

Wyrick excavated a great mound situated a mile southwest of the Licking River that meandered through Newark. There he found a wedge-shaped stone, six inches long and three inches wide. It tapered to a flattened surface about half an inch in diameter. A handle rested on the head of the wedge at the other end. On each of its four sides was a Hebrew inscription: *Melech Aretz* (King of the earth); *Toras Adonoy* (Law of the Lord); *Devar Adonoy* (Word of the Lord); and *Kodesh Kadashim* (Holy of Holies).

That find in June was followed by a much more important discovery in November. Wyrick unearthed a stone casket, 18 inches long and 12 inches wide. Within was a slab that was over 6 inches long, over an inch thick, and almost 3 inches wide. On one side was an etching of a fierce human figure dressed in priestly robes and turbaned; above him was the Hebrew word *Mosheh,* topped by an arched border carved with the Hebrew characters of the Ten Commandments. The letters were oddly shaped and similiar letters were found on a few broken stones unearthed nearby.

A short distance from this find was also uncovered a large wooden trough, rotted, within which lay a parcel of human bones, a locket of very fine black hair, and 10 copper rings.

None of these stirred as intense interest as did the stone figure of Moses and Ten Commandments which became called the "Holy Stones of Newark." Their authenticity was confirmed by a Dr. Nicol, Episcopalian minister of Newark. The Christian missionary, M. R. Miller, secured a loan of the "Holy Stones of Newark," brought them to Cincinnati, to two scholarly rabbis, Dr. Maxmillian Lilienthal and Dr. Bernard Illowy.

Lilienthal declared these stones to be "the strangest things he had ever seen." After careful examination he concluded that the "Moses Stone" was the oldest because of its earlier Hebrew script. Dr. Illowy concurred and suggested a number of ingenious interpretations of their origins.

The Chicago rabbi, Dr. Bernard Felsenthal was then visiting Cincinnati. He too studied them and sent an account of the find and stones to Dr. Abraham Geiger of Breslau, Germany, world renowned for his publication, *Wissenschaft des Judentums,* (the Science of Judaism). Felsenthal wrote to Geiger that "since the supposition that these are forgeries is scarcely admissible, it is worth the while of investigators for scientific reasons to devote attention to the interpretation of these stones."

Geiger carefully examined the accompanying photographic reproductions of the stones and concluded that "they were the bungling work of an unskilled stone mason and the strangeness of some letters as well as the many mistakes and trans-positions was his fault. The letters are not antique. This is not a relic of hoary antiquity nor is it of historical critical value for the Decalogue. I am unable to determine when and for what purpose this work of religious hocus-pocus was produced."

As their authenticity was being debated, printer Wyrick sold the "Holy Stones of Newark" to David M. Johnson of Coshocton, Ohio, about 30 miles northeast of Newark. David M. may have been a son or relation of David I. Johnson who was an Ohio pioneer and founder of the synagogue *B'nai Israel* in Cincinnati.

Then there was observed on a cliff above the Licking River a large black rock shaped like a hand that pointed towards the mound of the holy stones. R. E. Chambers, a medical doctor, advanced the following theory:

> This hand pointed to the mound that contained the last rabbi who ministered at the altar. Doubtless when his work was done his followers gave a burial that went to show their love and esteem, in the

mound they raised over his remains and the tablet that was as a guide to their faith, and then put the hand on the rock, pointing to the place of his burial.

David Wyrick died amidst the exciting controversy. Only then did the truth of his hoax emerge. In his office, bits of slate were found with crude Hebrew letters carved upon them, also a copy of the wood cut of the Moses figure chiseled upon the stone. Wyrick himself had manufactured the relics, hidden them in the mound, and dug them up in the presence of reliable, unimpeachable witnesses.

Why had he perpetrated the deception?

The answer was given by those who knew David Wyrick. So convinced was he that the American Indians descended from the tribes of Israel that to substantiate the theory he espoused with such fanatical zeal, Wyrick himself prepared and then planted the evidence.

Actually Wyrick accomplished the very opposite. All of the 10 tribes theories became ridiculed *ad absurdum, ad infinitum.*

In addition to the American Indian, nine other peoples were believed to be descended from the lost 10 tribes of Israel. This descent was claimed by families and tribes in the province of Manipur, India; Khaibar in Northern Arabia; the Abyssinian Falasha; Afghan Chiefs; Burmese Kareens; Japanese Shindai; Mesopotamian Nestorians of Armenia; also the Sinew-Pluckers, as Chinese called the Jews living in their midst for over two millennia; and last but not least, Anglo-Saxons.

The Anglo-Saxons who claimed descent from the lost tribes of Israel hailed from the tribe of Dan, who passing over into Denmark left its name upon that land. The Irish branch of the English Danites were said to have brought with them Jacob's stone, which the Bible relates, the patriarch used as a pillow the night he rested at Mount Moriah, site of the future Holy Temple of Jerusalem. That venerated rock has always been used as the coronation-stone of Scottish and English kings (now preserved in Westminster Abbey).

But, it would be asked, their appearance belied their descent from the Israelite patriarchs. It was claimed that Jews could be recognized not so much by the Moses they honored as by the noses they sported; it was not the Mosaic but the Nosaic that distinguished them. This argument became the subject of a witty discussion between an Irishman and a Jew.

Queried O'Flaherty, "If it's as yez say, that the Oirish bees wan av th' Troibees av Ishrael thot left the other troibes an' settled in Oireland, how come it that yez noses be so large while the Oirish have hardly any noses at all?"

Replied the German-Jew Hockenheimer: "Dot was soon egsblained. Ven your dribe left our dribes dey cut off dere noses to spite dere faces."

There were few who would declare in favor of the American Indian being descended from the ancient Israelite tribes when 30 years after the Wyrick hoax was exposed, there was unearthed in a burial mound at Bat Creek, in eastern Tennessee, under one of nine skeletons, a rock bearing a Hebrew inscription in the ancient Canaanite script. It was translated to read "for the Land of Judah." Skeptics soon learned that this was no hocus-pocus. It was a genuine stone, over 2,000 years old. Scholars concluded that in 534-531 B.C., a number of Jews had departed the port of Ezion Geber (present day Eilat, Israel) and sailed across the Mediterranean and Atlantic to the American continent.

At Clay City, Kentucky, there was found further evidence to substantiate this opinion. Coins dated the first century A.D., depicted the Bar Kokhba revolt against the Romans. These indicated subsequent crossings of Hebrews fleeing the ancient state of Judea after their last rebellion.

And the people in this country south of the Ohio were neither Anglo-Saxon, Negro, or Indian, nor had their ancestors descended from them. They were and are Caucasians, known as Melungeons, believed to be descendants of a Mediterranean people, of the "Land of Judah" according to the rock inscription.

Did Mediterranean people, such as those of the "Land of Judah," leave the names of their lands of origin engraved in rock? An inscription engraved on a cliff above Mount Hope Bay in Bristol, Rhode Island, discovered in 1780, announced in Punic: "Voyagers from Tarshish this stone proclaims."

Tarshish was a Biblical city on the southern coast of Spain, a major seaport in its day, and any large vessel capable of making a long sea voyage was referred to as a "ship of Tarshish." The Babylonian Talmud tells of Jews who traveled from the Land of Israel on to Spain for a voyage of one year, remained a year at their destination, and returned after an absence of three years.

On whose ships did these Israelites sail? Celtic Iberians ruled Iberia until about 533 B.C., when Tarshish was destroyed by the neighboring

Carthaginians from the opposite African coast. That the Celts had been in the New World was confirmed by such inscriptions as that found on Monhegan Island, ten miles off the coast of Maine, which read: "Cargo platforms for ships from Phoenicia" written in Celtic.

After the triumph of Carthage over Tarshish, a partnership between these peoples began and together they sailed to Celtic settlements in America, scattered from the Atlantic Ocean to the Mississippi Valley. They trapped, tanned, mined. Their valuable furs, hides, and metals were brought back across the seas to the lands of the Mediterranean. Celts had settled America as early as the ninth century B.C., when the Ten Tribes of Israel went into exile.

Thus we are left to ponder the enigma of the origin of the American Indian. Though the majority of ethnogenists, ethnologists, ethnohistorians, as well as anthropologists and other antiquarian researchers believe, as did those who rejected the ten tribes theory, absolute negative proof remains unsupported.

Of all American Jews, few felt a more common bond to the displaced Indian than the Mitchell brothers, Jacob, Hyman, and Louis, among the first of their people in the Arkansas Territory. They opened a trading post in Little Rock on the Arkansas River soon after the town was chartered in 1831. Branches were soon opened, one at Fort Smith, another in Oklahoma. In their dealings, they acquired an old Spanish land grant deed to the Hot Springs Mountain, located about 50 miles southwest of Little Rock.

Ignoring the title possessed by the brothers, the United States government set aside four sections of land around the hot springs. The Mitchell brothers contested the government action, arguing that the springs in question, over forty in all, had originally been discovered by the Spanish conquistador Hernando de Soto, in 1541. The thermal waters that flowed from the depths of the mountain had for hundreds of years prior to its discovery been a source of healing to the Caddo, Osage, and Quapaw tribes. Convinced of its healing powers, the Mitchell brothers claimed they legally acquired from the Spanish government the rights of ownership and that they sought to promote the region as a health resort.

Though the court ruled in favor of the federal government, the brothers appealed. Confident of victory, they built a hotel at the base of Hot Springs Mountain during their litigation in 1839. To facilitate the transportation of health seekers from Little Rock and eastern Arkansas, they ran a stagecoach between the steamboat center at Little Rock and the straggling little villages springing up around Hot Springs Mountain in the Ouachita Mountain Range.

Much of their time, energy, and funds was spent in the territorial courthouse during prolonged hearings on their appeal. After 50 years their plea was adjudicated. The Supreme Court of the United States ruled in favor of the federal government.

The Mitchell brothers began to feel a strong kinship with the dispossessed American Indians.

Judah Touro, Jewish philanthropist. *Courtesy Frick Art Reference Library*

Nefutzoth Yehudah (Touro Synagogue), New Orleans, was dedicated in 1850.

The Touro Block, New Orleans, built by Judah Touro.

Bark *Judah Touro,* one of Touro's cargo vessels.
Courtesy of Peabody Museum of Salem

Judah Phillips Benjamin, Attorney General of the Confederacy.
Courtesy American Jewish Historical Society

Plantation home of Judah Benjamin at Bellechasse, Louisiana.
Courtesy Dr. Bertram Wallace Korn

BILL OF SALE.—Printed at the Petersburg, Va., Intelligencer Office.

The State of South Carolina:

KNOW ALL MEN BY THESE PRESENTS, That I, ANSLEY DAVIS,

for and in consideration of the sum of *Four hundred & twenty five Dollars*

to *me* in hand paid, at and before the sealing and delivery of these presents, *by Abraham Tobias* (the receipt whereof I do hereby acknowledge) have bargained and sold, and by these presents, do bargain, sell, and deliver to the said *Abraham Tobias a female Slave named Savy about 15 years of age warranted Sound & Healthy*

TO HAVE AND TO HOLD The said Slave *with her future Issue & Increase*

unto the said *Abraham Tobias his* ——

Executors, and Administrators and Assigns, to *his* and *their* only proper use and behoof forever. And I, the said ANSLEY DAVIS, my

Executors, and Administrators, the said bargained premises unto the said *Abraham Tobias his* ——

Executors, and Administrators and Assigns, from and against all persons shall and will warrant and forever defend, by these presents.

IN WITNESS whereof I have hereunto set my Hand and Seal, Dated at *Charleston* on the *fourteenth* day of *December* in the year of our Lord one Thousand Eight Hundred and Forty-*four* and in the Sixty-ninth year of the Independence of the United States of America.

Signed, Sealed and Delivered } in the Presence of

M. Lopez

Ansley Davis [SEAL]

Slave bill of sale for Ansley Davis, 1844. *Courtesy Dr. Bertram Wallace Korn*

Mordecai Manuel Noah, publisher, politician, consul, sheriff, and grand sachem of Tammany Hall.

Courtesy American Jewish Historical Society

DISCOURSE

ON

THE EVIDENCES

OF

THE AMERICAN INDIANS

BEING THE DESCENDANTS

OF THE

LOST TRIBES OF ISRAEL.

DELIVERED BEFORE THE

MERCANTILE LIBRARY ASSOCIATION,

CLINTON HALL.

BY M. M. NOAH.

NEW-YORK:
JAMES VAN NORDEN,
No. 27 Pine-street.
1837.

Title page of address by Mordecai Noah (published 1837).

Henry Castro, colonizer of Texas Republic; background Castroville, Texas. *Courtesy El Paso Libr*

Jamaica-born Jacob de Cordova, Texas land agent and publisher.

Don Adolpho Sterne, fighter for Texas independence.
Courtesy Hoya Memorial Library and Museum

6

The Israelites' Role in the Conquest of the Southwest

Spanish Land Grants North of the Rio Grande

West and south of the Arkansas Territory lay a vast empty region that reached from the Red River to the Rio Grande. Spanish *conquistadores* first entered this land in 1541, led by explorer Francisco Vasquez de Coronado, in search of the "Seven Golden Cities of Cibola," glorified by Indian legend.

De Coronado and his troops learned from members of the Hasinai Confederacy who inhabited this land that they called it in their Indian tongue, *Tejas,* meaning "allies" or "friends." The Spaniards corrupted that name to read "Teyas" or "Texas."

After subduing a number of tribes south of the Rio Grande, the *Marrano* conquistador Luis de Carvajal y de la Cueva was declared governor general of the newly created state of Nuevo Reino de Leon (New Kingdom of Leon) in 1579. This encompassed the gulf lands from the port of Tampico 1,000 miles northward beyond the Rio Grande to the Indian village of Yanaguana (the future San Antonio, Texas) and extending inland 600 miles.

After successfully colonizing the region around Tampico, De Carvajal turned northward but before he could accomplish additional settlements the Holy Office seized him. After lengthy and tortured interrogations, he succumbed in 1590 in a dungeon-cell of the Inquisition in Mexico.

One hundred one years later, Father Damien Massanet, escorted by 50 soldiers, set up a mission at Yanaguana and christened the Indian encampment San Antonio. The next priest to arrive, Fray Antonio de San Buenaventura Olivares, founded in 1718 Mission San Antonio de Valero (later named the Alamo). Governor Don Martin de Alarcon erected nearby Villa de Bejar (later spelled Bexar) and stationed his troops there to protect the mission from Indian attack.

In the over 100 years after the mission was founded no more than 4,000 Spaniards herded their livestock to graze on the coastal gulf strip of Texas. Few ventured to settle north of the Rio Grande as they feared the cannibal Karankawa, the savage Apache, and the ferocious Comanche.

There were a few hundred settlers in San Antonio at the turn of the century. Spanish rule then began to weaken. Mexicans north of the Rio Grande were fired with the spirit of revolution. A Mexican deputation from the governing body of the province of Coahuila-Texas, consisting of General Bernado Guiteres and Captain Manshac, arrived in the U.S. outpost at Natchitoches, Louisiana. There Lieutenant Magee, a West Point graduate of 1809, was stationed. They offered him the command with the rank of colonel of the combined force of Mexicans and Anglo-Americans in that town.

Magee assumed command and wrote of his new role in Mexican freedom to his West Point colleague, Samuel Noah (son of Elias, and cousin of Mordecai Manuel Noah), who held the position of first lieutenant. Noah, allured by visions of adventure, set off to join Magee and lead the few undisciplined men camped on the Brazos River. He led this regiment to Fort Bahia, which they entered on November 14, 1812. The Spanish forces rallied and counterattacked with a force five times the strength of the garrison. At that critical moment, Colonel Magee sickened and died. Lieutenant Noah assumed command of the rear guard which on April 4, 1813, pursued and routed the Royalist Spaniards in sharp combat near San Antonio. Three days of fighting ensued and Noah triumphantly entered the capital of Texas, forcing the surrender of Governor Salcido with his entire force.

Samuel Noah, the uncrowned ruler of Texas, then learned of the United States' declaration of war against Great Britain. Loyal to his country, Noah covertly escaped from Mexican Texas and after many perils reached Washington, D.C., to fight with the American forces.

After Samuel Noah's flight from Texas, a Spanish force led by Don Joaquin Arrendondo slaughtered the rebels near the Medina River and at San Antonio executed the male population. He forced the women to grind corn into flour and bake tortillas for his troops.

The American revolt squelched, San Antonio was but a shell of its former self and Texas, an empty wilderness save for a pirate settlement, Campeache, on the Island of Galveston. There, since 1816, pirate Jean Laffite with his aide Jao de la Porta—a Portuguese *Marrano* Jew—ruled supreme as he had before the War of 1812 at Barataria in the Louisiana Bayou.

It will be recalled that after the War of 1812 President Madison pardoned the Laffite brothers and the buccaneers under their command. Many pirates took up a peaceful life as good citizens. But not the Laffites. Jean and Pierre Laffite, their fleet, buildings, and mansion at Barataria south of New Orleans destroyed, schemed to reorganize their pirate empire. But first they enrolled as undercover agents in the Intelligence Service of Spain, the very nation against whom Jean had vowed "eternal war." The Spanish believed that the Laffites, who were former patriotic Americans, had turned against the United States government for not compensating its destruction of their pirate empire.

Jean Laffite, operating as Secret Agent 13-2 and Pierre Laffite as Secret Agent 13-1, went to spy on New Orleanian citizens conspiring against Spain. They were to dispatch all information to their superiors in Havana, using code number 227-4916-6269-4766-5717-1327.

As the Laffite brothers were about to begin their new role, Havana was concerned over the occupation of Galveston Island on the Texas coast by Mexican rebels who were joined by privateers and pirates capturing Spanish vessels.

Unknown to Spanish authorities at Havana was the fact that heading the pirate forces were the other two Laffite brothers, Dominique You and René Béluche. Their square-rigged schooners wrought havoc with the Spanish ships. René, whom the revolutionist leader Commander Juan Batista de Arismandi called "Béluche the Gallant" named his vessel *General Arismandi*. Overhead their vessels they flew the flag of the "United Colonies" (Venezuela and New Granada).

Agents 13-2 and 13-1 dispatched to their superiors a classified communiqué wherein they suggested a plan to rid the gulf waters of all pirates and destroy the rebel stronghold at Galveston Island.

The plot was as simple as it was ingenious. A small fleet under the captaincy of Jean and Pierre Laffite, each vessel flying a privateer flag, would sail into Galveston Bay unchallenged and take the island by surprise. Incoming pirate vessels would then be confiscated, the crews placed in irons and sent off to Havana.

Jean Laffite's plan was approved and his request for funds was so convincingly presented that over $40,000 was advanced to him to establish a Spanish base at Galveston Island.

Jean Laffite sailed off to Texas with an entire fleet outfitted by Spain. He arrived to find the buildings deserted, the rebels and pirates gone.

Jean Laffite now set himself to the task to reorganize his pirate empire and prey upon Spanish shipping. In the old Spanish fort on the bayside of the snake infested sandy island the Spaniards had called *Islo Serpentine* he established temporary headquarters as he ordered his band to work. They built an entire fort: complete with arsenal, stockyard, boarding house, huts for themselves and their mistresses, houses for those with wives and children, and the most pretentious of all, Jean Laffite's lavish red mansion—*La Maison Rouge*.

"Campeache," as the pirate lair became known, attracted pirate vessels from all the gulf. The Laffite fort was located at the tip of Galveston Island by the inlet leading into Galveston Bay, a safe shelter from pursuing vessels and hurricanes. Most important, it was situated in New Spain, free from interference by the United States.

When pursued, Laffite's swift schooners would deliberately lure the captains of attacking vessels into the Bay. The pursuers, unfamiliar with its traps, would inevitably run afoul on one of the many hidden reefs, particularly "April Fool Pass."

Laffite's fleet increased to 50 great slooped schooners skimming the gulf waters in packs, in search of Spanish sail and returning with the treasure galleons.

Jean, who had spent eight months mapping the area between the Red and Sabine Rivers, had smuggled goods and slaves into Donaldsonville, about 50 miles west of New Orleans. From that station, river craft transported the slaves and merchandise north to St. Louis and to nearby New Orleans.

Their greatest danger was not the Spanish but the cannibal Karankawa. These Indian supermen were seven feet tall, handsome but ferocious, and included human flesh in their daily diet, which they carved from live as well as dead victims. In fact, it was they who were responsible for the refusal of Mexicans to cross north of the Rio Grande and settle in Texas.

Thus it happened one day on a hunting trip to the western end of Galveston Island that a few burly pirates raided a Karankawa camp and finding the men away carried off an attractive squaw each. But their pleasures were short-lived.

In the midst of their love-petting, the giant "Kronks" seized their captors, tied their hands and feet round trees. Slicing off their flesh, the fierce savages ate it raw in full view of their living larder.

In 1819, Jean Laffite learned that Spain granted the United States vessels permission to sail their territorial waters. He warned all his men not to attack any American ships, only those of Spain. It was then that Laffite's lieutenant, George Brown, nicknamed "Ferocious," requested of his captain to take leave and search out Spanish sail, declaring "If I take anything that isn't Spanish, you may hang me, Capitaine."

To which Laffite replied, and he was serious, "All right. If you do, I will hang you."

Once in the open Gulf, "Ferocious" exchanged fire with the United States cutter *Lynx,* which then pursued the pirate ship. Driven into a bayou, "Ferocious" and his crew tumbled ashore and made their way down the coast toward Campeache.

By the time the *Lynx* dropped anchor off Campeache, "Ferocious" had been hanged. The *Lynx* departed and a crisis had been averted.

Again in 1821, one of Laffite's captains disobediently attacked and scuttled an American vessel in Matagorda Bay. The United States dispatched to Galveston, the brig-of-war *Enterprise.*

Given the choice of getting out or being blown out, Laffite chose to leave and was given sixty days to disband and depart.

On Saturday night, March 3, 1821, the chief of the pirates of the Gulf, set torch to his Galveston colony. As he sailed off, *La Maison Rouge* engulfed in fiery scarlet, the Jewish pirate's heart beat with strong satisfaction for the Mexican Revolution had begun. He was confident that even as Argentina gained its independence from Spain in 1816, Chile in 1818, Colombia in 1819, so, too, would

New Spain's Mexico achieve its freedom. Soon the Inquisition in Mexico City would close its doors, after 300 years. His people had been avenged.

In September 1821 Mexico achieved independence. The Santa Fe Trail was opened for American traders and settlers to come to New Mexico, and they would be equally welcome into the former Spanish Texas.

It was then that Moses Austin who had in his youth been actively involved with the Gratz brothers in the development of the Ohio Valley, now in St. Louis, turned toward establishing an American settlement in Spanish Texas. In a meeting with Commandant General Arrendondo at his villa in San Antonio, Moses Austin in 1820 received confirmation of a Spanish land grant along the banks of the Rio de los Brazos de Dios (River of the Arms of God). However, 63-year-old Moses succumbed to pneumonia and was on his deathbed. His son, 27-year-old Stephen, swore to carry out the agreement.

He established two colonies, one settlement at Washington-on-the-Brazos and another, Columbus on the Colorado River. Further upriver others proceeded to found San Felipe de Austin.

These villages consisted of wretched wooden shanties and cabins scattered at random about a Main Street of tree stumps jutting freshly from the earth. The former Missourians, now Spanish nationals, cleared the land and hunted game. The men were envied by their wives, who dressed in drab calico and spent their days stirring hog and hominy with homemade wooden spoons, one of them remarking, "Texas is a heaven for men and dogs but hell for women and oxen."

News reached them after their arrival in 1821 that revolutionaries had triumphed and Mexico was at last independent from Spain. While they rejoiced that freedom had come to their new land, they were concerned about confirming their Spanish land grants.

Stephen Austin hurried off to the Mexican capital but had to remain there for an entire year, engaged in frustrating negotiations with a new Mexican government operating in confusion. Finally, in the spring of 1823, he managed to obtain a ruling recognizing the non-Hispanic colonies with land grants in Texas.

Austin's colonists welcomed their confirmed land titles. The Jew, Samuel Isaacs (Isaaks), from one of the original 300 families (comprised of 1,800 persons and 443 slaves), was allotted "a Spanish Grant of one league (4,428.4 acres grazing land) and one labor (177.13612 acres farming land)," situated about midway between the Gulf Coast and the upriver settlement of Washington-on-the-Brazos.

If Samuel Isaacs was a forerunner of the pioneer Isaacs of England who would soon settle in New York, Cincinnati, and elsewhere, he must have been the black sheep of the family, for Austin and his colonists, Isaacs included, had gone through the ceremony of affiliation with the Roman Church. The Mexican government diligently enforced its statues, withholding ownership of land from those not of the Catholic faith.

But the Mexican government was slipshod about the way foreigners were allowed to exercise political privileges without becoming citizens. It was satisfied with the strict standards set by Austin who required each colonist's character to be "practically unblemished, that he is a moral and industrious man, and absolutely free from the vice of intoxication."

As an extension of its encouragement to other Americans to settle in Texas and develop that northeastern section of Mexico neglected by Mexicans who feared the fierce Indian tribes, the Mexican government established in 1824 a democratic constitution. Attracted by Mexico's liberal attitude toward American immigrants, Adolphus Sterne, a rollicking young German Jew, upon the death of his parents in New Orleans in 1824, drifted there by way of Tennessee (where he met Samuel Houston, the future first president of the Lone Star State). Sterne took in stride the dangers and hardships of frontier Nacogdoches—Texas's easternmost settlement—and opened there a trading post.

Since its establishment in 1779, the Mexican outpost Nacogdoches, situated about 50 miles west of the Sabine River (the boundary between Mexican Texas and the United States), became a strongly garrisoned Spanish fortress after the Louisiana Purchase, and continued in the Mexican period to guard neutral ground between Mexicans and Americans. Nacogdoches military post at Mexico's northeastern border ranked in importance with other key garrisons spanning northern Mexico: Goliad, San Antonio, and Santa Fe along the Gila Trail; El Paso and Albuquerque along the Rio Grande; San Diego, Los Angeles, Monterey, and San Francisco along El Camino Real (King's Highway).

It had been Mexico's design to assimilate the American colonists and settlers into her own culture. However, American culture language, and religious differences as well as vigorous odds over slavery (forbidden in Mexico) dissipated all dreams of integrating the former Americans into the Mexican culture.

That its borders with the United States were becoming rapidly Americanized had become eminently clear in 1826 when Anglo-American Haden Edwards was granted a large land grant near the Sabine River for colonization. Arrogantly styling himself "military commander" instead of protecting the rights of earlier Spanish settlers, Haden demanded they show evidence of title many failed to keep. Those unable to produce the required proof had their lands sold to the highest bidder. Haden pocketed the proceeds.

When the Mexican officials received word of what was occurring they annulled Haden's grant and ordered him out of the country.

Without weighing the justice of the Mexican government's action, American settlers' aggressiveness asserted itself. Backed by Adolphus Sterne who supplied flints and powder secreted in bales of dry goods and barrels of coffee, "Commander" Edwards rode into Nacogdoches with a group of about 20 insurgents in the winter of 1826. They seized the old stone fort and proclaimed the Republic of Fredonia, combining the word "freedom" with the Latin "nia," meaning "place." Raising the red and white banner upon which was inscribed "Independence, Liberty, Justice," he demanded freedom for all American Texans.

A Mexican force drove Edwards and his followers across the Sabine River and out of Texas. Sterne was arrested in Nacogdoches. Tried and sentenced to be shot, he was chained in jail and awaiting execution when his life was spared through an amnesty granted by Stephen Austin.

Sterne's traitorous acts were soon forgiven and forgotten by the Mexican government and he was appointed to various offices, including postmaster, even elected and reelected *alcalde* (mayor) for many years.

By Gulf to Galveston

Twelve-year-old Dutch-born David Kokernot, living with his parents in New Orleans, fell in love with the Mississippi and apprenticed as a pilot to Captain John Summers.

By the time he was 19, the thrifty Dutch lad amassed $3,000 and started his first business venture. The daring Jewish lad bought flour, lard and bacon, and with his cargo sailed aboard the *George Washington* to Port au Prince, Santo Domingo. He returned to the Crescent City to establish himself there as a tradesman. But after six years the sea beckoned him once more.

On October 1, 1830, David Kokernot received his commission from President Andrew Jackson as an officer aboard the *Ingram* in the Revenue Cutter's Service of the United States.

Half a year passed when, after aiding in the capture of about nine smuggler sloops, the Jewish seaman got word from the collector of customs at New Orleans "to find a good schooner of light draught and about 150 tons burden and to charter same and report."

He chartered the *Julius Caesar* and reported. The customs collector handed him his mission—to embark on a three months cruise down the gulf coast to Galveston Island. There no trace remained of Campeache, which Jean Laffite had a decade earlier established as his pirates' lair—the first non-Hispanic settlement in Spanish Texas. The island was now alive with smugglers evading American customs.

Pilots warned Kokernot to postpone his departure date for all indications pointed to a heavy storm brewing in the Gulf. But ignoring their warnings he, with a crew of 10, cast off on March 20, 1831, as scheduled. There were 20 passengers aboard planning to settle in Texas. Twenty-six-year-old David felt he could take on any giant leviathan of the deep that the Gulf waters could spew forth. But Kokernot would never forget the following encounter:

> So on the 20th I set sail under a fine breeze to the northwest, making a fine run down the coast the first day. At 7 p.m. the wind veered to the northeast, blowing a tremendous tornado. Under close reef, foresail, about 1 o'clock p.m. the vessel sprang a leak. I set both pumps going, all my crew and passengers working for life to keep the water from gaining upon us. At daylight there were two feet of water in the hold, and it was still gaining upon us every moment and the hurricane raging. In all my travels and seafaring life I have never encountered such a storm. The entire coast, even to New Orleans, was lined with wrecks. Our only chance to save our lives was to drive for the shore. At 7 o'clock a.m. we descried the Sabine Pass, the breakers running mountain high. At the moment I saw two porpoises going for the shore and knowing that they always kept in the deepest water, I ordered all hands to go below, save Mr. Thompson, my mate, and two

men. We then ran for the shore in the wake of the porpoises. Mr. Thompson and one man lashed to the wheel, myself and one man to the rigging. The vessel was then running at the rate of fifteen knots per hour and we were expecting every moment that she would founder, and our only hope was to make the pass. As we drew nearer the breakers the wind hauled round east-northeast, trying itself. When we struck the breakers the deck was swept clean and the last boat taken. But, thanks be unto God, we were all saved. I ran the schooner to the shell bank near the Texas side of the pass, got out an anchor on the reef to keep her from sinking until I could get all hands ashore, then went to work cutting down the mast, spars and made a raft and in a short time we got off safe on the Texas shore. The schooner was a total wreck.

But their trials and tribulations did not end. They were without food or water, plagued by swarms of mosquitos, slimy snakes and alligators. Passing the juncture of the Neches River with the Sabine, faint and exhausted, Kokernot offered one of the men in his party $500 in gold for a little water he had yet in a bottle. The man refused. A few drank brackish water and died.

After a few days, all were hungry, tired, ill, and none thought survival possible. Kokernot wrote: "I thought of my home, of my dear wife and mother, and that I must die alone on this barren shore. But the thought came into my mind: make another effort—go on."

On and on the lone Jew struggled, the others dead or dying. He paused, rested, and resumed his march. Of this experience he wrote:

> I picked up my gun, which contained the last load of powder and shot, and started on, almost in despair. I soon saw ahead of me a large gang of cranes. Now was my time. Life or death depended on the shot. I crawled up behind some drift wood and, taking good aim, fired, bringing down one of the birds. I ran up, caught it, cut its throat and sucked the blood, tore it asunder and ate one-half of it raw. Rest assured it tasted extraordinarily well. The repast revived and strengthened me very much...

David Kokernot reached the small house of hunter Burrel Franks at Bolivar Point. Burrel and his wife were away, but their 12-year-old son, Elijah, nursed him back to health. A week later, the recovered Jew hailed a small schooner passing Bolivar Point, paid the skipper $400 to bring him and those who survived to Anahuac, a Texan port of entry at the mouth of the Trinity River. They arrived April 23, 1831, warmly received by American settlers, among them

William Barrett Travis whose name would be immortalized in his fight and heroic death for Texas independence.

David Kokernot liked the warm welcome and brought over his mother, wife and family to permanently settle there. Other Americans found entry more difficult, for the Mexican government then acted to prohibit further immigration from the United States, fearful of an American revolt.

Incident followed incident, a major one occurring in Anahuac in 1832: Colonel John Davis Bradburn was in command of the inland port town. Though an American, he took his Mexican citizenship seriously, preferred to be called Juan, and seeking to curry the favor of his Mexican government, imprisoned his countrymen on any pretext.

When five of Bradburn's Mexican soldiers gang-raped a settler's wife, William Travis organized a group of American avengers. They bushwhacked the rapists; they also tarred and feathered a soldier who may not have been one of the guilty.

In a chain reaction of events called the "Anahuac Scrape," another link was forged in the American Texans' battle for independence as the first Texas Navy was born. Those historic moments were preserved by David Kokernot who was a Captain in the Battle of Anahuac:

> Some time in June (1832), Col. Bradburn ... sent a squad of soldiers and arrested Travis, (P.C.) Jack, and Monroe Edwards, and threw them into the dungeon, or calaboose ... with the full determination to send them as prisoners to (Matamoros) ... whereupon a company of about forty was organized ... determined to rescue our friends ...
>
> Francis W. Johnson ... chosen to command ... He asked me if we had any boats. I told him we had three fine small schooners ... He then ordered us to fit them out with men, arms and provisions, for the purpose of blockading the town ... The "Stephen F. Austin" was commanded by Capt. William Scott (father of General Winfield Scott) ... "Water Witch" was commanded by Capt. James Spillman ... "Red Rover" was commanded by Capt. D. L. Kokernot ... Now, this was the first Texas navy.
>
> Out little army beseiged the fort by land and had several skirmishes, while our navy had no little sport by running near enough to provoke the fire of the enemy's guns, but received no damage thereby. We captured three boats as prizes loaded with provisions, such as butter, eggs, chickens, beef and pork, besides all sorts of dainties; and

you may be sure we lived high on Tory provisions. After some fighting the enemy surrendered, the redoubtable Bradburn making his escape by night and fleeing into Louisiana. Then we had great pleasure of liberating our friends from the prison.

There then arose a new champion of the people, American as well as Mexican, the politician-soldier General Antonio Lopez de Santa Anna. He was determined to dislodge the ensconced autocratic Mexican Regime. Elected to the presidency of the Mexican Republic in January 1833, Santa Anna proved himself an even greater autocrat. He not only contemplated returning Mexican troops into all of Texas but ordered every settler to take an oath of allegiance.

The Texan Americans took everything in stride and worked hard to develop towns, farms, ranches. David Kokernot took to ranching near Anahuac and one day in the spring of 1834 left for Nacogdoches to obtain land titles for himself and friends.

His seafaring legs now straddled a fine horse he rode on the trail. On the way he stopped to chat with fellow Texans, and offered condolences to Joseph Hertz, the Jewish doctor of Nacogdoches, grieving over the death of his brother, Hyman, who drowned in the Red River when the boiler of the sidewheeler *Pioneer* exploded and the steamer burned and sank. He had been en route from New Orleans to visit him at Nacogdoches.

Dr. Hertz's house calls required his traveling from his office by horse and buggy as far as 50 miles in various directions over the trackless plains. His services were in constant demand by day and night. He exerted himself to the extent that while strengthening others, he weakened himself. His health was deteriorating and he knew he would soon have to give up his practice.

At Nacogdoches, Kokernot met a number of Jewish realtors, and businessmen—all with the given name Simon. Simon Schloss and Simon Mussina were rival realtors. David Kokernot discussed land titles with them. Mussina gave kindly advice for he had made and lost several fortunes. David asked him if he did not regret having given away a large sum as charity. Simon Mussina shrugged and said, "It probably did the getters more good than it would have done me."

The Jewish trader, Simon Weiss, was loading his goods on a wagon to relocate on the Neches River. His new trading post is known to this day as Weiss Bluff.

David Kokernot never forgot that day, May 15, 1834, for his chance meeting with Samuel Houston, future president of the Republic of Texas. Kokernot recalled:

> ... as I walked up the street I noticed the finest looking man I ever saw, seated on the steps of Col. Thorn's storehouse. He was dressed in a complete Indian costume made of buckskin and ornamented with a profuse variety of beads, and his massive head was covered with a fine broad beaver hat. When he arose I stopped and looked at him with both surprise and admiration and bid him good morning. He asked me whence I had come. I told him from Galveston Bay, Middle Texas. Then he invited me to sit down and have a chat with him in reference to land matters, which I did for a considerable time. Our conversation ended, he invited me into the store to take a glass of wine with him, which I readily accepted ...

As they sat by the bar, the distinguished looking gentlemen said: "Now, my friend, tell me the news."

Kokernot replied: "The news is war; that Santa Anna, it was rumored, was gathering troops to send into Texas to disarm the inhabitants. But we are determined not to surrender our arms."

"Well, my friend," said the man, "how will you act in that case?"

"We will fight them to the last, or die in the attempt."

"That is right," agreed the chap in buckskin, "they shall never drive us out so long as we can fight them."

David noticed that as he made that remark his eyes sparkled with lightning flashes, and he ordered another bottle of wine.

"Now," said he, "the people ought to organize and get ready to meet him."

David Kokernot agreed.

"Who will command the army?" he asked.

David replied: "My dear sir, if I had the authority to make the appointment, you are the man; for you are the finest looking man I ever laid eyes on."

He immediately acknowledged, "Well, my dear sir, if I get the appointment of commander I will give you a commission."

He then pulled out a small pocketbook and asked the young man's name, entering in his book David Kokernot. Writing his own name, he handed the slip to the Jewish Texan, who on many a future occasion stated: "From that day I loved Sam Houston ... "

Kokernot returned home to learn that Anahuac and other Texas communities were on the verge of rebellion. Stephen Austin hurried to the nation's capital, hoping to obtain concessions sought by Texans, but was imprisoned.

The great among Texas leaders, Sam Houston, John A. Wharton, Don Carlos Barrett, and others, met at San Felipe de Austin and organized a temporary government. They proclaimed Texas a separate state of the Mexican Republic, and pledged loyalty to the democratic constitution of 1824. To this end, they announced their determination to fight, if necessary, against the dictator Santa Anna.

A spark, if now touched against the inflamed Texans, would mean war.

The spark came with the demand by a Mexican colonel at San Antonio that the Texans surrender a cannon they held at Gonzales. The small brass cannon had been given to them for defense against the Indians.

The usually quiet, oak-shaded town that sprawled in the valley of the Guadalupe River became a center of intense activity. Blacksmiths hammered out round shot from bar iron, men from other communities arrived. Word had reached them that the angered commander of the San Antonio garrison, who had hoped to welcome Mexico's General Martin Perfecto de Cos with the Gonzales six-pounder cannon, dispatched 100 soldiers to haul it to San Antonio. Many Texans greeted the soldiers, taunting them with "come and take it." The cannon was loaded with newly forged iron balls and the soldiers opened fire. The frightened Mexican troops vamoosed back to their base.

One of those Texans, a member of the first Texan revolutionary army, was the former sea captain, David Kokernot, arrived from Anahuac. He recorded:

> In the fall of 1835 a call came for men to march in the fields of conflict and repel the invading army of Mexico, under the command of General Cos, who was a brother-in-law of Santa Anna. Having mustered ten men, I set off post haste for Gonzales, where we were to rendezvous. We found all the settlers along the route ready to aid us by furnishing provisions and whatever else was necessary and in their power to bestow . . .
>
> On that day we reached Gonzales and were greatly rejoiced to meet Stephen F. Austin, the Father of Texas, who had made his escape from a Mexican dungeon and reached Texas in safety at this critical moment in her history.

During our stay in Gonzales a battle was fought at La Bahia, or old Goliad, in which the Texans were victorious.

At Gonzales, Kokernot and fellow Texans in arms learned that 50 volunteers led by Colonel Benjamin Milam and George Collinsworth were marching from the Lower Colorado by the Gulf and headed toward Goliad, its fortress on the San Antonio River of great military importance. Therein the Mexicans had stored $20,000 worth of military supplies, 300 muskets, and installed two cannons.

Goliad's fort, strategically situated about 80 miles southeast of San Antonio, that many miles closer to the Mexican bases on the Rio Grande. Whichever force controlled Goliad could conceivably control all of Texas. Fortunately for the Texans, General Cos left only 27 men to guard the Goliad fortress as he marched on with his force of 600 to San Antonio. The force of Milam and Collinsworth drove those few Mexican defenders from the Goliad garrison. That memorable day was October 9, 1835.

Kokernot told of the election at Gonzales by the proud Texan army of 101 cannons of Stephen Austin, commander-in-chief. He led them across the Guadalupe River to battle six times their number for possession of San Antonio. That little Jew, with nothing to do at Goliad, joined up with the Gonzales Army possibly at Salado where they camped. Their vigil relaxed, Comanches stampeded their horses at night, leaving them with only parched corn for food. One Indian crawled within 50 yards of Kokernot and fired, sending a ball whistling by the Jew's head. He returned the fire. A savage Indian cry pierced the night. This alarm set the Texans into motion again, this time on foot.

In the morning they were 10 miles south of San Antonio. General Austin ordered Captains James Bowie and James Fannin to call for volunteers to select a campsite near the city for his army. About 80 stepped forward, and Kokernot was among them. He was particularly fascinated by Captain Bowie's knife. A dozen or more processes had given the Bowie knife its unrivaled temper, which Bowie tested by whittling on a tough hickory axe handle for half an hour and then shaving an arm's hair with the blade.

Bowie had actually learned the secret from a smithy, James Black, when he lived in Washington, on the Upper Red River in the Arkansas Territory. There, the aforementioned Captain Abraham

Block, who probably earned his rank in the War of 1812, was one of his neighbors.

The volunteers set up campsite at Mission Concepcion, two miles below the city, in the bend of the San Antonio River.

Kokernot watched as Mexicans were gathering pecans nearby. One of them came into camp with a bag of "bolonces," which he sold at 25¢ apiece. The Jew, hearing what he thought to be "blintzes" bought a few as the vendor took a hard look at the camp and left. Captain Bowie then remarked: "Now, boys, we will have some fun." He revealed that the Mexican was an officer. Bowie had let him return to his command because he wanted them to attack, and announced: "We will get a fight tonight or in the morning."

The predicted assault came at sunrise. A thousand Mexican troops standing on the open prairie rushing toward the 80 some Texans dug into the horseshoe bend in the river. Kokernot and the others held their fire until the enemy came within 40 yards, and he noted: "Then we let fly at them, and, as the Kentuckian said, it would have done you good to have seen us drop them . . ." The enemy retreated with 120 lying dead on the open field. A number of Mexicans fell into the river mortally wounded. Only one Texan was killed by a grapeshot.

As the battle ended, the main Texan army arrived to encamp, rejoicing in the victorious volunteers. Urgent matters required Stephen Austin to return to his colony. He resigned in favor of Colonel Edward Burleson. Kokernot was assigned to the command of Colonel William Travis.

"Here," said Kokernot, "we had a jolly time, chasing the Mexican cavalry over the plains of San Antonio, with whom we had seven skirmishes, though neither of them proved very serious, except the "Grass Fight," in which a goodly number of Mexicans were killed and seven or eight of our men wounded . . ."

On December 5, 1835, Colonels Francis W. Johnson and Milam called for volunteers to take San Antonio. Over 250 men volunteered, Kokernot among them. He presented a detailed account of the conquest:

> . . . That night we took possession of the Veramendi house, situated in the northern part of the place. This gave us a fair chance to fire upon the Mexicans as they came to the cannon, which were placed across the street. From this house we broke through one house after another until we reached the Plaza . . . Col. Milam, one of the noblest and

bravest officers, fell in this heroic struggle, greatly lamented by all. The battle raged during four days (December 5 to 9), when Gen. Cos surrendered himself and army to Gen. Burleson. Thus some four hundred Texans had fought and vanquished fifteen hundred Mexicans in their fortified city. Our loss was comparatively small, while the enemy's was considerable. Every Texan was a sharpshooter, whose rusty Kentucky rifle seldom failed to bring down the game, while the enemy shot at random. Thus ended the campaign of 1835.

Within four days of fighting, the Texans, outnumbered four to one, scaled the high walls of the fort, took each house constructed of thick stone walls which were nothing less than a series of fortresses, then entered the citadel-like mission monastery, the Alamo.

Healing the wounded was Dr. Moses Albert Levy. Inspired by the determined ragtag Texans, armed only with rifles and lacking military training, the Virginian then in New Orleans influenced others to come to the aid of their fellow Americans. Sixty-six volunteers responded to his call.

Upon his arrival at the Texan encampment by the San Antonio River, he turned the young men over to General Burleson, offered his services as surgeon and was assigned to the post of Chief Surgeon.

Dr. Levy's description remains as one of the most vivid and candid, if nationalist colored, accounts of the taking of the Alamo. In a letter he wrote on December 20, 1835, at San Antonio de Bexar, the story unfolds:

> ... The Americans with a view to beseiging the town & fort which is the largest & strongest in all Texas, assembled themselves before its walls by slow degrees, but never at any one time amounting to more than seven hundred men, who had elected a general to command them. This General (Edward Burleson) unfortunately had not the slightest knowledge of military affairs and in short terms was a complete old Granny.
>
> When we reached the American camp after suffering a thousand deaths in traveling through and sleeping in the cold bleak prairies night after night without a tree or shrub to shelter us from the cold rain & wind (of which we had an abundance) we found the greatest state of confusion & dissatisfaction. The soldiers composed of men who had left their families and homes without any preparation or warning with a view to driving the enemy out of their country at once, and then returning home which indeed would have been quite an easy matter, but instead of this their miserable general thought proper to

starve out the enemy and prevented the Americans from immediately storming the place. The length of time this took tired out the patience of the soldiers who were all volunteers and some almost naked, and of consequence they continually returned home till the army was finally reduced to 450 men with scarcely any ammunition.

Finally affairs became so bad that the army broke up in confusion and desperate would have been the consequences for we would all have been cut by the enemy when I, *insignificant* I, and another individual a citizen of Texas called Milam, beat up for volunteers who would join us two in storming the town and fort that very night, (I should mention that from my mixing about a great deal with the soldiers and chatting and joking with them I had acquired some popularity among them). Our company, called the Grays, immediately and to a man signed their names, and mounting one of the baggage waggons (for we, as I have observed, were just ready for a hasty retreat) I harangued them for a few minutes and thus succeeded in getting 3 hundred men.

We laid our plans appointed our leaders, and about daylight marched up to the enemy's halls got into some strong houses in town and after a regular storm of five days and nights duration, during the whole of which the enemy kept up an incessant firing we forced them to surrender, thus achieving a victory perfectly unparalleled in history, a victory obtained by 225 disorganized and undisciplined men armed with muskets and bayonets in a well fortified fort with 30 pieces of cannon of different sizes.

Our men fought like devils, (even I fought). I worked in the ditches, I dressed the sick and wounded, I cheered the men, I assisted the officers in their counsels, for five days and nights I did not sleep that many hours, running about without a coat or hat, dirty and ragged, but thank God escaped uninjured. I received a slight wound on the forehead the first day which was entirely well before we took the town. I was much exposed to the fire of the enemy and all our men wondered how I escaped with my life. I have crossed a street when more than two hundred muskets were shot at me, our men begging me not to expose myself as I was a double man, being both soldier and surgeon . . .

Ten days following the Mexican surrender of its San Antonio bastion to Burleson and his force, Dr. Levy paused in the treating of wounded Texans to write his sister in Richmond. First he told her: "I have no time to make corrections. . . ." Then he requested: "Address me as Surgeon in Chief of the Volunteer Army of Texas . . ."

He then wrote his impressions of the events that embroiled Texas in a war for independence:

> Texas ... is decidedly the fairest portion of the whole republic [of Mexico], its soil is extremely fertile and it possesses a climate and salubrity of atmosphere not excelled by the South of France, Italy, or any other portion of the known globe. To this garden spot of creation our American citizens came a few years back, under the following circumstances.
>
> The Mexicans, well knowing the enterprising and daring spirit of the Americans, extended an invitation to all Citizen[s] from the United States to emigrate to and settle this State (which they had not the courage to do themselves as it is inhabited by large tribes of wild and ferocious savages;) and that they would bestow large & liberal grants of land for an eternal possession to them & their posterity forever. The Americans seeing such a perfect fairy land offered to them & laid open for their easy reception immediately settled large portions of the State and entered into a regular treaty with the Republic for a set of good and wholesome laws (called the Constitution of 1824). Several years thus passed on & Texas has improved beyond anything credible and now formed a valuable and rich state under American industry and enterprise. The Indians with the exception of one large tribe (consisting of 20,000) have all been destroyed or suppressed.
>
> The Mexicans perceiving of this envied them and coveted their possessions, and with a view to driving them away from here have annulled the former set of laws and enacted & endeavored to force on the Americans other laws oppressive and tyrannical & to which they are determined not to submit. They have therefore taken up arms resolved to resist to the death, and have strongly appealed to their brother Americans everywhere, to fly to their assistance and aid them in resisting their oppressors and their vile laws. They offer large grants of land in addition to pay as regular soldiers to all who will come and enroll themselves in the ranks of freemen assembled to oppose tyranny and oppression like our forefathers of imperishable memory.

While Dr. Levy reflected in his writing his pride as a Texan, he would soon happily add that the beaten General de Cos agreed not to oppose restoring to the Texans the Mexican Constitution of 1824 for which they had fought. Cos was allowed to leave with his troops for Mexico City.

Stationed at the Alamo, "we now began to think of home," wrote

Kokernot. "Our clothes were well-worn, we were bare-footed and winter had set in. Traveling through some severe weather, rain and northers, we reached home in safety." Less than 200 Texan riflemen remained to guard the Alamo, Antony Wolfe the only Jew known to be among them.

Upon the return of his beaten brother-in-law with his sulking troops, dictator General Antonio de Santa Anna seethed with rage. He set forth heading a fresh army of 4,000 to avenge the Texan takeover of the fortress of San Antonio de Valero.

Arrived on March 2, Santa Anna lay seige to the city walls. The sheer weight of wave upon wave of Mexican troops overpowered the Texans, who were outnumbered 20 to 1. As the heroic defenders of the city and Alamo were fighting for their liberty and their lives, Texan leaders were meeting that very day, that very moment, in a one-story partially finished wooden structure at the town of Washington-on-the-Brazos. Aware that Santa Anna was determined to destroy their freedom guaranteed by the Mexican constitution of 1824, they met in closed session. Cotton cloth was draped over the open windows to slow the force of the cold wind, and they solemnly proclaimed Texas an independent nation. They appointed Samuel Houston—the former governor of Tennessee—commander-in-chief of the armed forces of the new Republic.

General Houston issued a call that day for all Texans to rally in aid of the Republic of Texas at fortress Gonzales. The fateful day in the history of Texas and Mexico was March 6.

In response to Houston's call, David Kokernot led a number of his townsmen, as he mounted his mustang, armed and equipped for war. They rode out of Anahuac bound for Gonzales. Two days later, en route to Gonzales, his patriotism was rewarded in a most unusual recall:

> On the 8th, greatly to my surprise, I received a Captain's commission in the regular army of the Republic of Texas, from General Sam Houston, Commander in Chief of the Army, having long forgotten the promise of the General to send me a commission. This brought our first acquaintance and conversation vividly to mind.

Two more days of hard riding and Kokernot entered Gonzales, warmly welcomed by General Houston who then assumed a military stance. He ordered Kokernot to cross the Guadalupe, and march to the assistance of the defenders of the Alamo. But before they could mount their horses, a woman, Susanah Dickinson, staggered into Gonzales carrying a 15-month-old baby followed by a Negro boy slave of Colonel William Travis.

Mrs. Dickinson told a story that shocked the troops. Of all Texans in San Antonio only she and the boy had remained alive. They told of their fate at the Alamo, of the death of her husband, of the death of the slave's master, and all defenders of the San Antonio Mission. They described the horrors of the night of March 6 when the last of the Alamo defenders fought to the death with rifle butt, knife or club.

Among those last to die were Willie Travis, James Bowie, David Crockett, and the English Jew, Private Antony Wolfe, of Nacogdoches. Even the wounded in the hospital and field had been exterminated.

Santa Anna's overnight victory gave birth to the Texans' rallying cry: "Remember the Alamo!"

There would be another major defeat before achieving final victory. A second Mexican Army surrounded a Texas force at Goliad. James Fannin and his men were vastly outnumbered. They fought bravely but hopelessly. After an all night battle, the 300 surrendered in the hope of fighting another day, but they would not live another day. On March 27, at daybreak, the Mexican victors massacred them, with firing squads carrying out executions.

Among the Jews who were thus felled, was teenaged Edward Isaac Johnson, son of the Ohioan pioneer, David Israel Johnson. Edward had joined a volunteer company going to Texas. He landed at Matagorda in November 1835 with Captain Thomas K. Pearson's outfit. Pearson's men hauled a cannon—salvaged from the wrecked schooner *San Felipe*—to Burleson's army at Bexar. After the occupation of Bexar in December, Johnson joined Captain Burr H. Duval's company at Goliad, where he was cut down in the prime of life. His body along with all the Goliad defenders, was stripped of his clothing and valuables and thrown into heaps and burned. The order to kill them all had come from Santa Anna.

One who somehow escaped was a Jewish soldier, Benjamin H. Mordecai. But his life was cut short four years later, scalped by Indians somewhere in the western wilderness.

Commander-in-Chief of Texas forces, Sam Houston, in desperate need to bolster his untrained, poorly armed, and ill-provisioned

Texan troops, dispatched Adolphus Sterne, his longtime friend, to be his secret emissary to New Orleans, there to outfit an entire company of Americans.

Lively Don Adolfo, as the former Adolphus Sterne was called in Mexican Texas, drummed up volunteers at wayside taverns and stagecoach depots. A highly educated man, Sterne was proficient in languages. He spoke German, French, English and Spanish with great fluency and gained a speaking excellence in several of the Indian dialects in the Texas-Louisiana area. To the amusement of prospective volunteers and their astonishment, he mimicked himself in his capacity of auctioneer, bidding off articles in six different languages, including Yiddish and Choctaw.

Sam Houston, whom Sterne first befriended a decade earlier in Tennessee, took up residence in Nacogdoches in 1833. Houston became a permanent house guest of Senor Adolfo Sterne, who was *alcade* of the town. He found the kindness of Sterne's wife, Senora Eva Catherine Rosine Ruff, and the meals served by French-speaking Louisiana Negro slaves more desirable than the room and board offered at the Tavern on the Plaza or the Cantina del Monte where dancing and gambling continued throughout the night and there was a fandango once every week.

Sam Houston joined the Catholic Church, presumably influenced by the young Catholic wife of the Jewish *alcalde,* Eva Sterne. The baptismal waters were dispensed by her confessor, Père Chambondeau. The ceremony took place at the church in Nacogdoches, Eva Sterne acting as Sam Houston's godmother, after which ... he always addressed her as 'Madre Mio.' " After the conversion ritual, Don Adolfo Sterne gave a party on the porch of his home and opened many casks of wine.

On March 2, 1836, Sam Houston appended his signature to the Declaration of Independence, to free Texas from Catholic Mexico, his flowing autograph as bold as ever was the John Hancock of that Texan freedom document. Delegate Houston promptly sent his felicitations to Madre Mio—Citizeness Rosine Sterne of Nacogdoches—enclosing a pair of beautiful diamond earrings. She wore them each succeding year on March 2, the anniversary of Texas Independence and Sam Houston's birthday.

Events in the battle for Texas freedom moved fast. Santa Anna, following his conquest of the Alamo and Goliad and their accompanying massacres, confidently encamped his troops at the fork of

Buffalo Bayou on the San Jacinto River. The camp was located about a mile from the land tract acquired by David Kokernot at the time he first met Houston at Nacogdoches.

General Samuel Houston was encamped nearby, having arrived there the day previous, April 20, 1836, with a force of less than 400 men. Volunteers arrived, perhaps Sterne's recruits among them, to swell the number to 750. Nacogdoches merchant and landowner Albert Emanuel, a close friend of Sam Houston, took up his rifle in the Company of Cavalry of Captain Kimbo's Second Regiment of Texas volunteers. And there were other Jewish volunteers.

Surgeon-General Isaac Lyon headed the medical staff of troops commanded by Generals Thomas Jefferson Green and Tom Lee. A Jew named Kohn bore arms in the Texas Spy Company, and others, as Eugene Joseph Chimene, were to fight for Texas as a free and independent country.

On the next day, April 21, Santa Anna was discussing with his high officers the strategy that would annihilate the Texan rebels while his confident troops were enjoying their siesta. At the signal, Houston's troops overran the enemy camp awakened abruptly from their siesta, confused and bewildered. Within 18 minutes the Texans killed or captured in that decisive battle at San Jacinto 1,300 Mexicans; Santa Anna was taken prisoner.

Arrived too late to participate in the Battle of San Jacinto was the fiery, flamboyant Baltimorean Jew, Leon Dyer. He arrived in New Orleans early in 1836 to consummate deals in connection with his wholesale beef house, the first such in the United States. But typical of Dyer, he interrupted his business to join on February 3 the Louisiana Volunteers en route to join the campaign waged against the Seminole Indians in Florida. Serving as Regimental Quarter Master and aide-de-camp under General Sam Smith, Dyer occasionally met with Major General Winfield Scott for consultation. He would again meet General Scott in future campaigns.

Mustered out of the Louisiana Volunteers on May 12, upon returning to New Orleans he arrived in time to be appointed on May 18 aide-de-camp to Brigadier General Thomas Jefferson Green of the Army of the Republic of Texas. Aboard the steamer *Ocean,* Dyer reached Velasco harbor with 230 volunteers on June 1, 1836. There, Dyer was commissioned major, his rank signed by David G. Burnett, first president of the Republic of Texas.

But Texans rumored that "Old Baltimore" had backed out of "an affair of honour" before leaving New Orleans. Major Dyer threw up his commission, and embarked on the schooner *Fannin* to duel a man who had made an insulting remark about his religion. He met his antagonist at the usual hour of seven A.M. Both missed on the first shot. Their seconds regarded this as satisfaction enough for wounded honor and Dyer returned to Texas.

Major Leon Dyer was assigned to accompany the former Mexican dictator as guard of honor to Washington, D.C., from the port of Galveston. Santa Anna later sent Major Dyer a personal letter of thanks for the courteous treatment he accorded him.

Dyer left from the nation's capital to his home in nearby Baltimore where he operated the first meat packing house in the land with his brother Isidore, and brother-in-law Joseph Osterman married to his sister Rosanna. But Leon never forgot the new nation he helped create, the Republic of Texas and its capital, the village of Galveston. He would return.

Spanish Jews of the Republic of Texas

Before the ink was dry on the Treaty of Velasco, signed at that port-village where the Brazos River waters emptied into the Gulf of Mexico, on May 14, 1836, there sailed from New Orleans en route to Velasco the vessel *Columbia,* owned by merchantman Abraham Cohen Labatt, his the first to ply the gulf waters with super cargo between the United States and the Lone Star State.

Over 30,000 Texans comprised the new republic. That number would more than triple within a decade. The Americans of the Crescent City, which was the closest major U.S. city to Texas, had supplied during the war for Texas independence volunteers who fought at every major campaign.

After the victory, virtually all the commodities and goods Texans required were shipped from New Orleans. Businessman A. C. Labatt, a native of Charleston, South Carolina, in 1831 had settled in New Orleans. In 1836 he moved his residence to Velasco and seems to have been the leader of the Velasco Jewish Community. Records are sparse as to Jewish life in the village of Velasco during that early period. There is testimony that a Jew named Jacob Henry, at his death, left his fortune for the building of a much needed hospital.

One of the Jews of Velasco dispatched in 1837 a news report of the sudden death of a new Jewish citizen of the Texas Republic to

Mordecai Manuel Noah, publisher of the New York City *Evening Star*. The man was Noah's nephew, Levy L. Laurens, a native of Charleston, South Carolina, well known to Abraham Cohen Labatt prior to his leaving for the West.

Twenty-one-year-old Laurens had begun his career in journalism under the patronage of his uncle, working in the editorial department of the New York *Evening Star* prior to leaving for Texas's new capital, Houston. There the young reporter was appointed secretary to the Texan Congress at a salary of eight dollars a day, and was arranging for the establishment of a government paper.

Levy Laurens roomed with several young friends, and a Dr. Chauncey Goodrich, who came from Vicksburg, Mississippi, to serve as assistant surgeon of the fledgling republic's army. On rising one morning, Dr. Goodrich missed some of his money and charged young Levy with having stolen it. When the doctor refused to withdraw his accusation Levy challenged him. A dual was to be fought with rifles as weapons, at 65 yards.

The opponents met on the outskirts of Houston on June 25, 1837. At the first fire, Laurens fell, the ball of his antagonist having entered his right thigh and passed through his left; the doctor escaped unhurt. Levy Laurens died the next day.

Noah, who had like his nephew been driven to challenge, as was the custom of the country, appealed in his *Evening Star* that "it should be an established principle never to settle a point of honor with rifles. It is the weapon of the Brigand."

Dr. Chauncey Goodrich soon recanted. He stated in remorse his conviction that he was in error. Apparently he had misplaced the "missing" money.

High tribute to the young journalist was offered by Francis Moore, Jr., editor of Houston's *Telegraph and Texas Register*. It concluded with the eloquent thought:

> In him Texas has lost one of the first of that gallant and illustrious band of America's chivalry, which has so magnanimously rallied around the one-starred banner: displaying in the "land of Prairies" all that is admirable in fortitude, all that is lofty in heroism . . .

In the former Mexican/Spanish Texas these descendants of Spanish/Portuguese Jews and others were drawn to the new land of liberty—among them, the brothers Jacob and Phineas de Cordova. Jacob, first to arrive, entered into journalism as had Levy Laurens.

Jamaica-born Jacob de Cordova published the *Gleaner* at Kingston, but doctors ordered him to leave the damp Caribbean for the mainland. He left for Philadelphia, then New Orleans, but upon the emergence of the new Republic of Texas left for Galveston where he organized De Cordova Land Agency, one of the largest promotion companies for Texas land. His brother Phineas, born in Philadelphia, afterwards joined him.

But the humid Galveston climate forced Jacob de Cordova to seek relief. This time he took up residence in Houston. There too he suffered, and doctors advised him to settle west of the Brazos River or depart for the colder, dryer climate of the northern plains, as in Iowa Territory.

Jacob crossed the Brazos to live in the vicinity of Fort Waco. Expanding the activities of his De Cordova Land Agency, Jacob visited most of the organized counties in the republic to examine their records. He felt safe, for since 1837 the Texas Rangers had been dispatched to the borders including the frontier Brazos. Jacob could confirm the truth of the statement that the Texas Rangers "could ride like Mexicans, shoot like Tennesseans and fight like the very devil."

A very large portion of the deeds issued by the Texas Republic were based on certificates provided by the De Cordova Land Agency. In every case contested the De Cordova certificates were upheld by the courts.

The climate of the Brazos agreed with Jacob, and he remained there to see Waco rise. In fact, the government called upon him to lay out the town, former site of an Hueco Indian village, by Fort Waco. There he founded the Texas *Herald,* a newspaper copublished with his brother Phineas, largely a promotional project designed to attract Easterners.

He also published a basic reference volume: *Texas, Her Resources and her Public Men.* Of this work the *Galveston Civilian* said:

> This book contains more information about Texas than all the state papers issued by her President, Governors, Controllers and Treasurers combined.

Deeply involved in these and other contributions to the Lone Star State, Jacob apparently neglected his own affairs. He was land rich, owning more than a million Texas acres in his beloved Bosque County, northwest of Waco—an area larger than the present King

Ranch, the largest ranch in Texas, some 800,000 acres.

Jacob de Cordova, a learned Jew, was on rare occasions called upon to write Hebrew marriage contracts—written in the Aramaic language, but using Hebrew characters. He also performed the Jewish wedding rites. Though unrecorded, there were High Holy Day worship services held in the Lone Star State wherever 10 adult Jewish males assembled. Jacob de Cordova could repeat word for word liturgical chants. He could recite from memory the entire worship of the holy days, including the all-day prayers of the Day of Atonement, according to the Portuguese custom and order of Jewish worship.

Among those worshipers may well have been Henry Castro, who established a colony west of the Medina River, in the wild back country outside of San Antonio. He convinced the president of the republic, Sam Houston, that he could attract settlers if he be awarded a land grant in that far western region of Texas.

Castro's land grant proved to be four miles beyond the Medina, so he personally purchased the intervening strip so that his settlers would have the benefit of the riverside.

Born into a rich Parisian Jewish family, Henry Castro had been one of the guards selected to accompany Napoleon to Spain in 1806. Thereafter he was an officer in the First Legion of the National Guard of Paris. Inspired by the heroic Texans in their fight for independence, he emigrated to San Antonio. The new republic recognized in him an able negotiator, and in the interests of Texas he traveled overseas in 1838 to successfully arrange a loan for the Lone Star State's depleted treasury, with France.

From 1842 to 1844 Castro served the Republic of Texas as consul-general to France. While in Paris he worked hard to attract settlers to his colony in western Texas. Soon after he set his office in order in Paris in 1842, at his expense he dispatched the ship *Ebro* with 113 Catholic pioneers. He followed this with outfitting and dispatching the *Lyons* from Le Havre and the *Louis Philippe* from Dunkerque, bringing to nearly 400 the total Medina settlers.

In 1843, Henry Castro sent 300 more emigrants aboard the *Jean Key* and *Jeanette Marie,* to raise the total settlers to 700.

Letters received by their families and friends back in France brought thousands knocking at the doors of Castro's Paris office. At his expense, in 1844-45, 5,000 left French ports for Medina. Henry Castro became the greatest of all Texas colonizers.

He spent over $150,000 of his personal fortune to establish these colonies, providing them with food for one year, and supplying them with seed, farm implements, cattle, medical care and other essentials.

Texas Jews generally were model citizens and none more highly revered and respected than Castro the Jew. In his honor, his grateful Catholic colonists established a town on the west bank of the Medina, and named it Castroville.

The state of Texas, too, was indebted to him for his services and great achievement. He also founded the villages of Quihi, D'hanis, and Vandenburg. In recognition, the state named in his honor a western county—Castro.

Castro's colony, located on the very fringe of the frontier, was vulnerable to roving Mexican guerillas from the southwest and Indian forays from the northwest. His colonists fought off the sporadic attacks, as had other Texans.

The Mexican incursions began in 1841 when Mirabeau B. Lamar, president of the Republic of Texas, attempted to enlarge the Lone Star State and invaded New Mexico. The Mexicans captured the invading force before they reached Santa Fe. They were cruelly abused; Mexican officers kept a tally of the dead Texans by threading their ears onto rawhide thongs. Few survived the 1,200 mile march across desert wasteland to El Paso del Norte.

When news of their ill treatment reached Houston, the Texas government passed an act annexing six northern states of Mexico. When news of the attempted invasion of New Mexico reached Santa Anna, the Mexican dictator-general, claimed the move had relieved him of all obligations pledged in the treaty he signed at Velasco five years earlier.

Santa Anna sent an army into the Republic of Texas in the early months of 1842 to capture San Antonio and Goliad. Recalling the battle cries of '36—"Remember the Alamo" and "Remember Goliad!"—the Texas militia drove out the Mexicans. In September the Mexicans again took San Antonio, and after inflicting heavy damage, retired.

The mood of the day was reflected in a letter written by Dr. Moses Albert Levy who fought to take the Alamo in 1836. Now, in October 1842 he wrote from his office at Matagorda, 100 miles from San Antonio, to his nine-year-old daughter, Rachel, living with her mother in Richmond, Virginia:

> My dearest child,
>
> Your charming letter of August 16th has just reached me amidst a scene

of great confusion and trouble. The Mexicans have again invaded this wretched country and I am once more called upon to support her cause in the field. Tomorrow or next day I leave home for the army and God alone can say w(h)ether I shall ever return to behold my beloved wife and children, and this my Rachel may be the last letter your father may be permitted to pen to his adored child. If such be my fate may God the friend of the afflicted take my beloved ones in his keeping and shield them from all trials . . .

The Mexican incursions between 1842 and 1845 did not deter restless Americans from settling in the Republic of Texas. Some were attracted by that country's cheap land, many by its Homestead Law of 1839 which prevented a man's home, acreage, or implements from being seized as payment for debts.

The settlements on the far western Texas border were safeguarded by Henry Castro's ever-watchful vigil.

The Catholic colonists highly respected their benefactor. Those who accompanied him on trips into the backwoods to appraise and purchase additional land, watched him disappear into the forest and reverently awaited his return. They knew that he retired into the privacy of those woods to pray to the God of Israel.

The Mexicans of that region understood, for they knew of only two religions, the Catholic and the Jewish, which reemerged into the open after 1821 when Mexico became independent of Spain and abolished the Spanish Inquisition.

A Protestant who visited San Antonio in 1848 wrote: "They (the Mexicans) call us Jews, for they have never had an idea of any other religion than their own; and, as they never saw our marriages celebrated, supposed we lived in concubinage or had been married according to the Jewish rites."

San Antonio's Mexicans knew the Jew Louis Rose, a land agent, though it is not known if he was involved with Castro's colony. He left with a party of overlanders who took the Gila Trail to California in 1849, and Rose would be the first Jew to settle in San Diego.

But others came to San Antonio, two to gain immortality by the way they departed. Benedict Schwartz and Siegmund Moses Feinberg, both natives of Russia, became involved in a quarrel over a dog. Schwartz threatened Feinberg's life.

Two versions were told of what happened that fateful day (December 10, 1857). One was that Schwartz gunned down Feinberg who, after crossing his threshold, fell dead at his wife's feet. The other maintained that Feinberg was shot in a duel with Schwartz who was faster on the draw.

To the Mexicans and Texans such killing was part of life and deemed his death of normal causes.

Feinberg's beloved wife, Regina, was bitter. She interred her beloved in the recently acquired Hebrew burial ground and fenced off the grave and family plot with a high tan stucco wall, fronted by a wrought-iron gate. Thus she separated his grave from that to be occupied by Benedict Schwartz when his time would come.

Regina Feinberg ordered a tombstone from Philadelphia engraved there in accordance with her directions to commemorate the manner of his untimely dastardly death. It was boated downriver the Ohio and Mississippi to New Orleans then transported overland by oxcart to San Antonio. Over the Hebrew-English epitaph were sculptured two gentlemen clad in mid-Victorian long-frocked coats and stovepipe beaver hats, stolidly facing each others with arms raised, pistols pointed.

Benedict Schwartz was not prosecuted by human indictment, but divine justice was operative. An unknown assailant stabbed him to death in his pawn shop. That Feinberg was killed by Schwartz was regarded as a matter of honor in which he won the contest and the stabbed Schwartz was now extolled by the *San Antonio Weekly Express* as "A loving husband and father, a man of energy and enterprise, a good citizen and a most faithful and indefatigable worker, upholding the law."

But in those days it was every man for himself, for as it was admitted there was no law west of the Pecos or Brazos.

Lone Star Orbits into Stars and Stripes

The American frontier was moving westward, wagon trains were rutting the prairies of Texas where small farms were appearing in isolated regions, its population was over 100,000. Congress, in March, 1845, offered statehood to Texas and in December the republic entered as the 28th state.

Mexico, angered by Washington's annexation of Texas, insisted that the Nueces River was its northeastern boundary with the United States, while America claimed the Rio Grande as the border.

By writ of President James Polk, a unit of American cavalry, commanded by General Zachary Taylor, crossed the Nueces River and camped at the mouth of the Rio Grande to establish a kind of "squatter's rights" claim to the strip of land stretching north and south between the Nueces River to the east and the Rio Grande on the west. A body of Mexicans attacked and defeated the small American force at the Battle of Nueces.

Jewish attorney, David S. Kaufman, suffered a head wound in this clash. He returned somewhat a hero to his home in Nacogdoches. He would represent the Lone Star State in the congress of the United States; a Texas County (Kaufman County) would be named in his honor.

General Taylor regrouped his forces, returned, and drove the Mexicans across the Lower Rio Grande to Matamoros. The Jew, Abraham Charles Myers of South Carolina, fought in the two decisive battles at Palo Alto, the Resaca de la Palma on the Texas gulf coast.

Following these battles the United States declared war on Mexico, on May 13, 1846. General Taylor at the tiny gulf port of Matamoros at the mouth of the Rio Grande awaited additional troops. Throughout the nation the call was made for volunteers.

One company—organized in Baltimore and composed largely of Jewish immigrants—was announced in a dispatch from that city, dated July 3:

> Among the companies which have been formed here, one, for the most part of Jews, attracts particular attention. Almost for the most part composed of immigrants, they have given, by the raising of this company to fight with the native militia in behalf of our institutions, a splendid instance of their love and devotion for those and for their fatherland. Captain Henry Carroll, who was paymaster of the Fifth Regiment, has willingly resigned his position to accept the command of this patriotic company. Its other officers are Levi Benjamin, first lieutenant; Joseph Simpson, Samuel G. Goldsmith, third lieutenant; S. Eytings, first sergeant, and Dr. J. Horowitz, surgeon.

Of those who enlisted in the Baltimore company of Jewish volunteers, Lieutenant Joseph Simpson would be among the first to die in action.

But as they were about to sail to their final destination, Abraham Joseph Rice, rabbi of the Baltimore Hebrew Congregation, offered prayers for their well-being and safe return. Leon Dyer, who had rushed to the support of Texas during its war for independence in 1836, was now president of the congregation. But he resigned to reenlist. The membership presented him with a medal at a farewell party for seven years of exemplary leadership.

He arrived in New Orleans and joined the staff of General Winfield Scott, whom he had met during the Seminole Indian wars in Florida. Dyer was assigned to the post of Quartermaster-General. He would be rewarded with 640 acres of Texas soil.

Leon Dyer had an additional incentive to travel to Texas, for his brother Isadore and sister Rosanna and brother-in-law Joseph Osterman had moved to Galveston.

Both would bequeath their fortunes to the poor of the city. The beloved couple, however, would die untimely and tragic deaths. Joseph was shot to death when a weapon was accidentally discharged by a workman in a gunsmith shop. Rosanna, after a visit to Baltimore, was traveling aboard the steamer *W. R. Carter* and met her death when the ship's boiler exploded near Vicksburg, Mississippi.

Leon Dyer sailed from Baltimore to the Mexican gulf port of Matamoros, across from Brownsville, Texas, to join General Taylor's forces. They marched inland against the city of Monterrey, capital of Nuevo Leon.

Determined to crush the American force that penetrated northern Mexico, Santa Anna led an army of almost 20,000 troops against Taylor's 5,000. Fortunately, General John Wool arrived from Texas after a 900 mile march from San Antonio to join forces.

Though the Taylor-Wool troops were still outnumbered three to one, they fought heroically at the ranch of Buena Vista, southwest of Monterrey, against the backdrop of the towering Sierra Madre. Henry Seeligson, for his bravery, was highly complimented by General Taylor and offered a second lieutenancy in the Second Dragoons. Henry declined this rank but after he returned to his home town Galveston, accepted election to serve as its mayor.

Among the dead lay Sergeant Abraham Adler of the New York volunteers. His sacrifice was not in vain. The Americans under Taylor and Wool defeated the finest army Mexico could muster. That important battle was fought February 23, 1847.

By this date, all of northern Mexico had been taken by American forces, the Stars and Stripes waving over Texas, New Mexico, and California.

At Santa Fe, New Mexico's capital, Eugene Lott Leitensdorfer and his employee Solomon Jacob Spiegelberg, the Goldstone brothers, and other Jewish merchants, all former Americans, rejoiced on August 18, 1846 when General Stephen W. Kearny arrived with his troops.

To them, the victory was not only an American one, but also symbolized a Judaic conquest. Two centuries earlier, since 1610 when the Spaniards first founded Santa Fe as capital of Nuevo Mexico, the Inquisition hounded any Jews seeking to settle there. In 1662, New Mexico's governor, Bernardo López de Mendizábal, and his wife, Doña

Teresa de Aguilera y Roche, were arrested by the Holy Office, charged with being of Jewish ancestry. Bernardo was the great-grandson of a man sentenced in 1603 for the practice of Judaism.

Don Bernardo was accused of whipping a crucifix; additionally he and his wife Doña Teresa bathed before the Sabbath, and she, on the Sabbath eve, changed bed, table, and other linen and primped for the Jewish day of rest.

He was incarcerated, as had been the previous Governor Luis de Carvajal, for political reasons—because these men firmly believed in the authority of the state over the church. Like Carvajal, Mendizábal died in prison.

Two centuries had passed since and Santa Fe's Jews had good reason to rejoice that hot summer day in 1846 when United States General Kearny hoisted the American flag over the Palace of the Governors.

In mid-September General Kearny marched off with a thousand troops to conquer California. At the same time, he ordered Colonel Alexander W. Doniphan to lead some 300 Missouri volunteers down the Santa Fe Trail southward, through the Rocky Mountain ranges into Chihuahua, there to attack the flank of the Mexican Army. If successful, that Mexican force would be prevented from joining Santa Anna's troops then assembled at Monterrey to await General Taylor's oncoming army.

A story making the rounds amongst the Yankee troops told of two Jews in Santa Fe, one Abraham S. who arrived there in 1843 and the other, Isaac Finkerhaus, in 1844. Abraham convinced Isaac to make Spanish Fly, reputedly a sex stimulant, in order to earn a livelihood. The tale was first related as follows by Abraham:

"Isaac, you knows dis is Spanish country, don't you?"

"I spegs so," says Isaac, "pecause de people speags Spanish."

"Taint nuttin else," says I, "an ef de country is Spanish country, of course de flies, dey is *Spanish flies.*"

"Now is dey, Abraham?" says Ike.

"Well dey is," says I, "an' you knows dat Spanish flies dey prings four dollars a poun' in Germany. You can catch an' dry four poun' on 'em every day, an' dares twelve dollar made in one day."

"Tank Got," says Isaac, "an' vy you no tell me dat pefore? Me pegin dis day to catch him, an' me vill make de little start mit de Spanish fly."

So Isaac, he goes straight off, mighty trembly, wid his eyes open, he was so full of hope, an' he gits a big black bottle to put his flies in. He began to catch 'em in my store fuss. You would a'died a laughin' to see Isaac wid his bottle in his lef han', stoppered wid de forfinger, a goin' about de room catchin o' flies. He vould eeze his right han' up, half shot, close to a fly an' all at once, he vould give a sweep around, so, an' sure enough dare vould be de fly catched, an' sometimes more'n a dozen on 'em. Ike worked powerful in my storeroom, an' he sweated a heap ... ven I axed Isaac vot luck he had.

"Mine pottle pe no more as haef vull."

"Don't give up, Isaac," says I, "better luck nex' time. Now eat your supper, an' den dry your flies in de skillet."

De flies dat Ike cotched dat day veighed jess tree ounces. He hunted all de nex' day, an' didn't do quite vell. Ven he vas out at vork, I told John Jones, Solomon (Spiegelberg?) and Little Tom all about it, an' dey all come moghty near a dyin' a laughin'. De tird day, Little Tom, he muss go an' let all out to everybody.

Ven Isaac hearn how everybody vas a laughin' at him, he smell de rat, and know'd how bad he vas took in. He vas de maddest man I ever seed, an' ef now you vant to see a rale mad man, all you has to do is to talk before him about Spanish flies ...

Isaac swore that he even the score. He opened a general store did well and one day asked Abraham to lend him a thousand dollars. Abraham knew Isaac to be honorable and agreed. When the due date came, Isaac wanted to pay with merchandise. Abraham refused until he heard a rumor that Isaac was going bankrupt. He rushed to take the goods in payment. Leaving with the goods, Isaac told him of the ruse and said:

"Now, Abraham, you von't *fly* no more, vill you?"

Clerk Solomon Jacob Spiegelberg learned that Doniphan needed sutlers to supply his regiment. He promptly resigned his two year employment at E. Leitesdorfer & Co., and proprietor Eugene discovered that he was due $365. A firm member counted out the bills stating, "Jacob, this will give you luck. Here is one dollar for every day in the year."

With his earnings, Solomon bought a mule train which he loaded with supplies he obtained on credit from his former employer.

In December 1846 he went along with the troops departing Santa Fe. Driving his mule train over the bare, craggy mountains was breathtaking, the peaks over 7,000 feet high, on the winding stony Santa Fe Trail until they reached the pass that led down into El Paso del Norte, the town along the bank of the Rio Grande in a bleak setting of gray country and mountainous background.

The Mexican garrison at El Paso surrendered without a struggle. From El Paso del Norte they continued down the Santa Fe Trail toward the town of Chihuahua, capital of the state of Chihuahua. The traders' mules mixed indiscriminately with the army horses and cavalry, artillery, and infantry.

Outnumbered 13 to 1, the Missourian sharp-shooters killed over 300 Mexican troops, wounded an equal number, captured 40, while American losses were 2 dead, 7 wounded.

Captured booty included 1,000 lariats that the confident Mexicans brought with them for tying up the gringo soldiers.

Young Spiegelberg so inspired the troops with his lively support and help that upon their return to Santa Fe, in recognition of his popularity the officers chose him to be the sutler at the first American Military Post of New Mexico, Fort Marcy near Santa Fe.

During the Doniphan victory in Chihuahua, General Stephen Kearny led his men, nearly 1,000 strong over 1,000 miles through New Mexico Territory which included the future Arizona Territory into California, reaching San Diego on December 12, 1846. There he joined forces with Commodore Robert F. Stockton to attack Los Angeles.

Kearny learned that U.S. military explorer John Charles Frémont, an officer in the Army Topographical Corps, had on June 29 raised the American flag over San Diego. Moreover, Frémont had arrived in California's Sacramento Valley in February, many months before war was declared, possibly on secret orders to instigate hostilities with the Mexicans in California.

Ordered to withdraw from California by the order of the Mexican commander of the garrison in Monterrey, capital of the Mexican State, Frémont defiantly remained, camping about 25 miles away.

As a force of 200 Mexican volunteers rode into Monterrey to join the few troops stationed there, American Vice-Consul William Leidesdorff, reputedly a Jewish-Danish mulatto, directed a communication to Frémont to lower the Stars and Stripes over his camp and depart. It was anticipated, Leidesdorff pointed out, that a political rather than a military annexation of California to the United States would be effected.

As Frémont bided his time, there arrived Commodore John Drake Sloat who, while anchored at a port in western Mexico, at Mazatlán, quietly sailed out of the harbor to northern California and on July 7, captured Monterrey. His 250 marines encountered no opposition. A week later the flag of the United States was flying all over northern California settlements.

At *El Parage de Yerba Buena* (the place of the good grass, the future

San Francisco) stood a village of a few huts, one of these occupied by Lewis Adler, born Ludwig Simon Adler. This German-Jewish lad was converted to Christianity when he was 9 in 1829.

At a missionary school in London he apprenticed to a cooper, making beer barrels. After eight years he shipped on a whaler, sailing four years to all ports of the China Sea and Calcutta on the Indian Ocean, and to the northern Bering Sea.

Food was bad and pay was poor so he and other shipmates jumped ship and took an American whaler to the South Seas to remain at Tahiti.

Adler thought Tahiti to be the most beautiful place on earth and remained there for a year. The uncle of Queen Pomare offered him an entire island stocked with cattle if Lewis would but marry his daughter.

Lewis however reasoned that he was an Englishman. Once an Englishman always an Englishman and he could not live with a French girl and share his life with Frenchmen who ruled those islands.

He shipped out for *Yerba Buena* aboard the *Euthemia,* a Hawaiian brig, in 1846. There he set up shop as a cooper, buying old whale oil barrels and making wooden bathtubs and buckets. But there was not a great market in the Mexican pueblos for bathtubs so after three weeks he entered the employ of William Heath Davis, then Dixon & Hay.

When the American troops entered *Yerba Buena,* he was in business for himself. Having bought a boat from a whaler, he hired two Kanakas (Hawaiians) to row him across the bay and up Sonoma Creek to the Embarcadero at Sonoma. He traded his goods for hides, with leather dollars that served as actual money. The troops paid him his first American bills and coins. Lewis did well and soon set up a store in Sonoma, naming it the Commerce House, joined by one Charles Meyers.

Commodore Stockton replaced Sloat at Monterey and was joined by Kearny, as earlier noted, at San Diego. They set forth on December 29 to attack *El Pueblo de Nuestra Senora La Reina de Los Angeles del Rio de Porciuncula* (The Town of Our Lady, the Queen of the Angels by the River), which even long-winded generals called Los Angeles.

Lieutenant Colonel Frémont approached from the north. The pueblo of Los Angeles was entered on January 11, 1847. One American Jew was in town, the pioneer merchant, Jacob Frankfort. He first came to the cow town of Los Angeles in one of the first wagon trains into Mexican California in 1841. The town's sombreroed officials entrusted to Jacob the task of evaluating shipwrecked cargos, and he was regarded as a most expert appraiser.

It is believed that Jacob Frankfort left the town for a few years to sail on to the Philippines and China, returning to Los Angeles about 1846. He then opened a clothing store in the best spot in town, the corner of Bell's Row, the only two-story adobe, owned by Alexander Bell, at Aliso and Los Angeles Streets. Ranchers coming to town could see his store from far down the road leading into El Pueblo.

Jacob Frankfort was among the crowd of Mexicans who watched the Americans raise the Stars and Stripes at the Plaza in the center of Los Angeles.

Mexico Surrenders Its Golden Treasure

The conquest of Mexico's northern states accomplished, the victory of General Zachary Taylor at Monterrey achieved, there sailed from New Orleans an army under the command of General Winfield Scott, bound for the Mexican gulf port of Vera Cruz, entranceway to Mexico City.

Aboard the brig *Montezuma* in Scott's fleet of New York volunteers—in company "B," first regiment—was a Jewish enlistee, 16-year-old Jacob Hirschorn, who would be involved in every battle that led to the capture of the Mexican capital. In December 1846 he joined Scott's men at the Crescent City.

They set forth westward paralleling the Texas shore, turning south near Matamoros along the Mexican shore to Tampico and pausing at uninhabited Lobos Island about 200 miles from their destination, Vera Cruz.

After engaging for a week in combat against snakes, vermin, and assorted pests as well as drill and target practice, Hirschorn and his fellow soldiers headed southward.

Reaching Vera Cruz with 10,000 men aboard 80 ships on March 7, 1847 General Scott surveyed the situation from aboard the transport steamer *Massachusetts*.

Scott's army disembarked about five miles below the city and the next day, March 10, began the attack which was to last to the surrender on the 29th.

Young Hirschorn described the final days of the siege:

> Then (about March 27) the bombardment commenced by land and sea forces. So awful a sight, but still grand, I have never seen, especially at night, when one could follow the bomb-shells with the eye, as they were fired from the huge mortars on the frigates and line ships. The houses in

the city began to burn, and after two days' bombardment, the castle and city, capitulated, the Mexican flag came down, and the "Stars and Stripes" were hoisted . . .

Captain Jonas Phillips Levy, commander of the U.S.S. *America,* was commended for his leadership and appointed by General Winfield Scott to the high post of military governor of Vera Cruz.

Jonas Levy was a veteran of South American politics, having served the Peruvian government as a sailor of fortune.

Captain Levy's relations were among the American troops in Mexico. Levi Charles Harby was a captain in the Marines. He fought in the War of 1812, the Seminole and Texas Wars in the 1830s, and now was defending his home in the Battle of Galveston. Not only was he motivated by patriotism but he was protecting his most prized possession, his young wife. When he was stationed in 1842 at St. Marys, Georgia, he married in his 51st year Leonore Rebecca de Lyon, she but 14, a descendant of Georgia's first settlers.

Captain Harby's brother was playwright, George Washington Harby, born in the year the first president of the United States retired from office. Another brother, Henry Jefferson Harby, remained in his native Charleston, South Carolina, where he was the city blacksmith.

Jonas Levy's cousin, Robert P. Noah, was fighting with the Americans somewhere in Mexico. His father was the distinguished Mordecai Manuel Noah, now 60 years of age, living with unfulfilled dreams of establishing at the Falls of the Niagara a haven for all oppressed Jews and Indians.

But ironically, Jonas' brother, United States Naval Captain Uriah Phillips Levy, was in forced seclusion. Uriah Phillips Levy had not been given a ship to command since his court-martial and suspension a number of years earlier. Secretary of the Navy, the Honorable George Bancroft, testified in his favor and then remarked: "I perceived a strong prejudice in the service against Captain Levy, which seemed to me, in a considerable part attributable to his being of the Jewish persuasion . . ."

Uriah Levy's pride in being a Jew was a byword in the navy, ever since he had been assigned to his first post of prominence, sailing master aboard the 74-gun *Franklin.*

Upon reaching his home port, Philadelphia, Uriah attended a dance. Dressed in his well-tailored naval officer's uniform and adorned with gold epaulettes denoting his rank, he escorted his ladyfriend to the gala ball at Patriot's Hall. While dancing a polka, Uriah unintentionally collided with Lieutenant William Potter. Uriah politely excused himself, to which Potter retorted in a loud voice, "I hope you're a better navigator at sea than you are on the ballroom floor."

"I have said, 'I beg your pardon,'" Levy said, and continued with the dance only to be bumped intentionally by Potter. Restrained by his lady friend, Levy turned away.

Potter spouted, "Cowardly Jew, go home and sell old clothes."

"Sir, that I am a Jew I neither deny nor regret," Levy said with controlled anger. "If I am a coward the enemy did not discover it in the late war. As for old clothes, the clothes I am wearing I wear with more pride in my country than you seem to have."

The next day, one of the lieutenant's friends announced that Potter was challenging Levy to a duel. Unable to refuse without a loss of honor, Levy agreed, announcing his second.

On a cold, damp spring dawn under a cluster of oak trees by the New Jersey bank of the Delaware River (the laws against duelling were strictly enforced on the Pennsylvania side) Levy and his second, Aaron Marks, met Potter and his second. With the surgeon in attendance, the naval officers chose their pistols.

Twenty paces that would separate the two were stepped off by their seconds.

"Has either of the gentlemen anything to say?" asked the judge as Levy and Potter, backs to each other, stood at firing positions.

"Nothing!" said Potter.

"I wish to say a Hebrew prayer," Uriah replied, and recited the *Shema*.

There was a pause—then at the count of three both swung about and fired. Potter missed as Levy discharged his pistol into the air.

The judge ordered them to reload. Potter promptly complied. Levy reluctantly followed suit. The judge counted. Again Potter missed. Levy again fired toward the sky.

During the next reload Levy told Potter that he would hit the lowest hanging leaf on the tree over Potter's head. He aimed, pulled the trigger, and the leaf fluttered to the ground. He reloaded.

Potter's second thereupon tried to stop combat. Potter in a rage did not wait for the full count, fired and missed again. Levy's bullet found its mark—Potter's heart.

Uriah Phillips Levy's trouble with the navy began in earnest in 1839 when he commanded the U.S.S. *Vandalia*. His assignment was to influence Mexican officials to cease insulting American consuls and stop robbing American merchants. Mexican antagonism had begun three years earlier when Santa Anna was defeated and Texas was lost to the Americans.

Levy sailed the *Vandalia* into the Gulf of Mexico and anchored at the mouth of the Rio Grande. There he and other officers boated upriver the Rio Grande del Norte to Matamoros. With an armed guard of sailors, Uriah entered the town, escorted the American consul to the governor's office and gained apologies from him and promises of protection for American traders. From Matamoros the men returned to the *Vandalia* and Levy sailed to Tampico, his next port of call. At this dismal port in the tropics Uriah once again gained for the American consul there and American merchants the rights due them.

From Tampico, the *Vandalia* sailed south to Vera Cruz.

Approaching Vera Cruz, a French frigate of war was cruising off the nearby Island of Sacrificios. The U.S.S. *Vandalia* was coming in for anchorage in the small harbor, the French sloop of war alongside, in a parallel course. A sudden shift in the wind caused the two vessels to come dangerously close to each other. The *Vandalia,* headed off by the wind, was skillfully maneuvered by Captain Uriah Levy, who averted a collision, but not before it carried away some rigging, including the flying jibboom and fore royal mast; some tackle from the French sails fell to its deck. The French commander rushed to the rail nearest the *Vandalia,* shook his fist at the officers and shouted obscene insults.

Levy questioned the right of the French vessel to be in American waters. Indeed the Monroe Doctrine forbade this. As soon as the *Vandalia* found safe anchorage, Uriah ordered his gig and had himself rowed to hailing distance of the French vessel. Standing in the bow he shouted in French a demand for immediate apology. The French commander complied and the matter was closed.

Uriah demanded of his crew good conduct as well as good seamanship. All the while he was in Mexican waters, he had not once used a whip on an erring seaman. His methods, however, were most unorthodox. He ordered a drunken seaman confined until he was sober, with several wooden bottles hung around his neck, which effected the desired cure. Uriah Levy was determined to do away with brutal lashings inflicted for even minor infractions in traditional navy discipline.

Aboard the *Vandalia* officers constantly complained that they were being mimicked by cabin boy John Thompson. Uriah ordered the 15-

year-old lad to be tied to a gun, his trousers let down, circles of pliant pitch, each the size of a silver dollar, stuck upon each of his buttocks, and about six parrot feathers stuck into each dab of tar—the sight to be viewed for a few minutes by the other cabin boys.

Upon anchoring the *Vandalia* in Pensacola, Florida, Captain Uriah Phillips Levy, instead of being commended for upholding American honor was relieved of his command and ordered to appear before a court-martial.

To the Naval Court of Inquiry, Uriah Levy explained that tar holds no terrors to sailors, as their hands and entire bodies are frequently grimy from pitch. He pointed out that what he had done was a far cry from tarring and feathering and that the incident had been blown out of proportion. Certainly such punishment was preferable to the navy's customary flogging with a cat-o'-nine-tails—12 lashes upon the bare back, often leaving seamen disfigurement for life. Besides, Levy maintained that his humane punishment assured the finest discipline of any vessel in the United States Navy.

The naval court ruled that "Commander Uriah Phillips Levy is hereby dismissed from the Navy of the United States."

The sentence was forwarded to President John Tyler for review. The President read the indictment and mused: "A small quantity of tar was placed on the back of a boy and a half dozen parrot's feathers put on. It was substituted in place of 12 stripes with the cat, and for this Captain Levy is sentenced to be dismissed from the service." The President then directed the Naval Court to mitigate sentence from dismissal to suspension for a year.

Levy retired to his home, the Thomas Jefferson mansion that he purchased in Monticello, Virginia. Upon the death of his mother, Rachel Levy, a descendant of the first settlers of Georgia, Uriah and his brother Jonas and other family members interred her on the roadway leading to the mansion on the Monticello estate. There, along the path where Thomas Jefferson had strolled, Rachel Levy rests to this day inside a vine-covered alcove.

During the Mexican War and for a decade thereafter, while Uriah awaited reinstatement, he cared for the Jefferson mansion for he admired the liberalism and genius of the author of independence. In his 60th year (1852) Uriah carried across its threshold his bride, 18-year-old Virginia Lopez, his niece. Five years afterwards when he was reassigned, given command of the flagship of the Mediterranean Squadron, Virginia Lopez accompanied him. She was proud that her husband Uriah Phillips Levy was honored with the then highest rank in the United States Navy—commodore.

After Uriah's death, the Jefferson mansion was pilfered during the Civil War and his nephew, Jefferson Monroe Levy, restored the abandoned, abused, neglected, and pilfered estate at a cost of $1,000,000.

But during the Mexican War, Uriah, happy in caring for the Jefferson mansion was moody because of his having been deprived of a command.

Uriah's brother, Captain Jonas Phillips Levy, was 40 years old when he assumed the post of military commander of Vera Cruz. Married in New York to Francis (Fanny) Allen Mitchell, daughter of Abraham Mitchell, a one-time partner of Indian trader Joseph Simon, he sent for his wife as soon as travel was safe. In Vera Cruz she bore him a daughter, Isabella, whose name reflected Mexican influence.

And there was a nephew of Jonas and Uriah Levy who would become a congressman, Jefferson Monroe Levy. It was he who restored the Jefferson mansion acquired by uncle Uriah and in fact dedicated his life to this one great passion.

During the Mexican War, however, it was Jonas Phillips Levy who achieved the greatest distinction in a family of great American figures. As military commander of Mexico's leading seaport, Vera Cruz, he had an abiding interest in making the Gulf waters safe for American naval vessels. Under Jonas's control, Vera Cruz was a city serene and pacific, as though no war was being fought.

Camped outside the captured city of Vera Cruz in the spring of 1847, the American troops had no rest. The northers blew in from the sea, stirring the sand hills and all but blinding the troops. Sand could not be kept out of the food and water.

When orders were given to strike tent and march inland towards Jalapa, Hirschorn wrote:

> At Cerro Gordo (a mountain pass) we found Santa Anna entrenched on the heights with 20,000 troops and any amount of artillery. We had to pass there, no other way being passable, therefore general Scott, ordered, the next day at sunrise, an assault on the fortified heights. Step by step we had to pull our guns up by ropes, 40 or 50 men, attached with one hand to the rope, and with the other hand getting a hold on some grass cactus or any other old thing, so as to keep a footing and not to roll down again, with gun and all, and the Mexicans, continually firing on us, from above. It was a terrible battle, but after six hours fighting we conquered and the Mexicans fled "vamoosed" as they call it . . .

Of the 9,000 Americans storming the mountain pass, 431 officers and men were counted wounded or killed on April 18 and 19 as, according to one account, 13,000 of the enemy unloosed their firepower.

From the heights of Cerro Gordo, 60 miles northwest of Vera Cruz, the American force moved on to nearby Jalapa. There, Jacob Hirschorn watched as the imposing six-foot-two bearded Jewish general, David Emanuel Twiggs, arrived with his contingent to join Scott's army. Twiggs was affectionately called "the Bengal Tiger" by his troops because of his stalking stride and skillful military maneuvers.

David Twiggs's father, General John Twiggs, a Gentile, had fought in the Revolutionary War. David's mother, who was Jewish, Ruth Emanuel, was a sister of David Emanuel, Georgia's governor—the first Jewish governor in the United States.

At Jalapa the wounded and ill were housed in churches and convents swiftly converted into hospitals, while the combined army marched on to Puebla, which General Scott occupied on May 15. For three months Scott's army waited at Puebla for reinforcements to replace the overwhelming number of men who suffered dysentery after eating countryside fruit, presumably washed with unboiled Mexican water.

Additional supplies, too, were needed before attempting the major assault on Mexico City.

"Our situation at Puebla became a very alarming one," Hirschorn wrote:

> Every day there were deaths and more sickness, for the able men had to do twice as much in the way of guard duties, scouting, foraging, &c. By reason of the sick not being able to attend to these duties, we were in desperate straights. Remember, we had to hold down a population of 75,000 or thereabouts, besides any amount of guerillas, swarming round the city, to pick up outposts, stragglers, or so, and we only had about 4 or 5 thousand men fit for duty . . .
>
> Finally one fine day we saw a wagon train approaching the city. They had only a few supplies, no reinforcements, worth speaking of, but they had a mail and such a mail! When we got hold of the newspapers and we read of the proceedings in Congress, condemning the war with Mexico, hoping that the American army of invaders would meet with a hospitable grave at the hands of the Mexicans. Then we began to despair. Aimless and desponding the boys walked about, thousands of miles away from home in the interior of the enemies' country, with thousands

of sick and wounded comrades on hand, no supplies, no reinforcements and forsaken at home by our own government.

Another wagon train of about 300 wagons escorted by approximately 2,600 men and containing plenty of supplies, arrived four days later, which transformed the mood into one of rejoicing.

Finally the 12,000 men considered fit for action, including the Hirschorn lad who was yet a "greenhorn" for he spoke English with an accent, but he had mastered German and French. He was assigned to the quartermaster's unit, given the order on August 7 to move on Mexico City.

> The first battle took place at Contreras (about ten miles southwest of Mexico City, on August 19-20), where we encountered a part of the Mexican army under General Ampudia and his men fell back about six miles and joined Santa Anna, heavily fortified and entrenched at Churubusco (a small village, six miles south of Mexico City). At ten o'clock the same day, we attacked the enemy. Their strongest point was a bridge which our men would have to cross coming up from the main road. This bridge was strongly defended and the most vigorous defence was made by an Irish battery under Capt. Reilly, who had deserted the American army at Monteroy (Monterrey) with all accoutrement. They knew well what capture for them meant an ignominious, instant death. They fought bravely for their life and three times the regulars were repulsed under Worth and Twiggs . . .
>
> The next morning Reilly's battery was captured. A court martial convened, tried them and in a few minutes, sentenced them to be hanged, which sentence was carried into execution next day, after they had dug their own graves, a long and deep trench, into which their corpses were flung. Their captain (John Reilly, Riley, or O'Reily) was reserved for a worse fate . . .

In the action at Churubusco, Jacob Valentine, a Charleston Jew and the youngest soldier in the Palmetto Regiment, was badly wounded but recovered. Americans remained encamped there during a six-weeks' truce which permitted diplomatic negotiations. Nothing accomplished, General Scott ordered an advance on the Mexican capital.

The Battle of Molino del Rey, "the hardest contested battle of the whole war," was fought September 8. The American victory here carried the troops to their main objective, as further described by young Hirschorn:

> Next Chapultepec, the west point of Mexico built on a steep hill and surrounded by a high wall, well defended by Mexicans and splendidly

supported by the cadets, was to be assaulted. Here a call for volunteers from the different regiments was made to serve under the command of Major (Levi or Levy) Twiggs (a veteran of the Seminole War and brother of General David Twiggs) which command was called the "Forlorn Hope," because none of them ever expected to return alive.

Major Levi Twiggs was killed leading the assault. But Jacob Hirschorn lived to tell the tale of that battle:

> Under a terrible fire of artillery and muskets from the castle and wall we approached the wall, raised our ladders, and began to climb up. It was a terrible sight to see our brave fellows drop from the ladders, shot. Finally we reached the top of the wall . . .
> As soon as the glorious "Stars and Stripes" floated from the wall the Mexican flag came down. The defenders became demoralized and vamoosed . . . Having possession of the castle situated about three miles from the city, we advanced on the city. Our division [which] was to attack the garrita del Belen, were behind the breastworks. The Mexicans fought bravely, we forced them back however, and finally entered the city, opposed by the retreating enemy, who defended every foot of ground stubbornly and who were nobly assisted by hundreds of Mexican ladies, who from the tops of their houses (all flat tops) were pouring boiling water, boiling oil, rocks, anything they could lay their hands on, upon the very much exposed heads of our boys. Finally, about four o'clock p.m. we reached the "Plaza," the principal square of the city, planted the American flag on top of the Halls of Montezuma the palace of Mexico and Gen. Scott established his headquarters therein . . .

During a critical moment of the battle at Chapultepec, many of their officers fallen and the U.S. troops apparently about to be routed, the Jewish surgeon-general, David Camden de Leon, of Camden, South Carolina, took command. He had treated the ill and wounded soldiers of the Seminole War in 1836. At Chapultepec, he led inspired cavalry charges—as his commendation would state, "into the cannon's mouth," which helped immeasurably to turn seeming defeat into victory.

Expressions of gratitude were received from Congress; De Leon was praised as "The Fighting Doctor."

Fought September 12, Chapultepec was the Mexican War's final battle before the fall of Mexico City. While the Americans were ensconsed in Chapultepec, the commander of the deserted artillery company, Captain Riley, was court-martialed and sentenced, of which Hirschorn wrote:

... fettered with chains and balls [he] was to be taken to the place where all of our troops who could be spared were drawn up in a hollow square, the captain inside of the square to be attacked by the guard and (you may call him) the executioner, and a large D was to be branded with red hot iron on Capt. Riley's cheeks, D. standing for deserter. From thence he was taken in irons, to the castle Chapultepec, kept prisoner there during the term that the war lasted and when peace was declared and the army marched back to Vera Cruz to embark for home, he had to walk on foot at the head of the troops dragging his chains and balls on each foot. On arrival at Vera Cruz, peace had been declared [February 2, 1848]. He was then shipped back to New Orleans with the rest of the army ...

A day or two after, we were ordered to the city to witness the final punishment of Capt. Riley who was mounted on a donkey (chains and balls had been taken off) facing the tail of the donkey. The said donkey was marched through the streets of New Orleans a drum and fife corps playing Rogues march and finally Capt. Riley was drummed out of the service of the U.S.

Of the 1,200 New York volunteers who had left for Mexico two years previous, Jacob Hirschorn related that he was one of the approximately 260 that returned. He was decorated with the Silver Medal.

Highly honored of the Jewish fighters was "Old Davy, the Bengal Tiger," brevetted brigadier general for gallantry at Monterrey, and awarded by Congress the Golden Scabbard. His state of Georgia, upon his return, would present him with twin golden scabbards.

General David Twiggs, on September 14, 1847, led the vanguard of American troops, together with General Scott, into Mexico City.

Riding erect, General Twiggs entered as a conqueror into the heart of a land where his people had been forbidden to mount a horse, belt a sword, dress in silks or wear gold or silver adornments. He passed by the squares of Santiago de Thaltelelco and San Hipolito, which exactly two centuries earlier, in 1648, had been the site of one of Mexico's greatest mass *autos-da-fé* where Jews were burned at the stake.

Twiggs must have reflected that though Jews had inhabited every village or pueblo, from Acapulco and Antequera to Xicayau, Yucatan and Zumpango, the Jew dared not reveal his identity and live an open life.

He halted his mount upon reaching the Grand Plaza (present Zocalo); one of his regiments raised the Stars and Stripes over the National Palace, the band drummed "Hail Columbia" and "Hail to the

Chief." The never-to-be-forgotten day was September 14, 1847.

At the village of Guadalupe Hidalgo, near the Mexican capital, the treaty was signed in which Mexico turned over to the United States more than half its territory. Over 500,000 square miles of northern Mexico would one day become the states of California, New Mexico, Arizona, Utah, Nevada, and portions of Colorado and Wyoming. The United States now reached from the Atlantic to the Pacific.

But the greatest blow to Spain was about to be dealt. In their greed for gold, Spaniards killed thousands of Jewish *Marranos,* millions of Indians. But huge quantities of gold in northern Mexico undiscovered by Spaniards were to be United States possessions.

In the July 1849 issue of *Merchants Magazine and Commercial Review* it was written:

> The wealth of old Spain, drawn from the mines of Mexico and South America, involved the blood of millions, and the enslavement of the unoffending inhabitants of a continent. No wonder that prosperity thus obtained, did not command the blessings of heaven, and that the streams of gold, acquired at such a sacrifice, instead of fertilizing the land enjoying them, only paralyzed its industry, corrupted its morals, and, in the end, impoverished, weakened and degraded the people.

That gold would be discovered in such measure was undreamed of by the gold hungry *conquistadores.* Yet there it had been, its glittering nuggets sprinkled over the hills and dales inland of the Pacific coastal range and northward of the Gulf of California beyond the scanning range of Cortez and Pizzaro, reserved for a new nation, conceived in freedom, for men of all faiths, including the Jew.

At the very moment gold was discovered in California, a revolution was sparked. In the heart of Europe, in Austria and Bohemia, the masses rose up in arms against the reactionary governments. Jews were the scapegoats. They were violently assaulted, their homes in the ghettos pelted with stones, their property plundered, a few fatally wounded.

Shortly after the Vienna Revolution of March 1848, Leopold Kompert, a prominent Jewish novelist from Bohemia, appealed passionately to the Jews of the Austrian Empire to emigrate to the United States:

> On to America. No relief has been brought to us. The sun of liberty is up for the Fatherland; but for us it is a blood-red Northern Light. The larks of deliverance warble in the free air; but for us it is like the screaming of mews during a storm. Because servile hordes and sordid-minded people

have not understood and do not understand the spirit of liberty, we have to suffer . . . There is no other desire among us than to get away from this 'freedom.' . . . Let us go to America!

The clashes and conflicts between Czechs and Germans in Bohemia and between Poles and Germans in Posen spread throughout central Europe, aggravating the feeling of insecurity and alarm among the Jews. Families, even entire communities, began to emigrate to America, many to become "forty-niners."

Men of all nations, the dispersed Jews residing among them, raced to California. Aboard any sailing vessel that would float, Jews were among the first of the forty-niners who embarked from ports of all continents, from New York, London, Cape Town, Sydney and Shanghai. They suffered the rigors of the sea voyage that lasted over half a year until disembarking at San Francisco.

Other Jews, including American Jews, saddled a horse or joined wagon trains to cross what was then called "The Great American Desert" to Sacramento—Gateway to the Mines. They panned the Sierra streams, dug into its foothills, some striking bonanzas, others borascas; they tilled the soil, herded cattle, peddled, fought desperados.

The globe-trotting Jew, Benjamin II, met them in the mining camps and towns of the Mother Lode, dispersed in such remote diggings as at Grass Valley, Jamestown, and Shaw's Flat, as in the cities of Placerville, Jackson, and Columbia. Thus did Benjamin II describe the movement of mankind:

> From all points of the compass, all parts of the earth, all nations and tribes—they felt themselves drawn to this great magnet . . .

Of the forty-niners Benjamin II wrote:

> "They were witnesses of scenes which no other place, perhaps, and no other period had to show . . . El Dorado was found . . . Its call found ready and attentive listeners; a general migration began, as if a new Jerusalem was to be besieged, its golden temple robbed, its golden sepulchre captured, and its rich inhabitants driven away. With a wild adoration for that which lay buried in the mines of California, an adoration in its strength nothing less than that of a religious enthusiasm, they streamed to the promised land of California."

Epilogue

Forty-niner overlanders en route to the Mississippi ports and outposts to California found few Jewish communities; the few centers for Jewish settlers were Cincinnati and Louisville on the Ohio, Cleveland and Chicago on the Great Lakes, St. Louis and New Orleans on the Mississippi. But rarely did the gold seekers meet any of the early Jewish settlers, only recent immigrés like themselves.

A few adventurers may have sought in the Ohio or Mississippi valleys an uncle, a cousin, or relation who had preceded them, seeking freedom to work, marry and establish a family. If a Jew found his relative, he was either living with his non-Jewish wife and Christian children or interred in a family plot in a church graveyard.

To the generation of the forty-niners and succeeding ones it was clear that the Jewish people are unique, a clan apart and perhaps the key word is "more." They are more sentimental, more loyal, more tenacious, more religious, more adventurous and unfortunately more persecuted.

To the forty-niners who did not have to wait for over half a century to build a synagogue, who did not live in total isolation but organized congregations on the Pacific Coast that very year, it was easily apparent that the Jew of the Ohio wilderness was the Vanishing Jew—death, intermarriage, and atrocities decimated him; assimilation annihilated him.

But the generation of the German Jews, too, would be caught up in the transition to the modern Jew in a wave of imitating their Christian neighbors that resulted in reforming Judaism and which in no way made him a different person—only a changed person, the requirement for assimilation. Every synagogue they built in the three decades before the mass migration of European Jews to the United States was changed into a temple. When church organs were introduced, mixed choirs, with male and female as well as Jew and Gentile members; the Jewish house of worship had become a reflection of the individuals who themselves no longer kept the Sabbath, the kosher diet, ritual purity, or even the Covenant of Abraham. To prove their loyalty to their country, they struck from the prayer book all references to the Holy Land and as the Reform leader, Reverend Gustavus Poznansky of Beth Elohim in Charleston, South Carolina, declared upon the installation of an organ at its dedication: "this synagogue is our *temple,* this city our *Jerusalem,* this happy land our *Palestine,* and as our fathers defended with their lives *that* temple, *that* city and *that* land, so will their sons defend *this* temple, *this* city, and *this* land . . ."

The coming of the Messiah for the redemption of Israel was rejected by Reformers in favor of the concept of the Messianic Era ushering in peace for all mankind; the Temple of Jerusalem and its sacrificial cult was repudiated by those who no longer observed Judaism's precepts and ruled out Jewish nationalism in favor of the new temple of faith in America.

Only a few resisted intermarriage and assimilation—men like Joseph Simon of Lancaster in the 18th century and Joseph Jonas of Cincinnati in the 19th century.

But the majority of western Jews, isolated from their families and communities, with no one to pray with or mate with, intermarried and left no progeny to continue the chain of Judaism that linked them to their glorious heritage.

And even the descendants of Joseph Jonas, the Jew who formed the first Jewish community in the West and traveled east to marry a Jewess, would intermarry, as did grandson's Montrose who married Lucille Dorothy Herne and Robert S. Moses who married Laverne Conger. Niece Anne Elizabeth, daughter of Joseph's brother Abraham Jonas, married a Reverend T. B. Wells. No Jewish family in the West seemed to be without intermarried children or grandchildren.

But in consonance with the Jewish dictum that a born Jew is a Jew all his life, the unobservant as the observant, the intermarried as the intramarried, be they Indian trader or town merchant, soldier or mountain man, adventurer or renegade, peddler or pirate, along with men of all creeds and races, participated in opening a new frontier dedicated to the high principle of freedom.

Sources

List of Abbreviations of Publications

AJHQ	American Jewish Historical Quarterly
AOJD	Americans of Jewish Descent
CAJ	Colonial American Jew
EAJ	Early American Jewry
HJP	History of the Jews of Philadelphia
JLCHS	Journal of the Lancaster County Historical Society
MAJ	Memoirs of American Jews
PAJA	Publications of the American Jewish Archives
PAJHS	Publications of the American Jewish Historical Society
PEIS	Portraits Etched in Stone

1
Colonial Jewish-Indian Traders

page/paragraph

1/1 The Appalachian Mountains extend for more than a thousand miles parallel to the coast, and include the Catskill and Cumberland Mountains in addition to the Alleghenies. The latter extends for over 400 miles as part of the Allegheny plateau of the Appalachians.

1/2 *Ashkenazic* (German Jews and East European) call the Synagogue "Shul" or "Schule", Judeo-German (Yiddish) meaning "school." *Sephardic* (Iberian Jews) call the Synagogue "esnoga", Judeo-Spanish (Ladino) for the Hebrew "Beit Hakneses" meaning "House of Assembly".

Julius Friedrich Sache, *The German Sectarians of Pennsylvania 1899-1900* (2 vols.) 1:14, 27, 58, 114, 124; 2:372.

284 Sources

1/3 Sache, "Jacob Philadelphia, Mystic and Physicist" *PAJHS* 16: 74–83.

2/1 Max J. Kohler, "Some Jewish Factors in the Settlement of the West" *PAJHS*, 16:33–35. Appendix I, "Old War on Jews. Expulsion Edict of Louis XIII Just Found in Indiana . . . " (Chicago Inter-Ocean, October 1, 1899).
Le Code Noir, ou Edit du Roi (Paris, 1728) p. 2. "The edict of the late King Louis XIII, of glorious memory, dated April 23, 1615, shall be executed in our province and colony of Louisiana: this being done, We enjoin the Directors General of the said Company, and all our Officers, to drive out of the said country all Jews who may have established their residence there. These, as declared enemies of the Christian name, We command to leave in three months, counting from the day of the publication of these Presents, upon penalty of the confiscation of their persons and property."
Bertram Wallace Korn, *The Early Jews of New Orleans*, (Waltham, Mass., 1969), p. 3. "Such immigrants to Louisiana as Jacob David, shoemaker, Romain David, tailor, Robert and Genevieve Jacob, and a soldier named Louis Salomon, all of whom arrived in 1719, have been regarded as Jews . . . but no contemporary document identifies them as Jews . . . "
Arthur Daniel Hart, *The Jew in Canada*, (Toronto, 1926), p. 3. In New France Jesuit Biart, a descendant of Spanish Jews, arrived by 1611.
The Black Code as its name implied was directed against blacks. Negroes were known to have been apprehended in 1730 when the black Banbaras banned together with the Chickasaw tribe to kill all whites and set up an independent republic in Louisiana. The negro leader, Samba, and seven of his companions were captured, lashed to the rack, their bodies broken on the wheel; a negress hanged. There were probably about a thousand blacks in Louisiana at that time, for 600 were recorded enslaved in 1721 in that colony and in 1745, 2020.

2/3 Franklin Ellis and Samuel Evans, "*History of Lancaster County*, Philadelphia 1883." *PAJHS* 1: 121. Joseph Simon arrived in Lancaster in 1740.
Isaac Markens, *The Hebrews in America* (New York, 1888). Joseph Simon arrived "about 1735".

2/4 David Brener, "Lancaster's First Jewish Community 1715 to 1804, The Era of Joseph Simon," *JLCHS*, 80, no. 4 (Michaelmas 1976): 217–218.

3/2 Malcolm H. Stern, "New Light on the Jewish Settlement of Savannah," *AJHQ*, 52, no. 3 (March 1963): 191–192. Oglethorpe was defeated after he made an abortive attack on St. Augustine, Florida. While the British lines held, rumors of Spanish conquest frightened away the *Sephardic* Jews.

3/3 Brener, "Lancaster's First," *JLCHS*, 80, no. 4: 223.

3/4 Sterne, "New Light," *AJHQ*, 52, no. 3: 169–99.
Brener, "Lancaster's First," *JLCHS*, 80, no. 4: 225–26; 245.

4/2 Ibid. p. 223

4/3 Allegheny is derived from the Algonquin-speaking Delaware tribe. *Welhik* meaning "most beautiful" or "best" and *Hanna* or *Heny* meaning "stream."
The log cabin "Schul" is no longer extant. Neither is the old Jewish cemetery near Heidelberg, opened about 1732. The stone wall enclosing the burial ground, a plot about 30 by 60 feet, had monuments still standing about 1863. Today the ground of that cemetery, situated at the summit of Tower Hill, is neglected and covered with weeds.

CAJ, 1: 368–69; 471, 2: 732; 3: 1231. About the same time that Joseph Simon prepared to enter the west, Daniel and Moses Nunez Ribiero, the sons of Dr. Samuel Nunez Ribiero who fled the Inquisition, boated from Savannah, Georgia upriver the Savannah 125 miles to Augusta to trade with the Indians. Both learned the Indian languages, and married Indian women fathering broods of half-breeds. By 1750, Moses traded in present-day Alabama with the Upper Creek tribe. By 1756 he settled in Augusta, a western town of 500 (double that of Lancaster) to be numbered among its 18 leading citizens. There he married a mulatto and reared his children as Christians. *PAJHS*, 50, no. 3 (March 1961): 176–77. /To "Mulatta Rose" an f.w.c. (free woman of color) and his children Robert, James, Alexander and Frances he bequeathed his home and furniture, land tracts, thirteen Negro slaves, and "a full and perfect freedom from all Slavery and servitude in reward and as an acknowledgement of the faithful conduct and behaviour of the said Mulatta Rose towards me and my children." These progeny were probably those of his Indian wife.

4/7 *Babylonian Talmud*, "B'rokhot" Daf 28, side 2. Also, *Jerusalem Talmud*, "Sanhedrin" Daf 6, side 2.

5/1 Henry Necarsulmer. "The Early Jewish Settlement at Lancaster, Pennsylvania," *PAJHS*, 9 (1901): 29–44.

5/5 Arthur Daniel Hart, *The Jew in Canada: A Complete Record of Canadian Jewry from the Days of the French Regime to the Present Time*, (Toronto, 1926), p. 4.

6/2 E. M. Ruttenber, *History of the Indian Tribes of Hudson's River*, (Albany, 1872), p. 384.

Leon Huhner, "Daniel Gomez, A Pioneer Merchant of Early New York" *PAJHS*, 41, no. 2, (December 1951): 107–125. Gomez House six miles north of Newburgh by modern roads.

7/5 William Vincent Byars, ed., *B. & M. Gratz: Merchants in Philadelphia 1754–1798*, (Jefferson City, Missouri, 1916), pp. 58, 158. The beaver-hat reigned supreme, chiefly overseas, for a hundred years, until the 1840s, when silk from China, opened by the Opium War, replaced beaver. These hats were known as either "top hats" or because of their height, "stove-pipe".

8/1 Kosher signifies that which accords with biblical and rabbinic law. Kosher literally means that which is "proper" or "prepared" according to ritual law. Kosher is applied to all rituals in Jewish life, i.e., the Torah, Tefillin, or Mezuzah scrolls, marriage contract, bill of divorce, as well as to an individual who fulfills divine precept.

Kosher fish are possessed of fins and scales. Scales must be easily removable as an additional integument over the fish's skin, such as the ctenoid and cycloid. Among fish with cycloid scales are carp, herring, pike, and salmon. Among ctenoid-scaled fish are perch. The prohibited fish are those bearing ganoid scales as the garpike or placoid-scaled sharks, skates, or rays.

9/4 *AOJD*, p. 194.

JLCHS, p. 301.

9/5 *JLCHS*, p. 235.

10/2 *JLCHS*, p. 241, 272.

10/3 *JLCHS*, p. 239.

10/6 *CAJ*, 2: 54.
10/7 *CAJ*, 3: 1132-33.
Nathan Levy of Philadelphia is not to be confused with Nathan Levy of Phillipsburg. Of the latter John Farnsworth advertised in the *Pennsylvania Journal*, 1765, that he is no longer responsible for his wife's future purchases as she had run off with Nathan Levy, for "she likes said Levy better than me, and intends to live with him, as he will maintain her as a gentlewoman; I have waited on Levy respecting the affair, from whom I have received no other satisfaction than insolent language . . ."
11/1 Byars, *B. & M. Gratz*, pp. 57-58. Simon refers to waggoner Slough.
11/4 The Seven Years' War (1756-1763) involved nearly every nation in Europe, and extended to India in the east and Canada in the west. Control of Germany was contested between Prussia and Austria. Prussia won and became leader of the German states; England defeated the French and gained control of the seas. European boundaries however remained generally unaffected.

Though the mid-eighteenth struggle between the English and French for domination of the western wilderness had begun in 1754, the fighting that took place after the three-years lull, beginning in 1758, led to the decisive defeat of the French in 1760 and the Indians in 1763. The years 1758-1763 are therefore referred to as the period of the French and Indian War.
12/5 Samuel C. Williams, *Early Travels in the Tennessee Country* (Johnson City, 1928).
13-4 "The Simon-Henry Store at 2-4 East King St. disappeared early in the 19th century" according to John Ward Willson Loose, President and Editor of the Journal of the Lancaster County Historical, in a letter to the author dated December 31, 1976.
13/5 Victor Rosewater, *The Liberty Bell: Its History and Significance*, (New York, 1926).
14/6 Cyrus Adler, "Jewish Soldiers in the Colonial Period," *PAJHS*, 2: 180-81. See also, 29: 141.

Stuart E. Rosenberg, *The Jewish Community in Canada* 1: 42. Volunteer David David, who joined Captain Merrick's Company, should not be confused with the David David who at age thirteen donated in 1777 land he inherited from his father Lazarus David to Congregation *Shearith Israel* to build a synagogue. This lad was the first Jew born in Canada.
15/2 David Franks gained this enviable position acting as agent for the powerful English syndicate, Colebrooke, Nesbitt & Franks (the latter, New York born Moses Franks, a prominent merchant and shipowner, being David Franks' brother). The syndicate's army contracts with the Crown amounted to over 764,000 pounds. David Franks had ingratiated himself in the post when, following Braddock's defeat and the loss of their provisions when the Simon, Levy & Franks packtrain was destroyed, raised 5,000 pounds for the furtherance of the British cause in French-controlled Ohio.

CAJ, 2: 715. The syndicate's principals included notable and politically powerful merchants like Sir James Colebrooke, George Colebrooke, Arnold Nesbitt, Sir Samuel Fludyer, and Adam Drummond. When their fortunes waned and various partners left the syndicate, Moses Franks remained a constant member even into the 1780s.
15/3 *PAJHS*, 29: xxxvi; 31: 229-34. 31: 229-34. "Benjamin Franks, Merchant, and Captain Kidd, Pirate," by Samuel Oppenheim.

15/4 Kenneth P. Bailey, ed., *The Ohio Company Papers, 1753-1817,* (Arcata, California, 1947), pp. 36-173.
15/5 David deSola Pool, *Portraits Etched in Stone,* (New York, 1952), pp. 329-31.
Solomon Solis-Cohen, "Note concerning David Hays . . . " *PAJHS,* 2: 72.
15/6 Ibid.
Neil H. Swanson, *The First Rebel,* (New York, 1937), p. 30.
16/2 Jacob R. Marcus, "The Quintessential American Jew," *PAJHS,* 58, no. 1, (September 1968): 17.
Max J. Kohler, "Phases of Jewish Life in New York before 1800," *PAJHS,* no. 3: 82.
Goods sent by Heyman Levy to forts Detroit and Mackinac in the Michigan Territory ultimately reached as far west as the foothills of the Rockies.
Douglas Waitley, *Portrait of the Midwest* (New York, 1963), pp. 50-51.
16/3 Charles P. Daly, *The Settlement of the Jews in North America,* (New York, 1893), p. 52; *PAJHS,* 3: 81-82: Heyman Levy owned many vessels that preyed upon enemy commerce during the French and Indian War.
PAJHS, 66, no. 1 (September 1976): 27: Heyman Levy, headquartered in New York City, engaged in privateering. His vessels, the *Orleans* and *Dreadnought,* had a total of 14 guns. For a biography of Heyman Levy see *PEIS,* pp. 252-53.
17/3 *EAJ,* 1: 76-77.
17/4 Bernard Postal and Lionel Koppman, *A Jewish Tourist's Guide to the U.S.* (Philadelphia, 1954), p. 535.
17/6 John C. Fitzpatrick, ed., *Writings of George Washington* (Washington, D.C., 1931), 2: 190.
18/1 *PAJHS,* no. 20: 91; no. 31: 235-36. See also *Letters to Washington,* edited by Stanislaus Murray Hamilton (New York, 1899), 2: 32.
19/1 *PAJHS,* no. 35: 2. "William Pitt was now at the helm and, with Frederick of Prussia as his ally, to whom he entrusted the European phase of the struggle, he proceeded to concentrate all his strength on America, which he viewed as its real crux.
19/2 *JLCHS,* p. 236.
19/3 Ibid., p. 250. Potash Works was established at 230-250 West Chestnut Street. *PAJA,* 12, no. 1 (April 1960) 101-2. "Early Legal Records of Jews of Lancaster County, Pennsylvania" by Irwin S. Rhodes—"Deed Records" No. 62.
19/4 Ibid.
20/1 Ibid., p. 249.
20/5 Ibid., pp. 250-52.
JLCHS, pp. 250-252.
20/6 Francis Jordan, Jr., *The Life of William Henry of Lancaster: Pennsylvania 1729-1786* (Lancaster, 1910), p. 4.
21/1 *JLCHS,* p. 253.
21/2 Isaac M. Fein, *The Making of an American Jewish Community: The History of Baltimore Jewry from 1773 to 1920* (Philadelphia, 1971), p. 10.
21/3 Ira Rosenswaike, "Simon M. Levy: West Point Graduate" *AJHQ,* 61, no. 1 (September 1971): 69-73. Rosenswaike concludes that the "L. A. Levy

288 Sources

family of Baltimore had ties with the Magruders, as revealed by burial records for St. Paul's." But he is unaware of what that tie is. In an article entitled "Lancaster's First Jewish Community" by David Brener (*JLCHS*, p. 274), the author surmises that "obviously the Magruders were longtime employees of Levy far above the slave or servant status." In truth, the tie was Levy Andrew Levy's marriage to a Magruder.

21/6 *Pennsylvania Packet*, October 27, 1778.

21/1 *CAJ*, 2: 997.

22/5 Malcolm H. Stern, "Two Jewish Functionaries in Colonial Pennsylvania: Barnard Jacobs, Ritual Circumciser," *PAJHQ*, 57, no. 1 (September 1967): 39–45.

23/2 *CAJ*, 2: 795.

23/3 *HJP*, p. 64.

23/6 Throughout the period when France ruled the lands north of the St. Lawrence and Great Lakes, it was called New France. After 1760, when the British defeated the French, it became Canada, the name applied by the British to its possessions along Hudson's Bay and Nova Scotia since their earlier acquisition. Nonetheless, the names New France and Canada for France's possessions were interchanged in the early period. When Jacques Cartier in 1534 discovered the St. Lawrence and claimed the surrounding area for France, he called it Canada, taken from *Kanata*, meaning "village" in the language of the Iroquois Huron Indian tribe.

23/7 Max J. Kohler, "Jewish Activity in American Colonial Commerce," *PAJHS*, 10: 60. It was said that Gradis "controlled the trade of France with the West Indies."

24/2 Hart, *The Jew in Canada*, p. 9.

24/4 Ibid., p. 10.

24/5 *CAJ*, 2: 714.

25/1 Hart, *The Jew in Canada*, pp. 11–12.

25/2 Ibid., p. 12.

25/5 *PAJHS*, 50, no. 2 (December 1960): 123, note 12.

25/6 Hart, *op. cit.*, p. 14; *PAJHS*, 27: 490.

26/1 Hart, *op. cit.*, p. 4.

26/3 *PAJHS*, 35: 5. "Jewish Colonial Enterprise in the Light of the Amherst Papers (1758–1763)" by Frances Dublin. "There is record of a Jewish landowner at Halifax, by the name of Abrahams, specifically referred to as 'the Jew' . . . his ownership antedated 1762." Abrahams probably arrived with the ships that carried the Jewish sutlers to Nova Scotia in 1758.

26/1 Ibid., p. 4.

26/4 *Historical and Scientific Society of Manitoba*, 3: 14. Ferdinande Jacobs died in London in the early 1780s and was buried in an Anglican Cemetery.

Arthur A. Chiel, *The Jews in Manitoba* (Toronto, 1961), p. 5.

26/6 *PAJHS*, 50, no. 2 (December 1960): 123, notes 12 and 13. "Some Aspects of the Historical Development of the Canadian Jewish Community" by Louis Rosenberg.

27/2 *PAJHS*, 35: 6. General Jeffery Amherst was at this time attempting to reach Canada by way of Ticonderoga and Crown Point, New York. While building a fortress at Crown Point he was unable to reach Wolfe awaiting an opportune moment to storm Quebec. Amherst sent a Captain Kennedy with a few troops, including a Jewish soldier, Abraham (not the Abrahams who arrived to trade at Halifax and supply troops). Proceeding through the forests by way of Indian settlements, Kennedy offered them a large reward if they would guide them to Wolfe. But the Indians, instead of honoring his flag of truce, took them captives.

27/5 Hart, *The Jew in Canada*, p. 2.
27/6 Ibid., p. 14.
28/1 Point de Levis, originally Cap de Levis, was mentioned by Samuel de Champlain, explorer and founder of Quebec, in describing his voyage to Canada in 1629: "When my servant arrived with four small sacks of roots he told me of his having seen the English ships at a distance of a mile from our house behind the Cap de Levis." Cap de Levis thereafter referred to the region comprising the whole of the eight banks of the lake opposite the City of Quebec.

B. G. Sack, *History of the Jews in Canada* (Montreal, 1965), pp. 32–33.

28/2 Hart, *The Jew in Canada*.
28/3 *CAJ*, 1: 384–85.
29/4 *AOJD*, p. 69.

Bernard Postal and Lionel Koppman, *American Jewish Landmarks* (New York, 1977), p. 337. The site of *Shearith Israel*, New York, "just west of the rented wooden frame house then used as a sanctuary, was bought for 100 pounds, one loaf of sugar, and a pound of tea . . . " No doubt the tea was the beverage with which the consummation of the deal was toasted.

29/5 Morris A. Gutstein, *To Bigotry No Sanction* (New York, 1958), pp. 24–26.

PAJA 16: no. 1, (April 1964): 42. The "Touro Synagogue" *Yeshuat Israel* was designated a national shrine in 1954.

30/2 *PAJHS*, 50, no. 2 (December 1960): 125.
30/3 *PAJHS*, 4: 217.
31/1 *PAJHS*, 34: 273.
31/4 Byars, *B. & M. Gratz*, p. 47.

Anita Libman Lebeson, *Jewish Pioneers in America 1492–1848* (New York, 1938), p. 149.

32/1 *AOJD*, p. 64.
32/2 Byars, *B. & M. Gratz*.
33/1 *JLCHS*, p. 247.
33/2 *CAJ*, 1: 385–86. *PAJHS*, 35: 7–10. Captain Elias Meyer, presumed to be a Jew, was a member of the Royal American Regiment, composed largely of Germans. Stationed in 1761 at Fort Sandusky, he managed, after great difficulty in securing supplies, to complete the Block House by the end of that year. He had served for 13 years as a lieutenant, 11 as an engineer, and was the eldest Lieutenant in the Four Battalions, prior to his promotion to Captain in 1762.
33/2 Howard H. Peckham, *Pontiac and the Indian Uprising* (Princeton, 1947).

David E. Heineman. "The Startling Experience of a Jewish Trader during Pontiac's Siege of Detroit in 1763," *PAJHS*, 23: 31–35.

33/5 Howard H. Peckham, *Pontiac and the Indian Uprising* (Chicago, 1961), p. 122.

Sources

34/1 PAJHS, 35: 13. Abrams, a trader, was recorded in Fort Niagara in 1763. Peckham, *op. cit.,* 148, 198: Chapman, originally Kaufman; Abraham also Abram.

35/1 Ibid., 40, Part 1 (September 1950): 81–86.

35/1 John Heckewelder, *Account of the History, Manners and Customs of the Indian Nations* (Philadelphia, 1819).

35/5 Baggataway or lacrosse involves two opposing teams of ten players. Each player is armed with a long-handled stick, the paddle-like end suspending a webbed basket like that used in jai alai. The object is to send the ball through a goal.

35/5–7 David E. Heineman, "Jewish Beginnings in Michigan before 1850," *PAJHS,* 13: 49–50.

Alexander Henry, *Travels and Adventures in Canada* (New York, 1809), p. 105.

36/2 *PAJHS,* 23: 35.

36/3 *PAJHS,* 35: 19. "Levy had also been involved in transactions with . . . Gershon Levy and Partners, Montreal . . . "

36/4 *PAJHS,* 13: 55. Another Jewish trader was J. Levy in partnership with Richard McCarty, two large canoes of goods reaching Levy at Michilimackinac in 1774.

36/6 *PAJHS,* 35: 18.

PAJHS, 23: 32. Levy Andrew Levy was the trader referred to by Major Roberts in his "Diary of the Siege of Detroit"—his July 10 entry reading: "We heard today that the Miami Indians were gone off with Mr. Levy."

37/1 *PAJHS,* 35: 16.

37/5 Ray Allen Billington, *Westward Expanson* (New York, 1967), p. 138. Bouquet replied that he would try to distribute germ-laden blankets among the Indians " . . . as it is a pity to expose good men against them, I wish we could make use of the Spanish method, to hunt them with English dogs . . . who would, I think effectually extirpate or remove that vermin."

38/1 Bouquet Papers, 24, 1763, Public Archives of Canada, Ottawa, pp. 187–88.

38/2 Francis Parkman, *The Conspiracy of Pontiac* (New York, 1966), pp. 297–98.

Walker O'Mears, *Guns at the Forks,* (Englewood Cliffs, N.J., 1965), p. 233.

CAJ, 2: 92, 717.

39/2 *PAJHS,* 35: 16.

39/3 Howard H. Peckham, *Pontiac and the Indian Uprising* (Princeton, 1947), pp. 208–9.

40/1 Irving I. Katz, *The Beth El Story with a history of Michigan before 1950* (Detroit, 1955), p. 20.

41/6 Benjamin Monsanto had been expelled from New Orleans in 1769 together with his father Isaac Rodriguez Monsanto, brothers Jacob and Manuel, sisters Angelica, Eleanora, and Gracia. After confiscation of their property and valuables, the family, along with all Jews expelled, were allowed to return.

42/1 Korn, *The Early Jews,* pp. 20–23. Robert Fastio, a Jewish Monsanto associate, who failed to prosper, was not expelled.

42/4 The ambush at Sideling Hill west of Fort Loudon is located today by Lincoln Highway, U.S. Route 40.

42/5 Byars, *B. & M. Gratz,* pp. 69-71.

O'Mears, *Guns,* p. 228, note 8. In a typical listing of Indian and other goods listed in the books of Baynton, Wharton & Morgan are: "'britch clout,' buckskin britches, scarlet cloth, silk handkerchiefs, stockings, leggings, gun locks, 'riffle guns,' pipe tomahawks, Jew's harps, 'cags of rum,' venison, bear meat, corn, milk, window glass, horse bells, sleeve buttons, 'broaches,' rugs, ear bobs, scalping knives, spurs, laced coats, black wampum, tea, butter, vermillion paint, pumps, Madeira wine."

43/5 Billington, *Westward Expansion,* p. 139.

44/4 Byars, *B. & M. Gratz,* pp. 85, 88-89.

44/5 Ibid., pp. 69-71, 341-42.

PAJHS, 23b; 6.

45/2 "The Indiana Company," *CAJ,* 2: 754-57.

Samuel Wharton, *View of the Title to Indiana, a Tract of Country on the Ohio River* (Philadelphia, 1775).

Samuel Wharton, *Plain Facts: being an Examination into the Rights of the Indian Nations of America, to their respective countries* (Philadelphia, 1781).

Sydney G. Gumpertz, *The Jewish Legion of Honor* (New York, 1934), p. 71. "Joseph Simon fought the Indians at Bloody Run in 1763." The only evidence we have to this effect is his pack train that fought Pontiac on the economic front. "Indiana" was then situated south of the Ohio, west of the Monongahela, and north of the Little Kanawha. By the time of the Revolution, Indiana was applied to the region north of the Ohio River.

46/3 Byars, *B. & M. Gratz,* p. 120.

46/4 *PAJHS,* 35: 18. "Joseph Simon . . . made frequent excursions to the Ohio and Illinois country."

46/5 Ibid., p. 35.

Abram Vossen Goodman, *American Overture* (Philadelphia, 1947), p. 130.

PAJHS, 2: 121. A letter from General Thomas Gage, dated February 5, 1771, inquired whether the firm of Levy & Franks would provision "the Illinois" to the "Troops station'd at the Natchese & Iberville on the Mississippy."

47/4 Byars, *B. & M. Gratz,* pp. 11-14.

47/6 Ibid., p. 74.

48/1 Certification of *Kabalah* to Solomon Etting, 1782, signed by Barnard Gratz and Aaron Levy, Jewish Theological Seminary Library, New York City.

48/2 Byars, *B. & M. Gratz,* p. 84.

HJP, op. cit., p. 68.

48/3 Cahokia's name was derived from the Cahokia tribe of the Illini Confederacy. Founded as a mission among the Indians in 1699, it became a leading fur trading center in the Illinois country, with 3,000 population as compared to the present 800. Cahokia, north of Fort du Chartres, is five miles south of East St. Louis, Illinois.

Kaskaskia, founded like Cahokia by Jesuit missionaries, had rich bottomland soil along the Kaskaskia river where it emptied into the Mississippi. French farmers raised crops in this extremely fertile land for the soldiers at nearby Fort du Chartres, traders at Cahokia, as well as for its own community of Kaskaskia.

48/4 Robert Silverberg, *Mound Builders of Ancient America* (Greenwich, Conn., 1968), pp. 2–3.
49/1 Byars, *B. & M. Gratz*, p. 86.
49/2 Ibid., p. 109.
49/4 *CAJ*, 2: 743, 764.
Byars, *B. & M. Gratz*, p. 244. Michael Gratz, regarded as the founder of Gratzburg, New York, may have sold a portion of his tract to James Fenimore Cooper's father for his settlement, Cooperstown. Other lands taken in collateral from Croghan and others included 36,000 acres in Indiana.
50/2 Byars, *B. & M. Gratz*, p. 130.
PAJHS, 25: 119–21.
50/5 *CAJ*, 2: 760. *PAJHS*, 25: 120. Opinion of the English Jurists.
50/6 *CAJ*, 3: 1515, note 16.
51/1 Byars, *B. & M. Gratz*, pp. 130–31.
51/3 *CAJ*, 2: 760.
51/4 *HJP*, p. 72.
52/2 Byars, *B. & M. Gratz*, pp. 140–41.
52/4 *HJP*, p. 180, 433, note 94. "Michael Gratz in 1795 entered into negotiations with Stephen Austin (then in England but later one of the founders of the Texas Republic) to sell the land at the Falls of the Ohio to colonists or land promoters abroad. Some of it was sold to Robert Morris' fantastic North American Land Company, but some was retained . . ."
CAJ, 2: 711.
EAJ, 2: 173. Fort Fincastle, renamed Fort Henry, the future Wheeling.
54/1 *PAJA*, 12, no. 1 (April 1960): 101.
54/1 Lebeson, *Jewish Pioneers*, pp. 148–49.

2
American and Hebrew Revolutions

55/2 Morris U. Schappes, *A Documentary History of the Jews in the United States 1654–1875* (New York, 1950), pp. 38–40.
56/1 Leland Baldwin, *Pittsburgh: The Story of a City* (Pittsburgh, 1937), p. 89.
56/3 Byars, *B. & M. Gratz*, p. 151.
56/4 *JLCHS*, p. 271.
56/5 Journal of the Continental Congress, April 10, 1776.
56/6 Byars, *B. & M. Gratz*, p. 158.
57/3 *HJP*, pp. 74–75.
57/4 *PAJHS*, 20: 92.
58/1 *PEIS*, p. 477.
58/5 Schappes, *Documentary History*, p. 45, Francis Salvador lost 73,000 pounds through the failures of the Dutch East India Company and other interests in which he invested. Francis came to America to recoup his losses.

59/2 Abram Vossen Goodman, *American Overture* (Philadelphia, 1947), p. 165. *PAJHS*, 35: 6-7. Lieutenant Joseph Levey (Levy) served as a board member at the court martial of a deserter. The Cherokee, numbering 6,000 warriors, inhabited the region near the head of the Savannah River, extending westward. Since 1756, numbers of braves returning home from western Virginia where they aided British forces, now engaged in some depredations. Punitive measures were taken against the Cherokees in 1761. Lieutenant Levey saw action. During one such expedition led by Colonal Grant a Corporal deserted and Lieutenant Levey was called upon to serve in the case.

59/5 Schappes, *Documentary History,* pp. 45-47. Letter from Major Andrew Williamson, August 4, 1776, from "Camp, two miles below Keowee" to John Rutledge, President of South Carolina, Charlestown. According to Schappes his plantation was of 7,000 acres.

60/1 Samuel Rezneck, *Unrecognized Patriots* (Westport, Ct., 1975), pp. 41; 212-13. Patriot Mordecai Sheftall, later Deputy Commissary General of Issues for Georgia's troops and elevated to Colonel (to the General Staff of the Georgia Brigade) advanced money and goods for Colonel Wilkin's expedition against the marauding, murdering, Cherokee.

60/2 *PAJHS*, 9: 107-22. "Francis Salvador, A Prominent Patriot of the Revolutionary War" by Leon Huhner; No. 22, p. 188: "Additional Note on Francis Salvador" by Leon Huhner; No. 29, p. 142: "Jews of North Carolina Prior to 1800" by Leon Huhner.

Leon Huhner, "Francis Salvador, A Prominent Patriot of the Revolutionary War," *PAJHS*, 9: 107-22.

Huhner, "Additional Note on Francis Salvador," *PAJHS*, 22: 188.

Huhner, "Jews of North Carolina Prior to 1800," *PAJHS*, 29: 142.

60/4 *PAJA*, 17, no. 1 (April 1965): 29-32.

61/3 The Church of Jesus Christ of Latter-Day Saints, to author, 6 May 1977, Genealogical Department, Church of Jesus Christ of Latter-Day Saints. The letter contained the following data on the Kentucky Harts derived from the *Biographical Encyclopaedia of Kentucky of the Dead and living men of the nineteenth century* (Cincinnati, 1878), pp. 194-195.

Biographical Cyclopedia of the Commonwealth of Kentucky (Chicago, 1896), p. 193.

Thomas J. C. Williams, *A History of Washington County, Maryland* (Baltimore, 1968), pp. 89, 94, 102-5.

J. P. Young and C. L. Ficklen, comps., *Hart Family Genealogy,* forwarded to author by Mary E. Winter, Kentucky Historical Society Library, Frankfort, Ky. First of the clan was merchant Thomas Hart, who emigrated from London to Virginia about 1690. He seems to have been the Jewish ancestor of the Kentucky Harts and it was probably his Hebrew Bible that was preserved by his Kentucky descendants. He came to America with his only son, 11-year-old Thomas. Thomas Hart, Jr. married Susanne Rice, a Christian. Upon his death in 1755 he left six children: Thomas, John, Benjamin, David, Nathaniel, and Ann who, with their mother, moved to North Carolina about 1760. The oldest son, Colonel Thomas Hart, married Susanna Grey in North Carolina. They moved in 1780 to Hagerstown, Maryland, and in 1794 to Lexington, Kentucky. They named their eldest son Thomas. The other children were Nathaniel, John, Eliza, Susanna,

Nancy, and Lucretia (who married Henry Clay). General Thomas Hart, eldest son of Colonel Thomas Hart and Susanna, married Nellie Grush of Hagerstown, Maryland, and they named their eldest son, Thomas, who in turn married a Miss Gardner. They left no son whom they could name Thomas, after seven generations of reverencing the name of the first Thomas Hart to come to America.

Lewis N. Dembitz, "Jewish Beginnings in Kentucky," *PAJHS*, 1: 99. "Nathaniel Hart came out in 1774 with Richard Henderson to buy the Green River Country from the Cherokee Indians . . . in Kentucky he was known as a member of the Anglican Church."

61/5 "The Emigrant Indian Tribes of Wyandotte County," address delivered before the Kansas City, Kansas, high school, November 12, 1901 (Topeka, n.d.), pp. 16–18.

61/5 The Wilderness Trail (Wilderness Road), the only usable route through the mountains to the rich lands of Kentucky, began at the Block House in Virginia (one wonders if that house belonged to a forerunner of the Jewish Block family later settled in a number of Virginian cities and towns). The trail passed through the Powell River Valley, crossed the Cumberland Mountains through Cumberland Gap, and ended in Central Kentucky, at a settlement Boone built called Boonesborough, near present-day Lexington. Another branch of the Wilderness Trail led to Harrodsburg, the oldest settlement in Kentucky, named after James Harrod.

62/7 Frank J. Adler, *Roots in a Moving Stream* (Kansas City, Mo., 1972), p. 5. The daughter of Samuel Sanders became the mother of Quindaro Nancy Brown whose husband, Abelard Guthrie, was the first delegate to Congress from the original Nebraska Territory. Quindaro township in Wyandotte County, Nebraska, was named in honor of Quindaro Nancy Brown.

63/3 Samuel Rezneck, *Unrecognized Patriots, The Jews in the American Revolution* (London, 1975), pp. 200–201. "Levi was settled in Lexington, Virginia (probably in the Lexington situated in the Cumberland region of Virginia rather than Lexington in western Virginia or Kentucky).

63/4 Fort du Chartres was reconstructed in 1753 of sturdy limestone taken from nearby bluffs. Mississippi floods effectively destroyed most of the walls and structures. What remains is today housed in a museum in that former fort.

63/5 Leon Huhner, "The Jews of Virginia from the Earliest Times to the Close of the Eighteenth Century," *PAJHS*, 20: 95. *CAJ*, 1: 375–76.

64/2 *PAJHS*, 20: 95–96.

64/3 According to Levy's Pension Application, Levy was long stationed at Fort Vincennes, Indiana. Perhaps he was stationed there after the war. "Pension Application," National Archives, Washington, D.C.

65/1 *PEIS*, p. 416. The Daughters of the American Revolution placed a plaque honoring this veteran of the Revolutionary War at the foot of his grave in the old Portuguese-Jewish Cemetery on Chatham Street, New York.

Korn, *The Early Jews*, p. 273, note 46. There was a Simon Nathan in Kaskaskia during the period 1781–88. Another is recorded in Montreal in 1769. Perhaps the same Simon Nathan traveled to Canada and the Illinois on business; perhaps they are three different persons.

Militia duty was compulsory for virtually every able-bodied man, unless he purchased a substitute. A militiaman sometimes fought alongside volunteers, who were actual soldiers serving for extensive periods. Or a militiaman's service might be limited to patrol or police duty in his own community. Many militiamen, like Simon Nathan, were never involved in a skirmish.

65/2 Fort Sackville, retaken by Clark, was renamed Vincennes. From 1800 to 1813 it became the capital of the Illinois Territory.

65/4 Fitzgerald, ed., *Writings of George Washington*. The site of Middlebrook is about a mile from Bound Brook, New Jersey, and 45 miles from Easton, Pennsylvania. There was a continental army campground at Middlebrook.

65/5 Markens, *The Hebrews*, p. 83.

66/1 Joshua Trachtenberg, *Consider the Years* (Easton, Pa., 1944), pp. 71-72; 311, note 8.

67/7 This story appeared in a sermon by Rabbi David Hollander of Mount Eden Synagogue, Bronx, New York, in the Tercentenary Year 1955. He gave as its source the Hebrew/Israel publication, *Dvir*, Tel Aviv, 1954, but I have not been able to locate either that episode or its source. It is ascribed to "tradition." That soldier may have been Private Asher Pollock of the Second Rhode Island Battalion.

68/1 *PAJHS*, 25: 119-20. Petition of David Franks, William Murray and John Campbell, April 9, 1774, to Governor Dunmore, on behalf of the grantees, along with a copy of the Indian Deed, and the opinion of Lord Pratt and Yorke, dated April 1, 1772.

Essays in American Jewish History, American Jewish Archives. Cincinnati 1958, pp. 194, 202. "Illinois and Wabash Land Companies."

68/3 Byars, *B. & M. Gratz*, pp. 210, 215, 227-228.

EAJ, 2: 174-77.

SMW, *A Memoir: Susan Hart Shelby* (Lexington, Ky.), pp. 3-4.

69/1 Leon Huhner, "Captain Abraham Simons of the George Line in the Revolution," *PAJHS*, 33: 233. Simons was twice married to Christian women. When his widow remarried Reverend Jesse Mercer, a Baptist minister, the fortune of Abraham Simons built Baptist Mercer University in Macon, Georgia.

69/3 *HJP*, pp. 51, 125.

71/3 *PAJHS*, 64, no. 4 (June 1975): 298-99.

71/4 Malcolm H. Stern, "Two Jewish Functionaries in Colonial Pennsylvania: Mordecai Moses Mordecai (1727-1809)," *PAJHS*, 57, no. 1 (September 1967): 35-48.

Ira Rosenwaike, "The Jews of Baltimore to 1810," *PAJHS*, 64, no. 4 (June 1975): 298-99.

72/5 *PAJHS*, 57, no. 1 (September 1967): 39-40.

73/1 *PAJHS*, 64, no. 4 (June 1975): 308.

73/3 *CAJ*, 3: 1193. Dr. Jacob R. Marcus questions the assumption that Moses Simonson was a Jew on the basis of his Jewish-sounding name. He cites as proof, "Sam Moses who lived in Massachusetts in 1689, Isaac Cohen who roamed the Georgia back-country in 1758, and Solomon Abrahams, a native of King's Country, New York, who served as a soldier in the French and Indian War." They had three things in common: "Jewish" names, none was a Jew, and all three were Indians. Even if they had Jewish fathers, their mothers were Indian.

Sources

73/4   *CAJ*, 1: 216–17.
CAJ, 3: 1230.
CAJ, 1: 531. John (Jacob) Lumbrozo may have converted to Christianity, John being his baptized name. He was a tobacco planter, a merchant, an attorney, an appraiser, an innkeeper, and an Indian trader.
CAJ, 2: 534. Lumbrozo raised hogs and cattle.
CAJ, 2: 797. He faced as many charges as he had occupations: abortionism, attempted seduction, fornication, receiving stolen goods, etc.

73/6   *PAJHS*, 18: 213–14.
HJP, p. 33.

74/1   *CAJ*, 3: 1226.
HJP, p. 31.

74/2   *PAJA*, 27, no. 2 (November 1975): 113.

74/3   *PAJHS*, 66, no. 1 (September 1976): 28.

75/1   Trachtenberg, *Consider the Years*, pp. 55–67. Biography of Myer Hart.
PAJHS, 8: 187. Myer Hart (de Sira is the Anglicized version of Texeira in Spanish) was, like his wife Rachel de Lyon, of Portuguese stock.

75/2   Rachel, Rebecca and Zipporah de Lyon, were the daughters of Abraham and Esther de Leon of Lancaster (formerly pioneer settlers in Georgia in 1733). In 1761 the widow "Dylon" first appears in Easton's tax roll. She operated a shop and owned a house and a Negro, the latter two deemed of about equal value.

75/3   *HJP*, p. 417, note 70.
Trachtenberg, *Consider the Years*. Whether the ball occurred during Washington's first visit to Easton in 1778 or during his second in 1782 is questioned by Trachtenberg. It seems that 1782 was the correct date. Judith was age 20 and her marriage was the subject of controversy that year in Philadelphia. Undoubtedly the ball was held after, rather than during, the war.

76/6   "Mordecai letters" dated 25 Iyar, 5544; Marcheshvan 15, 5545; also "Congregational Decision" dated 5 Nisan 5545, *Mikve Israel Archives*, Philadelphia.
The *Parnas Presidente* or President served during the first half of the Hebrew year, from *Rosh Hashanah* (New Years Day) in the fall to Passover in the spring. The *Parnas Residente* or Vice-Presidente serving during the second half of the Hebrew year, from Passover to *Rosh Hashanah*.
The (orthodox) rabbi is primarily an expert on Jewish law and custom. Whereas minor questions were decided by learned Jewish laymen such as Manuel Josephson, complex questions were referred to the rabbi. There being none in America, their questions were sent either to Holland or England. Earlier in the 18th century there were rabbis serving in the Caribbean. Most questions confronting colonial Jewry were generally not of a profound nature, most relating to simple questions regarding marriage, conversion, burial or bastardy, or synagogue ritual.

78/1   Responsum/Inquiry by Manuel Josephson and Joseph Carpeles on behalf of the congregation *Mikve Israel*, to Chief Rabbi Saul Halevi Lowenstamm of the Ashkenazic Community, Amsterdam, Holland, 9 Nisan, 5545 (March 20, 1795), *Mikve Israel* Archives, Philadelphia.
Mordecai critique of Deposition, 25 Iyar, 5544 (1784); Mordecai letter sent

9 Heshvan 5544 and a second dated Marcheshvan 15, 5545, *Mikve Israel* Archives, Philadelphia.

Congregational decision regarding burial of Jew married contrary to Jewish tradition, 5 Nisan 5545, *Mikve Israel* Archives, Philadelphia. These documents were located in 1955 by the author in the company of Maxwell Whiteman, coauthor of the *History of the Jews of Philadelphia*. These were included in their entirety in the author's doctoral thesis, *Responsa Americana, 1636-1836*, Yeshiva University, New York, 1955, and in summation by Whiteman, pp. 128-31. Also summarized by Dr. Malcolm H. Stern in *AJHQ*, 57, no. 1 (September 1967): 41-46.

3
Jewish Settlers in Frontier Hinterlands

79/1 Isabella H. and Abraham S. Wolf Rosenbach, "Aaron Levy," *PAJHS*, 2: 157-63.

80/6 *Bar Mitzvah* (literally "son of commandments") refers to the entry of a thirteen-year-old Jewish boy into religious maturity when he is obliged to fulfill the positive as well as the negative precepts of Judaism, the latter enjoined since early childhood. Among his first positive obligations is the donning of phylacteries in daily weekday worship every morning. The *Bar Mitzvah* is honored with a call to the *Torah* when that sacred scroll is read (either Monday, Thursday, or Saturday morning, or the day of the New Moon or on holy days). The youth is reckoned as a member of the quorum required for public worship.

The *Torah*, "Five Books of Moses," is inscribed by the hand of a pious Jew with quill on parchment. Translated as "Law" the erroneous impression is rendered that the Jewish religion is purely nomistic, whereas in reality ethics balances the legalistic obligations. The highest ideal of the Jew was, and still is, the study of the *Torah*.

81/2 Sidney M. Fish, "Aaron Levy, Founder of Aaronsburg," *Studies in American Jewish History*, no. 1 New York: American Jewish Historical Society, 1951. Aaron Levy had at least 162 separate land tracts that he either purchased or acquired from individuals who found it too difficult to meet the terms of sale. They were located in Northumberland and Centre Counties. The tracts that Levy owned ranged from single lots to those of 26,000 acres. These western lands were purchased by potential settlers and speculators after a Provincial Land Office of Pennsylvania opened April 3, 1769, to sell lands recently acquired from the Indian Six Nations.

81/7 *PAJHS*, 20: 101, note 82. The western Virginia tract was situated in present day (1911) Fayette and Montgomery Counties in Virginia. This tract, obtained by Michael Gratz, was in alliance with James Wilson (a signer of the Declaration of Independence), Levi Hollingsworth, Charles Willing, and Dorsey Pentecost, all Pennsylvanians.

82/2 Byars, *B. & M. Gratz*, pp. 218; 247-48.

82/3 Herbert T. Ezekiel and Gaston Lichtenstein, *The History of the Jews of Richmond from 1769 to 1917* (Richmond, 1917), pp. 13-16, 17-20. Biographies of Isaiah Isaacs and Jacob I. Cohen.

82/4 *CAJ*, 2: 545-46.

PAJA, 23, no. 2 (November 1971): 198-212.

82/7 Eighteenth century Minutes, March 1782-September 1783, *Mikve Israel*

Archives, Philadelphia, pp. 33, 45, 57–60. Reverend Gershom Mendez Seixas was not a rabbi, but a *Hazzan,* as were all American spiritual leaders prior to the arrival of Rabbi Abraham Rice in 1840. In ancient times the Hazzan was an "Overseer," in charge of the Holy Temple utensils. After the destruction of the Temple, his duties were to recite the prayers in the synagogue and lead the congregation as well as read the biblical portion from the Scroll of the Torah. In the American colonies and well into the twentieth century United States, his services were expanded to include any and all religious responsibilities in communities where there was no rabbi (and rabbis too were burdened with manifold obligations): lay-rabbi (or rabbi), cantor, sexton, slaughterer of fowl and cattle, circumciser-*Mohel,* preacher, teacher, lecturer, fund raiser, and rallier for local, national, and overseas charities, interfaith representative, and in smaller towns to feed and at times board the wayfarer, particularly collectors for the Holy Land's Jewish communities and institutions.

83/1 *HJP,* pp. 126–127.

PAJHS, 17, no. 1 (September 1967): 40, note 83. *Essays in American Jewish History,* American Jewish Archives, Cincinnati, 1958, p. 90: "Elizabeth (Esther) Mordecai nee Whitlock, seems to have been denied burial in the Jewish Cemetery of Richmond for her epitaph is in the record at St. John's Episcopal Church."

83/2 *PAJHS,* 23: 11.

Ezekiel and Lichtenstein, *Jews of Richmond,* p. 15.

83/4 *EAJ,* 2: 187.

84/1 *EAJ,* 2: 187.

PAJHS, 20: 100.

PAJHS, 66, no. 1 (September 1976): 3.

84/3 *PAJHS,* 23: 12. Gratz, Kentucky (according to Dr. Malcolm Stern) may have been named for Benjamin Gratz; 66: 1 (September 1976): 3. The Gratzes launched the first passenger boats on the Ohio River, sending batteaux up its tributaries.

85/5 Max J. Kohler, "Some Jewish Factors in the Settlement of the West," *PAJHS,* 23: 25–26.

PAJHS, 31: 234. Abraham Franks, father of David Salisbury Franks, settled in Quebec in 1767; 23: 25–26. "Some Jewish Factors in the Settlement of the West" by Max J. Kohler.

85/6 *PAJHS,* 20: 24–25. Franks was on close terms with such leaders as Thomas Jefferson to whom Franks wrote on June 17, 1785, from Paris while on his diplomatic mission there, requesting a loan to help cover his debts incurred. Jefferson replied promptly:

Paris June 17, 1785.

. . . Your letter of this day distresses me not a little as it finds me utterly unable to give you the assistance needed. my outfit here, for the articles of furniture, clothes and carriage only has cost me fifteen hundred guineas. no allowance of this kind being made I have been obliged to run in debt for it . . . I am unhappily in a condition to feel much for your difficulties without a power to lessen them. nothing would have been more pleasing to me than the exercise of such a power . . .

Your most obedt. humble servt.
Th: Jefferson

85/7 Samuel Rezneck, *Unrecognized Patriots,* (Westport, Ct., 1975), pp. 34, 163; *PAJHS,* 10: 101, 163; 30: 88. David S. Franks was one of three marshals at Washington's inauguration, April 30, 1789; Reverend Gershom Seixas was one of 13 clergymen.

86/1 *PAJHS,* 16: 26-27, "Some Jewish Factors in the Settlement of the West" by Max J. Kohler. Havinghurst, Walter, *Wilderness for Sale,* New York 1956, p. 72: "Before relinquishing its claim on the Northwest Territory, Virginia reserved a tract of Military Lands north of the Ohio, extending between the Scioto and Little Miami Rivers."

88/2 David Philipson, "The Jewish Pioneers of the Ohio Valley," *PAJHS,* 8: 43.

88/6 *PAJHS,* 25: 96, note 6.

PAJHS, 24, no. 4 (June 1975): 307.

PAJHS, 61, no. 1 (September 1971): 69-73.

Francis B. Heitman, *Historical Register and Dictionary of the United States Army from . . . 1789 to . . . 1903* (Washington, D.C., 1903), 1: 629.

89/3 Moses Mendelssohn was celebrated for translating the Bible into Judeo-German, his commentary on the Bible, and as a philosopher. A collection of his works on philosophy, esthetics, and apologetics was published in Leipzig, Germany, in 1880. His grandson, composer Felix Mendelssohn, was known for such oratorios as *Elijah,* his overture to *A Mid-summer Night's Dream,* and as conductor of Gewandhaus Orchestra in Leipzig.

M. Kayserling, "A Memorial Sent by German Jews to the President of the Continental Congress," *PAJHS,* 6: 5-8.

PAJHS, 8:80.

PAJHS, 9:93-94.

Hans Lamm, "The So-called 'Letter of a German Jew to the President of the Congress of the United States of America' of 1783," *PAJHS,* 37: 171-84. The original of the Memorial appeared under the title, "Schreiben eines Deutschen Juden, an den Prasidenten des Congresses der Vereinigten Staaten," in *Deutches Museum,* Leipzig, 1783, pp. 558-66. It also appeared as a pamphlet in 1787 in Frankfort and Leipzig under the title "Schreiben eines deutschen Juden an den amerikanischen Prasidenten O." published by Moses Mendelssohn.

90/2 Joseph Heimberger, *Die staatskirchenrechtliche Stellung der Israeliten in Bayern* (Zweite Auflage, Tubingen, 1912).

Rudolf Glanz, *Studies in Judaica Americana* (New York, 1970), pp. 20-21.

Allgemeine Zeitung des Judentums 24 (1839): 420. " . . . the register *(Matrikel)* makes it little short of impossible for young Israelites to set up housekeeping in Bavaria; often their head is adorned with gray hair before they receive the permission to set up house and can, therefore, think of marriage . . . "

90/5 "Indentured Servants," *CAJ,* 2: 833-835.

91/2 Mark Wischnitzer, *To Dwell in Safety, The Story of Jewish Migration Since 1800* (Philadelphia, 1948), p. 6.

91/7 Fish, "Levy, Aaron, Founder of Aaronsburg," *Studies in American Jewish History,* no. 1, p. 5., note 4.

92/1 *HJP,* 186. Manuscript is in the possession of Edwin Wolf, II.

93/1 *CAJ,* 2: 793.

93/3 Richard Warren Welch, "The Assimilation of an Ethnic Group—The

German-Jewish Peddlers in the Upper Ohio Valley, 1790-1840: A Study in Historical Geography." MA Thesis, Michigan State University, 1972. Xerox copy, courtesy of American Jewish Archives, Cincinnati.

94/1 Isaac M. Wise, *Reminiscences* (New York, 1945), pp. 31-32.

94/5 John Howard Payne, "Trial Without Jury and Other Short Plays," American Short Plays Serials, edited by Codman Hislop and W. R. Richardson (Princeton, 1940), vol. 5, pp. 13, 25.

PAJHS, 33: 194.

94/6 *HJP*, p. 185.

95/3 Solomon Raphael's License as a Peddler, 1787, at the American Jewish Historical Society.

96/2 Welch, "The Assimilation of an Ethnic Group."

96/3 *PAJHS*, 9: 153.

PAJHS, 16: 25.

Joseph L. Blau and Salo W. Baron, eds., *The Jews of the United States 1790-1840, A Documentary History* (New York, 1963), vol. 1, p. 131.

97/2 Luke Shortfield, pseud., *The Zestern Merchant* (Philadelphia, 1849), p. 183.

97/4 Welch, "The Assimilation of an Ethnic Group."

97/6 *PAJHS*, 38, Part 1 (September 1948): 24.

Jacob R. Marcus, "From Peddler to Regimental Commander in Two Years: The Civil War Career of Major Louis A. Gratz."

MAJ, 3: 228-35. Louis Gratz laid out the Gratz addition to North Knoxville, Tennessee, and became its first mayor in 1889.

97/8 Glanz, *op. cit.*, p. 62. *MAJ*, Vol I, p. 359

98/2 Welch, "The Assimilation of an Ethnic Group."

99/2 *MAJ*, Vol I, pp. 390-342.

99/5 Glanz., *Judaica Americana*, pp. 59, 113.

Lewis A. Atherton, *The Pioneer Merchant in Mid-America* (Univ. of Missouri, 1939), no. 2, vol. 14, pp. 23-24.

99/7 Glanz, *Judaica Americana*, p. 75. *Die Deborah*, Cincinnati Vol. XIII (1867-1868) p. 31.

101/3 Welch, "The Assimilation of an Ethnic Group."

102/1 Harry Goldin, *Forgotten Pioneer* (New York, 1963), p. 37.

102/3-4 Abram Vossen Goodman, "A Jewish Peddler's Diary 1842-1843," *PAJA*, 3, no. 3 (June 1951): 99, 108-9.

MAJ, 2: 1-20.

104/7 Rudolf Glanz, *The Jew in the Old American Folklore* (New York, 1961), pp. 134-135.

Jewish Ledger, 12, no. 9: 15.

104/11 Ibid., p. 12.

Harper's Magazine, 19 (1859): 859.

105/1 James J. McDonald, *Life in Old Virginia* (Norfolk, Virginia, 1907), p. 299. Glanz, *Folklore*, p. 130.

105/2 *American Israelite, Deborah*, 6 (1860): 103.

4
Hebrew Patriots, Pioneers, Pirates

107/1 Willard Price, *The Amazing Mississippi* (New York, 1963), pp. 5–6. Ojibwa named the river Misisipi (*misi* "big" and *sipi* "river") Imaginative French explorers translated the name "Father of All Rivers." La Salle christened its valley, Louisiana, in honor of Louis XIV, King of France.

107/2 In 1780, a year after Clark's victories in the west during the Revolution, the British made a last and desperate attempt to regain the Mississippi Valley. They attempted to capture St. Louis on the west bank of the Mississippi River. However, the Spanish soldiers who manned Saint Louis' Fort on the Hill guarding Spanish Louisiana, were joined by the French-peopled town who never forgave the British conquest of Cahokia and Kaskaskia after the French defeat in the French and Indian War. They beat off a combined British and Indian attack in what was the westernmost battle of the Revolution.

108/5 Sidney M. Fish, "The Ancestral Heritage of the Gratz Family," *Gratz College Anniversary Volume, On the Occasion of the Seventy-fifth Anniversary of the Founding of the College 1895–1970*, ed. by Isidore David Passow and Samuel Tobias Lachs (Philadelphia, 1971), pp. 47–62.
PAJHS, 34: 19–20.
PAJHS, 41, no. 3 (March 1952): 26.

109/4 Donald Makovsky, (M.A. thesis, Washington University, St. Louis, Missouri, 1958). Microfilm at American Jewish Archives, Cincinnati.

109/7 *HJP*, p. 329.

110/3 Latin *trespass vi et armis* means "by force and armed power."

110/4 Blau and Baron, *The Jews*, vol. 3, pp. 842–44. In 1808 the town of St. Louis was incorporated.

110/5 Ibid., pp. 845–46.

111/10 David H. Coyner, *The Last Trappers* (Albuquerque, N.M., 1920), pp. 59–63. Captain Williams' party had been preceded into the unknown west only by the Lewis and Clark expedition which left St. Louis three years earlier to blaze a trail to the Pacific by way of the Missouri and Columbia rivers. Williams, an independent trapper, later trapped for the Missouri Fur Company.

113/1 The exclusive rights awarded to Laclede actually were worthless, for the Mississippi Valley, which included the Missouri Valley was surrendered by France that very year, 1763—the eastern bank to England and the western bank to Spain.

115/2 While a few churches possessed copies of works by Raphael, Rubens, and Veronese, not until half a century later did St. Louis evince an interest in the arts by organizing in 1879 the Saint Louis Museum of Fine Arts— the first art museum west of the Mississippi.

115/3 Makovsky, *op. cit.*

116/3 *AOJD*, p. 229.

116/4 Katz, *The Beth El Story*, p. 38.

116/6 Ibid., p. 22.

117/1 William L. Saunders, ed., *Colonial Records of North Carolina* (Raleigh,

N.C., 1886–1890), vol. 5, p. 980. Jacob Franks, Sr., may have been the "Jacob Franks" who traded with the Indians in North Carolina during the French and Indian War.

117/2 *PAJHS*, 16: 189. Will dated July 30, 1785, probated July 22, 1794.

117/4 *PAJHS*, 9: 151–52.

118/1 Katz. *The Beth El Story*, pp. 44–45.

Bayrd Still, *Milwaukee: The History of a City* (Madison, Wis., 1948), pp. 52–53. At this fine inland harbor, formed by the confluence of the three rivers which flow into Lake Michigan, Solomon Juneau, a Jewish French-Canadian fur trader, founded Juneautown in 1836. Byron Kilbourn and Morgan L. Martin, Yankee land promoters, acquired adjacent waterfront frontage for an urban settlement in which they invested thousands of dollars. Out of the union of Juneautown and Kilbourntown rose the city of Milwaukee. The journey from Green Bay to Milwaukee in pioneer days took four days, the distance being 130 miles.

118/2 *PAJHS*, 13: 53. One Captain Anderson who became a friend of Franks first made this statement in reference to uncle and nephew.

118/3 Blau and Baron, *The Jews*, vol. 3, pp. 835–36. In 1805, John Lawe purchased from his uncle, Jacob Franks, an equipped farm near Michilimackinac, the deed there executed on July 23.

119/1 *PAJHS*, 13: 52–53.

Katz, *The Beth El Story*, pp. 44–46. Many early American and Canadian Jewish families were intertwined by intermarrying cousins.

119/3 Chiel, *Manitoba Jews*, pp. 4–5. "The North West Company made so bold as to outfit a vessel, the *Beaver*, to secure as much of the trade in Hudson Bay as possible, thus challenging the Hudson's Bay Company in home territory!"

119/5 General William Harrison, from his headquarters at Vincennes, Indiana Territory, placed orders for food with H & S Gratz of Philadelphia. Likely they may have provisioned his troops as well.

120/3 Simon Wolf, *The American Jew as Patriot, Soldier and Citizen*, (Philadelphia, 1895), pp. 67–72: "Jewish Soldiers in the War of 1812."

120/6 Katz., *The Beth El Story*, p. 44. When the English withdrew from Mackinac after the war, the Americans broke into his home which they "wantonly pillaged." All who had supported England in the war were subjected to "unusual harshness."

120/7 Wisconsin State Historical Society *Collections*, Madison, 10: 94ff; 97.

121/2 Blau and Baron, *The Jews*, 3: 845. Clark was then at Fort Fincastle, Virginia (the future Wheeling, West Virginia).

121/4 Horace Carter Hovey, *Mammoth Cave of Kentucky* (Louisville, Ky., 1912), pp. 16–17, 30. Mammoth Cave, bought by a Mr. McLean in 1811 with surrounding 200 acres for 40 dollars, was soon sold by him to the Gratzes and Wilkins. This may have been the General Wilkins referred to by William H. Harrison in his letter to the Gratzes, dated Feb. 27, 1807:

    Mess/rs H. & S Grattz
        Merchants
           Philadelphia

                                      Vincennes Indiana Territory
                                            27th Feby 1807

    Mess/rs Hyman & Simon Grattz
        Gentlemen—Be pleased to send me by George Wallace Mr.

the following articles the amount of which shall be forwarded either to yourselves or to my friend Genl. Ino Wilkins as soon as I receive your account viz—one hundred pounds of Cofee one hundred Ditto Single refined loaf sugar six pounds best Tea ten Gallons Madeira Wine & fifty pounds of rice

        I am respectfully your
          Huml Servt [Humble Servant]
          Willm H Harrison

P.S.
To make a full barrel it will not be material if the quantity of coffee & sugar is encreased 20 to 25 lbs. each.

121/1 Ibid., 10: 132–33. After the war, Captain John Askin ordered Lieutenant Lawe to notify the Indians that further hostilities against Americans would be tolerated.

121/1 *PAJHS*, Vol. L. No. 3, Mar. 1961, p. 243 "The World of Hyman Gratz" by J. Solis-Cohen, Jr.

122/3 The Gratz brothers' role as soldiers is noted in "Jews in the War of 1812" by Leon Huhner, *PAJHS*, 26: 174–77. The story of Mordecai Myers role in the war was culled from *MAJ*, 1: pp. 50–75. Biographical data on Naphtali Phillips is presented in his historical sketch published in *PAJHS*, 21: 172–228. See also Harry L. Coles, *The War of 1812* (Chicago, 1971).

125/4 Stanley Clisby Arthur, *Jean Laffite, Gentleman Rover* (New Orleans, 1952). Of all the studies of Jean Laffite, I have found Arthur's to be the most accurate for it is based on primary sources and interviews with descendants.

129/5 Leon Huhner, *The Life of Judah Touro (1775-1854)* (Philadelphia, 1947), pp. 60–61.

   Brooks, Charles B., *The Siege of New Orleans* (Seattle, Wash., 1961), p. 268.

130/9 Arthur, *Lafitte*, p. 122. Jackson misspelled Laffite.

131/3 Ibid., pp. 123–24.

131/4 Ibid., pp. 131–32. President James Madison's Proclamation dated February 6, 1815, quoted in full.

131/4 The pirogue originated with the Indians. To paddle the bayous, the Bayougoulas and Mongoulachas of the lower Mississippi cut out or burned out the trunks of cottonwoods, and shaped the ends similar to canoes (Indians of the upper Mississippi used birch-bark canoes.) French traders improved the pirogue by felling cypress trees nearly 50 feet long and hollowing them so that they would carry from 20 to 30 men, or several tons of freight.

132/1 In 1795 France received the eastern part of Hispaniola—the Dominican Republic—from Spain. When the Dominicans revolted against the French in 1809, the country reverted to Spain. In 1821 the Dominicans again revolted, this time against Spain, and declared their country free.

132/5 The Inquisition did claim certain jurisdiction over unbaptized Jews. The Holy Office prosecuted Jews for a variety of offenses, including sorcery and witchcraft, blasphemy of personages or objects sacred to the Church, and for obstructing their co-religionists from converting to Catholicism.

   Among proofs advanced that Juan Colon, alias Cristobal Colon or Christopher Columbus, was a *marrano*, is the find of a Spanish document, dated 1494, currently at the University of Barcelona. Therein Juan de Baromeo, Duke of Angiere, "do hereby confess that I was forbidden to reveal the truth of this secret that was confided to me by Senor Pedro de Angiero, treasurer of the Catholic Majesties of Spain. However, since I wish to preserve this secret for the benefit of posterity and history, I hereby record the fact that the so-called Christopher Columbus, or Cristobal Colon, came from Majorca. The aforementioned Pedro de Angiero was convinced that for political and religious reasons Juan (Colon) of Majorca concealed his identity . . . "

133/2 Mendel Silber, "America in Hebrew Literature," *PAJHS*, 22: 112–14.

Ibn Verga, Solomon, *Shebet Yehudah*, Adrianople, 1550; Sabbioneta, 1554. Joseph ha-Kohen, *Emek ha-Baka, 1563–1575* (Vienna, 1852; Cracow, 1895).

133/3 Seymour B. Liebman, *The Inquisitors and the Jews in the New World, Summaries of Procesos, 1500–1810, and Bibliographical Guide* (Coral Gables, Fl., 1974), p. 40.

G. R. G. Conway, "Hernando Alonso, a Jewish Conquistador with Cortes in Mexico," *PAJHS*, 31: 9–31.

Arnold Wiznitzer, "Crypto-Jews in Mexico during the Sixteenth Century," *PAJHS*, 51, no. 3 (March 1962): 168–72.

133/4 The island of Hispaniola (Hispanola) or *La Espanola*, as called by Columbus, was renamed Santo Domingo after the Dominican Order, and not, as some historians allege, in honor of Colombus' father, Domingo, who in the eyes of the Church was a Jew, an unbeliever. So states Rafael Pineda Yanez, one of the foremost authorities on the Spanish colonial era in *La Isla Y Colon*, Buenos Aires, Argentina, 1955. It should further be noted that there was no priest aboard any of Columbus' three ships to christen the island.

133/5 Spain sent a Dominican mission headed by Domingo de Mendoza and Pedro de Cordoba to give no quarter in the war against sin and heresy in Hispaniola. As part of this antiheresy, Christianization campaign, Hispaniola was renamed after the Order.

134/1 No such rite exists in Judaism. Introduction of a son into Judaism requires the act of circumcision performed by an observant Jew as a religious act accompanied by a ritual which includes a benediction over a cup of wine. The prayers are recited on behalf of the newly initiated full-fledged member of Israel; a few drops of the wine are then placed upon the lips of the child.

134/6 The Cathedral was built upon the site of the Aztec Temple and constructed out of its stones, the Indian Temple having been demolished by the Spaniard conquerors.

Records of the Inquisition in the Western Hemisphere, set down in detail by the tribunals of the Holy Office in Mexico, and half a century later in Lima, Peru, and since the early seventeenth century at Cartagena, Colombia, disclose in detail the observances of Jewish rites by crypto-Jews, their imprisonment, torture, and the penalties meted out to them.

135/3 At New York's Portuguese Congregation, *Shearith Israel*, a bathing house was built over a spring in Mill Street, before the erecting of the first synagogue there. At Newport, Rhode Island, too, at *Yeshuat Israel*, wells were discovered not so long ago in the synagogue yard, long since covered over, that seem to have been connected with a ritual pool, the location of which can no longer be traced.

At Philadelphia's *Mikve Israel*, the river was used as a *Mikveh* for proselytes, but neglected by married women until the 1840s.

136/3 N. Taylor Phillips, "Family History of the Reverend David Mendez Machado," *PAJHS*, 2: 45–47.

136/5 Cecil Roth, *A History of the Marranos* (Philadelphia, 1941), p. 294.

136/6 The exit of the tunnel, no longer known, was recalled to the author by Mr. Martin Klein of Northridge, California who was a native of Newport, often visited the tunnel exit since sealed with earth to prevent entry thereby.

137/2 Gutstein, *To Bigotry*, pp. 37–38.

137/3 *PAJHS*, 66, no. 1 (September 1976): 13.

137/5 Records of the Inquisition in the Western Hemisphere were set down in detail by the tribunals of the Holy Office in Mexico; Lima, Peru; and Cartagena, Colombia. They detail the crime, manner of torture and penalties meted out after confession.

137/6 George Alexander Kohut, "The Trial of Francisco Maldonado de Silva," *PAJHS*, 11: 163–79.

139–1 Korn, *The Early Jews*, pp. 99, 296, note 16.

Arthur, *Lafitte*, p. 277. Jean Laffite's autobiographical "Journal" was contained in a series of small books, five or six inches in size, some 380 pages written in French, beginning "When I was three years old . . ."

139/6 *PAJHS*, 27: 475–79.

Blau and Baron, *The Jews*, 3: 786–90. During the 18th century and into the 19th, Jewish settlements flourished throughout the Caribbean, at Surinam, Dutch Guiana; Curacao, St. Eustatius, and Tobago, Dutch West Indies; Barbados, Jamaica and Nevis, British West Indies; St. Croix and St. Thomas in the Danish Virgin Islands.

141/2 Arthur, *Lafitte*, p. 223.

141/3 Ibid., p. 224.

Jane Lucas De Grummond, *The Baratarians and the Battle of New Orleans*, (Baton Rouge, La.), pp. 4–5.

145/3 Alexander E. Powell, *Gentlemen Rovers* (New York, 1913), p. 97.

145/7 Bertram W. Korn, "Jews and Negro Slavery in the Old South, 1789–1865," *PAJHS*, 50, no. 3 (March 1961): 171.

146/1 Ibid., pp. 174–75.

Columbus (Ga.) *Enquirer*, April 12, 1838. "Blow boys" were buglers who performed that function on the plantation.

149/4 Maxwell Whiteman, *The Kidnapped and the Ransomed* (Philadelphia, 1970).

150/3 *MAJ*, 2: 47–57.

150/5 Korn, *The Early Jews*, pp. 70–71. Governor William Claiborne's report to Secretary of State, James Madison, February 13, 1804, of his appointee.

151/2 Ibid., pp. 67–70, 72.

151/5 Ibid., pp. 104, 107, 163. Levy Jacobs and non-Jewish partner George Asbridge, exchange and commission merchants offering for sale or purchase goods, Negroes, etc.

152/2 Ibid., pp. 163–64.

152/5 "Alfred and Emily Seasongood," *MAJ*, 3: 68–69.
153/3 Korn, *The Early Jews*, pp. 94–98, "Jacob Hart, with some Incidental Comment on Jean Laffite."
154/1 The charges against Miguel Hidalgo y Costilla were spurious, flimsy, and contradictory, as in the cases of most convicted Judaizers. See Martin A. Cohen, intro., *The Jewish Experience in Latin America*, vol. 1 (New York, 1971), p. XLI. Reverend Hidalgo's head hung for ten years, until 1821 when independence was won.
154/3 Arthur, *Laffite*, pp. 25–26, 38.
154/6 Ibid., p. 133. Jean Laffite complained bitterly that "he saved the Union" for which he "received eulogies but not recompense." He usually added: "pas une decoration en bois!" (Not even a wooden medal!).

5
Judaism Takes Root in Western Wilderness

156/1 Wischnitzer, *Dwell in Safety*, p. 5.
157/9 *PAJHS*, 34: 49.
158/1 Trachtenberg, *Consider the Years*, p. 91.
158/2 Guide Kisch, "German Jews in White Labor Servitude in America," *PAJHS*, 34: 11–49. An idea of the number of Jewish bond-servants arriving in American ports may be gained from the "Record of the Indentures of Individuals Bound out as Apprentices, Servants, etc., and of German and other Redemptioners in the Office of the Mayor of the City of Philadelphia, Oct. 3, 1771 to Oct. 5, 1773," which included the following: Daniel Wolff, Jonas Katz, William Leib, Isaak Benjamin, Michael Levy, Jacob Katz, James Beer, Jacob Sucher.
159/3 W. D. Robinson, *Memoir Addressed to Persons of the Jewish Religion in Europe on the Subject of Emigration* (London, 1819).
       Blau and Baron, *The Jews*, 3: 879–84.
160/3 David Philipson, "The Jewish Pioneers of the Ohio Valley," *PAJHS*, 8: 44.
160/4 For biographical data on Joseph Jonas and the story of pioneer Jews in the Ohio Valley, see *Occident* (Philadelphia), vol. 1 (1843–1844): 547–50; vol 2 (1844–1845): 29–31, 143–47, 244–47.
       MAJ, 1: 203–15. A few months after Joseph Jonas arrived in America, Lyon Jonas, a London furrier who came to America during the Revolution but became a derelict, died in New York City in February 1817. They may have been related.
       David de Sola and Tamar Pool, *An Old Faith in the New World* (New York, 1955), p. 347.
160/6 Schappes, *Documentary History*, p. 224.
160/7 A *Mezuzah* is a rectangular piece of parchment on which are inscribed passages from Deuteronomy VI:4–9 and XI:13–21. On the outer side of the parchment is inscribed the name *Shadai* (meaning Almighty). The parchment is rolled and placed in a case with an opening to reveal the name *Shadai*. The case containing the parchment is then affixed in a slanted position to the doorpost on the right side on entry so that the upper part is inward and the lower part is downward. The *Mezuzah* is said to bring blessings to him that touches it but it must not be touched with unclean hands.

161/2 *PAJHS*, 8: 45.
161/5 *MAJ*, 1: 207.
       PAJHS, 8: 48.
162/1 *PAJHS*, 8: 43-44.
162/2 *PAJA*, 21, no. 2 (November 1969): 181. Ad in First City Directory of Louisville, Kentucky.
162/4 *PAJHS*, 8: 43-44, 55.
162/5 The corresponding secular name of Binyamin Leib is Benjamin Lyon. The Jewish (or Hebrew) name is cited in the memorial prayer or recited in religious services as at Torah blessings or on Hebrew documents as the wedding document, bill of divorce, or sale of leavened prior to Passover.
163/1 *PAJHS*, 10: 98. Joseph Jonas circular dated July 3, 1825. ". . . brought to be interred from Louisville a distance of near 200 miles." Travel by boat on the winding Ohio River added 70 miles to that of present-day roadways.
163/5 Rudolf Glanz, *Studies in Judaica Americana,* New York, 1970, pp. 351-53.
163/7 *PAJHS*, 1: 99-100. One of Jacob's daughters married James Clay, son of Henry Clay.
164/1 *HJP*, p. 341.
164/3 Korn, *The Early Jews,* pp. 162, 314, note 9. In 1820 Salomon left for New Orleans to assume his new position as cashier of the New Orleans branch of the Bank of the United States. One summer in New Orleans was too much for 43-year-old Ezekiel. He died on September 27, 1821.
165/2 *PAJHS*, 1: 100-101. "Kentucky Solomons, including the notorious Madame Diss de Bar, children of a scholar from Breslau . . . who claimed to a grandnephew of Haym Solomon."
165/3 *PAJHS*, 31: 241. Dr. Nicholas Schuyler of a famous New York family and his wife Shinah Simon had no children of their own. They adopted his niece Henrietta Ann who married her first cousin, Philip Van Rensselaer. Henrietta and Philip's first child was named Gratz Van Rensselaer, for her mother's adopted mother was an aunt of Rebecca Gratz. Gratz Van Rensselaer returned the favor and wrote a biography of Rebecca Gratz.
165/4 Byars, *B. & M. Gratz,* pp. 330-334.
       Gratz Van Rensselaer, "The Original Rebecca in Ivanhoe," *Century Magazine,* 24 (September 1882): 682.
       PAJHS, 37: 348-52. Estrangement between Joseph Simon and the Gratzes.
165/5 *PAJHS*, 61, no. 1 (September 1971): 69-73.
       PAJHS, 64, no. 4 (June 1975): 300-308.
166/1 Blau and Baron, *The Jews,* 1: 295, note 93.
       PAJHS, 16: 32.
166/2 *AOJD*, p. 65.
166/3 David Philipson, ed., *Letters of Rebecca Gratz* (Philadelphia, 1929).
167/1 Blau and Baron, *The Jews,* p. 289, note 47.
       HJP, p. 239. Sarah Matilda Hoffman, daughter of Judge Josiah Ogden Hoffman of New York. The Judge was married to Maria Elizabeth Fenno, a friend of Rebecca Gratz. Another version tells that Sarah Hoffman died April 26, 1809, of consumption. In her correspondence, Rebecca Gratz expressed concern and hope for her recovery.

167/3 *PAJHS*, 33: 196.
Blau and Baron, *The Jews*, 1: 290, note 53.
W. & W. p. 313.
167/4 *PAJHS*, 11: 189-190.
PAJHS, 22: 56.
167/5 *PAJHS*, 48, no. 2 (December 1958): 71-77. "Rebecca Gratz and the Jewish Sunday School Movement in Philadelphia" by Joseph R. Rosenbloom.
167/7 Philipson, *Letters*, introduction.
168/4 *PAJHS*, 16: 31. Mrs. Henry Clay, nee Lucretia Hart, was born in 1781 in Hagerstown, Maryland.
169/2 Philipson, *Letters*, p. xiii.
169/5 Harry Simonhoff, *Jewish Notables in America, 1776-1865* (New York, 1956), 1: 120.
169/9 Schappes, *Documentary History*, pp. 187-94.
170/1 *CAJ*, 2: 552-53.
170/4 *PAJHS*, 8: 46-47.
170/5 Makovsky, *loc. cit.*
171/1 Postal and Koppman, *Tourist's Guide*, pp. 511-12.
171/2 *PAJHS*, 22: 194-95.
PAJHS, 64, no. 4 (June 1975): 294, 310.
PAJHS, 23: 191. Another member of the Block family, Lazarus, came to Cincinnati from Bavaria in the 1830s.
172/1 Jacob Ezekiel, "The Jews of Richmond," *PAJHS*, 4: 26.
Letter from Malcolm H. Stern to author dated September 12, 1976: In Richmond, Va. Will Book 5, is the will of Simon Block, Jr. (probably Jr. to distinguish him from the Maryland Simon Block). He is "of Cape Girardeau, Mo."
172/3 Makovsky, *loc. cit.*
172/5 Glanz, , p. 115.
Eltone Out-and Outer Comic Songster (New York, 1839).
173/1 *MAJ*, 1:209.
PEIS, p. 372.
PAJHS, 8: 48.
173/2 *PAJHS*, 8: 150. Joseph Jonas elected first president.
173/3 *PAJHS*, 10: 98.
174/1 Ibid., p. 99.
174/3 Korn, *The Early Jews*, pp. 192-95.
PAJHS, 52, no. 4 (June 1963): 310-16. " . . . in 1826, (Jacob Solis) temporarily left his wife and children at Mt. Pleasant, New York, and went to New Orleans . . . " Having established himself as a commission merchant, Solis returned to New York to bring his family to their new permanent home.
J. Solis-Cohen, Jr., "Jacob S. Solis: Traveling Advocate of American Judaism," *AJHQ*, 52, no. 4 (June 1963): 310-16.
175/1 Fedora S. Frank, *Five Families and Eight Young Men: Nashville and her Jewry 1850-1861* (Nashville, Tenn.), p. 19. To Fort Nashborough (renamed

Nashville), founded in 1780 in the then western Virginia, Kentucky, Benjamin and Hannah Hays Myers settled. Hannah was the daughter of a prominent colonial family. Their daughter was born in 1795 in the fort.

175/2 Solomon Solis-Cohen, "Note Concerning David Hays and Esther Etting his wife, and Michael Hays and Reuben Etting, their Brothers, Patriots of the Revolution," *PAJHS*, 2: 71.

175/5 Ibid., pp. 64–71.
CAJ, 3: 1295.

175/6 *CAJ*, 1: 407.

176/2 *PAJHS*, 1: 117. Barrack's brother, Andrew Hays, had come to Montreal in the 1760s. Barrack (Baruch) Hays, first lieutenant in a militia company of the Revolutionary forces, switched loyalty during the war and was appointed by the British "Officer of Guides" under Generals Henry Clinton and Guy Carleston. Barrack Hays was a cousin of David and Michael Hays. David, loyal to the British, switched his loyalty after signing an address of loyalty to the British and swore an oath of allegiance to the new American government.

176/5 *PAJHS*, 16: 27–29.

177/2 In a log cabin of palisade construction John Hays maintained his St. Clair County Sheriff headquarters from 1798 to 1818. The single-story log courthouse built in 1735 still stands, a museum of French relics.

179/1 Joseph Levine, *John Jacob Hays: The First Known Jewish Resident of Fort Wayne*, Fort Wayne, Indiana, 1973.

179/3 *PAJHS*, 16: 30. Mrs. Eliza Brouillet of Dallas, Texas, granddaughter of John Hays, owned the Hebrew Bible and other evidences of his faith.

179/6 *PAJHS*, 20: 100. Ezekiel and Lichtenstein, *op. cit.*, pp. 14–15. Makovsky, *loc. cit.*

180/1 Ezekiel and Lichtenstein, *Jews of Richmond*, p. 90.

180/2 *Occident*, 15, no. 1 (April 1857).

180/4 *PAJHS*, 52, no. 4 (June 1963): 311, note 3. Jacob da Silva Solis, as all the American Solises, descended from *marranos*. Solomon da Silva Solis and his wife Isabel de Fonseca escaped from Portugal and married according to Jewish rites in Amsterdam in 1670. Jacob da Silva Solis, born in 1780 in London, was the son of Solomon da Silva Solis, born in Amsterdam in 1754, and arrived in America in 1803. At that time, Joseph Solis, settled in New Orleans, may have been a distant relation. Joseph's father Manuel was born in Boston about 1717 and Joseph's grandfather, also named Manuel, was born in Ireland. About 1755 Joseph Solis married Barbara de Rosas at Santiago de Cuba and lived as a Catholic.

180/5 Biographical material on Judah Touro includes *The Life of Judah Touro* by Leon Huhner (Philadelphia, 1946); *A Biographical Romance of Judah Touro* by Moses Wassermann (New York, 1923); and of especial importance is that data contained in *The Early Jews of New Orleans* by Bertram W. Korn (Waltham, Mass., 1969).

181/5 *PAJHS*, 50, no. 3 (March 1961): 154.

182/1 *PAJHS*, 52, no. 4 (June 1963): 310.
M. David Geffen, "Delaware Jewry: The Formative Years 1872–1889," *Delaware History*, 16, no. 4 (Fall-Winter 1975): 272–73.

182/6 Max Heller, comp., *Jubilee Souvenir of Temple Sinai 1872–1922* (New Orleans, 1922), p. 16.

Theodore Clapp, *Autobiographical Sketches and Recollections during a Thirty-Five Years' Residence in New Orleans* (Boston, 1857), pp. 101–3.
183/3   Korn, *The Early Jews*, pp. 192–95.
183/4   Ibid., p. 203.
184/1   Ibid., p. 205. There are a variety of recommended and accepted practices for positioning the corpse in a Jewish burial ground; one "that the feet ought to lay in the East," another suggested towards the south, a third, preferring the direction of the entrance to the cemetery.
184/3   Ibid., p. 196. Since the establishment of the State of Israel, a number of nonorthodox politicians have attempted to enact legislation that would deem any person of a non-Jewish mother to be accepted as a Jew so long as his father was Jew. Their apparent motive is to increase thereby Israel's Jewish population. The Chief Rabbinate of Israel have successfully frustrated such proposals.
185/4   Herbert Asbury, *The French Quarter*, New York 1938, pp 14, 100ff.
184/5   Ibid., p. 200.
184/6   Ibid., p. 332, note 1.
185/2   I. J. Benjamin, *Three Years in America 1859–1862* (Philadelphia, 1956), 1: 316–17.
186/5   Korn, *The Early Jews*, pp. 119–27.
186/8   Ibid., pp. 179–81.
187/4   Ibid., p. 179.
187/7   Ibid., pp. 65–66.
188/2   Ibid., pp. 230–31.
188/3   Ibid., p. 128.
188/4   Ibid., pp. 111, 299, note 44.
188/5   Ibid., pp. 296–97, note 28, 298, note 37.
189/2   Ibid., p. 70.
189/4   *PAJHS*, 50, no. 3 (March 1961): 153.
189/6   Max J. Kohler, "Judah P. Benjamin: Statesman and Jurist," *PAJHS*, 12, pp. 83–84.
190/2   Robert Douthat Meade, *Judah P. Benjamin, Confederate Statesman* (New York 1943), pp. 115–17.
191/1   Korn, *The Early Jews*, p. 166
191/5   *PAJA*, 3, no. 3 (June 1951): 87.
191/7   Korn, *The Early Jews*, pp. 199–200.
192/2   *PAJHS*, 52, no. 4 (June 1963): 315–16.
192/3   Israel Goldstein, *A Century of Judaism in New York: B'nai Jeshurun 1825–1925, New York's Oldest Ashkenazic Congregation* (New York, 1930), pp. 56–57. Hendricks' loan for a period of five years was at the nominal interest rate of one percent per annum. Upon learning that interest in such an instance is forbidden in Judaism, at the expiration of the period, Hendricks relinquished the interest.
193/3   Korn, *The Early Jews*, pp. 207–208.
David de Sola Pool, *An Old Faith in the New World* (New York, 1955), p. 434.
193/4   Ibid., pp. 194–95.

194/1 *Shearith Israel* Trustees' Minute Book, June 18, 1833, pp. 428–29. Copied by author at *Shearith Israel* Congregation, New York, in 1954 by permission of Rabbi David de Sola Pool, of blessed memory.

194/4 The names used in this factual anecdote recorded by Benjamin II, are unknown. Fictitious names are supplied to simplify the relationships. Any resemblance to persons living or dead is purely coincidental.

195/3 Throughout New Orleans water was encountered a foot to a foot and a half below the surface. As late as the 1840s New Orleans was known throughout the United States as the "Wet Grave" because of the difficulties encountered in burying corpses. Christians who disliked immersing the corpse of a dear one and could afford it would build a sort of brick oven on the surface of the ground, the coffin put in at one end and the door hermetically sealed. The hot sun on the white sepulchre baked the corpse. Mourners had the choice of baking or soaking the bodies of their beloved departed. After the 1840s burials, excepting those of Jews and poorer persons, were made in ovens or tombs.

195/8 Korn, *The Early Jews*, p. 202.

196/6 George Washington Harby produced, among other plays, *Tutoona, or The Battle of Saratoga*, in 1834, the same year his Protestant wife, Mary Olivia Lucas died. *Tutoona* opened at the American Theatre in New Orleans on February 22, 1835, in honor of George Washington's birthday. Critics praised it for "a score of hair breadth escapes, a great deal of action, and interesting incident," but felt that an excessive number of "scalping, whooping, trotting Indians," detracted from its possible success.

197/3 Ibid., pp. 240–45.

197/4 Ibid., p. 247. Gershom Kursheedt moved to New Orleans in late 1839 or early 1840.

PAJHS, 37: 213. Gershom Kursheedt came to New Orleans in 1835.

197/5 Circular addressed to Jews, New York, September 3, 1837, at American Jewish Historical Society, Lyons' Scrapbook III, item 129. Copied by author in his *Responsa Americana*, doctoral thesis, Yeshiva University, New York, 1955.

198/2 Rice Subscription, 1841, at American Jewish Historical Society. Included by author in *The Pioneer Rabbi*, a biography of Abraham Joseph Rice, in manuscript.

Korn, *The Early Jews*, p. 248.

198/4 *CAJ*, 2: 877. "By 1764 . . . the community at Newport called itself *Yeshuat Israel* (Salvation of Israel)."

198/5 *MAJ*, 1: 210.

199/2 *Occident*, 2 (1844–45): 246–47.

199/3 Heller, *Temple Sinai*, p. 3. Dr. M. Wiener, correspondent of the *Allgemeine Zeitung des Judentums*, visiting New Orleans in the early 1840s noted that there were "no less than 700 families of which only four households abstained from forbidden food and only two observed the Sabbath religiously."

200/1 Korn, *The Early Jews*, pp. 249–51.

200/2 Ibid., pp. 251–52.

200/3 Huhner, *op. cit.*, pp. 61–62; 66–67; 129–39.

PAJHS, 37: 213–20. In May 1855, Sir Moses Montefiore, the most prominent English Jew of the 19th century, and Lady Montefiore, together with his secretary and Gershom Kursheedt, set out from London to the Holy Land. They arrived in Jerusalem on July 18 to fulfill Touro's bequest of founding the Touro Almshouses and to mark thereby the creation of the new city outside the walls of Jerusalem. An uncle of Sir Moses, Joshua Montefiore, had come to America as early as 1803. From Philadelphia he traveled extensively, finally to settle in 1835, at the age of 73 in St. Albans, Vermont, on Lake Champlain near the Canadian border. Married to Elizabeth Maher, a Catholic, he died there in 1843. See: *PAJHS*, 40, Part 2 (December 1950): 119-34. "Joshua Montefiore of St. Albans, Vermont" by Lee M. Friedman.

201/2 Korn, *The Early Jews,* pp. 89, 293-294, note 43. The mystery deepens with the appearance in 1856 in New Orleans of John Touro as "ship's broker" of the ship *Judah Touro.*

201/4 Huhner, *op. cit.,* p. 140.

202/1 Ibid., pp. 118-20; Benjamin, *Three Years,* 1: 320-33.

202/5 Commodore Uriah Phillips Levy commissioned P. J. David d'Angers to fashion a likeness of his hero, Thomas Jefferson, which he presented to Congress that stands in the Capitol Rotunda.

202/6 Benjamin, *Three Years,* 1: 322-23.

203/1 *MAJ,* 2: 295.

203/3 *PAJHS,* 64, no. 4 (June 1975): 307.

204/2 Korn, *The Early Jews,* pp. 166-68.

204/4 Earliest Jewish fur traders, prior to the Gomezes, lived but temporarily, a few winters at the most, among the tribes at Albany, New York, and elsewhere.

205/3 Benjamin, *Three Years,* 1: 322-23.

205/4 *The Chronicles of Oklahoma* (Oklahoma City), 54, no. 4 (Winter 1975-1976): 497. Probably less than 300 Creeks died in transit, but, of the 10,000 or more resettled in 1836-1837, an incredible 3,500 died of "bilious fevers." There were no doctors or medicines to help the suffering Indians.

206/4 A. J. Messing, Jr., "Old Mordecai—The Founder of the City of Montgomery," *PAJHS,* 13: 71-81.

Alfred G. Moses, "The History of the Jews of Montgomery," *PAJHS,* 34: 267. According to a note by Dr. Malcolm H. Stern to the author's attention, Abraham was born ca. 1755; Jacob, b. Apr. 11, 1762; Isaac, b. Apr. 11, 1764; Joseph, b. Nov. 18, 1766. If Abraham was indeed the son of Moses Mordecai and Elizabeth Whitlock, he was born in England for they came to America in 1760.

206/6 *PAJHS,* 6: 40.

206/8 See page 4, note 3.

207/1 *CAJ,* 3: 1194. The most remarkable Indian Mordecai may have met in the wilderness was Isaac Cohen, his father having traded deep in Creek country since the 1720s and took to himself an Indian woman.

207/5 U.S. Bureau of American Ethnology, (Washington, D.C., 1912), no. 30, part 1, p. 719.

209/1 Robert Gordis, "Mordecai Manuel Noah: A Centenary Evaluation," *PAJHS,* 41, no. 1 (September 1951): 15-16.

210/1 Isaac Goldberg, *Major Noah: American-Jewish Pioneer* (Philadelphia, 1936), pp. 62–67.
210/2 Ibid., pp. 26–61.
210/5 Blau and Baron, *The Jews,* 3: 723–25.
211/3 Lee M. Friedman, "The Phylacteries Found at Pittsfield, Mass," *PAJHS.* 25: 81–85.
211/4 Blau and Baron, *The Jews,* 3: 767–70, 971, note 172.
212/2 Ibid., pp. 718–19, 723–25.
Max J. Kohler, "An Early American Hebrew-Christian Agricultural Colony," *PAJHS,* 22: 184–86.
S. Joshua Kohn, "Mordecai Manuel Noah's Ararat Project and the Missionaries," *PAJHS,* 55, no. 2 (December 1965): 174–87.
Kohn, "New Light on Mordecai Manuel Noah's Ararat Project," *PAJHS,* 59, no. 2 (December 1969): 210–14.
Bernard D. Weinryb, "Noah's Ararat Jewish State in its Historical Setting," *PAJHS,* 43, no. 3 (March 1954): 170–91.
212/3 John W. Vandercook, "Jungle Jews," *The Menorah Journal,* 14, no. 3 (March 1928): 238–46.
Richard Gottheil, "Contributions to the History of the Jews in Surinam," *PAJHS,* 9: 129–46. Die Joden-Savannah (the Jewish Savannah) was founded in 1632 when Holland gave Portuguese-Jews permission to settle upon the savanna (flat grasslands) in Dutch Surinam. At a hillock on the Paramaribo River about 60 miles from the coast, they built a synagogue in 1685. Following repeated attacks by runaway slaves from the sugar plantations they established during the 18th century their central village, the Jewish Savannah depopulated. When the last Jew died in that town in 1832, the blacks set the remaining buildings afire. Only ruins and broken tombstones remain as the jungle has reclaimed its former domain.
212/4 Blau and Baron, *The Jews,* 3: 892–93. Noah received letters of encouragement from Edouard Gans and Leopold Zunz, two leaders of the "Science of Judaism (Wissenschaft des Judenthums) movement," dated January 1, 1822, Berlin. They complimented him on his "meritorious undertaking . . . transplanting a vast portion of European Jews to the United States . . . of those who would prefer leaving their country to escape endless slavery and oppression."
214/3 *PAJHS,* 55, no. 2 (December 1965): 182–83.
214/4 *Truth Teller,* Microfilm, Brown University, 3 (1827): 54.
214/5 M. M. Noah, *Discourse on the Restoration of the Jews: Delivered at the Tabernacle Oct. 28 and Dec. 2, 1844, With a Map of the Land of Israel* (New York, 1845). Copy owned by the author.
214/6 Louis Ruchames, "Mordecai Manuel Noah and Early American Zionism," *PAJHS,* 64, no. 3 (March 1975): 195–223.
215/1 M. M. Noah, *Discourse on The Evidences of the American Indians Being the Descendants of the Lost Ten Tribes of Israel* (New York: James Van Norden, 27 Pine St., 1837). The Discourse is located at the American Jewish Historical Society. It was translated into German in 1838.
215/5 Due to the north winds, which endangered the life of an infant undergoing circumcision on his eighth day, the rite was postponed until after the arri-

314 Sources

- val of the Jews from the Sinai Desert into the land of the then Canaan—a period of forty years.
- 216/1 The Pentateuch forbad all marine life not having fins and scales as food for the Jew. While the Indians probably ate fish lacking fins, they did not eat eel, turtle, sea-cow. Such similarities in their eating habits strongly resembled the kosher dietary code.
- 216/2 Diego de Landa, . . . *Relacion de las Cosas de Yucatan* (Cambridge, Mass., 1941). In the Midrashic literature of the ancient rabbis it is related that the Sea of Reeds divided into twelve channels. Each of the Twelve Tribes of Israel passed between the transparent walls of congealed seawaters in their exodus from Egypt to the Sinai shore.
- 216/6 Terry Olendar Glick, "Jews in Central America," *B'nai B'rith Messenger*, Dec. 28, 1973, p. 24.
- 218/4 Elisabeth Levi de Montezinos, "The Narrative of Aharon Levi, alias Antonio de Montezinos, Related by him to Haham Menasseh Ben Israel in Amsterdam ANNO 5404 (1644) . . . ," *The American Sephardi* (New York: Yeshiva University, Autumn 1975-5736) vols. 7-8: 65-83.
- 218/7 *Jewish Encyclopedia*, 12 (1905): 252.
- 219/3 Lev: 26:29.
- 219/4 Lee M. Friedman, *Jewish Pioneers and Patriots* (New York, 1943), pp. 153-59.
- 219/5 Ps: 28:22.
- 220/2 Joseph B. Felt, *Ecclesiastical History of New England* (Boston, 1862), 2: 22.
- 220/6 *PAJHS*, 20: 81. Eliot's master work was his translation of the Bible into the Indian language of the Massachusetts tribes. Ibid., 42, no. 4 (June 1953): 361-70. "A Hebrew-Dakota Dictionary" by W. Gunther Plaut: Reverend Samuel W. Pond in 1842, a volunteer missionary of Puritan stock to the Dakota tribes studied Hebrew and prepared in manuscript a "Hebrew-Dakota Dictionary." This was in preparation for his projected Bible that he would translate directly from the Hebrew into Dakota. The "dictionary" is one of the treasures of the Minnesota Historical Society.
- 220/7 *PAJHS*, 20: 64.
- 221/2 Ibid., 17: 35, note 6.
- 222/3 Isaiah Sonne, "Jewish Settlement in the West Indies," *PAJHS*, 37: 355.
- 223/3 Lee M. Friedman, "Hebrew-Speaking Indians," *PAJHS*, 39, part 2 (December 1949): 185-89.
- 223/4 David de Sola Pool, "Notes on American Jewish History," *PAJHS*, 22: 172-73.
- 224/2 Robert Silverberg, *Mound Builders of America* (Greenwich, Conn., 1968), pp. 51-52.
- 226/3 David Philipson, "Are there Traces of the Ten Lost Tribes in Ohio?" *PAJHS*, 13: 37-46.
- 226/5 More recently, since the establishment of the State of Israel the Chief Rabbis have ruled that the Falashas are descended of the Tribe of Dan and are to be accepted as full-fledged Jews. This subject is fully discussed in *Contemporary Halakhic Problems* by J. David Bleich (New York, 1977), pp. 298-308. Also, about 100 Indians in the province of Manipur, India, claim to be descendants of one of the Lost Tribes of Israel and seek affiliation

with world Jewry. See *B'nai B'rith Messenger,* Los Angeles, Dec. 15, 1972, p. 1.

227/2 Rudolf Glanz, *Jew and Irish* (New York, 1966), p. 16.

227/5 Cyrus H. Gordon, *Before Columbus, Links Between the Old World and Ancient America* (New York, 1971).

228/1 Thomas Fleming, *Who Really Discovered America?*

229/1 George Alexander Kohut, "Arkansas," *PAJHS,* 6: 158.

6
The Israelites' Role in the Conquest of the Southwest

231/1 *Texas, A Brief Account of the Origin progress and present state of the Colonial Settlement of Texas* (Nashville, 1836).

231/4 Seymour B. Liebman, *The Enlightened, The Writings of Luis de Carvajal, El Mozo* (Coral Gables, Fl., 1967), p. 26.

PAJHS, 51, no. 3 (March 1962): 181-186. "Luis de Carvajal, Governor of the New Kingdom of Leon" by Arnold Wiznitzer. Seymour B. Liebman, *The Enlightened, The Writings of Luis de Carvajal, El Mozo,* Coral Gables, Florida, 1967, p. 26; *PAJHS,* 55, no. 3 (March 1966): 277. "The Autobiography of Luis de Carvajal, the Younger," Translated (from the Spanish) by Martin A. Cohen.

232/4 Max J. Kohler, "Incidents Illustrative of American Jewish Patriotism," *PAJHS,* 4: 90-93.

PAJHS, 20: 102. Samuel Noah was born in Virginia in 1873. Simon Wolf, *The American Jew as Patriot, Soldier and Citizen,* Phila., 1895, pp. 35-38.

232/5 Leon Huhner, "Jews in the War of 1812," *PAJHS,* 20: 180-81.

235/10 Arthur, *Lafitte.* Jose de San Martin, the "George Washington of Chile" and Simon Bolivar, the "George Washington of South America," by 1824 had broken the power of Spain in the New World for all time.

PAJHS, 54, no. 2 (December 1964): 175. "When the Inquisition cells were opened in 1820 (in Mexico City) by Captain Llop he found "a man of gigantic stature, who was a Jew . . . "

236/4 Federal Writer's Program, *Texas, A Guide to the Lone Star State* (New York, 1940).

236/7 A Spanish "league" was almost four miles.

Henry Cohen, "Settlement of the Jews in Texas," *PAJHS,* 2: 139.

237/1 Jewish genealogist Dr. Malcolm H. Stern has reservations about the Jewish origin of Samuel Isaacs.

Stanley F. Chyet, "The Political Rights of the Jews in the United States: 1776-1840," *PAJA,* 10, no. 1 (April 1958): 52. " . . . the religion of the Mexican nation is, and will be perpetually, the Roman Catholic Apostolic . . . "—Mexican Constitution (1824) Title I, Art. I, Sec. 3.

237/3 Korn, *The Early Jews,* p. 330, note 55.

"Diary of Adolphus Sterne," *Southwestern Historical Society Quarterly,* 32 (1928); 35 (1931). The frontier settlement's full name was La Villa de Nuestra Senora del Pilar de Nacogdoches.

238/5 Marquis James, *The Raven, A Biography of Sam Houston* (New York, 1929), pp. 209, 211.

PAJHS, 2: 142.

238/6 *Gonzales Weekly Inquirer*, June 22, 1878; and 70th Anniversary Issue, July 19, 1923, "Early Days in Texas" A biography of David Kokernot.
241/3 John Myers Myers, *The Alamo* (New York, 1948), p. 118.
       The *Pioneer* blew up, burned, and sank in the Red River in 1833.
242/1 *PAJHS*, 46, no. 2 (December 1956): 101. "The influx of some 20,000 Anglo-American immigrants in the decade following 1821 had alarmed the Mexicans. In an effort to stem the flow, the government forbade further immigration and began to enact measures directed at the newly arrived settlers. Finding this action intolerable, the colonists revolted."
245/5 *Arkansas, A Guide to the State* (New York, 1958), pp. 219–220.
247/4 Saul Viener, "Surgeon Moses Albert Levy: Letters of a Texas Patriot," *PAJHS*, 46, no. 2 (December 1956): 107–109.
248/1 Ibid., pp. 105–106.
251/2 Aside from the name and rank of Antony Wolfe, a thorough searching of Texas and other sources might yield biographical data of this Jew, one of the legendary defenders of the Alamo.
251/5 *PAJHS*, 2: 146. Edward Johnson was a volunteer in Captain King's Company.
251/6 Ibid.
252/1 Ibid., p. 142.
252/4 James, *The Raven*, pp. 203-4, 226.
253/2 *PAJHS*, 2: 144, 150.
253/3 Frederic Gaillardet, *Sketches of Early Texas and Louisiana* (Austin, Texas, 1966), p. 45.
253/4 Dyer was dispatched with groups detailed to mop-up operations. So, was Lieutenant Kokernot ordered by Sam Houston to arrest "Tories" after the Battle of San Jacinto, as described by Kent Gardien in "Kokernot and His Tory," *Texana*, 8, no. 3 (1970): 269–94.

       Ira Rosenwaike, "Leon Dyer: Baltimore and San Francisco Jewish Leader," *Western States Jewish Historical Quarterly*, 9, no. 2 (January 1977): 135–43. Documentary evidence points to Leon Dyer's volunteering in 1836 for duty in Texas. Rosenwaike states that none exists for his participation in the Mexican War a decade later, as claimed by Henry Cohen, "During the Mexican War, Leon Dyer acted as quartermaster-general for General Scott," *PAJHS*, 2: 148–49. Biographical data on the life of Leon Dyer is primarily drawn from Ira Rosenwaike's study. The Seminole War in Florida, in which Dyer participated in early 1836, was described that year by Lieutenant Myer M. Cohen of Charleston in his *Notices of Florida and the Campaigns*.
254/3 Little is known of the pioneer Jewish community in Velasco. Henry Cohen notes in *PAJHS*, 2: 139, that upon Abraham Labatt's arrival in 1831, he found in Velasco two Israelites who preceded him: Jacob Henry and Jacob Lyons, the former from England, the latter from Charleston, engaged in mercantile pursuits. When Jacob Henry died, childless, he left his fortune to the city of Velasco, to build a hospital at that port.
254/6 Ira Rosenswaike, "Levy L. Laurens: An Early Texan Journalist," *PAJA*, 27, no. 1 (April 1975): 61–66.
255/3 The first Hebrew Burial Ground in Houston was consecrated in 1844. Levy Laurens, as all other Jews who arrived before sufficient numbers were con-

	centrated in a given locality, was buried in a City or Church cemetery.
255/6	*Telegraph and Texas Register,* Houston, July 1, 1837.
255/7	*PAJHS,* 4: 13–14.
256/5	Ibid., p. 11. Lewis Nordyke, "Waco . . . The Jewel on the Brazos," *Texas Parade,* Sept. 1958.
257/1	Ibid., pp. 9–19.
258/1	*PAJA,* 8, no. 2 (October 1956, Western Issue): 72–73.
258/3	Henry Cohen, "Henry Castro, Pioneer and Colonist," *PAJHS,* 5: 39–43.
258/8	*PAJHS,* 49, no. 3 (March 1960): 204.
259/3	*PAJHS,* 5: 43. Henry Castro may have been related to the Brazilian Jewish Martyr, Isaac de Castro (Tartas), extradited to Portugal, burned alive on December 15, 1647. *PAJHS,* 47, no. 2 (December 1957): 63–75. The secretive manner of observing Jewish ritual among former *marranos* or those of *marrano* descent was maintained by some even in eastern cities, where women lit Sabbath candles in darkened rooms and even counted the beads of the rosary out of habit.
259/6	Norton B. Stern and William M. Kramer, "The Rose of San Diego," *The Journal of San Diego History,* 19, no. 4 (Fall 1973): 28.
260/4	Frances Rosenthal Kallison, "Was It a Duel or a Murder? A Study in Texan Assimilation," *PAJHS,* 62, no. 3 (March 1973): 314–20.
261/1	*PAJHS,* 2: 144.
261/2	J. George Fredman and Louis A. Falk, *Jews in American Wars* (Washington, D.C., 1954), pp. 36–37. Abraham Charles Myers married Marion Twiggs, daughter of General David Emanuel Twiggs.
261/3	Wolf., *op. cit.,* pp. 72–75: Jewish Soldiers in the Mexican War.
261/4	*New York Herald,* 12, no. 187 (July 17, 1846).
261/6	Although no documentary evidence has been found of Leon Dyer's participation in the Mexican War (see note 253/4 above), tradition could in time be borne out by source material yet to surface. Thus, in *A History of the Baltimore Hebrew Congregation 1830–1905,* by Adolf Guttmacher (Baltimore, 1905), pp. 30–31, "a medal was presented to him on October 1, 1847, by the Congregation" before leaving for Texas, it is noted that "The medal is in the possession of his son, Dr. J. O. Dyer of Galveston."
262/2	*PAJHS,* 4: 16. *PAJA,* Oct. 1956, p. 76. The Ostermans were observant Jews, kept a kosher home, prospered in business, and amassed a fortune, the bulk of which they bequeathed to the poor of Galveston. The steamer, *W. R. Carter,* exploded February 2, 1866.
262/5	*PAJHS,* 2: p. 150. Henry Seeligson was elected Mayor of Galveston in 1852.
262/6	Fredman and Falk, *American Wars,* p. 37.
262/8	"El Palacio," *New Mexican Historical Review,* 38 (January 1928): 83, 86.
262/8	Floyd S. Fierman, "The Spiegelbergs: Pioneer Merchants and Bankers in the Southwest," *PAJHS,* 56, no. 4 (June 1967). Fierman, "The Spiegelbergs of New Mexico, Merchants and Bankers 1844–1893," *Southwestern Studies,* 1, no. 4 (Winter 1964).
263/2	*CAJ,* 1: 51–52.

263/5 Rudolf Glanz, *Studies in Judaica Americana*, New York 1970, "Jew and Yankee: A Historical Comparison," pp. 347–49. *PAJHS*, 45, no. 1 (September 1955). "Henry Wadsworth Longfellow's Presentation of the Spanish Jews" by John J. Appel, p. 28. Another "fly" joke, told by Longfellow in 1839. It was after an evening of conviviality at a friend's house, that he recorded one of the stories told over the wine:
    A fellow lodging at the house of a Jew buys of him all the flies in the house, with permission to kill them as he pleases, for his amusement. He then cooly takes out his pistol and begins to shoot at them wherever they alight—on windows, lookingglasses, no matter where; bang! bang! till finally the Jew is glad to buy him off at a higher rate.

264/1 *PAJHS*, 56, no. 4 (June 1967): 380. "The Spiegelbergs: Pioneer Merchants and Bankers in the Southwest" by Floyd S. Fierman.

265/3 Oliver La Farge, *Santa Fe* (Norman, Okla., 1959), p. 335.

265/7 Rudolf Glanz, *Jews of California* (New York, 1955). William Augustus Leidesdorff operated a trading company, and owned the only hotel in *Yerba Buena*. He served as United States Vice-Consul at Monterey, capital of Mexican California. Descendants claimed he hailed from a Rabbinical family in Hungary.

266/6 Adam W. Adler, "My Father was born a Jew," *Western States Jewish Historical Quarterly*, 6, no. 4 (July 1974): 255–59.

267/2 Byrde Baker, "History of Judaism in Los Angeles County," manuscript in possession of the author.
MAJ, 2: 88–98. At the age of 73, Jacob Hirschorn, vividly recalled his adventures in the Mexican War of 55 years earlier. The year was 1903, the place was St. Louis. It was first printed in pamphlet form, then reprinted in *The American Israelite*, 50, no. 3 (July 16, 1903). See also Morris U. Schappes, *Documentary History of the Jews in the United States, 1654–1875* (New York, 1950), pp. 263–73.

268/1 Abram Kanof, "Uriah Phillips Levy: The Story of a Pugnacious Commodore," *PAJHS*, 39, part 1 (September 1949): 52.

268/3 Levi Charles Harby, born in 1793, was 19 at the beginning of the War of 1812. See *AOJD*, p. 67. The young midshipman was captured by the British and imprisoned at Dartmoor, England. A Jewish baker daily peddled bread among the prisoners. One day, after eighteen months of confinement, a loaf of the bread was offered to Harby, but he refused to buy. The bread peddler was so insistent that Harby finally bought it. Breaking open the bread, he found a newspaper telling of the American victory at New Orleans. Without waiting for formal release, Harby soon made his escape.
Fredman and Falk, *American Wars*, pp. 30–31. *PAJHS*, 26: 194. Levi Harby's middle name is mistakenly referred to as Myers. Levi Charles Harby was the son of Solomon Harby and Rebecca Moses. His uncle, Myer Moses, was married to Esther Phillips, sister of Rachel Phillips (wife of Michael Levy), the parents of Jonas Phillips Levy. Hence the relationship between Levi Charles Harby and Jonas Phillips Levy is in Levi's uncle being married to Jonas' aunt. This information was referred to me by Dr. Malcolm H. Stern.

268/4   Charles Reznikoff and Uriah Z. Engelman, *The Jews of Charleston* (Philadelphia, 1950), p. 283, note 82.
268/5   Isaac Goldberg, *Major Noah: American-Jewish Pioneer* (Philadelphia, 1936), p. 288.
268/6   *PAJHS*, 39, part 1 (September 1949): 25.
286/7   Ibid., p. 7.
269/13 Markens, *The Hebrews*, p. 134.
271/4   *PAJHS*, 39, part 1 (September 1949): 20–22, 38–40.
        MAJ, 1: 76–116.
272/3   *PAJHS*, 56, no. 3 (March 1967): 320. After the war, Jonas Levy settled in Washington, D.C. In 1857, Captain Levy was elected President of the Washington Hebrew Congregation, first in the nation's capital.
272/4   Charles B. Hosmer, Jr., "The Levys and the Restoration of Monticello," *PAJHS*, 53, no. 3 (March 1964): 219–52.
274/2   Reznikoff and Engelman, *The Jews of Charleston*, p. 105.
275/1   *PAJHS*, 17: 194. "Major Levy Twiggs . . . killed at the storming of Chapultapec."
275/2   Fredman and Falk, *American Wars*, p. 61.
276/1   Schappes, *Documentary History*, pp. 263–73, 634–37.
276/2   Fredman and Falk, *American Wars*, p. 36.
276/6   In 1857, over 100 Jews assembled to discuss building a synagogue in the capital of Mexico. Not until 1918 was the cornerstone laid for Mount Sinai, Mexico's first synagogue.
276/6   *PAJHS*, 59, no. 4 (June 1972). "Mexico—Another Promised Land?" by Corinne A. Krause, pp. 325–26: "From 1856, the date of the first laws of the Reform Government, the government of Mexico pursued a policy of encouragement of immigration without regard to race or creed." In 1857 a liberal Constitution was established. That year, over 100 Jews in the capital city of Mexico assembled to discuss building a synagogue. However, various factors intervened to delay the building of a Jewish house of worship for over half a century. In 1918 the cornerstone was laid for Mount Sinai, Mexico's first synagogue edifice.
277/6   Guido Kisch, "The Revolution of 1848 and the Jewish 'On to America' Movement," *PAJHS*, 38, part 3 (March 1949), p. 198. "On to America!" First Call to Emigration; Leopold Kompert's translation of the original German "Auf, Nach Amerika!"
278/5   Benjamin II., *op. cit.*, 1: 121–22.

Index

A

Aaronsburg, Pa. 80, 81, 91
Abraham, Isaac, 69
Adair, James, 222
Adams, Catherine, 171
Adler, Abraham, 262
Adler, Lewis, 266
Agnes, Rachel, 173
Aguilera y Roche, Teresa de, 263
Aid society, 93
Alamo, 232, 247-48, 249-50, 251, 252, 258
Alarcon, Don Martin de, 232
Albany, N. Y., 312
Alcohol, 19, 71, 113
Alden, John, 73
Algonquin Indians, 6, 7
Allegheny Mountains, 4, 283, 284
Allen, William, 211
Alonso, Hernando, 133, 134
American Fur Company, 119
American Society for Meliorating the Conditions of the Jews, 210, 212, 268
Amherst, Jeffrey, 37
Anahuac, Tex., 240-41, 243

Anderson, Minerva Campbell, 168
Angiero, Pedro de, 303
Anglo-Saxons, 226
Ansley, Benjamin, George, Solomon Davis Co. (Davis Co.), 146-47
Apache Indians, 232
Appalachian Mountains, 283
Argentina, 235
Arismandi, Juan Batista, 233
Arkansas Territory, 228
Arrendondo, Don Joaquin, 233, 236
Asbridge, George, 151, 152, 305
Ashkenazic, 283
Astor, John Jacob, 112, 119
Astoria, Ore., 119
Attakullaculla (Indian chief), 59
Audler, Helene, 189
Audler, Solomon, 189, 203-4
Augusta, Ga., 207
Austin, Moses, 236
Austin, Stephen, 236-37, 238, 243-44, 245, 246, 292
Austin, Tex., 236, 244
Austrian Jew, 277
Aztec Indians, 218, 219
Aztec Temple, 134, 304

321

B

Baggataway, 35, 290
Bahia, Fort, 232
Bailey, Charlotte, 124
Bailey, William, 124
Baker, Isaac, 97
Baltimore, Md., 21, 69, 71, 72, 163, 165, 197, 261
Bancroft, George, 268
Bank of St. Louis, 114
Barataria Bay, 125, 143, 144, 145, 150, 151, 154, 233
Bar mitzvah, 297
Barnett, Edward, 189
Barnett, Maurice, 128, 151-52, 188, 189
Barnett, Maurice, Jr., 189
Barrett, Don Carlos, 244
Bavarian Jew, 90, 91, 155-56, 197-98, 279, 299
Baynton, Wharton, & Morgan, 39, 42, 43-44, 45-47, 49, 50, 291
Bear baiting, 100
Beatty, Charles, 221
Beaver pelts, 7, 112, 285
Bedford (Hills), N. Y., 175
Bees, 87
Bell, Alexander, 267
Bellechasse (estate), 189
Benjamin, Israel Joseph, 202, 203, 205
Benjamin, Judah, 189-91
Benjamin, Levi, 261
Benton, Thomas Hart, 114, 168
Bernheim, Isaac Woolf, 98
Beth Din, 3, 76, 77, 82-83
Beth Elohim, 280
Bexar, 232, 251
Big Bottom massacre, 87-88
Black, James, 245
Blackbeard, 144
"Black Boys," 42
Black Code, 2, 5, 14, 24, 25, 29, 107, 284
Blackfeet Indians, 111
Blackfish (Indian chief), 62
Black Hawk (Indian chief), 114
Blacks, 185-86, 186-87, 284. *See also* Slavery

Blanque, Jean, 126
Bloch, Andrew, 108-9
Bloch, Jacob, 108
Bloch, Jonathan, 108
Bloch, Solomon, 108
Bloch, Zevi Hirsch, 108
Block, Abraham, 179-80, 246-47
Block, Andrew, 108-9
Block, Annie, 171
Block, Eliezer, 172, 173, 179
Block, Elinor, 173
Block, Ezekiel, 109
Block, Jacob, 171, 172
Block, Jonas, 171
Block, Lazarus, 308
Block, Levi, 172
Block, Louisa, 173
Block, Phineas, 171
Block, Resna, 171
Block, Simon, 171, 172, 308
Block, Wolf, 171
Block & McCune, 171
Block & Philipson, 171
Bloody Run, 39, 45, 291
Blue Jacket (Indian chief), 88
B'nai Israel, 173, 198-99, 225
B'nai Yeshurun, 192, 199
Bodlye, Laura Cary, 168
Bohemian Jew, 277
Bolivar, Simon, 315
Boone, Daniel, xi, 61, 62, 82, 83-84
Boonesborough, Fort, xi, 61, 62-63, 68, 294
Boswell, Anna Maria, 166
Boude, Samuel, 19
Boudinot, Elias, 210-11, 212
Bouquet, Henry, 20, 37-38, 290
Bourdeaux, Rose, 191
Bowie, James, 245, 246, 251
Bowie knife, 245
Boxing, 99-100
Boyd, Stephen, 157-58
Bradburn, John Davis, 241
Braddock, Edward, 14, 15, 27, 166, 175
Brandeau, Esther, 5
Braxton, Carter, 57
Brazil, 134-35
British taxation, 49, 55

Brou, Marie Emeronthe Becnel, 188
Brouillet, Eliza, 309
Brouillet, Mary Louise, 179
Brown, George, 235
Brown, Quindaro Nancy, 294
Bryan & Morrison Co., 113
Bryand, Caroline C., 168
Buffalo, 112
Buffalo, N. Y., 212
Bunker Hill monument, 200
Bunn, Hiam Solomon, 3-4, 6, 9
Bunn, Rose, 9-10
Burial, Jewish, 77, 162, 184, 309
Burial mounds, 48, 224, 227
Burleson, Edward, 246, 247, 248
Burnett, David G., 253
Butler, Richard, 57
Butler, William, 130

C

Cadillac, Antoine, 221-22
Cahokia, Ill., 46, 48, 63, 64, 176, 177, 291-92
Cahokia Indians, 40, 42, 51
Calhoun, John C., 176, 177, 178
California, 263, 265-67, 278, 279
Campbell, John, 51, 52, 56
Campbell, Robert, 56
Campeache (settlement), 233, 234, 235, 239
Canada, 53-54, 67, 115-16, 119-20, 286, 288
Canter, John, 209-10
Cape Girardeau, Mo., 171
Carib Indians, 133
Carlisle, Pa., 33
Carpeles, Joseph Wolf, 77, 296
Carroll, Henry, 261
Cartier, Jacques, 288
Carvajal y de la Cueva, Luis de, 231-32, 263
Castro, Henry, 257-58, 259
Castroville, Tex., 258
Catawba Indians, 205, 222
Cayuga Indians, 45
Cazenave, Pierre Andre Destrac, 201
Cemetery, Jewish, 4, 77, 162-63, 167, 172, 183-84, 194, 284, 309, 316

Cerro Gordo, 272, 273
Chambers, R. E., 225-26
Champlain, Samuel de, 45, 289
Chapman, Abraham, 33, 34-35, 116
Chapultepec, Mex., 274-75, 319
Charleston, S. C., 146, 209, 254, 255, 268, 280
Charlottesville, Va., 180
Che-ku-ka-tes, 111-12
Cherokee Indians, 43, 58-59, 61, 65, 102, 205, 206, 222, 294
Chesse, Margarite Basilique, 188
Chew, Samuel, 92
Chickasaw Indians, 205, 222, 284
Chicago, Ill., 120, 121, 279
Chihuahua, Mex., 264, 265
Chile, 235
Chimene, Eugene Joseph, 253
Chippewa Indians, 34, 88, 219
Choctaw Indians, 127, 129, 205, 206
Choteau, Rene Auguste, 113
Choteau's Pond (camp), 113
Churubusco, Mex., 274
Cincinnati, Ohio, xvi, xviii, xix, 85, 147, 160-63, 167, 170, 171, 173-74, 183, 198, 225, 279, 308
Circumcision, 3, 22, 74, 215, 304
Claiborne, William C. C., 111, 126, 127, 141-42, 150, 154
Clapp, Theodore, 182
Clark, Abraham, 170
Clark, Clarissa, 170
Clark, George Rogers, 63, 64, 65, 67, 68
Clark, William Rogers, 121, 302
Clary, Marie Louise, 114
Clary, Robert Emmett, 114, 115
Clava, Benjamin Moses, 77-78
Clay, Henry, 120, 147, 164, 168, 293
Clay, James, 164, 307
Clay, Thomas Hart, 168
Clay City, Ky., 227
Cleveland, Ohio, 105, 279
Code Noir. *See* Black Code
Coffey, John, 128
Cohen, Charles Clemens Coleman, 169-70
Cohen, Isaac, 312
Cohen, Jacob I., 82-84

Cohen, Jacob Raphael, 74
Cohen, Karl, 205
Cohen, Simon, 128
Cohen & Isaacs, 82
Colebrooke, George, 15, 286
Colebrooke, James, 15, 286
Colebrooke, Nesbitt & Franks, 286
Collinsworth, George, 245
Colombia, 142, 145, 235
Colombus, Tex., 236
Columbus, Christopher, 303, 304
Comanche Indians, 232, 245
Concklin, Seth, 149
Conger, Laverne, 280
Connersville, Ind., 170
Connolly, John, 53
Cooperstown, N. Y., 292
Coquataginta (Indian chief), 56
Cordoba, Pedro de, 304
Coronado, Francisco Vasquez de, 231
Cortes, Hernando, 133
Cos, Martin Perfecto de, 244, 245, 247, 249
Cotton gin, 207-8
Crawford, Charles, 219
Crawford, Hugh, 35
Crawford, William, 35, 219-20
Creek Indians, 127, 205-9, 312
Crockett, David, 251
Croghan, George, 42, 49-50, 292
Crow Indians, 111
Cumberland Gap, 61, 294
Cuming, Sir Alexander, 12-13
Curvalla Indians, 207

D

Da Costa, Rachel, 176
Dalton, Margarite, 188
Dalyell, James, 39
D'Angers, David, 312
Danites, 226
Da Silva, Benjamin, 202
David, David, 286
David, Jacob, 284
David, Romain, 284
Davis, Jefferson, 114, 190
Davis, William Heath, 266
Dearborn, Fort, 120

De Cordova, Jacob, 255-57
De Cordova, Phineas, 255, 256
De Cordova Land Agency, 256
De Costa, Isaac, 77
De Jonce, Solomon F., 128
De Lancey, Oliver, 73
De Landa, Bishop Diego, 216
De Lassus, Chevalier, 109
Delaware Indians, 7, 15, 37, 38, 43, 46, 56, 62, 81, 84, 87, 89, 221
De Leon, Abraham, 296
De Leon, David Camden, 275
De Leon, Esther, 296
De Levis, Gastogne Francois, 27-29
De Levis, Point, 289
De Lyon, Abraham, 3, 5, 70, 136
De Lyon, Leonore Rebecca, 268
De Lyon, Rachel, 75, 296
De Lyon, Rebecca, 75, 296
De Lyon, Zipporah, 70, 75, 77, 296
De Maria, Vicente, 134
Dembitz, Lewis N., xvi
De Morales, Francisco, 134
De Morand, Aime Dauqueminil, 187
De Pere, Wis., 119
De Sequeyra, John, 82
De Silva, Francisco, 137-39
Detroit, Fort, 33-34, 35, 38, 39, 63, 64, 65, 67, 120-21, 221-22
Devil River, 118-19
"Devil's Dance Chamber," 6
Dickinson, Susannah, 251
Dickson, Robert, 121
Diet, kosher, 3, 8, 48, 65, 91, 101-2, 216, 285, 313
Dinwiddie, Robert, 14, 15
Dixon, Robert, 121
Dixon & Hay, 266
Dohla, Johann Conrad, 74
Dominican Republic, 303
Donaldsonville, La., 234
Doniphan, Alexander W., 263, 264, 265
Dow, Robert, 187
Drayton, William Henry, 59
Drummond, Adam, 286
Dubois, Louise, 116
Ducre, Felicite, 151, 189

Index 325

Duquesne, Fort, 14, 19, 175
Duran, Diego, 219
Dutch Jew, 157
Dutch peddler, 93-101, 102-5
Duval, Burr H., 251
Du Vale, William, 82
Dyer, Isidore, 254, 262
Dyer, Leon, 253-54, 261-62, 316, 317
Dyer, Rosanna, 254, 262

E

Easton, Pa., 70, 74-75, 158, 296
Ecuyer, Simeon, 37, 38
Edgeworth, Maria, 103
Edwards, Haden 238
Eliot, John, 220-21
El Paso, Tex., 264
Emanuel, Albert, 253
Emanuel, David, 273
Emanuel, Ruth, 273
English Jew, xviii, 160-74, 199
Esnoga, 283
Essenecca (village), 59, 60
Etting, Edward Johnson, II, 169
Etting, Elijah, 48, 169
Etting, Frances, 169
Etting, Horatio, 169
Etting, Reuben, 169
Etting, Samuel, 169
Etting, Solomon, 48, 169, 291
Evans, Margaret, 73
Evans, Peter, 73
Ewing, Samuel, 166
Eytings, S., 261
Ezrath Orechim, 93

F

Falashas, 226, 314
Fallsway, Md., 71
Fannin, James, 245, 251
Farmar, Robert, 41, 42
Farnsworth, John, 286
Fastio, Robert, 290
Fechheimer, Sam, 152
Feinberg, Regina, 260
Feinberg, Siegmund Moses, 259-60
Felsenthal, Bernard, 225
Fibemann, Feibel, 61
Fincastle, Fort, 53, 292, 302

Finkerhaus, Isaac, 263-64
Fish, 8, 285, 313
Fludyer, Samuel, 286
Fond du Lac, Wis., 118
Forbes, John, 19
Fort. *See word following Fort as Dearborn, Fort.*
Fort (du) Chartres, 40-41, 42, 43, 44, 46, 63, 292, 294
Fort Wayne, Ind., 177
Forty-niners, 278, 279
Francisco "Cacique," 217-18
Frankfort, Jacob, 266-67
Franklin, Benjamin, 53-54, 72, 95
Franklin & Framfield, 146-47
Franks, Abraham, 299
Franks, Benjamin, 15, 286
Franks, Burrel, 240
Franks, David, xi, 11, 13, 15, 16, 17, 18-19, 31, 47, 50, 51, 52, 55, 73-74, 117, 286
Franks, David Salisbury, 85-87, 88, 119, 299
Franks, Elijah, 240
Franks, Jacob, 50
Franks, Jacob, Jr., 117-19, 120, 302
Franks, Michael, 14
Franks, Moses, 15, 50, 286
Franks, Phila, 73
Franks, Rebecca, 119
Fredonia, Republic of, 238
Freehold, N. J., 170
Fremont, John Charles, 265, 266
French and Indian War, 12-20, 23-29, 59, 286
French Jew, 25, 155, 257
Friedman, Isaac, 147-49
Friedman, Joseph, 147-49
Friedman, Levi, 148, 149
Fronty Fort, 79
Fuller, John, 114
Fulton, Robert, 21, 192-93
Fur trade, 7, 12, 40, 44-45, 52, 55, 68, 108-9, 112, 115-16, 116-17, 118, 119, 177

G

Gage, Thomas, 42, 46, 63, 291

Gallipolis, Ohio, 85, 87
Galveston, Tex., 254, 256, 262, 268, 317
Galveston Island, 233, 234, 235, 239
Gambino, 145
Garrick, David, 31
Geiger, Abraham, 225
George, Fort, 123
Georgia, 3, 12-13, 271, 273
German Jew, xvii, 3, 89-91, 93-94, 99, 155-57, 158-59, 188, 197-98, 199, 279, 283, 306
Getty, John, 209, 210
Ghent, Treaty of, 128
Gibson, George, 44
Gibson, John, 68, 209, 210
Gist, Christopher, 166
Gist, Maria Cecil, 166, 168
Gist, Nathaniel, 166
Gladwin, Henry, 33, 35
Gold, 277, 280
Goldsmith, Samuel G., 261
Goliad, Tex., 245, 251, 252, 258
Gomez, Daniel, 58, 137, 204
Gomez, Jacob, 137
Gomez, Manuel, 26-27
Gomez, Matthias, 204
Gonzales, Tex., 244-45, 250
Goodrich, Chauncey, 255
Gradis, Abraham, 24-25
Gradis, David, 23-24, 25, 288
Gradis (David) & Sons, 23, 24, 41
Grand Island, 212, 213, 214
Grand Isle, 153
Grand Portage, Minn., 116, 119
Grand Terre (island), 125, 145
Grant, Campion & Co., 176
Gratiot, Charles, 113
Gratiot & La Croix, 63
Gratz, Alexander, 168
Gratz, Anderson, 168
Gratz, Anna, 168
Gratz, Barnard, 32, 47-48, 52, 55, 56-57, 67, 69, 76-77, 108-9, 291
Gratz, Benjamin, 164-65, 166, 167-68
Gratz, Benjamin III, 168
Gratz, Charles Cunningham, 169
Gratz, Cora, 169

Gratz, Ella, 168
Gratz, Frances, 169
Gratz, Heinrich, 169
Gratz, Henry Howard, 168
Gratz, Hermine Cary, 168
Gratz, Hyman, 81, 121-22, 302, 303
Gratz, Hyman Cecil, 168
Gratz, Jacob, 122, 303
Gratz, John Johnstone, 168
Gratz, Joseph, 122, 184-85, 303
Gratz, Louis, A., 97, 300
Gratz, Maria, 166, 168
Gratz, Mary Cecil, 168
Gratz, Michael, 47-48, 52, 55, 56-57, 67, 69, 81-82, 108-9, 164, 166, 292, 297
Gratz, Miriam, 81, 82, 165
Gratz, Rebecca, 164, 165, 166-67, 185, 307
Gratz, Richea, 175
Gratz, Sarah Campbell, 168-69
Gratz, Simon, 80, 81, 121-22, 165, 168-69, 302
Gratz, Ky., 84
Gratz, Pa., 81
Gratz & Gibson, 68
Gratz (B. & M.) Co., 47, 49-54, 56, 68, 84, 96
Gratzburg, N. Y., 49, 292
Gratztown, Pa., 81
Gray, Henry, 189
Great Dismal Swamp, 83
Green, Thomas Jefferson, 253
Green Bay, Wis., 117, 121
Grey, Susanna, 293
Griesinger, Theodor, 100
Grush, Nellie, 293-94
Guadalupe Hidalgo, Treaty of, 277
Guiteres, Bernado, 232
Gumilla, Joseph, 218
Gutheim, James Koppel, 202
Guthrie, Abelard, 294

H

Hagerstown, Md., 293-94
Haldimand, Frederick, 25
Halifax, Nova Scotia, 25
Hamilton, Henry, 63, 64
Hamilton, Laura J., 168

Hanukah, 65, 66, 67
Harby, George Washington, 268, 311
Harby, Henry Jefferson, 268
Harby, Isaac, 196
Harby, Levi Charles, 268, 318
Harby, Samuel, 196
Harby, Solomon, 318
Harrington, 103
Harris, Hyam, 183-84
Harris, John, 80
Harrisburg, Pa., 80
Harrison, Benjamin, 63
Harrison, William Henry, 119, 179, 302
Harrod, James, 294
Harrodsburg, Ky., 62, 164, 294
Hart, Aaron, 25-27, 28, 29-30, 61
Hart, Henry, 21, 61
Hart, Jacob, 128, 153
Hart, Jacob Naphtali, 153
Hart, Judith, 75-76, 296
Hart, Leah, 65
Hart, Louisa, 65
Hart, Lucretia, 69, 168, 293, 307
Hart, Michael, 65-67, 158
Hart, Moses, 25, 61
Hart, Myer, 75, 296
Hart, Naphtali, 158
Hart, Nathaniel, 68, 88, 293-94
Hart, Rachel, 75
Hart, Sarah Simpson, 68-69
Hart, Thomas, 88, 168, 293-94
Hart, Thomas, Jr., 293-94
Harvie, John, 82
Hays, Abigail, 177
Hays, Andrew, 308-9
Hays, Barrack, 176, 309
Hays, Benjamin, 175
Hays, Benjamin Etting, 175
Hays, Catherine, 181
Hays, Charity, 174-75, 179, 180, 183
Hays, David, 15-16, 19, 82, 175, 309
Hays, Esther, 175
Hays, Hannah, 175
Hays, Hetty, 82, 179
Hays, Jacob, 175-76
Hays, John Jacob, 176, 177-79, 309
Hays, Michael, 175, 309

Hays, Michael Solomon, 176-77
Hays, Moses Michael, 181
Hays, Reyna, 180, 181
Hays, Samuel, 175
Hays, Solomon, 176, 177
Hazzan, 297-98
Heidelberg, Pa., 22
Henderson, Richard, 61, 294
Hendricks, Harmon, 192-93, 310
Henriques, Isaac Nunes, 3, 4
Henry, Alexander, 35
Henry, Jacob, 108, 254, 316
Henry, Michael, 108
Henry, Patrick, 63, 83
Henry, William, 20-21
Henry, Fort, 17, 36, 292
Hermann, Louis Florian, 188
Hermann, Samuel, 128, 188
Hermann, Samuel Edmond, 188
Herne, Lucille Dorothy, 280
Hertz, Hyman, 242
Hertz, Joseph, 242
Heyman Levy Company, 16
Hickory oil, 207
Hickory Town, Ind., 2, 3, 4
Hidalgo, Miguel, 154, 305
Hirschorn, Jacob, xi, 267-68, 272, 273, 274, 276, 318
Hispaniola, 132, 303, 304
Hockfre, Captain, 130
Hoffman, Josiah Ogden, 307
Hoffman, Sarah Matilda, 167, 307
Hogun, John 147, 148
Hollingsworth, Levi, 297
Holy Stones of Newark, 225, 226
Horowitz, J., 261
Hot Springs Mountain, 228-29
Houston, Samuel, 237, 243, 244, 250, 251-53, 257
Houston, Tex., 255, 316
Hudson's Bay Company, 116, 119, 302
Huntington, W. Va., xv-xvi
Huron, Indians, 34, 35, 38, 45
Hyman, Henry, 162

I

Iberian Jews, 283
Illini Confederacy, 40, 42, 50, 51

Illini Indians, 40
Illinois, 68
Illinois Territory, 177, 295
Illinois Company, First, 50
Illinois Company, Second, 51-52, 67-68
Illowy, Bernard, 225
Immigration, 90-93
Incas, 218
Indentured servants, 90-93, 156-58, 306
Indian, American, 3, 6-7, 8-9, 13, 33, 34-35, 39-40. *See also names of tribes as* Cherokee Indians
  land, 45-46, 49, 50-51, 55, 56, 178
  massacres, 35, 36, 39, 52, 59, 79-80, 87
  Revolutionary War, 56, 58-59, 63, 65, 67, 68
  ten tribe theory, 215-16, 228
Indiana, 67, 291
Indiana Company, 45, 47, 67
Intermarriage, x, xvi, xvii-xviii, 69, 73-77, 163, 167, 170, 184, 188, 198, 280-81, 302
Iroquois Confederacy, 45, 81, 88, 297
Irving, Washington, 167
Isaac, Lazarus, 19
Isaacs, Aaron, 94
Isaacs, Frances Isaiah, 179-80
Isaacs, Isaac, 211
Isaacs, Isaiah, 82, 83, 84, 179
Isaacs, Samuel, 236-37, 315
Isaacs, Solomon I., 194
Israel, 296, 310, 314
Israel, David, 170
Israel, Eliza, 170
Israel, Phineas, 170
Ivanhoe, 167

J

Jackson, Andrew, 126-28, 129-31, 154
Jackson, Solomon H., 212
Jacob, Genevieve, 284
Jacob, Robert, 284

Jacobs, Barnard Itzhak, 22, 95
Jacobs, Felix, 184
Jacobs, Ferdinande, 26, 288
Jacobs, Isaac, 98
Jacobs, John I., 163-64
Jacobs, Levy, 151, 152, 305
Jacobs, Manis, 183-84, 191-92, 193-94, 195
Jacobs, Moses, 163
Jacobs, Solomon, 202, 203, 204
Jacobs, Theresa, 184
Jacobs, Thomas P., 163-64
Jacobs & Asbridge, 151
Jalapa, Mex., 272, 273
Jefferson, Thomas, 68, 82, 271, 298, 312
Jesus Christ, 104
Jew, The, 212
Jew Company, 82
"Jewish Cemetery at Newport, The," 200
Jew peddler, 93-101, 102-5, 163
Jews. *See also under country of origin as* Bavarian Jew; Portuguese Jew
  black code, 2, 5, 14, 24, 25, 29, 107, 284
  burial, 77, 162, 184
  integration, 74, 124, 159-60, 279-80
  marriages, x, xvi, xvii-xviii, 69, 73-77, 83, 163, 167, 170, 184, 188, 198, 280-81, 302
  population, xi, xix, 73
  prejudice, 103-5, 163
  surnames, xvi-xvii, 295
Jews' harp, 43
Johnson, "Boggy," 171
Johnson, David Israel, 170, 171, 225, 251
Johnson, David M., 225
Johnson, Edward Isaac, 170, 251, 316
Johnson, Francis W., 246
Johnson, Frederick A., 170
Johnson, Phineas Israel, 170
Johnson, Selena, 170

Johnson, William, 45
Jonas, Abraham, 161, 172, 173, 280
Jonas, Anne Elizabeth, 280
Jonas, Joseph, 160-61, 163, 173-74, 198, 199, 280, 306, 307, 308
Jonas, Lyon, 306
Jonas, Montrose, 280
Jonas, Sarah, 173
Jonau, Antoine, 187
Jones, John Beauchamp, 101
Josephson, Manuel, 16-17, 77, 296
Josephson, Meyer, 61
Judah, Dorothea Catherine, 29
Juliana Library, 20
Juneau, Solomon, 301

K

Kabalah, 48, 291
Kahal Kadosh Lancaster, 72
Kahal Kadosh Mikveh Israel, 69
Karankawa Indians, 232, 235
Kashita Indians, 207
Kaskaskia, Ill., 40, 44, 46, 48, 49, 63, 291-92
Kaskaskia Indians, 40, 42, 51
Kaskaskia River, 40, 44
Kaufman, David S., 261
Kaufman County, Tex., 261
Kearny, Stephen W., 262, 263, 265, 266
Kehillah, 69-70, 77, 78
Kennedy, Sarah, 158
Kentucky, 58, 61-63, 68, 81-82, 83-84, 96, 166, 293
Kentucky rifle, 20
Keowee River, 59
Kickapoo Indians, 40, 43, 178
Kidd, William, 15
Kilbourn, Byron, 301-2
King George's War, 12
Kingsborough, Viscount, 218
King William's War, 12
Kittredge, Sarah, 172
Koasati Indians, 207-8
Kohn, Abraham, 102-3
Kohn, Joachin, 188
Kohn, Samuel, 128, 186, 188, 205

Kohn, Samuel Arthur, 188
Kohn, Simon, 187
Kokernot, David, 238-43, 244-45, 246, 250-51, 316
Kompert, Leopold, 277
Kosher diet, 3, 48, 65, 91, 101-2, 216, 285, 313
Kursheedt, Gershom, 197, 198, 199, 200, 201, 311, 312
Kursheedt, Israel Baer, 197-98

L

Labatt, Abraham Cohen, 254, 316
Laclede, Pierre Liguest, 113, 301
Lacrosse, 35, 290
Laffite, Alexandre Frederic (Captaine Dominique), 126, 127, 128, 129, 130, 131, 143, 233
Laffite, Henry Elias (Rene Beluche), 126, 127, 129, 131, 143, 233
Laffite, Jean, xi, 125-32, 137, 139, 141, 142-45, 151, 152, 153-54, 233-35, 239, 303, 305-6
Laffite, Pierre, 126, 127, 128, 130, 132, 141-42, 143, 144, 233-34
Lafitte, La., 131
Lake of the Woods, 115
Lamar, Mirabeau B., 258
Lancaster, Pa., 4, 9, 10, 48, 70, 72, 80, 81, 284, 287
"Land of the Forks," 7-8, 9-23, 52
Larned, Sylvester, 211
Laurens, Levy I., 255, 316
Lawe, John, 118, 119, 121, 302
Lazarus, Hyman, 97
Leach, John, 171
Le Blond, Joseph, 110
Le Boeuf, Fort, 14
Ledoux, Modeste, 189
Lee, Tom, 253
Leeser, Isaac, 97, 200
Leggett, Samuel, 212
Legionville, Pa., 72
Leib, Binyamin, 162-63, 306-7
Leidesdorff, William, 265, 318
Leitensdorfer, Eugene Lott, 262, 264
Le Loup Blanc (Indian chief), 17

"Les Sirenes," 153
L'Estrange, Hamon, 220
Levine, Cristiana, 141
Levy, Aaron, 79, 80-81, 91-92, 291, 297
Levy, Asser, 73
Levy, Barnard, 75-76, 77
Levy, Barnett Lazarus, 75
Levy, Ezekiel, 69, 73
Levy, Gerson, 33, 36, 116
Levy, Henrietta, 74
Levy, Heyman, xi, 16, 287
Levy, Isaac, 63-64, 73, 74, 294
Levy, Isabella, 272
Levy, Jefferson Monroe, 272
Levy, Jonas, 161
Levy, Jonas Phillips, 268, 271, 272, 318-19
Levy, Joseph, 59, 293
Levy, L. A., Jr., 203-4
Levy, Levy Andrew, xi, 10, 21-23, 31, 36-37, 38, 39, 47, 51, 56, 70-71, 88, 165-66, 203, 288, 290
Levy, Mary Simon, 10
Levy, Michael, 318
Levy, Moses Albert, 247, 248-49, 258-59
Levy, Nathan, 11, 14, 73, 286
Levy, Rachel, 74, 79, 80, 258, 271
Levy, Samson, 74
Levy, Samson, Jr., 74
Levy, Simon Magruder, 88, 89, 165, 203
Levy, Susannah, 21-22, 36-37, 70, 165
Levy, Uriah Phillips, 202, 268-72, 312
Levy & Franks Co., 11, 13, 19, 291
Levy, Franks & Simon, 13-14
Levy, Lyon & Co., 17
Lewis, Alexander, 115
Lewis, Meriwether, 112
Lewis and Clark expedition, 112, 301
Lexington, Ky., 167, 168, 184, 294
Lexington, Va., 294
Lexington and Ohio Railroad, 168
Liberty Bell, 14

Lilienthal, Maxmillian, 225
Limpieza, 151
Liquor, 19, 71, 113
Little Rock, Ark., 228
Little Turtle (Indian chief), 88, 89
Livingston, Edward, 130
Logan (Indian chief), 52
Longfellow, Henry Wadsworth, 200, 317-18
Lopez, Virginia, 271-72
Lopez de Mendizabal, Bernardo, 262-63
Lorimier, Louis, 109
Los Angeles, Calif., 265, 266, 267
Lost Tribes of Israel, 210-11, 212, 213-14, 215-29
Louis XIII, king of France, 284
Louisbourg, fortress of, 2, 25-26
Louisiana Purchase, 124, 159, 186
Louisiana Territory, 48-49, 107, 112, 124-31, 284, 300
Louisville, Ky., 53, 162, 163, 279
Lowenstamm, Saul, 78, 296
Lowrey, Alexander, 46-47
Lumbrozo, Jacob, 73, 295-96
Lushington, Richard, 82
Lyon, Benjamin, 17, 26, 33, 35, 36, 116, 162-63, 306-7
Lyon, Emanuel, 98
Lyon, Isaac, 253
Lyons, Jacob, 316

M

McCarty, Richard, 290
McClure, Alexander K., 169
McClure, David, 10
McCoy, Isaac, 177
Mackinac Company, 116
Mackinac, (Michilimackinac), Fort, 33, 35, 39, 40, 67, 116, 119, 120, 302
McNair, Alexander, 112
Madison, James, 131, 150, 151, 177, 233
Magee, Lieutenant, 232
Magruder, Christiana, 165
Magruder, Susannah, 21-22, 36-37, 70, 165, 288

"Maid and the Magpie, The," 94
Malaria, 49, 63, 87
Mammoth Cave, 121-22, 302
Manasseh ben Israel, 217, 218, 219, 222
Manhattan Island, 9
Manshac, Captain, 232
Marchegay, Delphine Blanchard, 186
Marietta, Ohio, 85, 87
Marks, Aaron, 269
Marks, Albert J., 195-97, 199
Marranos, 132, 133, 136, 137, 138, 277
Marriages, mixed, x, xvi, xvii-xviii, 69, 73-77, 163, 167, 170, 184, 188, 198, 281-82
Marshall, Henry Clay, 168
Marshall University, xvi
Martin, Marie Thalie, 188
Martin, Morgan L., 301-2
Martin, Natalie Saint, 189, 190
Marx, Frances, 169
Massanet, Father Damien, 232
Matamoros, Mex., 270
Matrikel, 90, 155, 299
Matzah, 183
Maumee Falls, Ohio, 88-89, 115
Maya Indians, 216-17, 218
Mayflower (ship), 73
Mendelssohn, Felix, 299
Mendelssohn, Moses, 89, 299
Mendes da Costa, Emanuel, 60
Mendez, Antonio, 150-51, 180
Mendizabal, Bernardo Lopez de, 262-63
Mendoza, Domingo de, 304
Menominee Indians, 117-18
Menorah, 66
Mercer, Jesse, 295
Mercer University, 295
Merrick, Joseph, 210, 211
Mexican Revolution, 153-54, 235-36
Mexican War, 260-77, 316, 317
Mexico, 133, 236, 237-38, 241-54, 258-59, 260-77, 315, 319
Mexico City, Mex., 236, 273, 274, 275, 276

Meyers, Charles, 266
Mezuzah, 160-61, 306
Miami Indians, 35, 37, 81, 84, 178, 290
Michigamea Indians, 42
Michigan, 67, 116
Michigan Territory, 120
Mickve Israel, 135
Middlebrook, N. J., 65, 295
Middletown, Conn., 156
Mikveh Israel, 29, 74, 75, 76, 77, 93, 95, 167, 296, 304
Milam, Benjamin, 245, 246-47, 248
Miller, John, 19
Milligan, James, 44
Milwaukee, Wis., 118, 302
Mingo Indians, 37, 38, 52, 53, 56
Minis, Abigail, 181
Minyan, 5
Miranda, George, 3
Miranda, Isaac, 2-3, 26-27
Mississippi River, 11, 300-301
Missouri, 114
Missouri Fur Company, 301
Mitchell, Abraham, 44, 272
Mitchell, Francis Allen, 272
Mitchell, Hyman, 228
Mitchell, Jacob, 228
Mitchell, Louis, 228
Mobile, Fort, 40-41
Mohawk Indians, 17, 36, 45, 79
Mohawk Trail, 211
Mohegan Indians, 211
Molino del Rey, Battle of, 274
Monsanto, Angelica, 187, 290
Monsanto, Benjamin, 290
Monsanto, Eleanora, 290
Monsanto, Gracie, 290
Monsanto, Isaac Rodrigues, 41-42, 187, 290
Monsanto, Jacob, 187-88
Monsanto, Manuel, 290
Monsanto, Sophia, 187, 188
Monsanto Company, 41-42
Montcalm, Marquis de Louis Joseph, 27-28
Monterey, Calif., 265, 266, 318
Monterrey, Mex., 262, 263, 267

332 Index

Montezinos, Antonio de, 217-18
Monticello, 271-72
Montreal, Que., 29
Moore, Francis, Jr., 255
Mordecai, Abraham M., xi, 206-8, 312
Mordecai, Benjamin H., 251
Mordecai, Esther, 70, 72, 82, 83, 206, 298
Mordecai, Isaac, 206, 312
Mordecai, Jacob, 83, 206, 312
Mordecai, Joseph, 206, 312
Mordecai, Mordecai Moses, 19, 69-72, 75-78, 83, 206, 312
Mordecai, Zipporah, 70, 75, 77
Morgan, General, 130-31
Morgan, George, 44, 46, 108-9
Morris, Robert, 82, 292
Morton, Jeremiah Rogers, 168
Moses, Isaac, 72
Moses, Morris, 161, 173
Moses, Phineas, 173
Moses, Rebecca, 318
Moses, Robert S., 280
Mound builders, 48
Mount Pleasant, N.Y., 182
Mulatto, 187
Murray, John, Lord Dunmore, 51, 52-53
Murray, William, 48-49, 50, 51, 52
Mussina, Simon, 242
Mussina, Susanna, 114
Mussina, Zachary, 112
Myers, Abraham Charles, 261, 316
Myers, Benjamin, 124, 175, 308
Myers, Esther, 14
Myers, Hannah Hays, 308
Myers, Isaac, 14
Myers, Jacob, 14
Myers, Mordecai, 14, 122-24, 303
Myers, Sarah, 175
Myers-Cohen, Bilah, 3, 4
Myers-Cohen, Rachel, 4, 32
Myers-Cohen, Richea, 32
Myrtilla, 13-14

N

Nacogdoches, Tex., 237, 238, 242, 252, 261, 315

Nadrimal, Abhorad, 132, 137, 138
Nadrimal, Zora, 132, 137, 139, 141
Nahum Keike (Indian village), 220
Naphtalites, 222
Nashville, Tenn., 175, 308
Natchitoches, La., 232
Nathan, Asher Moses, 188
Nathan, Benjamin, 22-23
Nathan, Marie Virginie, 188
Nathan, Simon, 64-65, 75-76, 77, 294
Nebraska Territory, 294
Nefutzoth Yehudah, 198, 199-200, 202
Nesbitt, Arnold, 15, 286
Neville, John, 56
Newbold, Maria, 169
New Dunkers, 1-2, 3
New France, 11, 12, 23-31, 45, 48-49, 53, 284, 288
  black code, 2, 5, 107
New Judea, 1, 3
New Madrid, 108
New Mexico, 258, 262-63
New Mexico Territory, 265
New Orleans, La., xviii, 2, 41-42, 127, 128, 143-44, 150, 151-52, 154, 180, 181, 182, 183-89, 191-92, 193, 194, 198, 199-200, 202, 279, 284, 290, 310-11
  battle of, 124-31, 154
Newport, R.I., 29, 122, 136-37, 139, 180, 198, 200, 304, 311
New Spain, 41-42, 48-49, 107, 124, 315
New York, N.Y., 29, 175, 192, 193, 289, 304
Niagara, Fort, 121, 122-23
Nicolls, Edward, 125
Noah, Elias, 232
Noah, Mordecai Manuel, 209-10, 211-16, 232, 255, 268, 312
Noah, Robert P., 268
Noah, Samuel, 232-33, 315
Nolte, Vincent, 129
North American Land Company, 292
Northumberland, Pa., 79-80
North West Company, 116, 119, 302
Northwest Ordinance, 85

Northwest Territory, 84-89, 107-8, 159
Nueces, Battle of, 260
Nunez, Esther, 70
Nunez Ribiero, Samuel, 135-36

O

Oconostata (Indian chief), 59
Octaroon, 187
Ogden, Birdie Virginia, 168
Ogilvie, Gillespie & Co., 117
Ohio, 89
Ohio Company, 11, 12, 52, 166
Ohio River, 7, 8, 13
Ohio Valley, 5, 9, 14, 54, 56, 60-61
Ojibwa Indians, 35, 39, 45, 300
Oklahoma, 205, 208
Olivares, Fray Antonio de San Buenaventura, 232
Oneida Indians, 45
Onondaga Indians, 45
Orah, Lucy, 173
Oregon, 119
O'Reilly, Don Alejandro, 42
Oriental Jews, 200
Orphan Asylum, 168, 182
Osterman, Joseph, 254, 262, 317
Ottawa Indians, 33, 39, 45, 120
Ottoleungui, Jacob, 181

P

Pakenham, Edward M., 128-29, 130
Parker, Lucretia, 172
Parnas President, 76, 296
Parnas Residente, 76, 296
Patterson, Daniel, 129
Paul Revere & Son, 192
Payne, John Howard, 94
Pearson, Thomas K., 251
Peach Bottom, Pa., 157
Peddler, 93-101, 102-5
Penn, William, 221
Pennsylvania, 3, 14, 47, 52-53, 54, 57, 221, 269, 297
Pennsylvania Botanic Garden, 122
Pensacola, Fla., 125
Pentecost, Dorsey, 68, 297
Peoria Indians, 42, 51
Pernauille, Angelique Charlotte Jacinthe, 192

Peters, Abraham, 93
Petersburg, Va., 146
Pettigrew, James, 75-76
Philadelphia, Jacob, 1-2
Philadelphia, Pa., xvii-xviii, 13, 29, 56, 72, 73, 93, 96, 167, 286, 304
Phillips, Alexander, 128
Phillips, Asser, 203
Phillips, Esther, 318
Phillips, Jonas, 69
Phillips, Levy, 95
Phillips, Naphtali, 122, 210, 303
Phillips, Rachel, 92, 318
Philipson, Amanda, 114
Philipson, Esther, 114-15
Philipson, Jacob, 112-13, 114, 115, 171
Philipson, Joseph, 112, 113-14, 115
Philipson, Lavinia, 115
Philipson, Louis, 114
Philipson, Philip, 114
Philipson, Rosa Adelaide, 115
Philipson, Simon, 114, 115
Philipson & Brothers Company, 112
Piankishaw Indians, 40
Pickawillany (Indian village), 11
Pietersen, Solomon, 73
Pike, Zebulon Montgomery, 116
Pirogue, 131, 303
Pitt, Fort, 14, 19, 175
Pittsburgh, Pa., 7-8, 19, 21, 31, 37, 44, 52, 53, 56, 70, 71-72, 89, 96. *See also* Duquesne, Fort; Land of the Forks; Pitt, Fort
Pittsfield, Mass., 210-11
Plattsburgh, N.Y., 124
Plauche, J. B., 128
Point Pleasant, W. Va., 53
Pollock, Asher, 295
Pontiac (Indian chief), 33-34, 35, 39, 40, 42, 43, 260, 291
Population, Jewish, xi, xix
Porta, Jao de la, 233
Port au Prince, Haiti, 139-40
Portuguese Jew, xvii, 3, 5, 24, 29, 77, 132-39, 188, 198, 313
Potawatomi Indians, 35, 120, 178
Potter, John, 212
Potter, William, 269

Pouillot, Marie Ulalie, 196
Poznansky, Gustavus, 280
Prairie du Chien, Wis., 117
Prather, Henry, 44
Pratt, Lord Charles, 50
Prietto, Antonio, 115
Prussian Jew, 91
Pue, Elizabeth, 74
Puebla, Mex., 273
Puritans, 220
Putnam, Rufus, 85

Q

Quadroon, 187
Quaker traders, 39, 42, 43-44, 45-47
Quebec, 24, 27-28, 45, 120
Quebec Act, 53-54
Queen Anne's War, 12
Queenstown, Battle of, 122-23

R

Rabbi, 296, 297
Rapely, Richard, 58
Raphael, Solomon, 94-95
Reilly (Riley), John, 274, 275-76
Reubenites, 217, 218, 219
Revere, Paul, 192
Revolutionary War, 56-59, 63-68, 294, 300
Reynolds, Michael, 127
Rhode Island, 221
Rice, Abraham Joseph, 197, 261, 297
Rice, Susanne, 293
Richmond, Va., 82, 83, 109, 146, 171, 172, 179
Rivera, Diego Lopez, 137
Rivera, Jacob Rodriques, 137
Robert, Jean, 153
Roberts, Major, 290
Robinson, William David, 158-59
Rochelle, Reuben Levin, 128, 150, 188
Rogers, Lucius, 169
Rogersville, Ky., 152
Romain, David, 284
Rome, N.Y., 45
Rose, Edward, 111-12

Rose, Louis, 259
Ross, John, 42
Roxbury, Mass., 220
Royal Humane Society, 109
Ruff, Eva Catherine Rosine, 252
Russell, Philip Moses, 72

S

Sabbath, 8, 10, 69, 102, 164-65
Sacerdote, Simon, 187
Sackville, Fort, 43, 46, 63, 64, 65, 295
Sacramento, Calif., 278
Saginaw, Mich., 36
St. Asaph's, Fort, 62
St. Clair, Arthur, 85, 88
Saint Dominque, 139-41
Sainte Genevieve, Mo., 113, 171
St. Louis, Monsieur, 34
St. Louis, Mo., 48-49, 107, 109, 110-11, 112-14, 121, 170, 171, 279, 300-301
St. Louis Brewery and Distillery, 113
St. Louis Museum of Fine Arts, 301
St. Louis Sawmill, 113
St. Mary's, Ga., 268
Salimen, Isaac, 92
Salomon, Ezekiel, 164-65, 307
Salomon, Haym, 69, 83, 164
Salomon, Isaac, 100
Salomon, Louis, 284
Saltpeter, 121-22
Salvador, Francis, 58, 59-60, 292, 293
Salvador, Joseph, 58, 60
Samuel, Wolf, 156-58
San Antonio, Tex., 232, 233, 244, 245, 246-48, 250, 251, 258, 259
Sanders, Samuel, xi, 61-63
San Diego, Calif., 259, 265
Sandusky, Fort, 33, 36
San Francisco, Calif., 266, 278
San Jacinto, Tex., 253, 316
San Martin, Jose de, 315
Santa Anna, Antonio Lopez, 242, 243, 250, 251, 252-53, 258, 262, 263, 272, 274
Santa Fe, N.M., 258, 262, 263
Santa Fe Trail, 236, 264

Santa Maria, Pablo de, 138
Santo Domingo, 132, 133, 304
Sauk Indians, 35
Savannah, Ga., 135
Schafferstown, Pa., 3
Schiff, Hart Moses, 128
Schloss, Simon, 242
Schomberg, Alexander, 27, 28, 30-31
Schuyler, Henrietta Ann, 307
Schuyler, Nicholas, 165, 307
Schwartz, Benedict, 259-60
Scioto Company, 86
Scott, Sir Walter, 167
Scott, Winfield, 123, 253, 261, 267, 268, 272, 273, 274, 275, 276, 316
Seagrove, James, 207
Seasongood, Alfred, 152
Seeligson, Henry, 262
Seixas, Abraham Mendes, 146
Seixas, David G., 145-46
Seixas, Sarah Abigail Mendes, 197
Seixas, Gershom Mendes, 29, 83, 172, 297-98
Seminole Indians, 206, 253, 261
Seneca Indians, 45
Sephardic, 283
"Serpent Women," 153, 187
Seven Years' War, 286
Shanarai Chasset, 183, 189, 191, 195-96
Shawnee Indians, 7, 9, 15, 35, 37, 38, 44, 46, 53, 56, 62-63, 81, 89, 119, 120, 207
Shearith Israel, 29, 85, 135, 175, 192, 286, 289, 304
Sheftall, Mordecai, 83, 293
Shepherd, Regin D., 129
Shiff, Edward, 188
Shiff, Hart Moses, 150, 188
Shiff, Louisa, 188
Shloshim, 193
Shochet, 3, 22
Shortfield, Luke, 101
Shul, 1, 2, 3, 283, 284
Silberstein, Moses, 100
Silver, Rabbi Eliezer, xvi
Simon, Erasmus H., 214

Simon, Joseph, 2, 3, 4-11, 12, 13, 15, 19, 20, 21, 31-33, 36, 44, 46-47, 51, 52, 70, 71-72, 82, 112, 164, 165, 169, 272, 280, 284, 291
Simon, Miriam, 47
Simon, Shinah, 165, 307
Simon & Boude, 19
Simon & Campbell Co., 53, 55
Simon & Henry Forge, 20-21
Simon & Levy, 44
Simon & Milligan, 44
Simon & Mitchell, 44
Simon & Nathan, 22
Simon, Levy & Franks, 14, 15, 16, 17-18, 23, 43-44, 45-47
Simon, Levy, Trent & Company, 31, 44
Simon, Levy, Trent & Franks Company, 38, 42
Simon, Mitchell & McClure, 44
Simons, Abraham, 69, 295
Simons, Nancy Mills, 69
Simonson, Moses, 73, 295
Simonson, Rebecca, 73
Simpson, Joseph, 261
Sioux Indians, 121
"Sirenes, Les," 153
Six Nations, 45, 81, 88, 297
Slavery, 139-40, 144, 145-53, 154, 186, 187, 189-90, 234, 238
Sloat, John Drake, 265, 266
Slough, Mathais, 11, 286
Smallpox, 37-38, 290
Smith, Ethan, 211
Smith, Mary, 165
Smith, Sam, 253
Smyth, Alexander, 123
Smyth, Sarah E., 169
Soho, N. J., 192
Solis, Jacob da Silva Solomon, 174-75, 179, 180, 182, 183-84, 189, 192, 193, 308, 309
Solis, Joseph, 180, 189, 309
Solis, Manuel, 309
Solis, Solomon de Silva, 309
Solomon, Esther, 25
Solomon, Joseph, 3
Solomon, Levi, 25, 116, 170

Solomon, Samuel D., 109-10, 121
Solomons, Alexis, 116
Solomons, Ezekiel, 25, 33, 35-36, 40, 116, 307
Solomons, Ezekiel, Jr., 116, 119
Solomons, Lewis, 116, 119
Solomons, Mary, 119
Solomons, Sally, 172-73
Solomons, Samuel, 116, 119
Solomons, William, 116, 119
Sonoma, Calif., 266
Soria, Aaron, 139-40
Soule, John, 73
South Carolina, 58, 60
Souza, Victor, 191
Spain, 132, 276, 315
Spanish fly, 263-64
Spanish Inquisition, 41, 132-39, 259, 262, 276, 303
Spanish-Portuguese Jew, 3, 41, 132-37, 255
Spiegelberg, Solomon Jacob, 262, 264, 265
Sports, 100
Standish, Myles, 73
Standish, Sarah, 73
Stanwix, Fort, 45, 49
Statue of Liberty, 114
Steamboat, 21, 97
Steigel glassware, 19
Sterne, Adolphus, 237, 238, 252
Sterne, Eva, 252
Steward, Edward Warren, 114
Still, Peter, 147-49
Still, Vina, 149
Still, William, 149
Stix, Lewis, 98-99
Stockton, Robert F., 265, 266
Stone, Charles P., 114
Stove-pipe hat, 285
Stowe, Harriet Beecher, 147, 149
Straus, Oscar Solomon, 202-3
Stuart, John, 59
Sully, Thomas, 166
Summers, John, 238
Sunday School, 167
Surinam, 313
Surnames, Jewish, xvi-xvii

Sydnor, Frances, 73
Symmes, John Cleves, 85
Synagogues, 1, 2, 5, 29, 69, 72, 135, 136-37, 138, 160, 173-74, 175, 183, 192, 193, 196, 198, 199-200, 280, 283, 319

T

Talome, Susanna, 21
Tamenend (Indian chief), 21
Tampico, Mex., 270
Tarshish, 227-28
Taylor, Zachary, 260, 261, 262, 263, 267
Tea, 55-56
Tecumseh (Indian chief), 119
Tennessee, 104
Ten tribe theory, 210-11, 212, 213-14, 215-29
Texas, 231-33, 235, 236-37, 238, 241-62
Texas Rangers, 256
Thomas, Gabriel, 221
Thompson, John, 270
Thompson, Martha Lampley, 74
Thomson, Ga., 69
Thorowgood, Thomas, 219, 220
Tippecanoe, 119
Tomato, 82
Toomer, Joshua W., 210
Top hats, 285
Torah, 297
Toronto, Ont., 120
Torquemada, Tomas de, 132
Touro, Isaac, 180, 181, 198
Touro, John, 311, 312
Touro, Judah, 129, 180-83, 192, 198, 199-202, 309
Towerculla, Isaak, 208
Trader's Path, 7
Trahan, Marie Celeste, 151, 188-89
Trail of Tears, 205, 206, 208
Transylvania Company, 61, 68
Transylvanians, 60, 61
Transylvanian University, 167-68
Travis, William Barrett, 241, 246, 251
Trent, William, Jr., 31, 45

Trenton, N. J., 31
"Trial Without Jury," 94
Troy, Mo., 172
Tubal, Moses, 101
Turner, Frederick Jackson, ix-x
Turtle Town (village), 178
Tuscarora Indians, 45
Tuscumbia, Ala., 147, 148, 149
Tutoona, 311
Twiggs, David Emanuel, 273, 276, 316
Twiggs, John, 273
Twiggs, Levi, 275, 319
Twiggs, Marion, 316
Tyler, John, 271

U

Underground railroad, 149

V

Valentine, Jacob 274
Van Rensselaer, Gratz, 307
Van Rensselaer, Philip, 307
Velasco, Tex., 254, 316
Velasco, Treaty of, 254, 258
Vera Cruz, Mex., 267-68, 270, 272
Vincennes, Fort de, 2, 5, 41, 42, 43
Vincennes, Ind., 164, 294, 295
Virginia, 47, 51-52, 52-53, 54, 57, 68, 297

W

Wabash Company, 67-68
Waco, Tex., 256
Wade, Benjamin F., 190
Wagontown, Pa., 17
Warburg, Daniel, 186
War of 1812, 120-31, 154
Warriors' Path, 61
Washington, George, 11, 14, 15, 16, 18-19, 52, 54, 65-67, 68, 74, 81, 85-86, 88, 166, 175, 209, 296
Washington, D. C., 123
Washington, Tex., 236, 250
Watson, Elkanah, 210, 211
Wayne, Anthony, 88
Wea Indians, 178
Weis, Julius, 149-50

Weiss, Simon, 242
Weiss Bluff, Tex., 242
Wells, T. B., 280
West Point Military Academy, 89
Wharton, John A., 244
Wharton, Samuel, 53-54
Wheeling, W. Va., 53, 292
White, John, 220
White Oak Spring, Fort, 68
White Raccoon's Village (settlement), 178
White Thorn Grove (settlement), 80
Whitlock, Elizabeth, 82, 206, 312
Wildcat Hill, 81
Wilderness Trail, 61-62, 294
Wilkins, Charles, 121, 293, 302
William Henry, Fort, 17, 27
William, Maimi, 187, 188
Williams, Ezekieh, 111, 301
Williams, Roger, 221
Williamson, Andrew, 59-60, 293
Willing, Charles, 297
Wilmington, Del., 182
Wilson, Ellen, 201
Wilson, James, 297
Wisconsin, 115, 117-18
Wise, Isaac Mayer, 167, 169
Wissahickon, 2
Wolfe, Antony, 250, 251, 316
Wolfe, Benjamin, 172
Wolfe, James, 25, 27-28
Wool, John, 123, 262
Wurzburg University, 156
Wyandotte Indians, 7, 36, 37, 87
Wyoming Valley Massacre, 79-80
Wyrick, David, 224, 225, 226

Y

Yanaguana (Indian village), 231
Yellow Creek, 52
Yeshuat Israel, 29, 136, 138, 289, 304, 311
Yorke, Charles, 50
York, Ont., 123
York, Pa., 169
Yuchi Indians, 215